Fourth Edition

PUBLIC BUDGETING
IN AMERICA

Thomas D. Lynch

Florida Atlantic University

PRENTICE HALL, *Englewood Cliffs, New Jersey 07632*

Library of Congress Cataloging-in-Publication Data

Lynch, Thomas Dexter, (date)
    Public budgeting in America / Thomas D. Lynch. -- 4th ed.
       p.   cm.
    Includes bibliographical references and index.
    ISBN 0-13-735846-6
    1. Budget--United States.   I. Title.
    HJ2051.L93   1995
    350.72'2'0973--dc20   94-519
                                     CIP

Editorial Director: CHARLYCE JONES OWEN
Assistant Editor: JENNIE KATSAROS
Editorial/production supervision and
  interior design: ELIZABETH BEST
Copy Editor: KATHRYN BECK
Cover Design: EDSAL ENTERPRISES
Production Coordinator: ROBERT ANDERSON
Editorial Assistant: NICOLE SIGNORETTI

© 1995, 1990, 1985, 1979 by Prentice-Hall, Inc.
A Paramount Communications Company
Englewood Cliffs, New Jersey 07632

Printed in the United States of America

10 9 8 7 6 5 4

ISBN 0-13-735846-6

Prentice-Hall International (UK) Limited, *London*
Prentice-Hall of Australia Pty. Limited, *Sydney*
Prentice-Hall Canada Inc., *Toronto*
Prentice-Hall Hispanoamericana, S.A., *Mexico*
Prentice-Hall of India Private Limited, *New Delhi*
Prentice-Hall of Japan, Inc., *Tokyo*
Simon & Schuster Asia Pte. Ltd., *Singapore*
Editora Prentice-Hall do Brasil, Ltda., *Rio de Janeiro*

CONTENTS

☆

PREFACE, xi

1 PUBLIC BUDGETING IN CONTEXT 1

WHAT IS PUBLIC BUDGETING? 2
    Perspectives on Budgeting 2
    A Public Manager's Perspective 5
    An Operational Definition 6
    Budget Realities 7
    Political Realities 9
THE BUDGET CYCLE 10
    The Nature of the Cycle 10
    Budget Phases 11
    Local Government Budget Cycles 14
CONTEXT OF AMERICAN BUDGETING 14
    Ideology 14
    Federalism 17
    Decision-Making Models 18
ECONOMIC INFLUENCES ON BUDGETING 21
    Twin Evils 21
    Influence of Economics 24
MONETARY POLICY 25
    Central Bank 25

Effectiveness   26
Monetary Policy and Public-Budgeting   26
FISCAL POLICY   27
Policy Goals   27
Role of Government   27
Using Fiscal Policy   29
Fiscal Policy and Public Budgeting   31
OTHER ECONOMIC TOPICS   32
REVIEW QUESTIONS   32
REFERENCES   33

2   **TOWARD MODERN BUDGETING   35**

PRELUDE   35
Parliament versus the King   35
Colonial America   37
Budgeting in the 1880s   37
Progressive Reform Movement   38
EVOLUTION   39
Prior to 1921   39
Budgeting and Accounting Act of 1921   40
Post–1940 Reforms   42
Approaches to Budgeting   42
AN EXECUTIVE FOCUS   46
Planning and Analysis   46
Management by Objectives   49
Zero-Base Budgeting   50
TBB and Envelope Budgeting   52
Reagan and Bush   53
A LEGISLATIVE FOCUS   54
The 1974 Budget Reform Motivations   54
Unified Congressional Budget Reforms   54
Backdoor Spending   58
Impoundment   59
Reconciliation   61
Sunset Legislation   63
Federal Budgetary Madness   63
State and Local Challenges   67
REVIEW QUESTIONS   68
REFERENCES   68

3   **BUDGET BEHAVIOR   70**

POLITICS AND PERSPECTIVE   71
Four Institutional Roles   71

Role Objectives and Enemies   73
Cultivation of an Active Clientele   75
Agency Budget Office   77
Perspective of the Budget Officer   77
Agency Budget Behavior   82
Four Views   85
Develop Confidence   87
Results   89
Preparing for Hearings   91
STRATEGIES   93
Reviewers versus Reviewed   93
Spender's Strategies   95   ✓
Cutter's Strategies   97
New Program   100
Cautions   100
REVIEW QUESTIONS   101
REFERENCES   101

4   **BUDGET FORMATS AND PREPARATION   103**

BUDGET FORMAT   103
The Important Means   103
Distinguished Budgets   105
Ends Defining Means   108
BUILDING THE BUDGET   112
Program Financial Schedule   112
Budget Call   112
BUDGET REVIEWS   116
Executive Budget Hearings   116
Executive Budget Document   118
Congressional Budget Timetable   119
Legislative Considerations   121
LEGISLATIVE ADOPTION   124
REVIEW QUESTIONS   125
REFERENCES   125

5   **ANALYSIS APPLIED TO BUDGETING   127**

THEORETICAL FOUNDATION   128
A Budget System Approach and Accountability   128
Program Impact Theory   131
APPLICATION DIFFICULTIES   134
Mix-Up   134
Types of Output Measures   135
Staff and Service Units   135

Nonperformance Option   136
DATA MEASURE CONSTRAINTS   136
ELEMENTARY ANALYSIS   138
    Defining Relationships   138
    Marginal Cost and Discounting   139
CROSSWALKS   140
    Conceptual Bridge   140
    Determining Consistency   142
REVENUE FORECASTING   142
    Three Approaches   142
    Econometric Forecasts   144
    Forecasting Practices   146
EXPENDITURE FORECASTING   148
    Bargaining and Unit Cost Approaches   148
    Time Series Methods   149
    Expenditure Econometric Model   151
PRODUCTIVITY ANALYSIS   152
    Productivity   152
    Simple Regression Analysis   153
    Productivity and Budgeting   155
THE BENEFIT-COST CONCEPT   159
    Concept: What and Why   159
    Procedures   160
    Alternative Choice Methods   160
    Benefit-Cost Ingredients   161
    Benefits and Estimation   161
    Discount Rate   162
    Externalties, Risk, and Other Considerations   162
REVIEW QUESTIONS   163
REFERENCES   164

6   ANALYTICAL PROCESSES   166

PROGRAM ANALYSIS   167
    Selecting Issues   167
    Issue Assessment   168
    Commentary on Analysis   170
    Presentation of Results: Some Prescriptions   172
    Role of the Chief Executive   173
BUDGET EXAMINATION   173
    Information Sources   174
    Code of Ethics   174
    Services Performed   178
    Program Inputs and Outputs   179
    Emphasis and Change   182

Responsiveness 184
Effectiveness and Efficiency 185
Exploring Private Options 186
Forecasting 187
Politically Sensitive Subjects 188
Detailed Budget Examination 189
Automation 190
PROCESS ANALYSIS 193
Focus 193
Steps 194
Advantages 199
Context Is Important 200
Needed Interpersonal Skills 201
Honesty 202
Cooptation 202
PROGRAM EVALUATION 202
AUDITING 205
Purpose of Auditing 205
Internal versus External Audits 206
Auditing Principles 207
USE OF ANALYTICAL PROCESSES 209
REVIEW QUESTIONS 210
REFERENCES 21

7 **OPERATING BUDGETS AND ACCOUNTING 213**

DESIGNING CONTROL 214
Fixing Responsibility 214
Budget Execution 214
Pitfalls to Avoid 217
Current-Year Adjustments 218
BUDGET CONCEPTS AND REPORTS 219
Allotments and Budget Concepts 219
Expenditure Controls 224
Cash Internal Control 225
Management Information Systems 227
CASH MANAGEMENT AND INVESTMENTS 228
Cash Management 228
Commercial Bank Services 234
Controlling Payables 236
Investment Marketable Securities 237
Types of Marketable Securities 239
Portfolio 240
ACCOUNTING FUNDAMENTALS 242
Accounting Norms and Budgeting 243

FINANCIAL ADMINISTRATION   245
    Basic Governmental Accounting   246
    Accounting System Design   247
REPORTS AND ANALYSES   248
    Statement of Revenue   248
    Appropriation and Expense Ledger   249
    Fund Balance Change   251
    Balance Sheet   254
    Inout and Output   257
REVIEW QUESTIONS   257
REFERENCES   258

8   CAPITAL BUDGETING AND DEBT ADMINISTRATION   260

STATE AND LOCAL DEBT   261
    Definitions   261
    Classifications of Debt   262
    Short-Term Debt   265
    Early Developments in the Debt Concept   266
    Capital Financing in the 1980s   267
NONTRADITIONAL   270
    Tests and Limits   277
    New York City Financial Crisis   280
    Government Financial Emergencies   281
CAPITAL BUDGETING   282
    Operating versus Capital Budgeting   282
    Capital Facilities Planning   284
    Capital Budget Cycle   285
BONDING   285
    Designing an Issue   285
    Bond Prospectus, Notice of Sale, and Sale   290
    Debt Records and Reporting   292
    Bond Ratings   292
REVIEW QUESTIONS   299
REFERENCES   300

9   REVENUE SYSTEMS   302

INTERGOVERNMENTAL REVENUE SYSTEMS   302
    Historical Background   302
    Significant New Trend   305
PROPERTY TAX AND CONTROVERSY   308
    A Simple Idea   308
    Criticisms   308
    Property Tax Reforms   310
    Serrano v. *Priest*   311

ASSESSMENT AND TAXATION   314
  Taxable Property and Assessment   314
  Testing Assessments   316
  Assessment Cycle, Taxation, and Foreclosure   319
OTHER REVENUE SOURCES   322
  Income Tax   322
  Sales Tax   323
  User Charges   324
  Other Taxes   326
REVIEW QUESTIONS   326
REFERENCES   326

10   INTERNAL SERVICE FUNCTIONS   328

PROPERTY MANAGEMENT   329
  Preliminary Review   329
  Purchasing   330
  Procurement   330
  Selected Purchasing Challenges   332
  Central Stores and Inventory   334
  Property Control   335
  Bar-Code Technology   336
PROPERTY MAINTENANCE   338
RISK MANAGEMENT   338
  A Practical Necessity   338
  Exposure Identification and Risk Evaluation   339
  Risk Control   344
  Risk Funding and Self-Insurance   346
  Insurance   348
  Administration   349
PENSION FUNDS   351
  Budget Concerns   351
  The Investment Process   352
  Policy Issues   353
REVIEW QUESTIONS   358
REFERENCES   358

GLOSSARY   360

INDEX   378

PREFACE

This fourth edition updates the earlier one by using the more empirically related literature of public budgeting and financial management. Since the third edition, the literature has significantly improved, making it easier to report on existing conditions in the profession itself. Of particular note is the added use of analysis in the budget process. In the continuing drama of the federal budget crisis, much has been written and many laws have been passed. Unfortunately, the crisis continues and the details associated with the crisis have become more complex without adding to the understanding of the essential problem. My solution was not to write about some of the more recent federal budget reforms but instead to focus on the problem itself. In general, I am impressed that academic inquiry and the professional field have both improved—the notable exception being the federal budget process itself.

I acknowledge my appreciation to everyone who has contributed to this edition. I wish to thank the Prentice Hall reviewers, David. C. Ringsmuth, *California State University-Northridge*, and Richard L. McAnaw, *Western Michigan University*. Special thanks to Jennie Katsaros and Elizabeth Best of Prentice Hall, and Rita Kramer of Florida Atlantic University.

Thomas D.Lynch

1

PUBLIC BUDGETING

IN CONTEXT

Public budgeting is a mystery to most people—even to many professionals working in the government. People are aware that chief executives propose budgets to legislative bodies and that these groups in turn make decisions on taxes and what programs will receive financial support. If they work in government, they know that material is prepared to justify "the budget" and that detailed controls exist that often prohibit simple management decisions. In the personal lives of most people, the family budget is a source of tension because of the need to live within one's income. Most people assume that public budgeting must deal with similar matters but that it must involve much more complex accounting techniques.

This chapter examines what public budgeting is and the contextual factors necessary to understand public budgeting in the American context. Public budgeting is an activity, and many people view that activity from their own perspectives. Thus, the meaning of *public budgeting* is very much dependent upon perspective. The primary contextual factors in American budgeting are the ideologies of democracy and capitalism, federalism, decision-making theory, and economics. Each helps define how we approach and understand the purpose of public budgeting. This chapter should help the reader understand:

1. the various significant perspectives on budgeting, including that of the public manager;
2. important budgetary and political realities;
3. the nature of the budget cycle (that is, phases, cycle variations, overlapping of cycles) and the activities associated with each budget phase;

4. the significance of ideology in influencing how we approach public budgeting;
5. the role of federalism as a factor in budgeting;
6. the significance of normative decision-making theory to public budgeting;
7. the major tools of monetary policy, what aspects of the economy they primarily affect, and their significance to public budgeting:
8. the variety of ways in which the federal government can act to stimulate or depress the economy and the theory behind such actions; and
9. an explanation of how economic policy has and has not worked since the 1960s.

WHAT IS PUBLIC BUDGETING?

Perspectives on Budgeting

One can define a term by seeking out the common usages or one can create a definition for one's own intellectual and conceptual purposes. The former approach is particularly useful when one is trying to understand the various perspectives that people bring to a given activity. The latter approach is useful when an author is attempting to establish a reasonably uniform body of thought. Both approaches are used here.

Public budgeting can be viewed from many perspectives, as illustrated by Professor Sydney Duncombe in Exhibit 1–1. Reading the variety of statements helps one to appreciate the various academic and practical perspectives found in the practice of public budgeting. There are many such perspectives, of which none is exclusively "correct." The parable of the three blind men and the elephant helps us understand the significance of perspective. One of the blind men examined the tail and pronounced his description of the animal. Another felt a large foot and leg and then argued that the first man's description was inaccurate. The third man, after examining the beast's trunk, said that the other two were quite wrong in their descriptions. The storyteller was said to laugh at the foolish arguing among the blind men because the storyteller could see all of the elephant. The point of the parable is not the importance of "better" perspective but rather the foolishness of the storyteller for not recognizing that he himself was blinded by arrogance because he was sighted. Each person was correct and each was wrong because our individual perspectives always prevent us from easily understanding another's "truth."

When one works in the world of public budgeting, each perspective is used by various key actors in the budget process. The person trained as a lawyer sees the phenomenon called budgeting as a sort of legal process. The economist and politician describe the phenomenon differently based on their perspectives. The public manager sees budgeting differently from the others. None is incorrect, because all of them define the phenomenon based on their educational or professional perspectives. They become incorrect, like the storyteller, when their arrogance blinds them to the significance of perspective when defining and understanding the phenomenon of public budgeting.

EXHIBIT 1–1 What Are the Main Purposes of Budgeting?

I view the budget system as *a means of balancing revenues and expenditures.* Our constitution requires a balanced budget and in preparing our budget we first make careful estimates of revenues for the next year. We then reduce agency budget requests to our revenue estimates for the next year.

I look on the budget process as a *semi-judicial process* in which state agencies come to the Legislature to plead their case just as I plead the case of my clients in court. Our job as a legislative committee is to distribute the available funds equitably among state agencies.

The main purpose of the budget system is *accountability.* The people hold the Legislature accountable through the electoral process. The Legislature holds state agencies accountable by reviewing their budgets, setting the appropriation levels the people want, and letting state agencies know how the people want their money spent through statements of legislative intent.

The most important single reason for a budget system is *control.* State agencies would spend the state bankrupt in two years if there weren't an adequate means of controlling their spending. The appropriations are the first line of defense against overspending. Important second lines of defense lie in allotment systems, position controls, and controls over purchasing.

The executive budget document should be *an instrument of gubernatorial policy.* When a Governor comes into office there are certain programs and policies he would like to see accomplished during the term of office. Many of these program and policy changes cost money, and the Governor will have to either raise taxes or cut expenses to pay for these changes. The people expect the Governor to show accomplishments and the budget is a major means of showing these accomplishments.

Budgeting is *public relations.* I write my budget justifications in the way I think will best gain the appropriations I need. If the budget examiner likes workload statistics, we'll snow the examiner with statistics. If a key legislator would be influenced by how the budget will affect constituents, we put that in the request.

A budget is *an instrument of good management.* Careful use of workload statistics, performance accounting, and standards of performance will tend to insure that personnel are effectively utilized.

A budget is really a *work plan with a dollar sign attached.* As an agency official, I am committing myself to certain levels of program which I promise to attain if I receive my full budget request. When the Governor and the Legislature discuss cutting my budget, I describe as accurately as I can the reduction in program level that will result.

The budget is an instrument for *planning.* A good budget system requires agency officials to project costs and program levels at least several years ahead. Such a system requires agency officials to examine the costs and benefits of alternatives to present programs in order to plan changes in programs where necessary. In short, budgeting should be an annual means for agency heads to reexamine the objectives of their programs and the effectiveness of the means used to accomplish these objectives.

Budgeting is *the art of cutting* the most fat from an agency request with the least squawking.

Source: Prepared by Sydney Duncombe, 1977.

For the purposes of this textbook, the more important perspectives are those of the politician, the economist, the accountant, and, especially, the public manager. Given a democratic society, budgets are the tool used to frame much public policy; thus, the politician's perspective is important. Both economists and accountants have professional perspectives that greatly influence how we understand budgeting and how we believe we should practice it. Economists give us theories and techniques that help us define how we should budget, what factors should be weighed, and how to weigh these factors in making budget policy decisions. Accountants give us conceptual frameworks in which to execute and evaluate budgets. Public managers must understand each of the previous perspectives when managing the affairs of government through the budget process.

Political leaders are often painfully aware that many of the most important policy decisions are made during the budget process. Former New York City Mayor Abraham Beame was reported to have said that "the budget is everything" when that city was undergoing its fiscal crisis during the 1970s. Mayor Beame was quite sensitive to the financial crisis of his city and the resulting policy dilemmas confronting him. Henry Maier, the former mayor of Milwaukee, once said, "The budget is the World Series of Government." This mayor in the early 1980s had to support a 20 percent increase in property taxes. Both mayors were aware that many—if not most—of the major political decisions are made when a chief executive proposes the government's budget and a legislative body (for example, the city council) adopts it.

The budgetary process can be viewed as a political event conducted in the political arena for political advantage. Politics—being a reflection of human nature—has its best and worst sides. In some instances, politicians or individuals who influence politicians are seeking money for themselves. In other instances, the political advantage sought is to further some ethical position or to aid others selflessly. Motivations differ, but the seeking of political advantage is constant. Thus, one significant perspective on budgeting is political.

Economists view budgetary decisions with the assumptions that budget decisions are made within restricted financial conditions and that economic analysis can therefore help identify the best decision. Every budget decision involves potential benefits which may or may not be obtained; it also involves *opportunity cost*. If the available money is spent for one program, then another program is not funded or is funded at a lower level. In other words, opportunities are lost in every budget decision, and there never seems to be enough money for every program. When choices have to be made, economic analysis can help one to evaluate the comparative benefits and costs, including opportunity cost. This view of budgeting focuses on decision making and places a high premium upon the value of analysis in helping decision makers make "better" decisions.

Accountants stress the importance of capturing accurate financial information. To the accountant, the budget is the statement of desired policy, and information on actual expenditures is compared with the budget to judge whether policy has been followed, as well as to question the wisdom of the original policy. The accountant's view largely defines how public managers understand how they should execute the budget and how some of their evaluators will judge their actions.

None of these views—the politician's, the economist's, and the accountant's— is incorrect. Each perspective is valuable in getting a more comprehensive understanding of public budgeting. Interestingly, the perspective of the public manager most closely approximates that of the storyteller in the parable. Public managers must try to achieve a more comprehensive view, but they cannot fall into the trap of arrogantly believing that such a view is anything more than one valid perspective among others.

A Public Manager's Perspective

Viewed from a public manager's perspective, the budget is often the principal vehicle for developing government plans and policies. There can be a separate planning process, but often such a process develops vague statements without stressing relative priorities. The budget states specific dollar amounts relative to proposed government activities and these decisions reflect the government's plans and policies much more accurately than most planning documents.

The budget also represents the chief executive's legislative program. It states which programs are to be active, emphasized, or ignored given the limited resources available to the government. Other public statements may be made that discuss a mayor's or governor's legislative program, but the comprehensive and detailed presentation is presented in the budget.

There are several different ways to categorize the request for funds to finance a government, but they all outline planned functions, programs, and activities. Program and performance budgets more clearly explain the relationship of money requested and government activities. However, even line-item budgets, which focus on specific items to be purchased with the budget, provide the knowledgeable reader with a detailed outline of planned government activities.

Most budgets present the planned program for the year against a background of past experiences and future needs. Even zero-base budgets normally cite past experience to demonstrate the type of activities likely to be funded in the planned year. In some instances, budgets project future needs beyond the planned budget year in order to suggest the future-year implications of budget-year decisions. This past and future information is highly useful to decision makers: the past gives them an impression of what the program can accomplish and the future gives them warning of the long-run implications of current budget-year decisions.

Strictly speaking, the budget is a request for funds to run the government. The request is normally made by the chief executive to the city council, legislature, or Congress. It also states the revenue and other sources of resources (for example, debt financing) needed to balance the suggested expenditures. Once the budget is modified or approved, the executive branch develops operating budgets for the budget year. Traditionally, the document sent to the legislature by the chief executive is called *the budget*. In the federal government, Congress receives the budget but passes several appropriation bills which constitute the modified approved federal budget.

An Operational Definition

As can be noticed from the previous discussions, the term *budget* is used in a variety of ways. Each may be quite correct given the perspective of the user of the word. In public administration, the following definition is normally an excellent operational definition:

> *Budget* is a *plan* for the accomplishment *of programs* related to *objectives* and *goals* within a definite *time* period, including an estimate of *resources required*, together with an estimate of the *resources available*, usually compared with one or more *past periods* and *showing future requirements*.

The budget always represents what someone wishes to do or have someone else do. It is a tool to help us control our affairs. Once the money is spent, it can be contrasted to the plan but it no longer represents something called a budget; rather, it represents actual obligations or expenditures. Prior to that time, the budget may change many times. The document sent to the legislature by a chief executive is normally considered to be "the budget," whereas the plan used by the bureaucrats during the budget year is normally called the "operating budget."

People writing budgets have programs and program accomplishments in mind. Admittedly, those people may have rather vague notions of the exact nature of each program and their desired goals and objectives. Dealing with and avoiding vagueness is one of the major challenges of public budgeting. But in spite of vagueness, people preparing budgets do believe that the requested funds will be used for some set of activities and that those activities will result in accomplishments.

Budgets are focused on a specific time period called the *budget year*. In some instances, the year used corresponds to the calendar year, but normally an arbitrary year called *fiscal year* (for example, October 1 to September 30) is defined. The money is planned to be spent or obligated in the budget year. Years prior to the budget year (BY) are called prior or past years (PY), and the current time period in which the government is operating is called the current year (CY). Future fiscal years beyond the budget year are referred to as budget year plus one (BY + 1), budget year plus two (BY + 2), and so on. For example, let us say we are preparing the budget for the fiscal year (FY) 2000 but we are actually in FY 1999. The BY is 2000. The CY is 1999. The PY is 1998. The BY + 1 is 2001.

Budgets are planned for a specific time period, and an estimate is always made of the resources required during that time period. The estimates include the revenue as well as the expenditures. Estimating is another challenge of budgeting as one can never be certain that a specific dollar sum will be raised or that the government can live within its proposed expenditures. The latter is more easily controlled, but unexpected emergencies or problems do occur.

In order to facilitate a better understanding of the requested resources, the budget usually compares the BY requests against the PY and CY actual obligations or expenditures. This provides a basis for comparing and permits the decision maker to focus on the difference or increment between the CY and the BY. This is called *incremental budgeting*. In *zero base budgeting*, one ignores the differences and demands that the whole BY amount be justified. As will be explained later in more depth, this distinction between incremental and zero base budgeting is overstated. Increasingly, budgets also go beyond the BY and show BY + 1, BY + 2, BY + 3, BY + 4, and BY + 5. This showing of future requirements helps the decision maker realize that BY decisions have an effect beyond one budget year. Thus, a policy maker may decide that a given set of decisions may be affordable for the budget year but are not wise decisions, given the likely future requirements. Unfortunately, policy makers often ignore future implications, and this situation represents yet another challenge of public budgeting.

Budget Realities

If you examine a budget, there will be many tables and charts. If you work in government, there will be many forms that must be completed so that a budget can be prepared, executed, and evaluated. The details in the forms and tables are an essential part of budgeting, but you can never understand public budgeting by examining those forms and tables per se. The numbers and the formats used to present the numbers are merely some of the means and not the ends of public budgeting.

Budgeting is a good reflection of actual public policy and often a better reflection than formal speeches or written statements. Politicians must get elected to hold office, and clarity of expression may be dysfunctional because it makes needless enemies. Also, it is often difficult to verbalize policy. The budget states the planned priorities and the programs in a meaningful way to the people who must carry out the policy. This is not to say that all policy is reflected in the budget, because some important policy matters have no fiscal implications. Nor is it to say that all budgets clearly present policy. But an expert can read the message that will be operationalized by the bureaucracy.

A budget focuses on a given year (the budget year), but its preparation, execution, and evaluation take place over a period of several years (the *budget cycle*). Going back to the FY 2000 example, the preparation and approval of the 2000 budget should have been finished just prior to the beginning of the fiscal year (October 1, 1999). In order to have an approved budget on time, the preparation and approval process must begin much earlier. Sometimes the preparation begins a full year or more before the beginning of the budgeted fiscal year. During FY 2000, the operating budget is used to guide obligations and expenditures, but after FY 2000 no more money can be obligated, though some money can be spent to fulfill the FY 2000 obligations. The period in which to fulfill obligations can be open-ended, but sound practices place a one- or two-year limit so that the books can be closed. The final stage in the budget cycle is auditing and evaluating the program resources obligated in the earlier budget year. This can take place one to several years after the completion of the fiscal year. In other words, the FY 2000 budget cycle can start as early as 1999 and end as late as 2003.

Budgeting is highly emotional, detailed, and a great deal of work. When policy makers decide to fund or not to fund programs, people are profoundly affected, lives are changed. Not surprisingly, budget decisions evoke strong emotions because the stakes are high and the consequences are important. Budgets are also detailed. The one cardinal sin for a budget officer is to make an arithmetic error because that is one mistake everyone can catch and criticize. The budgets are often hundreds and thousands of pages long, filled with tables. Each number is usually important to someone and mistakes are not treated lightly. The preparation of this mass of information requires much work. Deadlines drive the process and require intensive fifty- to sixty-hour-plus work weeks, especially prior to a major deadline such as submission of material to a legislative committee. The work is consuming and requires almost complete devotion. The work is also extremely interesting because of the interrelationship of budgeting and politics.

Students of public budgeting must use concepts developed in political science, economics, accounting, the behavioral sciences, finance, and other disciplines. Political science helps the budget person understand the political nature of government and the public policy-making process. Economics provides useful analytical tools and highly influential theories. Accounting provides the means to keep track properly of the complex array of dollars. The behavioral sciences help the budget person understand the human as a part of the budget process. Finance gives the practitioner some conceptual tools to use, especially relative to the revenue aspects of budgeting. Public administration helps bring this information together and adds some concepts of its own. Students of public budgeting should be able to draw upon a broad interdisciplinary background so that they can more easily deal with their challenging problems.

Public budgeting does require highly specialized knowledge, critical behavioral patterns, and important skills. These can be learned through experience, and the learning process can be facilitated through formal education. This text sets out the primary knowledge useful to those involved in public budgeting as well as those wishing to better comprehend government by understanding public budgeting. Public budgeting requires more than knowledge. To be effective, certain important behavioral patterns should be mastered and that requires a learning laboratory or experience. Also, certain skills must be acquired, such as being able to translate possible policy positions into dollars and cents almost instantly in order to deal effectively in active political bargaining situations. Public budgeting is one of the most professionally challenging and often most emotionally rewarding activities in public administration.

Budgeting is a constantly changing field. In Chapter 2, the history of budgeting in the United States is explained in more depth. At the federal level, the key budget reform years were 1921 and 1974. In the federal executive branch, Presidents Johnson, Nixon, Carter, and Reagan each made major budget reforms that have endured to varying degrees. Debates at the highest level continue to occupy public attention in spite of the complexity of the subject.

One last public budgeting reality should be stressed. Public budgeting involves very big money. The 1992 federal budget outlay was about $1.5 trillion. In 1990, all levels of government expenditures in the United States made up about 35 percent of the gross national product. State and local government budgets are also huge today. For example, in 1929, the combined federal, state, and local expenditure was $10.4 billion; in 1989, the states of Wisconsin, Minnesota, Georgia, Virginia, and Washington had budgets in that same range, with California's expenditures being about $64.5 billion. Many cities, counties, and school districts have budgets over $1 billion.

Political Realities

Budgets are decided through politics; analysis is only ammunition in the decision-making process. Sometimes the politics are crude and unethical; sometimes reason and ethical views prevail. Often the decisions involve complex, conflicting values supported by minimal analysis, but they are decisions that must be made. The analyses used in public budgeting are only significant to the political actors if those actors use the analyses in their deliberations. Even when used and not ignored, the analyses are merely some of the ammunition used to persuade other political actors. In some cases, an appeal, such as to the nation's pride, may be more significant than an elaborate analysis. In other situations, an analysis can be the key to persuading political actors how they should vote on a major policy matter.

Budgets are proposed plans. The budget presentations sometimes can make the difference for a program, but, in some instances, the presentation will make no difference because the program is politically weak. In other instances, the program may be so politically strong that even a bad budget presentation will not defeat the program. Often the proposed plan or budget of the executive is a significant factor in the public decision-making, and the quality of the presentation is considered to be a reflection of the managerial competency of the program.

Political "sacred cows" do exist. An influential member of Congress or political executive can successfully demand a specific project or program. The appropriateness of the project or program is irrelevant, but the power of the political actor is very relevant. In public budgeting, the professional must learn to tolerate this unless a moral or legal question is involved. The nature of the American political system almost ensures the existence of sacred cows. Some of them are prompted by campaign promises and some by less desirable motivations. The percentage of programs and projects that are sacred cows will vary, but normally they are the exception. If the program decisions are dominated by sacred cows, then public management will suffer as foolish programs or projects cannot be stopped except by highly political and time-consuming debate.

Public budgeting is strongly influenced by the political causes of the day. The causes vary over time, but some contemporary causes include national security, energy, environment, poverty, recession, and inflation. Policy makers who decide on budgets are keenly aware of the political causes because their positions on those causes influence people to vote for or against them. Therefore, politicians wish to know how budgets relate to those causes. Not surprisingly, budget justifications are often cast in terms of those causes or, at a minimum, the agency is prepared to answer questions involving the program and the politically sensitive topic. For example, in a time of recession, with large numbers of people unemployed, a major defense project will be justified first on the basis of providing jobs and second on the basis of national security.

THE BUDGET CYCLE

The Nature of the Cycle

The *budget cycle* takes place in four phases which can extend over several years. The first phase is *planning and analysis.* Here, the issues are explored and the agency budget is prepared. The second phase is *policy formulation*, which involves extensive executive and legislative reviews and decisions. The third phase is *policy execution and reinterpretation* when the budget becomes operational. The final stage involves *audit and evaluation.* The beginning of the third phase is a key date. On that date, the operating budget goes into effect, to end in one year. Prior to that date, enough time must be provided to consider the issues, conduct analysis, prepare the budget, and permit various executive and legislative groups to modify the evolved budget. After the end of the operating budget, time is needed to close accounts and to audit and evaluate the programs. This latter phase can take place in a few months, but often involves several years.

Cycles vary from one government to another and from one agency to another. If the government or agency is small, then the smaller numbers of people normally require a briefer budget cycle. In a large agency with many field units, coordination is difficult and more time is needed to prepare the document.

The federal budget cycle is particularly important because state and local governments sometimes use the federal government as a model and—more importantly—local and state governments are dependent upon federal transfer payments, such as revenue sharing and grant programs. If the federal government delays, many other groups are affected.

One confusing reality of public budgeting is that the budget person and agency must operate with overlapping budget cycles. On the same day, a budget person may have to review the evaluations covering last year's program, prepare readjustments in the current year or operating budget, and answer congressional questions on the budget year covering the next fiscal year. This can be and is confusing. Not surprisingly, people working in budgeting learn to refer to their work by specific fiscal years to minimize confusion.

Budget Phases

Planning and Analysis.   The planning and analysis phase was popularized by planning-programming-budgeting (PPB) in the 1960s, but the phase was not original to PPB reforms. The New York Bureau of Municipal Research encouraged planning and analysis at the turn of the century. Almost all budget preparation did and does involve some analysis, but the amount and sophistication were greatly increased during the PPB reform era. Planning and analysis can take many forms, but most of the techniques were developed in the disciplines of economics, operations research, and systems analysis. Techniques including modeling, sensitivity analysis, and survey research are used, but are not covered in this text because they are not closely associated with budgeting. Other techniques, such as forecasting and cost-benefit, cost-effectiveness, and marginal utility analyses, are introduced in various sections of this text.

The planning and analysis phase takes place at the beginning of the budget cycle, but analysis does occur at other periods in the cycle. In the policy formulation stage, time is a key factor, so there is not the luxury of being able to prepare elaborate analyses. Only quick original analysis or reapplication of earlier analyses can be used in this phase. There is little analysis, except for forecasting, done in the policy execution phase. A great deal of analysis is done in the audit and evaluation phase. The techniques, analytical problems, and focus of analysis do change somewhat when this budget phase occurs relative to other budget activities.

Policy Formulation.   In the policy formulation process, the budget is developed and approved. Policy positions become operationalized as the budget is prepared. The agency is the preparer and significant advocate of the budget. The agency's clientele group and elements in the legislative and the highest levels of the executive branch may also support the agency's budget or aspects of the budget, but the agency is the advocate. The reviewers and modifiers of the budget include the department, the chief executive and his or her staff, and the legislature. A variety of conflicting influences converge on the budget process from various levels in the executive branch, the legislature, clientele groups, the media, and even sometimes the judiciary branch.

The federal process is elaborate, but it does illustrate the complex steps in the policy formulation process. Prior to this phase, the agency has submitted quarterly program financial plans which give budget reviewers initial indications of likely fund requests five years beyond the budget year. At the beginning of the phase, the central executive branch budget office (that is, the Office of Management and Budget) issues guidelines to the departments and agencies for the development of the new budget. Then the various agencies issue their budget calls to agency personnel in order to compile the necessary information for the budget. The agency uses this information to prepare its budget.

The remaining portion of the policy formulation phase involves budget reviews and, eventually, decisions on the budget. The agency submits the budget to the department budget office. The format can vary in style from a line-item to a program budget to decision packages. The department budget office and the highest officials review the budget and decide upon the department's recommended budget. The agency makes the necessary changes and the revised budget is submitted to the Office of Management and Budget. Again the budget is revised, the OMB arrives at its recommendations, and the president revises and eventually approves the budget. In some cases, the president permits an appeal from the department. In the federal government, a current services budget is submitted to Congress with the president's budget in January. The Congress then reviews the submission and passes appropriate bills prior to the beginning of the new fiscal year.

Policy Execution. In the policy execution phase, the budget is used as guidance for specific decisions by bureaucrats. This phase takes place during the current year, and all obligations must be made in this year if they are to be attributed to the fiscal year. The executive branch can sometimes reinterpret policy during this phase by not spending the planned resources or by shifting funds from one activity to another. As a general practice, the latter does not occur at the federal and state levels, but does occur sometimes at the local level. The executive policy not to spend appropriated funds is an *impoundment*. The nonspending can take the form of a delay in spending in the intended budget year or of a recision from the budget. On the state level, some executives have the power of line-item vetoes or impoundment, depending on the state constitution.

At the agency and department level, the rate of obligation and disbursement of resources can be controlled by *allotment*. This power is intended to assure that funds are available when needed for proper economic and managerial purposes. With the greater emphasis upon macroeconomics, the federal government is more carefully controlling the rates of both obligation and disbursement. Sometimes the allotment power is used for political purposes, such as ensuring maximum and timely obligations on key programs at the correct moment in a political campaign. The allotment power might be abused and treated as an illegal impoundment, but no evidence of such abuse has been raised yet publicly. Normally, allotments are used entirely for economic and managerial purposes.

Authorizations and *appropriations* are often phrased in technical budget language. The technical wording can be significant to the operating budget. The normal appropriation is for the budget year only, but the language need not be so limiting. For example, the appropriations may be for no-year funds, thus permitting the agency to obligate the funds in subsequent fiscal years if the money is not entirely obligated in the current year. Other technical devices are *contract* and *bond authority*. Congress can also place special conditions on appropriations. For example, the appropriation can read, "$150 million is appropriated under section 204 of XYZ legislation but none of this money can be used to build a flag pole in front of the Bureau of Standards building nor can any money be spent on the ABC project." Often such detailed conditions are not included in the appropriation language, but are included in the nonlegally binding report that accompanies the appropriation bill. Agencies are sensitive to such requests and normally will comply unless some very unusual circumstance exists. Another technical budget device is for the appropriations committee to negate yearly contract authority by saying that no more than a specific amount can he obligated during the budget year.

The federal and state government use of the authorization and appropriation distinction is extremely useful, given the complex budget decisions that are made. Many local governments do not make the authorization and appropriation distinction because a two-stage process is not as useful to them. There are normally fewer city councilors or county supervisors, so a more elaborate two-stage process is not needed to coordinate decision making.

Once the allotments have been made, the agency can prepare its operating budget. Normally, the operating budget is not the desired sophisticated managerial tool that has proper linkages to accounting, management-by-objectives and progress reporting, and program evaluation. The operating budget should inform the agency's units how much and at what rate resources can be obligated and disbursed. The operating budget should reflect the decisions made in the management-by-objective (MBO) process. The recording of progress and accounting of actual obligations and disbursement should be used in a classification scheme so that management can verify that budget and MBO decisions were executed. Also, proper program evaluations can be done only if the program direction is understood and necessary cooperation exists among the evaluators, managers, and budget persons.

Audit and Evaluation. The final phase takes place after the current year is complete. Some audit and evaluation work can and should be started much earlier in the cycle, but the focus of the work and the preparation of the final reports take place in this final phase. Audit and evaluation activities are conducted by such groups as the agency, the department, the General Accounting Office (GAO), and the Congress itself through its oversight function. Audits are often focused on checking if the agency properly recorded its transactions and obligated resources legally. Increasingly, auditing has been expanded to include program evaluation, especially by the GAO. However, program evaluation is often done in separate agency and departmental program evaluation units. To a limited extent, legislative bodies conduct oversight hearings and investigations which can be considered program evaluations.

Laws are sometimes quite specific in requiring audits and evaluations. States have audit agencies, and states require auditing in and of local governments. States often require a local government to submit its annual audit to the state. The audit is often examined by the state itself. States sometimes have legislative review commissions which perform program evaluations. Often, audit agencies are staffed by accountants who are reluctant to perform program evaluations because they are not trained in that activity. However, the trend is for audit agencies to become more involved in program evaluation and for new evaluation groups to be established. In the federal government, the law often requires that a portion of program funds be set aside for program evaluation.

Local Government Budget Cycles

There are some differences between federal and state government and local government budget cycles. Revenue estimation is very important in local as well as state government, particularly in the planning and analysis phase. The estimation is normally done by the finance or central budget office. Budget formulation practices vary in local government, but often there is a small central budget staff. Procedures are much more informal, but sometimes state law or local charters require more formal practices such as public hearings. Often the budget is prepared by a budget office that receives input from the city agencies and guidance from the city manager or mayor. The chief city executive sometimes serves as the person who resolves outstanding issues and as a court of appeals. The exact procedure depends upon each local government, with some having the agency heads reporting directly to the city council or county elected board of supervisors.

Local governments vary greatly in their review and power over the budget. Normally, budgets are detailed line-item documents which part-time nonexpert board members must review and approve in a short time. Not surprisingly, budgets are confusing and frustrating to board members. They usually focus their attention on small comprehensible items or pet projects rather than conducting a comprehensive review of the submitted budget. Often, local governments conduct public hearings in connection with the legislative deliberations on the budget.

Once the budget is approved, the focus of the budget is on control. In some local governments, almost every change in the line-item budget must be approved by the legislature. In other local governments, almost any change can be made by the city manager or department head. The money is controlled, but the ability to make changes in the budget during the operating year varies.

CONTEXT OF AMERICAN BUDGETING

Ideology

Public budgeting is best considered in the context of the ideological culture of a nation. Budgeting practices in Canada, the United States, France, Panama, Israel, Yemen, India, Russia, Japan, and the People's Republic of China are not identical because the budgeting process relates to the fundamental political and economic value schemes of each society. Techniques and concepts can be similar across societies, but how those techniques and concepts are applied meaningfully depends upon the society's culture.

Ideas are powerful, especially when shared by many people, because they can guide behavior by discouraging "bad" and encouraging "good" activities and actions. Ideas can be and often are used to place a value on people, things, activities, and even other ideas. Sometimes ideas can be logically consistent or nearly consistent and form belief systems. These systems in turn can be shared by many people and can guide entire civilizations. These belief systems are called *ideologies*, and every culture has them.

In the United States, two important ideologies, both of which influence the way public budgeting is conducted, are democracy and capitalism. Other belief systems and subsystems are important, but are not central to this simplified sketch. *Democracy* is a term that can have many meanings, as illustrated by its use in American and many communist societies. Democracy as defined in the United States evolved from a desire to have a limited representational government that respected the political rights of minorities. In the agriculture-oriented colonies, certain rights, such as freedom of the press, were considered essential and were built into the Constitution. These rights were viewed as a means to prevent tyranny and permit the peaceful selection of a new government. In time, the definition of *voter* extended from white male adult landholder to an adult citizen of either sex and any racial or religious background.

The American democratic system of government evolved into a pattern partially explained by the Federalist Paper No. 10 of the 1780s. Parties and groups interact to influence government in a manner deliberately designed to decentralize and diffuse political power. People continually learn that they can best influence government by acting in groups and directing their political efforts at partisans in the political process. The partisans interact and adjust policy based on the relative strengths of lobbying forces and varying influential ideologies. The strength of policy in some instances may be due to economic interests, but often that strength rests upon shared and effectively argued belief systems.

In America, the notions of partisan bargaining, minority and fundamental human rights, diffusion of power, and the influencing of partisans through collective action over time together constitute the meaning of *democracy*. The activity called public budgeting tends to reflect that ideological culture. Thus, budget decisions are made through partisan bargaining in a system of diffused political power. Decisions made by partisans are influenced over time by a process called *lobbying*. Public agency clientele groups (that is, those affected directly by the agency's activities) can and do lobby the legislature and the executive. The agency's actions are thus largely determined by the complex influence of executive, legislature, and clientele; and the mechanism of that influence is often the budget. Freedom of information and "sunshine" legislation, logical extensions of minority and fundamental human rights, are taken seriously; and discussion of these issues opens up much budget detail to the media and the general public. In America, budget decisions require a melding of executive and legislative will to achieve the necessary policy mandates as prescribed in the Constitution. Often the influence of democratic ideas has even extended to requiring public hearings on budget decisions. The belief system called *democracy* does greatly influence the way Americans think public budgeting should be conducted.

The second major American ideology is *capitalism*, which does not exist in the strictest sense of the term. Unlike democracy, capitalism is subject to active ideological challenge, which has led to a blending of logically conflicting belief systems. Strict capitalism evolved from a reaction against the extensive English-government-dominated mercantilism of the 1760s and was reinforced by the Social Darwinism of the late 1880s to the 1930s. The desire was to limit the role of government in the economic activities of society. The capitalist ideology does have a role for government, but it is limited to "public goods" like national defense, and possibly could be extended to include:

1. coping with public allocations for the general good, like public education and pollution control; and
2. avoiding inconvenient private monopolies on such things as highways, bridges, and water systems.

Advocates of capitalism raise severe protests when subjects such as redistribution of wealth and the use of government control to achieve economic stabilization and growth are raised.

From the 1890s to the present, contrary economic (and related political) belief systems arose. One advocated a predominantly guiding role for government over society. Another argued for total governmental control over society. The guiding role was advocated by the Progressives. They felt that government should intervene in the social and economic conditions in society in order to ensure that national concerns were being met. Progressives were quite successful politically and their accomplishments included child labor laws, the income tax, the Federal Reserve System, social security, a national park system, and other landmark legislation.

Communists and some Socialists advocated a total role for government in society. They felt that government should run the society and curb the economic abuses of the wealthy elites. The most visionary advocates of this belief system expected that a classless society would eventually evolve, eliminating the need for government to act as the people's trustee. At one time, in over one-third of the world, that belief system was dominant. In the United States, the socialist belief system challenged the social conscience of the nation and aided in the passage of many Progressive reforms such as the reduced workweek and worker safety requirements.

After 1932, the Progressives and many of the less radical American Socialists merged politically into the liberal movement. They have played an active role in such matters as the advocacy of consumerism, the protection of the environment, the fight for equal opportunity, and the implementation of workplace and product safety.

The correct mix of the public sector and the private sector in the United States continues to be the major issue dividing partisans in many major political battles. For purposes of public budgeting, the important point to understand is that this ongoing ideological debate is taken very seriously and affects budgeting. The very size and scope of government is at issue; thus the question of what is and should be budgeted is also at issue. Attitudes about how government can and should influence the overall national or regional economy are critical to the way budgeting is conducted. The stress on economy, efficiency, and productivity arises out of capitalism and its economic doctrines. The use of enterprise funds and government corporations also evolved from the ideological debate. A later unit in this chapter will discuss current economic thinking and its influence on budgeting.

Federalism

The United States is a federated government, and budgeting differs on each level. The scope, size, and different nature of programs lead to the differences in budgeting. In public budgeting, the similarities are more striking than the dissimilarities. However, the differences are important and are discussed here.

In the national government, more effort is focused on the expenditure as opposed to the revenue aspects of budgeting. Taxes are important, but more effort is channeled into controlling, managing, and planning expenditures. The state of the economy and the role of the budget in stimulating the economy are actively debated and are very significant in shaping both presidential and Congressional budgets. The revenue side of the budget is considered in terms of its influence on the economy. The typical agency budget officer does not consider the revenue aspects of the budget. At the highest levels in the OMB and in Congress, attention is addressed to macroeconomics and the analysis of proposed expenditures. There is a strong desire to improve the analysis associated with public budgeting; productivity is considered important.

The national government manages many of its programs in cooperation with state and local governments. Sometimes the federal government interacts directly with citizens, as is the case with veterans' programs. In many programs, categorical and block grants are provided to state and local governments, which manage the programs. The government also has a revenue-sharing program with local governments. The result is that many federal activities are really intergovernmental in nature, with the actual services being provided by local government.

Unlike the federal government, state and local governments must balance their budgets. Sometimes that legal requirement is not met, but it does exist. Revenue and expenditure forecasts are thus important for state and local governments in developing balanced budgets.

State governments have a great deal of potential power over local governments. States commonly focus their efforts on highways and education, with increasing interest being addressed to health, environmental control, and welfare issues. Like the federal government, state governments provide assistance to local governments, often acting as pass-through agents for the federal government. Unlike the federal government, state governments can control local governments directly. Many local budgeting requirements are established by state law.

The form of local government varies from large cities to small villages and townships. Each unit of government has a budget process. Each is concerned with balancing revenue and expenditure. Local governments provide direct services, including public safety, education, and sanitation. Many local government activities require large expenditures for capital items like schools and roads; thus debt administration is an important aspect of local government. Transfer payments in the form of grants and revenue sharing are an important source of revenue.

The complex overlapping jurisdictions, economy of scale, and the growth of suburban areas and decline of cities are important to local government budgeting. The overlapping of jurisdictions means that tax collection is more complex and coordination of services is difficult. The existence of small governments means that many services are provided without the advantage of economy of scale. The declining tax base for cities is putting extreme pressure on city budgets. The increased population of suburban areas has strained the expertise and capability of the suburban governments to cope with the challenge. They must develop budgeting expertise while dealing with massive program growth. Each problem is significant and helps explain the challenge of local budgeting.

Decision-Making Models

Public budgeting is a decision-making process. Not surprisingly, there are several theories as to the way public policy decisions should be made. These theories or conceptual models are important because many people take them seriously and try to reform public budgeting using one of the theories as their guide. To better understand contemporary public budgeting reforms, these theories must be understood. But first, a criterion must be developed to judge the conceptual models, and the concept of conceptual models itself must be explained.

A conceptual model can be viewed as a tool which enables the user to understand and deal with complex phenomena. A tool can be judged "good" or "bad" in terms of the user's purpose. A hammer, for example, may be a good tool for building a shed, but it is bad for chopping wood. Professionals should judge conceptual models or theories in terms of the model's usefulness in helping them accomplish their tasks. Those tasks must be accomplished within a decision-making context largely induced by the ideologies of the culture.

Public budgeting in the United States must be conducted in a political, human, and often practical environment. The democratic ideology has helped to define the political environment. Consensus and partisan adjustments best explain the political context. Public budgeting is conducted by humans and it affects humans; thus emotional drama, error, pride, and other human characteristics help define the context of budgeting. In public budgeting, the practical is often a significant factor because decisions must be made. Even a so-called nondecision often represents an allocation of resources in budgeting. If the data or analyses are not available, then the decision maker must make do with conventional wisdom or personal, biased judgment. Thus the "do-able" or practical is significant.

Decision-making models can be judged in terms of their applicability to the decision-making environment of the public budget person. If the model is not in harmony with the decision-making environment (which is unlikely to be changed) then the model is "bad." That is, the model is not appropriate to the user's purposes. This value judgment must be limited to the decision maker discussed here.

Some major and commonly noted decision-making models are the *incremental change model*, the *satisficing model*, and the *ideal-rational model*. To this list, a provocative but little-cited model called the *stages of problem solving* model can be added. The incremental model is used for descriptive and normative purposes, but just because something exists in a certain way does not mean that it should continue to exist. The focus in this and subsequent paragraphs shall be on the normative use of the model. In the incremental model, major public policies evolve through cautious incremental steps; political forces mutually adjust their positions and, over time, public policy changes. This is an inherently conservative approach, and it biases the decision makers against more radical, innovative alternatives.

An agency develops a budget that it advocates to its department, to the Office of Management and Budget, and to Congress. In the major phases of the budget approval process, the agency takes the role of an advocate; the reviewer (for example, the Office of Management and Budget) questions the wisdom of the proposal; and the reviewer makes a tentative decision, which is often appealed to the secretary, the president, or the Senate. This model is consistent with the incremental change model in that policies are mutually adjusted because someone advocates and someone accommodates.

The satisficing model points out that decision makers develop a criterion to judge acceptable policy alternatives for a given problem. They then search the alternatives and select the first acceptable alternative they discover. Time is significant in the satisficing model. Alternatives are considered, but the ideal is not sought. The acceptable is the standard for judgment. Like the incremental change model, the satisficing model is used for both descriptive and normative purposes; the consideration here is only on the normative use. The reasons for the limited search are the lack of time for an exhaustive search and the opportunity costs of such a search.

The rational model is most commonly cited as the ideal way to reach decisions, especially major public policy decisions such as those in public budgeting. Its assumptions are deeply rooted in modern civilization and culture. The model systematically breaks decision-making down into six phases:

1. establish a complete set of operational goals, with relative weights allocated different degrees to which each may be achieved;
2. establish a complete inventory of other values and resources with relative weights;
3. prepare a complete set of the alternative policies open to the policy maker;
4. prepare a complete set of valid predictions of the cost and benefits of each alternative, including the extent to which each alternative will achieve the various operational goals, consume resources, and realize or impair other values;
5. calculate the net expectations for each alternative by multiplying the probability of each benefit and cost for each alternative by the utility of each, and calculate the net benefit (or cost) in utility units; and
6. compare the net expectations and identify the alternative (or alternatives, if two or more are equally good) with the highest net expectations.

In fewer words, using the rational model is merely defining one's goals, analyzing the available alternatives, and selecting the alternative that best meets the goals.

Although similar to the rational model, the stages-of-problem-solving model is amenable to observation and analysis, but it too can be a normative model. The starting point is the perception that a problem exists—not the formulation of goals. This perception permits the possibility of multiple value perspectives, whereas in formulating goals, one tends to ignore the possibility of multiple or conflicting values. Either formally or informally, the decision maker defines the problem, considers the solutions, and analyzes the alternatives in a manner similar to that of someone using the rational model. A key decision is then made either to reconsider the nature of the problem or to plan to resolve the problem. (This reconsideration step is not a part of the rational model.) If the decision is to proceed, the necessary action steps are taken and outcomes are evaluated. (This second reconsideration is also absent from the rational model.) From evaluation, the decision maker may either start over by reconsidering the problem or replan his or her action steps.

The incremental change model is an excellent tool for understanding the political environment of public policy making, but it is not useful for explaining the more technical difficulties associated with analysis. On the other hand, the rational model helps us comprehend the technical difficulties of analysis, but is relatively useless in explaining the highly important political environment.

With the incremental change model, the public budget person can better understand how the budget process is dominated by the strategies employed by and the conflicts that arise among the participants (clientele groups, agencies, departments, the Office of Management and Budget). Definable strategies exist that require such practices as agency cultivation of an active clientele, the development of confidence among other reviewing government officers such as budget examiners, and skill in following tactics that exploit temporary opportunities. Analysis in the budget process must serve to aid the key factors involved in making public policy. Reasoning from the incremental change model, program and budget analysis must be timely, must be able to be used to seize political opportunities, and must be comprehensible to those who must use the analysis in partisan bargaining situations.

The satisficing and ideal-rational models are useful for understanding difficulties associated with decision making. The satisficing model dramatically emphasizes that decisions are made under pressure, and severe limitations make achieving even a satisfactory alternative a significant accomplishment. The problem with the model is that one is often not satisfied that the best alternative has been selected. On the other hand, the desire for deciding on the best alternative is reflected in the ideal-rational model. The problem with that model is that the best alternative often cannot be achieved because of practical concerns such as a lack of time. We seem to be trapped between our desire for quality and the necessity to cope with our daily pressures.

The stages-of-problem-solving model can be contrasted to the ideal-rational model. In the problem-solving model, the starting point is the perception that a problem exists, that permitting one to consider the significance of culture, time, and perspective. By contrast, in the rational model, the starting point is the definition of one's goals. Next in the problem-solving model, the person formulates the problem, defines alternatives, gathers information, and tests proposals. In the rational model, the next steps cited are defining alternatives and gathering information. In the problem-solving model, the last steps are planning action, taking action steps, and evaluating outcomes. Again in contrast, the rational model is limited to deciding a given matter with the intention of maximizing goals. The rational model does not extend to taking action steps and evaluating outcomes. Another distinction is that the rational model does not include reconsideration as a factor, whereas the problem-solving model does.

The problem-solving model can help people working in public budgeting understand the nature of analysis. The rational model serves as the primary theoretical explanation of how analysis should be conducted, but the rational model cannot be attained. The problem-solving model serves as an alternative theoretical explanation of how analysis should be conducted in the budget process. The problem-solving model permits cycles of defining one's problem, producing alternatives, and testing alternatives. It implicitly recognizes that any given analysis will depend upon the ingenuity of the analysts, the kind of data available to them, the amount of resources at their command in undertaking the analysis, and other factors. Also the problem-solving model helps the public budgeting person relate budgeting, management-by-objectives, progress reporting, accounting, auditing, and program evaluation.

None of the models by themselves is adequate. The problem-solving and the incremental change models help the bureaucrat to understand the role of program and budget analysis in the budget-making process. They can be significant, but there are some constraints in using them. The problem-solving model helps the bureaucrat to understand the context in which intelligence, knowledge, and analytical techniques must be used. Together, the models meet the criteria.

The rational model, the theoretical basis for some budget reforms, can lead individuals to create false and naive expectations. That model ignores the political context and demands the impossible in terms of analysis. This can encourage some individuals in the budget process to neglect timeliness, seek needlessly expensive data, search for needless alternatives, and quest for clarity in objectives that will not be forthcoming. The rational model can be useful, but not in the manner commonly assumed. The usefulness is more to point out the impossible rather than serve as an ideal for the possible.

ECONOMIC INFLUENCES ON BUDGETING

Twin Evils

As noted earlier in this chapter, capitalism as modified by socialism provides the ideological economic climate for the United States. The dispute between capitalism and socialism centers on the role of government in society and thus on the appropriateness of what should be included in a public budget. Today there is a belief that government can make a difference in the overall economy, but disagreement exists on the question of what government should and should not do to help the economy achieve the desired condition of minimum unemployment with minimum inflation.

The agreed-upon twin evils are *severe unemployment* (mild unemployment is called a *recession* and a severe recession is called a *depression*) and a *sustained increase in price without an equal increase in value* (a mild increase is called *inflation* and a radical increase is called *hyperinflation*). Both result in significant hardships for the people of the world. Unemployment means that many people in the economy who want jobs cannot find them. Usually, during a recession, the economy is not growing or is growing very slowly; as a result, families do not receive adequate money for a decent existence. Inflation often means that people can buy fewer goods and services with the same amount of money. People on fixed incomes or slow-rising incomes are more likely to be hurt by inflation.

Exhibit 1–2 shows the U.S. employment rates from 1929 to 1992. The reader can easily understand why the 1930s are called "the Great Depression," since more than 5 percent unemployment is normally considered unacceptable, and the unemployment rate in that era reached a high of 24.9 percent. Some inflation is common,

EXHIBIT 1–2   Unemployment Rates for Selected Years 1929–92 (% of Civilian Work Force)

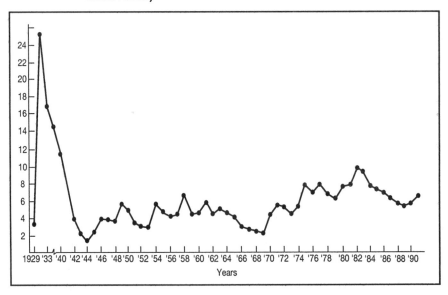

Source: U.S. Department of Labor, *Economic Report of the President*; U.S. Department of Commerce, *Statistical Abstract of the United States*. Washington D.C.: Bureau of the Census 1983 and 1992.

but the rate of inflation can rise to hyperinflation levels. Prices can rise so fast that no one is willing to receive or hold money. In Germany in 1923, the rate of hyperinflation was so high that paper currency became almost worthless and was used as wallpaper; barter reasserted itself as the principal method of trade. However, Western civilization has evolved to the point where it cannot sustain itself with a barter economy. Hyperinflation exists when a government enormously expands the money supply to finance large-scale expenditures. Mild inflation exists for reasons which will be discussed later.

Recession and inflation have been with us throughout modern society. Economic theory largely addresses these twin problems: How do they occur? What can be done to avoid them? In the last quarter of the twentieth century, our tools to deal with these problems are monetary and fiscal policy. Both involve public budgeting.

Exhibit 1–3 is a Phillips curve which helps describe the relationship between the unemployment rate and the rate of inflation. Note that there is an inverse relationship. In the exhibit, as unemployment goes down, inflation goes up. Also note the odd locations of the points for 1970 and 1971, which reflect a different pattern from those for the 1960s.

EXHIBIT 1–3   Phillips Curve

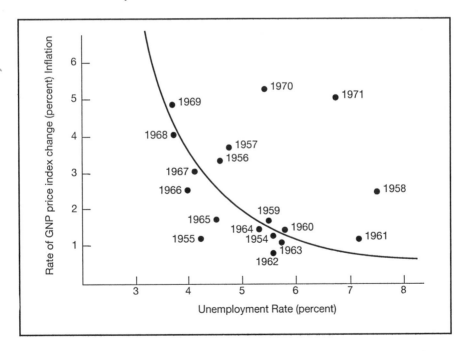

Source: Lloyd G. Reynolds, *Economics*, 4th ed. Homewood, Ill.: Richard D. Irwin, Inc., 1973, p. 174. Used by permission.

Influence of Economics

When Franklin D. Roosevelt became President of the United States, the country was in the Great Depression. He advocated and the Congress strongly agreed that action was necessary and that jobs had to be created. FDR was not motivated or influenced by economic theory. He was influenced by the large number of unemployed people, as cited in Exhibit 1–3.

The Great Depression was a political turning point for the United States. Before that time, social and economic thinking called for minimum or laissez faire government. The works of Adam Smith, Herbert Spencer, and Charles Darwin were highly influential prior to 1929. The least government was considered the best government. Nature and business should take their courses without interference as if they were guided by invisible forces or laws which would enable society to evolve into a higher, improved state. The Great Depression was a harsh awakening. In 1933, the unemployment rate was 24.9 percent. This was not an improved state. Voters and many intellectual leaders felt the old theories were unacceptable.

The idea that government could and should be used as a positive instrument in society gained widespread approval. No longer was the least government the best government. FDR launched massive public works programs for the times. Today, most economists agree that he was not bold enough. The spending for World War II is probably what got the United States and the world out of the depression. FDR's New Deal programs convinced many Americans that a strong, active federal government was "a good thing." World War II and the subsequent Cold War convinced even more Americans that the United States must remain a strong military power. Thus, the public's view of the role of government in American society has been greatly altered since 1929.

In the mid–1960s and 1970s, economic theory guided some of our most significant government decisions, and a variety of government units have arisen as the institutional means to consider and implement economic policy. Especially at the national level, economic theory has become the context in which major decisions are made.

The institutional mechanism is complex. In the executive branch, there is the Council of Economic Advisors, the Office of Management and Budget (OMB), and the Department of the Treasury. Each helps consider economic policy, and the OMB is the major implementer of fiscal policy once decisions are made by Congress and the President. In the legislative branch, the Congressional Budget Office (CBO), the Joint Economic Committee, the House and Senate Budget and Appropriations Committees, the House Ways and Means Committee, and the Senate Finance Committee all play important roles. The CBO and the Budget Committees are particularly important in setting overall fiscal policy. Partly independent of both Congress and the President, the Federal Reserve System largely establishes the nation's monetary policy. The detailed workings of each group are beyond the scope of this text, and readers are encouraged to take economics courses to pursue these subjects.

For both the legislative and executive branches, the primary device to establish fiscal policy is the federal budget. The primary device to establish monetary policy is the Federal Reserve System.

MONETARY POLICY

Central Bank

The Federal Reserve System is the central bank for the United States. It attempts to control the economy's supply of money and credit. This supply in turn affects unemployment and inflation. The Federal Reserve tries to expand money and credit to foster greater employment and to contract money and credit to combat inflation. The Federal Reserve banks have tools which influence member banks, and they in turn influence business and the public. These tools are based on the facts that banks maintain a reserve-to-loan ratio and borrow money from the Federal Reserve System banks. The three main Federal Reserve tools are:

1. open-market operations;
2. discount-rate policy; and
3. changes in the legal reserve requirement of the member banks.

Two other less significant tools are (4) "moral suasion" and (5) selective controls over *margin requirements* for loans made to buy stocks.

The most frequently used tool is that of *open-market operations*. The Federal Reserve's Open Market Committee frequently meets to decide to buy or sell government bonds or bills. Selling results in tightening and buying results in expanding the money supply. For example, selling $10 million in government bonds depresses the overall money supply. The buyers of the bonds will draw checks at a member bank, and the Federal Reserve will present the checks to the member bank for payment. That bank will then lose an equivalent amount of its reserve balance. This will contract the money supply, often by $50 million. This anti-inflationary tactic results in decreasing the total money supply.

Another tool is the *discount rate*, which is the interest the Federal Reserve (Fed) charges member banks for short-term loans. An increase in the discount rate increases interest rates, which makes money more expensive, thus discouraging people from borrowing. This contracts the economy. The reverse Fed action will stimulate the economy.

The third tool, *changing the reserve requirement*, is the most powerful, but most clumsy, tool. In a previous example, a 20 percent reserve requirement was assumed. The Federal Reserve Board has the limited power to raise or lower that required legal ratio within congressionally established limits. The Fed can tighten the money supply by requiring a greater reserve be maintained, thus shrinking the loan amount available. The converse increases the money supply. Changing reserve requirements is the most powerful tool, but it is used infrequently because of its awkward nature.

The minor tools are also useful. "*Moral suasion*" (for example, "jawboning") might mean merely appealing directly to key banks. The appeal alone may be sufficient. *Selected credit controls* are another important tool, as they involve stock margin requirements. The Federal Reserve establishes how much credit a person is allowed to use in the buying of common and preferred stocks. This selective control acts in the same manner as the reserve requirement.

Effectiveness

The major advantages of monetary policy are:

1. decisions can be reached and applied rapidly due to the less political nature of the Federal Reserve; and
2. monetary policy does work if the proper vigorous action is taken, especially in combating some types of inflation.

The advantages are significant, but the use of monetary policy should be understood in terms of its effect on society. Federal Reserve policy severely affects companies in industries such as housing that depend heavily upon external credit. When banks are forced to restrict loans, the higher credit groups will have preference; thus, smaller and newer businesses will suffer. Therefore, tight monetary policy will affect certain sectors of our economy more than others and certain groups (for example, the young and the minorities) more than others. The events of fall 1966 illustrate the dangers of restrictive monetary policy. At that time, the policy:

1. brought the capital market to the brink of crisis;
2. caused a radical decline in home construction;
3. threatened the solvency of intermediaries (for example, banks), and
4. left banks reluctant to make long-term loans.

Monetary Policy and Public Budgeting

Monetary policy is significant to public budgeting in at least two important ways. First, all levels of government borrow and invest. Monetary policy affects available credit and especially interest rates. The interest paid and earned is important to any government. This shall become more apparent in subsequent chapters. Second, many government programs (for example, housing, environment) are heavily influenced by monetary policy. Budget justifications and intelligent budget reviews would not be possible without a thorough understanding of the effects of monetary policy on those programs.

FISCAL POLICY

Policy Goals

The principal macroeconomic goals are:

1. *Full employment*: Practically, this means about a 4 percent unemployment rate in the United States. At this rate, there are about as many people looking for jobs as there are jobs available.
2. *Maintenance of price stability*: Inflation increases prices. This brings a shift in the distribution of real income from those whose dollar incomes are relatively inflexible to those whose dollar incomes are relatively flexible. Thus, those on fixed incomes such as the elderly are hurt by inflation.
3. *Steady constant economic growth*: As the population increases, economic growth is essential, not only to maintain the past standard of living but to improve that standard.
4. *An adequate supply of collectively consumed goods*: Some activities are public in nature and involve services for the good of the society. These include police protection, national defense, highways, schools, and so on.

In fiscal policy, there is an assumed relationship between the total spending level in the economy and the existence of either unemployment or inflation. Total spending can be thought of in terms of the gross domestic production of the society. The *gross domestic product* (GDP) equals personal consumption plus gross private domestic investment plus government purchases of goods and services plus net exports of goods and services. The *gross national product* (GNP) is the total productive activity in a country during a certain period of time.[1] If GNP is at the target level, then the unemployment rate and the inflation rate are at acceptable levels. As mentioned earlier, the reader will notice in Exhibit 1–3 the inverse relationship between the unemployment rate and inflation. The best possible rates in the United States are debatable, but many consider them to be about 4 percent unemployment and about 3 percent inflation. These optimal rates occurred in 1966 and 1967. All the macroeconomic or fiscal policy goals were being achieved. In the other years, the goals were not met.

Role of Government

How does a society reach these goals each year? This is the challenge of macroeconomics. Examine again the definition of GNP. Notice the key ingredients are both private and public. Exhibit 1–4 defines the ingredients of the GDP in billions of current dollars.

---

[1]Economists commonly define GNP as "the sum of final products such as consumption goods and gross investment (which is the increase in inventories plus gross births or productions of buildings and equipment)."

EXHIBIT 1–4   1991 Gross Domestic Product (in billions of dollars)

Personal consumption expenditure		$3,889.1
Gross private domestic investment		726.7
Net exports of goods and services		-30.7
Government purchases		1,087.5
Federal	445.1	
National defense	323.5	
Non-defense	121.6	
State and local	642.4	
Gross Domestic Product		$5,672.6

Source: U.S. Department of Commerce, *Survey of Current Business*, vol. 72, no. 4, April 1992, p. 9.

    Today, the GDP is well over $5 trillion, but the key relationships are the same. The private sector is the most significant (about 81 percent), but the public sector is large (about 19 percent). Notice that state and local government represents about 57 percent of the public sector and 73 percent of the federal government is defense. The key is total GDP. If the private sector is inadequate, then the government can act positively by changing its level of spending or influencing the private sector. If the level is too high, the economy will probably suffer inflation; and if the level is too low, the economy may suffer unemployment. The fiscal powers can be viewed as operating in pairs.

GOVERNMENT POWERS	EXAMPLES
1. Buy or sell	1. Purchase of goods or sale of stockpiles
2. Take or give	2. Taxes or rebates
3. Lend or borrow	3. Surplus or deficits in the budget

    The economy can be influenced by government action. Buying as a consumer stimulates the economy. Selling depresses prices. Increasing taxes depresses the income because consumers and corporations have less to spend. Giving tax rebates stimulates the economy. A budget surplus will depress the economy and deficit spending will stimulate it. Fiscal powers exist through government action because the federal government is a major actor in the economy.

    There is no one fiscal policy solution to an economic problem. An examination of the paired powers of government listed above implies that policy makers reasoning from macroeconomic theory can disagree on the appropriate fiscal solution. This does not imply that all methods or techniques will give the same results. For example, if faster consumer stimulation is desired, then rebates are probably better than deficit spending because the latter takes much longer to be felt in the economy. On the other hand, if the problem is chronic, then deficit spending may be the best solution. Possibly the economic problem is temporary and concentrated in one major product, such as steel. Then the solution may be to stockpile the goods to stimulate jobs or to sell the stockpile to depress inflationary price increases.

Macroeconomic theory does not necessarily condemn the existence of a public debt or a national budget deficit. If the debt can be easily serviced, then there is no difficulty in having a public debt (as pointed out in a later chapter). Having a chronic national debt may lead to serious difficulties. The debt payments may interfere with the government's ability to finance other useful projects. Large interest payments can mean an equitable or nonprogressive redistribution of income. Note that these problems are manageable and do not speak against a deficit in one or more particular years. Also, there are beneficial aspects of a large national public debt:

1. the public debt provides the means for the Federal Reserve to increase or decrease the money supply in connection with reserve requirements;
2. it provides needed liquidity for all the financial and nonfinancial businesses; and
3. it provides a safe investment for the unsophisticated and unwary investor.

There are built-in fiscal stabilizers in the U.S. economy. Several fall outside the scope of this text, but one that is important for public budgeting is transfer payments. These payments rise substantially during periods of recession and fall during prosperity. When people are unemployed, they receive unemployment compensation and eventually they may receive welfare and food stamps. Farm prices are likely to fall so agriculture price support programs automatically start working. Emergency public works programs can also begin automatically. During prosperity, these transfer payments shrink. These are commonly referred to as entitlement programs, and they constitute a large share of the national budget.

Using Fiscal Policy

In the early 1960s, the unemployment in the nation was excessive. In fiscal terms, the actual GNP was less than the desirable GNP level, but prices were stable. The fiscal policy adopted was a tax cut. The Investment Tax Credit of 1962 and later, the Revenue Act of 1964 were passed. The former stimulated the private sector to increase investment, thus stimulating income, employment, and the economic growth rate. The latter reduced tax liabilities, thus stimulating consumption. The policy was successful. In 1965, further tax reductions were enacted and the fiscal policy seemed sound.

By early 1966, unemployment fell below 4 percent, and, predictably (see Exhibit 1–3), the price level (inflation) was rising. Only modest steps were taken to increase taxes, but government purchases rose sharply. This was a period of "guns and butter"—a war in Vietnam and a war on poverty. In 1967, President Johnson did ask for a temporary tax surcharge, but Congress took no action. The Fed acted as noted earlier. The excessive use of monetary policy tools caused a credit crunch with high interest rates and a recession in the home-building industry. In early 1968, the situation was getting worse. President Johnson requested another "war tax," but the Congress refused to enact this politically unpopular tax. Finally, in June 1968, a compromise tax surcharge was passed, but it proved ineffective.

President Nixon inherited an economic problem. Monetary policy continued to be quite restrictive. The U.S. role in the Vietnam war began to diminish and government purchases were cut. The Vietnam war boom ended by late 1969, and a recession started by 1970.

The 1960s experience with using fiscal policy indicates that it is not a flexible policy easily applied. Quick action might be desired, but Congress is slow to act, especially on unpopular tax increases. Thus, a significant lag occurs.

Look again at Exhibit 1–3 and notice the points representing 1970 and 1971. Unlike the other years, they are not on the Phillips curve. We experienced both relatively high unemployment and inflation. The Phillips curve seems to have shifted to the right. In other words, we experienced a time in which both unemployment and inflation were at unacceptable levels at the same time. Economists call this *stagflation*—stagnation accompanied by price inflation.

Economists and political leaders argued about this phenomenon. In August 1977, a Treasury Department official was quoted as saying of President Carter: "I don't think that he understands why there's high inflation and high unemployment at the same time. But, then neither does anyone else" (Samuelson, 1977).

Some facts can help us to understand the phenomenon, but confusion on this subject continues. The recession fell disproportionately on narrow groups—particularly the young and blacks. Monetary policy curbed economic activity in the sectors of the economy dependent on borrowing, but the nation has evolved into a service economy, which is not as affected by monetary policy. Inflation originated most in food and oil price increases, which rippled throughout the economy. The new labor and industry custom of applying automatic cost-of-living increases prevents the traditional groups from absorbing the inflation loss, thus lengthening the inflation effects. In other words, the American economy after 1975 was more complex than before, and the aggregate monetary and fiscal policy actions of the 1960s were apparently not as effective as they once were.

President Reagan approached the stagflation economy with a new economic theory largely developed by Professor Arthur B. Laffer then of the University of Southern California. The heart of this theory is the relationship between tax rates and tax revenues. The Laffer curve is presented in Exhibit 1–5.

In this exhibit, the vertical line represents tax rates and the horizontal line represents tax revenues. The two extremes of zero tax rate and 100 percent tax rate produce no tax revenue. In between, the curve demonstrates that at some point an increase in tax rates actually reduces tax revenue. This is because at the higher rates individuals reduce their taxable work effort, spend more time seeking ways to reduce tax liabilities, and engage in more nontaxed activities. The implication for budgeting is that if marginal tax rates have exceeded that key point, then, ironically, a reduction in tax rates will actually lead to an increase in tax revenues.

EXHIBIT 1–5 Laffer Curve

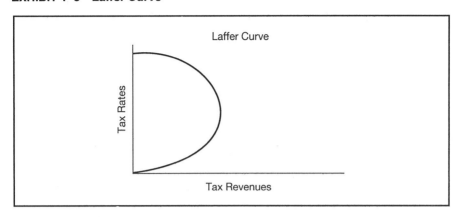

Source: Dom Bonafede, "Reagan's Supply-Side Policies Push Economics Writers into the Spotlight," *National Journal*, 1337 (September 26, 1981), p. 1723.

President Reagan and his economic advisors felt that the way to get the American economy out of stagflation was to cut the tax rates. Because such a cut would result in higher budget deficits, they advocated cutting government expenditures (with the exception of military expenditures, which they increased). The immediate result was lower inflation, higher unemployment, and a larger federal debt. Given the automatic fiscal stabilizers built into the government programs, the federal budget expenditures grew to offset rising unemployment and revenues fell because there were fewer taxpayers. The larger federal debt, coupled with a monetary policy of high interest rates, and with other factors, resulted in high interest rates which retarded economic growth and recovery.

Fiscal Policy and Public Budgeting

At the national level, fiscal policy largely influences federal budgets. Once policy is determined, using macroeconomics, then those policies influence the following budget concerns:

1. the overall size of the budget, including revenue and expenditure totals;
2. the types of spending, such as capital investment versus direct payments;
3. the timing of spending programs;
4. the balance of activities—federal programs do work at cross purposes, and it must be decided which to emphasize and which to deemphasize;
5. the size of entitlement programs, and the amount available for the controlled programs;
6. the building or selling of stockpiles;
7. jawboning big labor or big corporations; and
8. tax policy.

A federal budget professional and most state and local budget officers must understand fiscal policy. Macroeconomics is the theory used to make many key budget decisions. Budget justifications and reviews are often done using macroeconomics. With the CBO and budget committees, Congress is likely to be more effective in using fiscal policy than it was in the 1960s, but political forces will still discourage the use of tax increases.

OTHER ECONOMIC TOPICS

In a text of this nature, all aspects of economics important to public budgeting cannot be covered in a single chapter. Subsequent chapters use various economic concepts, but the important contribution of economics to public budgeting is still not stated fully. Students are encouraged to read various economics texts, especially public finance books. The following subjects are worth investigating at greater length:

1. multiplier effect;
2. economic growth;
3. balance of payments;
4. regional economics;
5. public interest, including Rawl's "justice is fairness" implication to economics;
6. pareto-optimum;
7. welfare economics;
8. labor economics;
9. public goods theory; and
10. public choice theory.

REVIEW QUESTIONS

1. Explain the various perspectives one can have on public budgeting and how the definition of public budgeting can be affected by each perspective.
2. Assuming policy is defined as "a guide to action," explain how budgeting is policy. Why and in what way is this understandably significant to policy makers and public managers?
3. What is the budget cycle? How does the local budget cycle differ from the federal one?
4. In what ways are American ideologies significant in shaping public budgeting?
5. Explain the federal context of American budgeting and the significance of that context.
6. What are the major normative decision-making theories and how do they affect public budgeting as a practice?
7. Explain why inflation and unemployment rates act in inverse relationship.

8. What happened in 1970 and 1971 that cast doubt upon macroeconomic theory?
9. Why does the shift in the American economy from an industrial to a service economy have significance to the effectiveness of monetary policy?
10. How can liberals and conservatives disagree on fiscal policy but still base their thinking on macroeconomic theory?
11. Why is public debt not bad *ipso facto?* Explain why entitlement programs are consistent with macroeconomic theory.
12. Explain the economic theories upon which Reagan relied in making his economic recommendations. Contrast them to the other, more accepted macroeconomic theories.

REFERENCES

BAKKER, OEGE. *The Budget Cycle in Public Finance in the United States.* The Hague: W. P. Van Stockum, 1953.

BARTIZAL, JOHN R. *Budget Principles and Procedures.* Englewood Cliffs, N.J.: Prentice Hall, 1942.

BRUNDAGE, PERCIVAL FLACK. *The Bureau of the Budget.* New York: Holt, Rinehart & Winston, 1970.

BUCHANAN, JAMES M. *The Demand and Supply of Public Goods.* Chicago: Rand McNally, 1968.

BUCK, A. E. *Public Budgeting.* New York: Harper & Row, 1929.

BURKHEAD, JESSE. *Government Budgeting.* New York: Wiley, 1965.

———— and JERRY MINER. *Public Expenditure.* Chicago: Aldine, 1971.

Center For The Study Of American Business. *The Supply-Side Effects of Economic Policy.* St. Louis, Mo.: Washington University, 1981.

DAHL, ROBERT A. *A Preface to Democratic Theory.* Chicago: University of Chicago Press, 1956.

DAVID, JAMES E., JR. (ed.). *Politics, Programs and Budgets.* Englewood Cliffs, N.J.: Prentice Hall, 1969.

DORFMAN, ROBERT. *Measuring the Benefits of Government Expenditures.* Washington, D.C.: Brookings Institution, 1965.

DUE, JOHN F., and ANN F. FRIEDLAENDER. *Government Finance.* 5th ed. Homewood, Il: Richard D. Irwin, 1973.

HAVENMAN, ROBERT H., and JULIUS MARGOLIS. *Public Expenditure and Public Analysis.* 2nd ed. Chicago: Rand McNally, 1977.

LEE, ROBERT D., and RONALD W. JOHNSON. *Public Budgeting Systems.* Baltimore, Md.: University Park Press, 1973.

MILLER, RODGER L. E. *Economics Today.* 4th ed. New York: Harper & Row, 1982.

MOAK, LENNOX L., and ALBERT M. HILLHOUSE. *Local Government Finance.* Chicago: Municipal Finance Officers Association, 1975.

Municipal Performance Report, 1, 4 (August 1974).

MUSGRAVES, RICHARD A., and PEGGY B. MUSGRAVES. *Public Finance in Theory and Practice.* New York: McGraw-Hill, 1973.

NICHOLS, DOROTHY M. *Modern Money Mechanics.* Chicago: Federal Reserve Bank of Chicago, 1975.

RABIN, JACK, and THOMAS D. LYNCH. *Handbook on Public Budgeting and Financial Management.* New York: Marcel Dekker, 1983.

REYNOLDS, LLOYD G. *Economics,* 4th ed. Homewood, Il: Richard D. Irwin, 1973.

SAMUELSON, PAUL A. *Economics*, 10th ed. New York: McGraw-Hill, 1976.
SAMUELSON, ROBERT J. "The Enemy Among Us," *National Journal*, 9, 42 (October 15th, 1977), 1619.
SWAN, WALLACE K. "Theoretical Debates Applicable to Budgeting." In Jack Rabin and Thomas D. Lynch (eds.), *Handbook on Public Budgeting and Financial Management*. New York: Marcel Dekker, 1983.
TRUMAN, DAVID. *The Governmental Process*. New York: Knopf, 1951.

2

TOWARD
MODERN BUDGETING

This chapter examines public budgeting, reflects on how it has evolved into its present condition, and reflects on its significance in the larger context of public administration. Some attention is given to explaining what knowledgeable people define or characterize as public budgeting. Particular attention is focused on the critical issues which shaped the evolution of public budgeting. This chapter should help the reader understand:

1. the major historical reforms that have shaped public budgeting in America, and how the issues implicit in these reforms are still influencing what we perceive to be the "proper" role of budgeting in our government;
2. the executive focus on contemporary budget reforms;
3. the legislative focus on contemporary budget reforms; and
4. the state of modern budgeting in America.

PRELUDE

Parliament versus the King

Public budgeting in the United States is very much influenced by early English history. The word *budget* seems to have originated in the Middle English *bouget*, meaning bag or wallet. A great leather bag was used by the king's treasurer—later called the exchequer—to carry the documents explaining the king's fiscal needs. That bag was called the budget. Over time the document came to be called the budget, and the system used to prepare and execute the document came to be called budgeting. The bag was used primarily when the king's treasurer went to Parliament seeking funds for the king.

English history is largely a story of struggle between the king and the Parliament over the control of the nation. To a greater extent than other feudal realms, the newly established Norman kingdom of England in 1066 stressed the power and authority of the king over all others, including the important nobles. In England, the elite barons, who controlled large landed estates, actually held their estates as tenants-in-chief of the king rather than being actual property owners, as the concept is understood today. By 1215, the kingdom was ruled by King John—a descendant of William the Conqueror. King John lost the continental portion of his kingdom, which included Normandy, and he engaged in a civil war with many of his English barons and other nobles. In an attempt to achieve peace, the king signed the Magna Carta. The twelfth article of that document stated that no taxes could be imposed "unless by the common council of the realm." The "council of the realm" became Parliament.

In the important Reformation period, the power of the king versus that of Parliament was tested to its utmost. By 1649, not only had the Parliamentary forces prevailed over King Charles I in battle, but also King Charles had been beheaded. From the Parliamentary forces, Oliver Cromwell emerged as a military leader and became dictator of England, Scotland, and Ireland. A few years after his death, key elements of the army rebelled against Cromwell's son and supported the restoration of King Charles II in 1660. The tension between the Crown and Parliament continued. Charles II and the other Stuart kings favored a divine-right-of-kings interpretation of power and seemed to consider adopting Catholicism as the state religion. In 1688, James II was forced from the throne, and King William and Queen Mary (the sister of James) were asked to share the throne. A key product of that era was the English Bill of Rights of 1688. It established that no man could be compelled to pay a gift, loan, or tax "without common consent by Act of Parliament." The concept of a shared legislative and executive power was established. By 1770, the king even agreed to an annual specified grant of funds that were controlled by the Parliament.

This struggle, or tension, between the legislative (the Parliament) and the executive (the king) is also one of the most important characteristics of public budgeting in the United States. At the time of the American Revolution in 1776, the stress was upon legislative supremacy, and the use of executive power was greatly suspect as a principal of proper government. The Revolution was fought against the "tyranny" of the king. From the end of the Revolution to 1789, the country was run under a weak executive system as established by the Articles of Confederation.

With the adoption of the Constitution in 1789, the principles of proper government shifted away from a weak central government, with a weak executive, toward a strong executive authority and a national government. James Madison was particularly influential in arguing for continued legislative-executive tension. He believed that such tension was not only functional, but even necessary. He argued that power should be separated, especially between the legislative and executive branches. This separation of powers would prevent an executive abuse of power yet still permit strong executive leadership to exist.

Since the beginning of the Republic, almost every budget reform addresses or affects this intended tension and balance of power between the legislative and executive branches of government.

Colonial America

In colonial America, the revenue was generated within the colonies, and the various state houses had a great deal of control over revenues and expenditures. The king's representatives administered the government. The legislatures became the place where the leading colonists gathered. They became accustomed to exercising power, with a separate group actually administering the government programs. The separation from England, abetted by the primitive means of transoceanic transportation, fostered independence. But the need to live within their own resources and to decide how to apply their own resources using a locally elected legislative body were the important factors leading to self-reliance.

Many of the causes of the American Revolution relate directly to public budgeting issues. England decided to impose taxes (for example, the Stamp Act) on the colonies largely because of the expensive French-Indian War. This unilateral act seemed unfair given the legislative authority over tax matters and the reasoning of such documents as Magna Carta and the Bill of Rights. Of course, many other reasons as well explain the emotions leading to the American Revolution, but issues concerning public budgeting were some of the most emotionally charged subjects of that era.

Not surprisingly, those strong feelings helped shape the U.S. Constitution. For example, Article I, Section 9 of the Constitution requires that all matters dealing with revenue must originate in the House of Representatives. The founders of the United States were not content to say that Congress had to act on revenue matters, as the English Bill of Rights had said of Parliament a century earlier. Rather, they stated that this matter had to start with the chamber of Congress that was to be *the* representative of the people. Today, the president presents his budget somewhat as the king's treasurer did. The House passes the appropriation bills first. The Senate often acts as an appealing body and eventually the two chambers agree upon the appropriations. However, the House is still considered the leading chamber on matters concerning revenue and appropriations.

Budgeting in the 1800s

For the first few years of the federal government, Alexander Hamilton was the influential secretary of the Treasury. He viewed his role as being much like that of the English exchequer, and his department was the most significant nonmilitary department. The national government's revenue source was customs duties, and the

Coast Guard was an important force in ensuring their proper collection. Hamilton also effectively had the very large Revolutionary War debt retired.

Hamilton, a leader of the Federalist faction, argued in favor of strong executive in government. He not only felt that government was responsible for the welfare and defense of the country but also that the nation's leaders should act as trustees for the people. To Hamilton, strong executive leadership was important, and the government's budget and financial affairs were primary tools of his leadership. The Federalist view was influenced by contemporary England, where the ministers dominated the Parliament and the executive activities.

Thomas Jefferson came to be the leader of the anti-Federalist faction, which opposed Hamilton. Jefferson thought not only that the separation of powers was critical, but also that policy matters, including budgetary decisions, were the dominion of the Congress. Executive leadership on comprehensive budget matters was considered improper by some presidents, but, interestingly, Jefferson's administration was characterized by the strong leadership of Secretary of the Treasury Albert Gallatin.

Congress started with a unified and comprehensive approach to public budgeting. The Ways and Means Committee was extremely powerful, as it made decisions on revenues and appropriations. With few exceptions, the executive branch did not have a unified approach. The Treasury Department did compile the expenditure estimates from all the agencies, but it did not edit or analyze the estimates. Such activities were considered to be legislative in nature.

As the nineteenth century evolved, the Congress eroded its unified approach to the budget, and the executive branch did not attempt to assert itself. By 1865, a separate House Appropriations Committee was established so that revenues and expenditures were considered separately. By 1885, there were eight separate committees that recommended appropriations. This disunity lessened the budgetary focus of power; but, except for periods of war or depression, the federal government was not concerned about tight budgets. In this era, there was a constrained view of what government should do in society, so budgets tended to be small. And, the major revenue source—the customs—was providing more revenue than was needed by the demands for expenditure, so that Congress had the unusual problem of dealing with large surpluses.

Progressive Reform Movement

What is commonly considered "modern budgeting" started in the Progressive era with the Progressives' reactions against corruption in local government. Largely due to the efforts of popular newspapers and book writers, called "muckrakers," the Progressive political movement gained popular support, which included demands for municipal reforms to curtail corruption. The political views of the Progressives were similar to those of Alexander Hamilton, but much of their political philosophy was influenced by German political philosophers such as Georg Wilhelm Friedrich Hegel and conservative English philosophers such as Edmund Burke. The most effective municipal reformers were the National Municipal League (founded in 1899) and the New York Bureau of Municipal Research (1906).

The latter group is one of the most remarkable in American history. One of the leaders was Charles Beard, who was a noted historian and founder of the academic discipline of political science. Luther Gulick and other members of that Bureau were also instrumental in founding public administration as a study and practice. The research arm of the Bureau moved to Washington, D.C., and evolved into today's Brookings Institution. The training arm was moved to Syracuse University in 1925 and became the Maxwell School of Syracuse University. The Bureau served as a model and "mother house" for many other bureaus throughout the country. The members of the Bureau led and staffed almost every major governmental reform committee between 1910 and 1950.

Not surprisingly, the New York Bureau of Municipal Research was highly influential in budget reforms. One year after its creation, it prepared the first detailed report demonstrating the need for adopting a municipal budget system. In that same year, the Bureau produced an object classification budget for the New York City Department of Health. By 1912, the reforms of the Bureau were reflected in the Taft Commission report, which called for object (line-item) classification budgeting in all federal departments and agencies.[1] By the 1920s, most of the budgets of major American cities were reformed. In 1929, A. E. Buck, a staff person of the Bureau, wrote the first (and very influential) text on public budgeting.

Budget reform was stimulated by a desire to strengthen the executive authority. Influential reformers such as Woodrow Wilson believed that executive authority could be strengthened if citizens could vote for candidates who had the power to carry out their promises. Wilson argued against a government dominated by the Congress. He felt the chief executive should be stronger and that budget reform was one of the best ways to strengthen the executive. Wilson, like other Progressives, argued for a professionalization of the career administrators who would report to elected decision makers.

EVOLUTION

Prior to 1921

In the early 1900s, the federal government started to experience large federal expenditures and budget deficits. The customs revenue was not adequate and a federal income tax was passed. This new tax solved the fundamental revenue problem, since the tax rate could be increased to provide the necessary revenue. This tax also attracted the keen attention of the business community, as they now had a vested interest in minimizing the money that the government took from them as corporations and individuals. Business interests dominated the times. Business and many citizens stressed the importance of economy, efficiency, and government retrenchment. Many felt that the least government was the best government.

President Taft issued a report prepared by the Commission on Economy and Efficiency Goals titled "Need for a National Budget." The report stressed that the president should be responsible for preparing a unified executive budget. The rationale was motivated by two themes: (1) economy and efficiency, and (2) strengthening democracy. A budget would better enable the president to plan government activities so that maximum economy and efficiency were achieved. A president's budget would also strengthen the president's power—thus citizens could vote for or against a person who had the power to fulfill campaign promises. President Taft was not successful in his reforms and Woodrow Wilson's income tax temporarily took the pressure off.

Prior to 1921, agencies still followed the Jeffersonian tradition of preparing their estimates and transmitting them to the Treasury Department, which passed them on to Congress. Treasury conducted no analyses. The various congressional committees considered the estimates with minimum coordination among themselves. The agencies did sometimes overspend the appropriations and Congress felt obligated to appropriate the overspent amount. The president did not participate in the budget process and there was no overall executive branch plan.

Budgeting and Accounting Act of 1921

President Taft's reforms were largely enacted in 1921. Pressures for budget reform continued, especially with the expense of World War I. The Budget and Accounting Act of 1921 provided for a national budget and an independent audit of government accounts. The law specifically required the president to submit a budget, including estimates of expenditures, appropriations, and receipts for the ensuing fiscal year. The new legislation created the Bureau of the Budget (BOB) in the Treasury Department. Section 909 of the legislation states:

> The Bureau, when directed by the President, shall make a detailed study of the departments and establishments for the purpose of enabling the President to determine what changes (with a view of securing greater economy and efficiency in the conduct of the public service) should be made in (1) the existing organization, activities, and methods of business of such departments or establishments, (2) the appropriations, (3) the assignment of particular activities to particular services, or (4) the regrouping of services. The results of such study shall be embodied in a report or reports to the President, who may transmit to Congress such report or reports or any part thereof with his recommendation on the matter covered thereby.

This landmark legislation greatly strengthened the president and created the powerful BOB as an arm of the president. The agencies were required to submit their estimates and supporting information to the BOB. Agencies were not allowed to initiate contacts with Congress. Also legislation established that all recommended legislation from agencies had to be sent to the BOB for review and clearance. This clearance function greatly increased presidential power because it allowed the president to ensure the executive branch was in step with presidential policy. The Bureau could and did prepare the president's budget, which was the executive branch (president's) proposal to the Congress. The agencies and departments in the executive branch were and are required to support the president's budget.

Budgeting is largely a story of relative legislative-executive strength. With Hamilton, executive strength was asserted but short-lived. After Jefferson, legislative strength in the budget area dominated but was diminished by the nonunified approach that evolved in the Congress. With the passage of the 1921 legislation, executive branch strength started to grow in spite of the fact that the Congress largely initiated the legislation. The power of the Congress was not diminished, but the 1921 Act did increase the power of the president.

The Budget and Accounting Act of 1921 also created a congressional agency called the General Accounting Office (GAO) to audit independently the government accounts. This agency is headed by the comptroller general, who is appointed to a fifteen-year term by the president. The purpose of the audits is to verify that government funds are being used for legal purposes. The independence of the agency prevents improper pressure being exerted upon it by members of the executive branch.

The president's 1937 Committee on Administration Management (Brownlow Committee) recommended the strengthening of the BOB's management activities. The 1921 legislation had given the bureau certain managerial responsibilities, but they were not exerted. The Brownlow Committee's report eventually led to the Reorganization Act of 1939. This, in turn, led to establishment of the Executive Office of the President and the transfer of the BOB to that new office. President Roosevelt defined the duties of the Bureau as follows:

1. to assist the president in the preparation of the budget and the formulation of the fiscal program of the government;
2. to supervise and control the administration of the budget;
3. to conduct research in the development of improved plans of administrative management, and to advise the executive departments and agencies of the government with respect to improved administrative organizations and practice;
4. to aid the president in bringing about more efficient and economical conduct of the government services;
5. to assist the president by elevating and coordinating departmental advice on proposed legislation and by making recommendations as to presidential action on legislative enactment, in accordance with past practices;
6. to assist in the consideration and clearance and, where necessary, in the preparations of proposed executive orders and proclamations;
7. to plan and promote the improvement, development, and coordination of federal and other statistical services; and
8. to keep the president informed of the progress of activities by agencies of the government with respect to work proposed, work actually initiated, and work completed, together with the relative timing of work between the several agencies of the government, all to the end that the work programs of the several agencies of the executive branch of the government may be coordinated and that the monies appropriated by the Congress may be expended in the most economical manner possible with the least possible overlapping and duplication of effort.

The Bureau became the right arm of a strong president.

Post–1940 Reforms

During World War II, the Bureau became even more important, with all activities directed toward the war. Taxes were increased, and record deficits were incurred. The Bureau assumed added duties, including supervision of government financial reports and establishing personnel ceilings. In 1945, the Bureau's budget function was extended to include the government corporations. And, accounts had to be maintained on a program basis, and full cost information was required. The Government Corporations Act of 1945 also directed the GAO to appraise the corporations in terms of their performance rather than merely in terms of the legality and propriety of their expenditures. This provision was eventually extended to all GAO reviews.

The Full Employment Act of 1946 called for economic planning and a budget policy directed toward achieving maximum national employment and production. The late 1940s saw the addition of more duties to the BOB. The Classification Act of 1949 required the director to issue and administer relations involving agency reviews of their operations. The Travel Expense Act of 1949 assigned the director regulatory functions on travel allowances.

President Truman appointed the Hoover Commission in 1947, and a report was submitted in 1949. The Commission recommended that

1. a budget based on functions, activities, and projects, called a "performance budget," be adopted;
2. the appropriation structure be surveyed and improved;
3. the budget estimates of all departments and agencies be separated between current operating and capital outlays; and
4. the president's authority to reduce expenditures under appropriations "if the purposes intended by the Congress are still carried out" be clearly established.

Several reforms resulted from the Hoover Commission, but the Budget and Accounting and Procedures Act of 1950 was particularly important. It recognized the need for reliable accounting systems and the president was given the authority to prescribe the contents and budget arrangements, simplify the presentations, broaden the appropriations, and make progress toward performance budgeting.

The Second Hoover Commission (1955) led to more technical but equally important budget reforms. Agency accounts were to be maintained on an accrual basis. Cost-based budgets were encouraged. Synchronization between agency structure and budget classifications were encouraged. The President's Commission on Budget Concepts in 1967 did not address any fundamental budget reforms but concerned itself with smaller technical issues. In summary, the post-1940 period saw many reforms that continued to strengthen the executive budget process.

Approaches to Budgeting

By the 1950s, there were three accepted formats for budgeting—*line-item, program,* and *performance*—with two underlying philosophic perspectives on budgeting—*incremental* and *rational.* In *line-item budgeting* (Exhibit 2–1), the

EXHIBIT 2–1 Hennepin County Line-Item Budget

MAJOR PROGRAM: COMMUNITY SERVICES & ECONOMIC ASSISTANCE	PROGRAM ACTIVITY BY LINE ITEM	BUDGET YEAR 1980
PROGRAM: COMMUNITY SERVICES : SUBPROGRAM MANAGEMENT & PLANNING ACTIVITY	DEPARTMENT COMMUNITY SERVICES	PROGRAM CODE 8831

Account No.	Description	1979 Budget	1979 Actual & Estimated	1980 Department Request
	Personal Services (8000)			
8002	Salaries & Wages-Reg	$1,586,573	$1,673,696	$1,763,765
8004	Salaries & Wages-Temp	14,137	25,000	24,000
8006	Overtime	11,117	12,000	13,000
8008	Intern Stipend	–	–	–
8014	On Call	–	–	–
8016	Emergency	–	–	–
8020	Shift Differential	–	–	–
8022	Sunday Differential	–	–	–
8048	Long Term Disability Insurance	14,694	15,308	11,789
8052	Life Insurance	1,456	1,422	1,489
8054	Health Insurance	70,401	80,619	77,388
8060	FICA	82,649	91,050	102,421
8062	PERA	106,810	111,275	104,828
8064	MERA	–	2,658	2,951
8066	Severance	–	–	–
8068	Stability	37,242	37,242	40,330
8070	Supplemental Retirement	13,236	13,789	11,851
8072	Unemployment Compensation	6,915	3,400	3,600
8074	Worker's Compensation	4,872	4,872	5,424
8080	Other Personal Services	10,000	10,000	10,700
8099	Personal Services-Contra	–	–	–
	Subtotal	$1,960,102	$2,082,331	$2,173,536
	Commodities (8100)			
8012	Office Supplies	$ 38,557	$ 43,000	$ 49,000
8103	Photocopying	22,181	15,000	16,500
8104	Film & Photographic	33,900	25,000	27,500
8110	General Supplies	6,000	2,000	2,200
8120	Food & Beverages	–	500	500
8130	Clothing & Linens	–	–	–
8134	Kitchen & Dining	–	–	–
8140	Surgical & Medical	–	–	–
8142	Drugs & Medicine	–	–	–
8150	Laboratory	–	–	–
	Subtotal	$ 100,638	$ 85,500	$ 95,700

Source: Hennepin County, Minnesota, Budget.

items necessary to run a government process (for example, salaries, supplies) are identified for each government unit, and the sum of money required for each item is identified by year. *Program* and *performance budgeting* are more sophisticated approaches. In the former, a logical grouping of government activities is defined, and money is allocated to these activities. Performance budgeting goes one step further—identifying specific program outputs—which are associated with specific program money requests. Exhibit 2–2 illustrates performance budgeting.

Those working in budgeting in the 1950s tended to follow either the *incremental* or the *rational philosophic* perspective. The former stressed that budget decisions should be viewed as essentially incremental, with the fiscal year serving as the base upon which the new year is judged. This is why budget formats often show the PY, CY, and BY (and, normally, BY-CY)—so that the incremental difference can be examined. The latter perspective, popularized by economists, stresses that rational decision making requires examining budget decisions for a set of objectives, using analytical techniques to help discern the best decision possible.

Critics of incrementalism stress that the CY numbers may remain the same in the BY, but that significant policy shift can occur even if the numbers remain constant. Agencies may focus their arguments on the BY-CY difference, but their success rate on such requests is low. Incrementalists agree that this is true, but insist that it does no harm to their original arguments, because decisions still focus on the current services in the CY and the proposed difference in the BY. Critics of the rational philosophic perspective argue that it is a logical absurdity and is inconsistent with a pluralist political system that accepts a multiple-value culture. A counterargument used by rationalists is to stress that the analytical techniques associated with the perspective do help executive branch decision makers.

There are three common purposes behind the budget activity: *control, management,* and *planning.* If control is the main purpose, then budget formats are designed to ensure that the money is spent according to established policy and that no resources are used for illegal purposes. If management is the purpose, then budget process stresses directing people in the bureaucracy and achieving efficiency and economy in those programs. If planning is the purpose, then the process emphasizes improvements in the political decision-making process. These three stresses are not mutually exclusive. All of them exist in most budget processes, but the three-purpose distinction is conceptually useful. Reformers in various eras tended to emphasize one budget purpose over the others, but the other purposes did not cease to exist.

If reformers are stressing control, they wish to guarantee fiscal accountability. They are fearful of corruption and of leaving the decisions of public employees unchecked. Those arguing for greater control are supported by arguments to increase the strength of the chief executive (which will also achieve greater economy and efficiency in government). Strong chief executives can enhance their strength through improved budget control mechanisms. Strong control can also mean that inefficient and uneconomical activities are increased because not enough management flexibility is permitted to deal with changing situations. The added procedural requirements can result in more workers and less productivity.

EXHIBIT 2–2   Hoover Commission Performance Budget Model

MEDICAL CARE

Summary: This appropriation request in the amount of $43,648,008 is to provide for the care of a daily average of 28,696 sick and injured, maintenance and operation of 34 hospitals, 2 medical supply depots, 2 medical storehouses, 6 medical department schools, 11 research facilities, operation of 432 other medical activities ashore, instruction of personnel in non-naval institutions, and care of an estimated 1,859 dead; and for Island Government—6 hospitals, 80 dispensary beds, and instruction of native practitioners. Specific programs are as follows:

1. Medical and Dental Care Afloat— to provide technical medical and dental equipment, supplies, and services for an average of 232,485 personnel at sea, and initial outfits for 4 new naval vessels to be commissioned in 1948	$ 2,822,923
2. Medical and Dental Care Ashore	48,419,168
3. Care of the Dead—to provide services, supplies, and transportation for an estimated 1,859 deaths in 1948	502,700
4. Instruction of Medical Department Personnel	2,645,347
5. Medical and Dental Research—to provide civilian employment of 328 and supplies and equipment to operate and maintain 6 research facilities and 5 field research units in 1948	2,519,742
6. Medical and Dental Supply System	2,936,396
7. Island Government	1,910,463
8. Departmental Administration—to provide civilian employment of 550, travel, telephone, telegraph, supplies, and equipment for the departmental administration of the responsibilities of the Bureau of Medicine and Surgery in 1948	1,432,100
Appropriation Request, 1948	$43,648,008

Source: Hoover Commission, 1949.

Early American public budget literature stressed the control function. Given the well-publicized political corruption of the era, the stress on control is certainly understandable. The reforms included such well-known budget features as the following:

Annual budget: revenues and expenditures presented for one fiscal year period;

Comprehensive budget: all revenues and expenditures included in the budget;

Detailed line items: presenting the exact amount planned to be spent for every separate thing or service to be purchased;

Identification of all transactions: recording every obligation and transfer of money and liquidation of obligation; and

Apportionments and allotments: an executive branch mechanism to regulate the rate and actual spending of authorized funds.

Stress on budget control comes with a price tag. Extreme control limits management flexibility, which might be essential in many situations. Interestingly, the reform for efficiency can lead to inefficiency because management cannot easily adapt to more efficient procedures. Budget control is a high administrative cost activity. Recording all transactions and every line item requires many people even in this era of the computer. Another cost of budget control is more subtle in its effect upon government. By stressing control, the emphasis is on detail, and the big policy decisions tend to be ignored. Thus government becomes less responsive to the problems of society.

If reformers are stressing management, they view the budget as a tool of the executive to achieve effective operational direction with greatest efficiency. The budget can be used as a mechanism to guide the massive bureaucracy. Reforms like performance budgeting (that is, categorizing the planned activities to stress the relationship of money to achievement) and productivity improvements (that is, getting greater results for relatively fewer resources) are stressed. Often reformers decentralize the details to the agency level while stressing means to achieve greater centralized direction. Normally those reforms are more conservative and business-oriented, and, not surprisingly, these reforms were stressed more in the 1920s, early 1930s, 1970s, and 1980s, when conservative Republicans were president.

If reformers are stressing planning, they view the budget as a way to bring greater rationality into the public policy-making process. These reformers are appalled at the poor decision-making situation of top policy makers and the noncoordinated nature of many decision-making processes. They believe that coordinated and rational decision making is important and that more planning and greater use of analysis will improve the decision-making process. Those reformers stress the importance of analysis, data, and categorizing the budget to facilitate analysis. In the 1960s, PPB (planning-programming-budgeting) and the use of analysis was stressed in public budgeting. In the 1970s, ZBB (zero-base budgeting) also stressed analysis.

AN EXECUTIVE FOCUS

Planning and Analysis

Planning-programming-budgeting (PPB) was an attempt in the federal government—continuing today in some state and local governments—to institutionalize analysis in the executive branch decision-making process. The advocates of PPB believed public budgeting was the key to most of the important decisions made in government and that public policy making lacked enough analysis for top-level decision makers. They believed that procedural reforms could insert essential analysis into the public budgeting process, thus improving public policy making.

PPB was not a new creation in the 1960s. In 1907, the New York Bureau of Municipal Research developed the first Program Memorandum. The Hoover Commission advocated performance budgeting and budgets were organized into programs in the 1940s. In the 1930s, welfare economics developed many of the same techniques later associated with PPB. In the 1950s, operations research and systems analysis also developed techniques later associated with PPB.

PPB was popularized in the 1960s by Secretary of Defense Robert McNamara and spread by President Johnson to the whole federal government. Secretary McNamara had a strong analytical background and asked Charles Hitch to apply the concepts developed at Rand Corporation to the Defense Department. Most people, and especially President Johnson, were impressed with the McNamara management of the Department of Defense. In 1965, President Johnson ordered that PPB be used in every federal department and agency. In time, PPB also spread to many state and local governments as well as to governments around the world.

The era of PPB was one of guns and butter. The United States was fighting a war on poverty and a war in Vietnam. There were strong, intelligent people (then called the "best and the brightest") running the country, but the goals outmatched the available talent and resources. This was true with PPB because the goals were visionary, but the resources, including talented people, were inadequate for the challenge.

PPB was an attempt to embody the rational model of decision making into the executive branch's policy-making process. The attempt and PPB were declared dead in the Nixon administration, but the verdict was too harsh. PPB was officially deleted from the U.S. Office of Management and Budget (the renamed Bureau of the Budget) official guidelines, but federal agencies continued to use it. In some federal agencies PPB worked, in many others it was never really tried, and in some agencies it just didn't work.

A common misunderstanding of novices about budgeting is to equate PPB and analysis. PPB was and is an attempt to institutionalize analysis into the public budgeting process. PPB is not analysis or a form of analysis. It does encourage the application of marginal utility analysis, cost-benefit studies, cost-effectiveness analysis, sensitivity analysis, pay-off matrix, present values, and other techniques.

Analysis can be characterized as various art forms—many would argue sciences—that examine alternatives, view them in terms of basic assumptions and objectives, and test as well as compare alternatives. All this is done with a purpose of finding "useful" information or conclusions concerning policy questions. The techniques vary and were developed in several different disciplines.

PPB was operationalized through the use of several mechanisms. The use of analysis was stressed, particularly in the early stages of the budget cycle. A categorization of government programs called a "program structure" was required to facilitate analytical comparisons. A greater use of data associated with the programs was encouraged. Output measures and five-year projections beyond the budget were considered essential. Analysis was further encouraged by the use of mandated special studies and analyses addressed to specific major program issues.

What are the lessons which can be learned from the PPB experience? They can be summarized as follows:

Theoretical and Conceptual Issues

1. Program budgeting, policy analysis, and other related concepts are vague, and thus present a difficult challenge to the practitioner who wishes to apply the concepts. A great deal of effort and creative talent is necessary to tailor and operationalize these concepts.
2. The rational model, as an ideal for practitioners, can result in serious mistakes.
3. The use of one program structure does not strengthen but rather limits policy analysis. Subjects of analysis vary and one categorization greatly limits the necessary range of analysis.
4. Government programs often do not have and may never have logical, consistent operational objectives. Policy makers recognize the value of vagueness in achieving necessary political consensus and know that vagueness often hides conflicting views on the proper direction of a program. Public administrators inherit this confusion and must deal with it even though most analytical techniques cannot work with such ambiguity.
5. Analysis normally is helpful only for relatively narrow but often important policy questions. The use of analysis is constrained by such things as the ability of the analyst and the nature of the subject being examined. Analysis is often most useful on technical questions.

Implementation

1. A significantly large amount of money and many talented people must be devoted to making a reform like PPB work.
2. A phased implementation plan should be adopted so that agencies and portions of agencies most likely to accept the change can be introduced to the innovation first, and resisting agencies can be introduced to the change last. As a matter of realistic strategy, one can expect resistance from some top management which will effectively prevent successful implementation. Training and hiring policies can minimize the problem, but such effective resistance cannot be avoided entirely.
3. The key person for ensuring effective policy analysis is the agency head. A desire and ability to use policy analysis effectively should be one criterion for hiring a person for this position. Then a tailor-made, brief orientation course could be given new agency heads that could include the use of policy analysis in public policy making.
4. One particularly difficult problem is to achieve coordination of policy among the policy analysts, planners, the budget officer, the accountants, the lawyers, the public affairs officer, the analysts preparing the agency's progress reports, and the program managers within an agency.

Political Factors

1. The use of plans covering five years does not appear to limit the political options available.
2. Public analysis rarely addresses the political costs and benefits of a program to specific key individuals such as legislators, but good analyses do address analytical questions that set out political costs and benefits in general.
3. The political advantages of not using analysis with explicit objectives may be critical to reaching some decisions in some specific political situations, but there is no reason to believe there is a common circumstance.

Human Factors[1]

1. People in an agency must believe that the reform is a significant and legitimate undertaking. The real test for them will be how seriously key people (like the agency head) and key agencies (such as the Office of Management and Budget) treat the reform. If these people and groups continually demand and use the products of this reform, then significance and legitimacy will be established.
2. Positive and politically practical recommendations must be the products of the reform. If they are not generated, the people directly responsible for operationalizing the reform in the agency will lose effectiveness both among organizational peers and also among the key decision makers who use the products.

Management

1. Systematic attempts to institutionalize policy analysis do tend to centralize governmental decision making.
2. Reforms like PPB do not greatly influence government reorganization.

Management by Objectives

At the beginning of the second term of the Nixon administration, the White House and the Office of Management and Budget strongly encouraged the federal departments and agencies to use a technique called *management-by-objectives* (MBO). MBO is the setting out of specific objectives for agencies and requiring regular, high-level, periodic reports on the progress toward achieving those objectives. The Nixon administration's use of MBO varied from the conventional MBO, especially by not stressing lower-level participation in the formulation of objectives. Also, the adoption of MBO was not done through the OMB regulations, as PPB had been, but was required through the use of the informal memorandum from the OMB to the various departments and agencies requesting information to a specific MBO format.

Serious government-wide presidential use of MBO was short-lived and died with the Nixon administration. The reform did have a significant influence on many federal departments and agencies as the technique was integrated into their standard operating procedures.

In a few agencies, there was an attempt to link MBO and public budgeting. Such a linkage is theoretically possible but is rarely done. The linkage is accomplished by using a matrix table with MBO objectives and budget activities. The matrix table squares contain the amount of money needed to carry out the objective during the budget year. A given program may have multiple objectives; therefore, the money cited would not be placed in mutually exclusive categories. Also, not all program activities would be covered by the objectives used in MBO. The advantage of the linkage is to ensure that resources are available to meet the high-priority objectives of the government.

[1] Some items were covered under "Implementation."

Zero-Base Budgeting

Zero-base budgeting is an approach to public budgeting in which each budget year's activities are judged in a self-contained fashion, with little or no reference given to the policy precedents of past years. ZBB is contrasted to incremental budgeting, in which the budget justification is focused on the difference between the current year (CY) and the budget year (BY). In making the distinction between ZBB and incremental budgeting, a false impression can be given of both concepts as they are practiced. In ZBB, the analysts normally will want information on past funding levels and past accomplishments, but the analysts could also ignore such data. In incremental budgeting, the analysts normally will want information on all activities being planned in the budget year, but their focus will be on the program changes from the current year. The analysts already know much of the program information from reviewing last year's budget.

In 1964, the U.S. Department of Agriculture used a ZBB approach to prepare its budget. It was an additional exercise on top of the normal budget process. ZBB required voluminous documentation and a great deal of departmental time and energy. Critical evaluators of the approach concluded that, except for a few small decisions, the department reached the same conclusions as it would have reached with the less expensive incremental approach. The higher-level officials did feel that they gained a much fuller understanding of their organization because of the ZBB experience. However, ZBB was abandoned.

Peter A. Pyhrr used ZBB in the private sector and popularized its wider use. Mr. Pyhrr used it successfully in Texas Instruments and wrote a book titled *Zero-Base Budgeting*, and also authored an extremely influential 1973 article in *Harvard Business Review*. The then-governor of Georgia—Jimmy Carter—read about ZBB and invited Mr. Pyhrr to help him apply the approach to the state of Georgia. Presidential candidate Carter talked a great deal about the virtues of ZBB, and President Carter required its adoption by the federal government.

The use of ZBB in the private sector has been confined primarily to overhead activities (that is, expenses needed to maintain the organization versus expenses needed to produce the product). There is a great deal of difference between public and private budgeting, but they are the most similar in the area of overhead. In private budgeting, revenue comes from sales, which can fluctuate due to a variety of factors. If sales are up and unit costs are constant or lower, then the company has more money to spend or give back to the investors. In public budgeting, revenue comes from taxes, which normally are intended to buy certain services. The focus is on the services, which are sometimes difficult to define—for example, national defense preparedness. In the private sector, overhead is meant to be a service to the organization, much as government is a service to the society. Not surprisingly, the private sector has had little difficulty budgeting for its major functions, but has had greater difficulty budgeting for its overhead functions. ZBB has proved to be a useful budgetary approach for the private sector's overhead activities.

The use of ZBB in the public sector is a recent development, with the exception of the Department of Agriculture experience. ZBB was adopted by a few cities and several states (including Georgia, New Jersey, Idaho, Montana, and Illinois). The assessment of its success and failure is unclear, but its initial advocates were enthusiastic. Problems have arisen similar to the ones experienced with PPB, but conclusions are unclear, with the few empirical studies generally negative.

There are several different ZBB approaches. This is appropriate, as ZBB should be tailored to each government's unique circumstances. Normally, the ZBB process consists of preparing budget proposals and alternative levels of spending grouped into "decision packages." Program and higher-level managers then rank those decision packages in the order of priority. The lowest levels don't get funded.

Decision packages are self-contained units for budget choice containing input and output data (that is, resources needed to operate the program and the products of the program) as well as the expected levels of performance for each defined level of expenditure. These packages are prepared by the manager responsible for each discrete activity at the lowest level of an organization capable of formulating a budget request. Alternative decision packages are prepared and ranked, thus allowing marginal utility and comparative analyses. Often the guidelines stipulate that a package should be prepared for the minimum cost essential to carry out the activity effectively, but some guidelines recognize the extreme latitude given the manager using that type of guidance. Some states have selected arbitrary percentages to ensure that an amount smaller from last year's request is considered. They do this by stipulating that one alternative must be 50 or 80 or 90 percent of last year's request.

Decision packages are then ranked by managers and executives by priority. Other, lower-cost packages within each activity are necessarily given higher priority over the more costly packages. The packages are ranked by the managers preparing the packages and by executives at each level above the manager. A chief executive can and does establish a cutoff point for the government as a whole, as well as for each agency. Only the packages above the cutoff are included in the executive branch budget submitted to the legislature.

There are some serious problems in using ZBB. The most obvious is that it can be a paper monster that buries executives in an avalanche of documents. ZBB necessarily means thousands of decision packages. For example, in Georgia there were 10,000 decision packages, and no chief executive can review each one. Mechanisms must be created to manage the paperwork, limiting it to only the critical decisions. Another problem is dealing with programs which are effectively uncontrollable in the budget, such as veterans' benefits, social security, interest on the debt, retirement, and food stamps. ZBB cannot address them, yet they represent over 75 percent of the federal budget and are significant in many state and local budgets as well. The technique does not help judge priorities between budget activities such as defense, welfare, and the environment. Also, the technique does not lend itself to demanding responsive grant programs (for example, grant-in-aid programs), which are designed to let communities largely define objectives and priorities. Marginal analysis of the budget packages cannot be used in those programs because the granting agency cannot accurately forecast benefit. The agency does not know who will qualify or what the funds will be used for and therefore what benefits should result. Also, a very serious question still exists: Are government decisions different from private sector decisions, or is there something to which government decisions are being compared?

There are some apparent advantages to ZBB. In programs involving clear operational missions, such as highways, recreation, and public works, the technique is analytically relevant to the program analysts and decision makers. The approach shifts budget attention away from adding to the current-year program and focuses consideration on increases to the minimum level of operational support. The approach is successful in educating higher-level executives and their staffs on the nature of government programs. Also, the approach may stimulate redirection of resources within budgets and programs into more productive activities.

TBB and Envelope Budgeting

There is a nonrational approach to budgeting that rejects PPB and its foundations but does require extensive budget expertise, including analytical capacity; it is called *target-base budgeting* (TBB) in several U.S. cities and was called envelope budgeting in Canada. In contrast to PPB, TBB is a top-down rationing process that is concerned with establishing priorities and limits at the top as a means to force choice among alternatives at the bottom. The targets are revenue driven and are adjusted due to political choice. Target-based budgeting uses the rational or satisficing decision-making models for the discretionary or policy reserves. Priorities are set, and they are used in making decisions. Major government units are required to submit their budgets within the targets, but they can request added funding from discretionary or policy reserves (for example, 5 percent) that are set aside in TBB for additional funding possibilities, such as new proposals.

TBB does not require an enormous amount of analysis, but the analysis done is often similar to that found in zero-base budgeting. It works well with cost accounting, productivity studies, performance measurement, strategic planning, and MBO. TBB does require some cost-accounting capability, is top-down in that allocations are centrally determined, and encourages department-head prioritizing and innovation, in that lump-sum allocations permit a variety of management trade-offs within departments, between line items, between programs, and sometimes between capital and operating budgets. With TBB, department staff can propose revenue enhancements, action designed to achieve productivity increases, and alternative means to avoid service and personnel cuts when targets cut into the base. Generally, departments have more autonomy under TBB than under other forms of budgeting.

TBB is adaptable to political priorities, as they can be put in either the base or the reserve for new projects. How this is done depends on the jurisdiction, but they can insist that departments include the politician's ideas in the department's budget proposals. Sometimes under TBB, a department can then decide to include the suggestions in its budget base, thus not funding some other projects or putting the suggestions in the department's list of new requests.

As reported by Irene S. Rubin (1991), TBB does have its problems. The political decision to include a new program in the budget base may encourage department heads to obscure service level reductions in other areas that resulted from funding the new initiatives. Thus, the implicit trade-offs would be obscured, and the inaccurate budget document would not enlighten the decision making process. TBB permits nonrational reallocation decisions such as across-the-board cuts and political trade-offs among departments.

Reagan and Bush

President Reagan advanced and strengthened the executive in terms the budget process by adding a third important executive power. The first power was the pulling together of the agency budget requests and their organization into the president's budget recommendation. The second was the OMB legislative clearance process (see Exhibit 2–3), which covers agency legislative proposals, agency reports and testimony on pending legislation, and enrolled bills. The OMB ensures that proposals, reports, and testimony conform to presidential policy and coordinates agency recommendations on presidential vetoing of enrolled bills. The third power was added in 1981 by Executive Order 12291. All federal agencies that have proposed regulatory changes must send them to the OMB for its clearance on regulatory budget and economic implications. This greatly strengthens the OMB's influence, especially over entitlement programs.

EXHIBIT 2–3   Executive Legislative Clearance Process

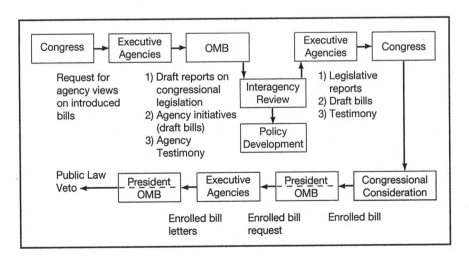

A LEGISLATIVE FOCUS

The 1974 Budget Reform Motivations

The Congressional Budget and Impoundment Control Act of 1974 is one of the landmark pieces of budget reform legislation in this century. The law's passage is dramatically related to the events surrounding President Nixon's resignation. The 1974 legislation created a unified congressional budget reform, and it made the Congress a coequal branch with the executive on budgetary matters. President Nixon and the Democrat-controlled Congress were constantly in battle. Nixon wished to decrease the role of government in society, and Congress passed legislation seeking government action to redress various societal problems. Nixon had the advantage because it is much easier to defeat programs than it is to initiate them. One tactic employed by President Nixon was to use the disputed presidential impoundment powers on a wide range of programs, including those he had vetoed with the veto being overridden. Another tactic was to stress that the Congress was acting in an irresponsible manner because of its piecemeal and uncoordinated approach to appropriations. As Herbert Jasper—an important actor in developing the legislation—pointed out, the Congress was most upset at Nixon's charge of reckless congressional spending.

The Watergate crisis weakened President Nixon and strengthened the Congress. The 1974 Act was one of several reforms directed toward strengthening the legislative branch. The congressional Research Service and the General Accounting Office were expanded. Various reforms were passed to improve the congressional oversight activities. The important legislation was to achieve a unified congressional budget approach and neutralize the presidential impoundment powers. There was a great deal of difficulty in drafting the Act because it affected the strength of some of the most powerful legislators in both the House and Senate. Congress was able to overcome its internal struggles and passed the legislation in 1974 so that it could deal more effectively with President Nixon.

The 1974 legislation should be viewed in the context of the historical tension between the executive and legislative branches built intentionally into our system of government. After the Jefferson administration, the purse strings were clearly controlled by Congress, but Congress itself fractionalized the power over the years. This was not particularly significant, as the executive branch did not attempt to exercise leadership in this area. With the passage of the 1921 legislation and a series of strong presidents, the power of the executive branch greatly increased against a fractionalized Congress. With the 1974 legislation, Congress once again focused its purse-string powers and could deal with a strong executive.

Unified Congressional Budget Reforms

The 1974 legislation made several changes. It created the new Senate and House Budget Committees, created a new congressional Budget Office, required current services estimates, and required various reforms addressed to the presidential budget. The new congressional committees' duties included drafting overall budget targets. They could prepare reconciliation bills between budget resolutions and appropriation bills. Also, the new committees were intended to, and have, put pressure on Congress to meet established budget deadlines.

Linda Smith, a former House Budget Committee staffer, pointed out in *The Bureaucrat* that the concept of a unified budget approach to congressional budgeting was challenged, but the process worked, at first. However, the unified approach has not resulted in a balanced, or even a nearly balanced, yearly federal budget. One hope was that the annual appropriation bills would be passed prior to the fiscal year in which they were to become effective. This has rarely occurred. The process resulted in the appearance of a comprehensive examination of the budget, but the reforms have made it easy for political interest groups to get their programs funded and even give single-issue-oriented groups an easy means to threaten the whole budget to further their policy aims.

The Congressional Budget Office (CBO) is a source of nonpartisan budget expertise for both chambers of Congress. The office is charged with presenting the Congress with respectable and viable alternatives on aggregate levels of spending and revenue. The office must also make cost estimates for proposed legislation reported to the floor and provide cost projections for all existing legislation. The Act requires the CBO to prepare an annual report covering "national budget priorities" and "alternative ways of allocating budget authority and budget outlays." One last important duty is to keep score on administration and congressional actions related to the budget. See Exhibit 2–4 for a complete list of responsibilities.

The CBO has proven to be a successful policy aid to the Congress. Its economic forecasts have proven to be more accurate than those produced by executive branch agencies. The scorekeeping reports have proven particularly useful. The CBO is not the congressional counterpart to the executive branch OMB. That type of power rests with the budget and appropriation committees. The CBO provides essential information so that the Congress knows the fiscal implications of various proposals and can act in a deliberate manner on fiscal policy matters.

Other innovations prompted by the 1974 legislation are the OMB *current services estimates* and the CBO *baseline budget projections.* The OMB submits its current services budget authority and outlay estimates covering the next and future fiscal years. These estimates must assume that the existing services shall continue at current levels. They can and should reflect inflation and other factors that may raise costs but do not reflect a change in policy. A parallel concept is the CBO baseline budget projections, which are an extrapolation of budget trends, typically for the next five years. The estimates also assume current policies remain and the projections reflect inflation, workload changes mandated by law, and other nonpolicy factors. For most programs, baseline projections are higher than current funding levels.

The President's budget is submitted no later than February for the fiscal year that begins the next October 1. Congressional budget actions are (1) adoption of budget resolutions, (2) passage of appropriations bills, and (3) passage of other budget-related legislation such as authorization legislation, reconciliation bills, tax changes, modifications of entitlement programs, and adjustments to the debt limit. Congress is not bound by the president's recommendations in preparing its budget actions.

Within six weeks after the President's budget submission, each House and Senate committee must submit its *views and estimates report* on budget matters relevant to its committee. The House and Senate Budget Committees use these reports and the CBO analyses including the baseline projections to prepare their budget resolutions. The *budget resolution,* which should be adopted by April 15, contains revenues and spending levels for five years, but only the first year is binding. Being a concurrent rather than a joint resolution, the budget resolution is not signed by the president and does not have statutory effect.

The budget resolution has three main sections: *aggregates, functional allocations of spending*, and (optionally) *reconciliation instructions*. The aggregates include total revenues and any desired changes in those levels, total new budget authority, total outlays, the budget surplus or deficit, the debt limit, and the total new direct loan obligations and new primary loan guarantee commitments. The new budget authority, outlay, direct loan, and loan guarantee levels are allocated among twenty functional categories such as national defense, international affairs, energy, and agriculture. Reconciliation instructions direct specific House and Senate Committees to report legislation conforming spending, revenue, or debt-limit levels under existing law to current budget policies.

Budget resolutions are not always effective. Budget targets in those resolutions are not established by programs or accounts. Instead, they are based on nonbinding assumptions that are sometimes contained in the reports of the budget committees. Congress should meet its own April 15 deadline if the 1974 process is to be effective. Unfortunately, it does not, and the House rules even permit consideration of appropriations bills after May 15 if the budget resolution has not been adopted.

The annual appropriations are decided in thirteen regular appropriations bills under the jurisdiction of parallel House and Senate appropriations subcommittees, which recommend spending levels to the full committees. The appropriation committees subdivide their spending amounts among their subcommittees. When the entire House or Senate considers appropriations legislation, the recommendation can be compared with the amount decided by the respective appropriation committee. In some circumstances, a parliamentary point of order can bar consideration of an appropriation measure if the measure breaches the assigned limit.

Although intended to create a uniform comprehensive approach to budgeting within the Congress, the 1974 reforms have failed. Appropriation bills and others such as revenue and entitlement legislation come to the respective chambers individually but they affect the overall budget levels. Normally, Congress does not pass the appropriation bills by the start of the fiscal year as required. An interim device is the *continuing resolution*, which provides appropriations for a few months while Congress continues to deliberate. In some years, the continuing resolutions have been substituted for the appropriation bills. Congress also enacts supplemental appropriations to provide additional funding not covered in regular appropriations bills.

EXHIBIT 2–4   CBO Responsibilities

Budgetary Estimates

Scorekeeping.   Each spring, the Congress formulates and adopts a concurrent resolution on the budget, setting expenditure and revenue targets for the fiscal year to begin on the coming October 1. In September, the Congress reviews the detailed spending and taxing decisions it had made during the summer in the form of individual bills. It then arrives at and adopts a second concurrent resolution, reconfirming or changing the totals in the spring resolution. While the first resolution sets targets, the second establishes an actual ceiling for spending and a floor for revenues. The CBO keeps score of congressional action on individual bills, comparing them against targets or ceilings in the concurrent resolutions. The CBO issues periodic reports showing the status of congressional action.

Cost Estimates.   Four types of cost estimates are required of the CBO by the budget Act.

The CBO prepares, to the extent practicable, a five-year estimate for what it would cost to carry out any public bill or resolution reported by Congressional committees (except the two appropriating committees).

The CBO furnishes to a reporting committee a report on each committee bill providing new budget authority. Each report shows: (a) a comparison of the bill with the most recent concurrent resolution, (b) a five-year projection of outlays associated with the bill, and (c) the amount of new budget authority and resulting outlays provided for state and local governments.

The CBO also furnishes to a reporting committee an analysis of each bill, providing new or increased tax expenditures. The reports cover: (a) an assessment of how the bill will affect levels of tax expenditures most recently detailed in a concurrent resolution, and (b) a five-year projection of the tax expenditures resulting from the bill.

As soon as practicable after the beginning of each fiscal year, the CBO prepares a report that analyzes the five-year costs of continuing current federal spending and taxing policies as set forth in the second concurrent resolution. The purpose of these projections is to provide a neutral baseline against which the Congress can consider potential changes as it examines the budget for the upcoming fiscal years.

Fiscal and Programmatic Analysis

Fiscal Analysis.   The federal budget both affects and is affected by the national economy. The Congress thus must consider the federal budget in the context of the current and projected state of the economy. To provide a framework for such considerations, the CBO prepares periodic analyses and forecasts of economic trends. It also prepares analyses of alternative fiscal policies.

Inflation Analysis.   Beginning in 1979, the CBO prepared estimates of the inflationary effect of major legislative proposals and, more generally, identifies and analyzes the causes of inflation. These estimates are intended to provide the Congress with guidelines, as it undertakes new programs, of the cost in terms of inflation that these programs might entail.

(continued)

EXHIBIT 2–4   CBO Responsibilities (continued)

Program and Policy Analysis.   The CBO undertakes analyses of programmatic or policy issues that affect the federal budget. These reports include an examination of alternative approaches to current policy; all reports are nonpartisan in nature. These reports are undertaken at the request of: (1) the chairman of the committee or subcommittee of jurisdiction of either the House or the Senate; (2) the ranking minority member of a committee of jurisdiction of either the House or the Senate; or (3) the chairman of a Task Force of the House Budget Committee.

Annual Report on Budget Options.   By April 1 of each year, the CBO furnishes to the House and Senate Committees on the Budget a report that combines many aspects of the functions outlined above. The annual report presents a discussion of alternative spending and revenue levels, levels of tax expenditures under existing law, and alternative allocations among major programs and functional categories.

The CBO's analyses usually take the form of published studies comparing present policies and programs with alternative approaches. The responsibilities of the CBO are (1) budgetary estimates, and (2) fiscal and programmatic analysis.

Source: 21.S. Congressional Budget Office, 1982.

Backdoor Spending

One of the concerns of the advocates of the 1974 reform was the use of *backdoor spending* (the commitment of federal funds outside the effective control of the appropriation process). Reformers argued that backdoor spending is contrary to the concept of a unified consolidated congressional budget because some activities cannot be balanced against the competing claims of other activities. The 1974 legislation outlaws or tries to control backdoor spending, with some major exceptions. The major exceptions were necessary, or the legislation would not have passed.

There are various forms of backdoor spending. One is *permanent appropriations*, by which the program is allowed to spend whatever is necessary. This blank check is theoretically possible, but is not found in practice. Another is *contract authority*, by which government officials can obligate the government through legal contracts, and Congress must pass subsequent appropriations to fulfill the obligation. *Borrowing authority* is similar to contract authority, except the government official can borrow money, and the Congress must pass subsequent appropriations to liquidate the debt. Yet another method is mandatory for *entitlement spending*, such as unemployment compensation, food stamps, payment on the national debt, veterans' benefits, and so on. The payment levels are established by programmatic rules set down in legislation and administrative regulation. If there is a recession, the government will *automatically* pay more in unemployment compensation, welfare, and food stamps, and the Congress must pay appropriations to fulfill the obligation. *Earmarked revenue* is considered by some to be backdoor spending because funds from a specific source (for example, gasoline tax) can be spent only for a specific activity (for example, highways). This earmarking prevents a unified consolidated consideration of the budget. Use of the *unexpended balance* (that is, money appropriated but not spent in the last fiscal year) by carrying it over to the budget year is also contrary to the unified approach, but it is allowed in many programs.

The backdoor spending exceptions cover about 75 percent of each year's budget. The 1974 prohibition applies only to *new* contract authority, budget authority, and entitlement programs. Other major exceptions are as follows:

1. all Social Security trust fund programs;
2. all trust funds that receive 90 percent or more from designated taxes rather than from the general revenue (for example, highways);
3. general revenue sharing;
4. insured or guaranteed loans;
5. federal or independent public corporations; and
6. gifts to the government.

Impoundment

As was pointed out earlier, the extensive use of impoundment by President Nixon was quite upsetting to the Congress. Nixon impounded large sums of money because he did not favor the programs that Congress had enacted and funded. The impoundment was not used because the executive branch found it could accomplish the congressionally mandated purpose with less money. It was used because it was a type of veto that could not be overridden by Congress. Interestingly, in some cases the Nixon administration impounded funds for programs that had been preserved by the Congress by overriding a presidential veto. Congress felt that Nixon violated the spirit if not the letter of the Constitution.

The judicial branch concurred with the majority of Congress. In every instance that someone took the expense and time to battle the Nixon administration on impoundment, the president lost and was forced to spend the money. Court challenges take months and often years, so the delay tended to establish, de facto, the impoundment. The program administration was crippled by this executive-judicial decision-making process because of the extreme delays.

The 1974 legislation redefined the impoundment powers. The Congress and the courts pointed out that neither the Constitution nor the law granted the president the impoundment power. The executive branch argued that ample precedent existed over the many years of the nation's history. Congress recognized the best solution was to redefine the impoundment powers so that the president could not cripple a program regardless of the true validity of the impoundment powers. Congress pragmatically wanted to prevent a president from overruling the will of Congress on government spending issues.

Today there are two types of impoundments, each handled somewhat differently. If the impoundment is to defer the spending appropriated by Congress, then *either* the House *or* the Senate can force the release of funds by passing a resolution calling for their expenditure. If the impoundment is to cut or rescind the appropriations, then *both* the House and Senate must pass recision resolutions within forty-five days of the recision or it is not valid.

The deferral type of impoundment has been challenged successfully on constitutional grounds. In *Immigration and Naturalization Service* v. *Chadha*, the Supreme Court struck down the one-house legislative veto as unconstitutional. Thus, the implication is that there was no way to overturn presidential deferrals except by passing a law which the president could then veto. This left the president with a de facto line-item veto. At first the Reagan administration did not attempt to use this apparent advantage, but it was eventually employed. Not surprisingly, the reaction was a legal suit. The plaintiffs argued that the Congress had never intended to give the president the deferral power that resulted from the Chadha case. At the district level, the federal courts agreed and found in favor of the plaintiffs.

One technical problem in writing the 1974 law was how to deal with a president who might not inform the Congress of an impoundment. The threshold of trust between the Congress and the president was at a low ebb in 1974. The legislation required the president to send a message to Congress requesting impoundment and setting forth the rationale for it. The legislation then stated that if the president did not comply with the law, then the comptroller general (a congressional employee) would report the impoundment to the Congress. If the president did not comply, the comptroller general was directed to go to the courts to get a court order forcing compliance.

The ultimate strategy involved is complex. The Constitution provides for a means to impeach the president and requires the president to execute faithfully the laws of the nation. If the courts rule against the president after the new procedure has been applied faithfully, then the president has an extremely weak defense against the argument that he refuses to execute the law faithfully. Under the procedure, both the Congress and judicial branch would have said he must comply. The Congress would be in an excellent position to impeach the president under such circumstances.

The first minor test of the impoundment process occurred in the Ford administration. The president did send the required impoundment messages to Congress and did comply with the will of Congress except for one situation. On April 15, 1975, the comptroller general of the United States filed a lawsuit in U.S. District Court for the District of Columbia. Named as defendants in the suit were Gerald Ford, President of the United States, James T. Lynn, director of the Office of Management and Budget, and Carla A. Hills, secretary of Housing and Urban Development.

The new legislation was being tested. On October 4, 1974, President Ford transmitted his impoundment messages, including the deferment of approximately $264 million in contract authority for the section 235 housing program, but the legislation was due to lapse on August 22, 1975. The comptroller general reasoned that this would permit only 52 days to obligate the money, thus it was a de facto recision, and, under the law, the comptroller general reported the error in a formal message to Congress. This meant that Congress had forty-five days to act or the money had to be spent; it did not act, nor did the president release the funds. The comptroller general then notified Congress of his intention to bring a lawsuit and the Senate passed a resolution in support of the comptroller general. The Ford administration challenged the 1974 legislation on the grounds that (1) the comptroller general was improperly carrying out an executive function by instituting the lawsuit, and (2) the Constitution provided means other than the courts for resolving disputes between the branches of government. The legal arguments continued, but the case came to an abrupt end without a court resolution. On October 17, 1975, Carla Hills announced that the section 235 program would be reactivated and there was no longer a need for the suit. The Congress had won.

Exhibit 2–5 presents the early history of post-1974 impoundments. Ford won cancellation of only 7 percent of the funds he proposed for recision. Carter was more successful. Reagan's success rate needs to be seen in two parts. In his first two years, he had a 62 percent success rate, but it dropped to 2 percent in his last years in office. The difference reflects the change in the make-up of the Congress. The impoundment power can be a useful presidential tool only when a president has greater influence in the Congress. The impoundment power certainly does not equal that of a governor's line-item veto but it can be significant under the correct conditions.

EXHIBIT 2–5   1975–88 RECISIONS AND DEFERRALS (dollars in millions)

TYPES OF IMPOUNDMENTS	PROPOSED	ACCEPTED	% ACCEPTED
Rescissions			
Ford (1975–77)	$7,405	$ 530	7.2
Carter (1977–81)	6,946	2,580	37.1
Reagan (1981–82)	23,269	16,080	69.1
Reagan (1983–88)	20,011	400	2.0
Total Rescissions	57,631	19,589	34.0
Policy Deferrals			
Ford (1975–77)	22,904	14,145	59.2
Carter (1977–81)	12,905	7,314	56.7
Reagan (1981–82)	6,788	6,174	91.0
Reagan (1983–88)	22,333	7,736	34.6
Routine Deferrals			
Ford (1975–77)	16,623	16,610	99.9
Carter (1977–81)	17,943	17,928	99.9
Reagan (1981–88)	66,817	66,284	99.2
Total Routine Deferrals	$101,383	$100,820	99.4

Source: U.S. Office of Management and Budget. Cited in Allen Schick, *The Capacity to Budget*. Washington, D.C.: The Urban Institute Press, 1990. P. 112.

Reconciliation

The major architect of the 1974 Budget Act, Richard Boiling, was surprised by the ploy that was tried in the Congress by the Republicans and the conservative

Democrats (called "Boll Weevils") soon after President Reagan took office. Although the reconciliation provision of the 1974 Act clearly says that a concurrent resolution on the budget may "determine and recommend changes in laws, bills, and resolutions...," the Democratic congressional leadership had carefully avoided serious confrontation with their powerful committee chairmen. With Ronald Reagan's election in 1980, the Republicans not only captured control of the White House and the Senate, but also gained a working majority in the House of Representatives by joining forces with Democratic conservatives. President Reagan and his aides worked with their congressional allies to use effectively the reconciliation power stated in the 1974 Act but not previously used.

The confrontation and its success were a surprise to the House leadership, as illustrated in Exhibit 2–6. The Republican-controlled Senate concurred with President Reagan's budget suggestions (for example, increased national defense, reduced taxes, and a huge cut in domestic spending). It passed the necessary instructions to other committees in its first concurrent budget resolution. The real confrontation occurred in the House, where the Democratic budget resolution was dramatically overturned on the House floor by a Republican/Boll Weevil coalition that supported the president's views. This monumental budget resolution, called Gramm-Latta I, contained instructions for budget reductions in fifteen House committees and fourteen Senate committees, required very large outlay reductions (that is, of $56 billion), and provided reconciliation savings of discretionary and entitlement programs. The congressional committees responded as called for by the 1974 Act, but the result was unacceptable. The next ploy was a quickly fashioned, massive reconciliation bill called Gramm-Latta II. This extraordinary law (see Exhibit 2–7) changed eligibility rules for entitlement programs (for example, food stamps), limited programs earlier authorized, and rewrote major parts of substantive law. No hearings were held on the law; amendment possibilities were strictly limited; debate lasted only two days; and the law was passed in a single vote rather than in a section-by-section vote. Speaker O'Neill's reactions are not surprising. Reconciliation was clearly demonstrated to be a powerful budget tool, but the reconciliation tool was altered to be instructions with the first budget resolution. Although reconciliation remains important, it has been significantly changed and its potential effectiveness has been diminished.

EXHIBIT 2–6   House Speaker Thomas P. O'Neill, June 25, 1981

I have never seen anything like this in my life, to be perfectly truthful. What is the authority for this? Does this mean that any time the President of the United States is interested in a piece of legislation, he merely sends it over? You do not have any regard for the process, for open hearings, discussions as to who it affects, or what it does to the economy? But because a man, who does not understand or know how our process, sends it over, are we to take it in bulk? ...Do we have the right to legislate? Do we have the right to meet our target or can he in one package deregulate, delegislate, the things that have taken years to do?

Source: Congressional Record, June 25, 1981, #3383–85.

Sunset Legislation

In many states and in the federal government, *sunset legislation* is being considered and implemented. The sunset concept is that government programs should automatically expire unless positive action is taken to renew them every few years. The form of the legislation varies. In most instances, the sunset provisions permit the program to remain on the law books, but the authorization for funds expires. In other words, the program technically exists but no money can be spent on the program unless the legislature reenacts the authorization section of the law. The cycle for renewal varies, but often a staggered five-year cycle is used.

The states of Colorado and Florida have taken the lead in sunset legislation. Colorado was the first state to enact major sunset legislation, but it is limited to the state's regulatory agencies. In June 1976, Florida also passed sunset legislation directed toward regulatory agencies, but it set termination dates for both the agencies and substantive laws.

The federal government considered enacting sunset legislation. In fact, many authorization bills were approved with sunset provisions in them. Comprehensive sunset legislation has not passed the Congress. In sunset legislation, the termination schedule is staggered so that programs within a budget function can be reviewed at the same time. Some programs are exempt, such as interest payments on the national debt, retirement, health care, and disability programs. The review process is controlled on a day-to-day basis so that Congress can decide the form, scope, and time allotted for each review appropriate for the subject.

Sunset legislation is misleading. The title and the first explanation lead people to believe that there will be wholesale terminations of government programs. This is unlikely. If there is a strong enough reason to create and fund a program, then there is strong enough reason to reenact the authorization section of the legislation. Some programs will expire, but not on a wholesale basis. The legislation will mean a great deal more paperwork addressed to justifying programs, and, potentially, to a situation in which Congress may not be able to handle the generated volume of justifications.

Federal Budgetary Madness

During the Reagan-Bush years, the federal budget process was inadequate. Naomi Caiden (1982) described the process as "preventing consistent policy making, and encouraging deadlocks, blackmail, and symbolic voting." Typically, the Congress passes not timely appropriation measures, but makeshift continuing resolutions after the beginning of each fiscal year. Federal agencies braced for payless paydays during yearly budget crises, members of Congress were weary of endless rounds of budget decisions, and brinkmanship politics best described budget decisions between the Republican president and the Democrat-controlled Congress.

Federal budget reform will continue to be a major policy issue, especially given the chronically high yearly deficit budget levels. Exhibit 2–7 shows the growth in the federal deficit and Exhibit 2–8 shows the related growth in net interest paid to service the debt over those same years. Exhibit 2–9 shows the growth of the national debt in terms of its relationship to gross national product. A key year was 1982, when the early Reagan administration was able to achieve a significant tax cut but not an equally significant expenditure reduction. Public-interest politics—called the "necessary evil" by James Madison—makes significant cuts in government programs very difficult for members of Congress to support. The alternative means to cut the deficit—raising taxes—is literally impossible to achieve when a Republican president vetoes such laws and his party has enough votes to prevent an override vote of the veto. The resulting political tension has resulted in various major attempts to reform the budget process since 1974, but all of them except the 1993 law failed to prevent a rapid increase in the yearly federal deficit. The deadlock that caused the continual yearly deficit was broken in 1993 largely due to the American people selecting a Democrat as President of the United States. With absolutely no assistance from Republicans, President Clinton by a margin of only one vote was able to get Congress to pass a law that raised taxes, lowered expenditures in many federal programs, and significantly lowered that year's deficit. There is reasonable hope that the yearly federal deficit might remain relatively small and a little more hope that a balanced budget might eventually be achieved.

EXHIBIT 2–7   Federal Budget Deficit in Billions

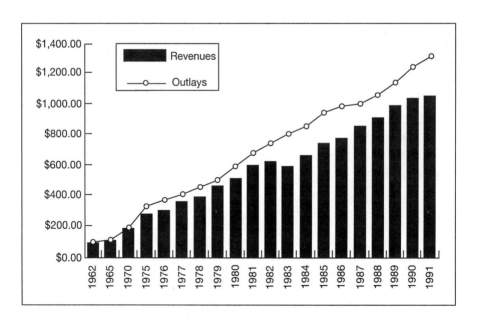

Source: Congressional Budget Office. *The Economic and Budget Outlook: Fiscal Years 1993–1997.* Table D–2, 3 and 6, pp. 114, 115, 118. Washington, D.C.: Government Printing Office, January 1992; U.S. Advisory Commission on Intergovernmental Relations. *Significant Features of Fiscal Federalism*, Vol. 2 Revenues and Expenditures. Table 20, p. 44. Washington, D.C.: Government Printing Office, January 1991.

EXHIBIT 2–8   Federal Budget Interest Paid

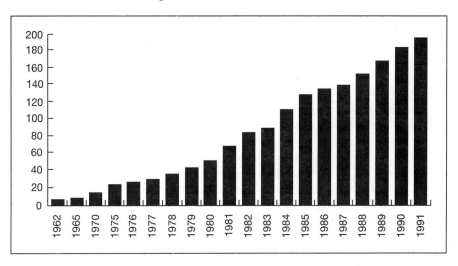

Source: Congressional Budget Office. *The Economic and Budget Outlook: Fiscal Years 1993–1997*. Table D–2, 3 and 6, pp. 114, 115, 118. Washington, D.C.: Government Printing Office, January 1992. And U.S. Advisory Commission on Intergovernmental Relations. *Significant Features of Fiscal Federalism*, Vol. 2 Revenues and Expenditures. Table 20, p. 44. Washington, D.C.: Government Printing Office, January 1991.

EXHIBIT 2–9   Deficit as Percent of GNP

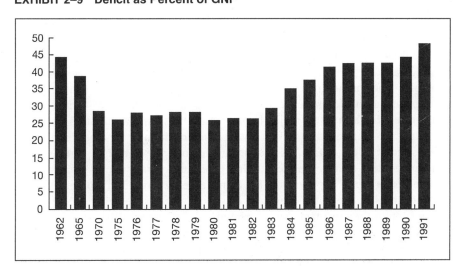

Source: Congressional Budget Office. *The Economic and Budget Outlook: Fiscal Years 1993–1997*. Table D–2, 3 and 6, pp. 114, 115, 118. Washington, D.C.: Government Printing Office, January 1992. And U.S. Advisory Commission on Intergovernmental Relations. *Significant Features of Fiscal Federalism*, Vol. 2 Revenues and Expenditures. Table 20, p. 44. Washington, D.C.: Government Printing Office, January 1991.

In 1983, Carl Grafton and Anne Permaloff characterized the failed federal budget process as follows: (1) it is concerned more with many special political interests to the disadvantage of the larger public interest, (2) it is fragmented with little connection between programs and money, (3) key officials do not take the necessary time to familiarize themselves with budgets, (4) key officials are willing to accept less than the best from the process, and (5) key decision making takes place in unreasonable and unrealistically short time frames.

Allen Schick (1990) calls this failure "improvisational budgeting" and notes that established procedures have broken down, with the result that budgeting is now a contentious, unstable process. Schick says the three underlying causes for this failure are persistence of high deficits, erosion of the government's capacity to ration resources, and a failure to adapt budgeting sufficiently to the changed composition of federal expenditures. Schick believes that successful budget reform is impossible until the yearly deficit is reduced significantly and only then can budget practices be changed to discourage a recurrence. The imbalance problem occurred primarily in 1982. Leading causal factors include indexing programs to force budget growth, less positive national economic growth, rising mandatory payments and entitlements that consume more of the budget, an unwillingness to raise taxes to keep up with the rise in spending, and an unwillingness to cut expenditures radically so that the budget becomes balanced. Schick argued that the solution to the deficit problem must be a combination of a tax increases and spending cuts. That was done in 1993, but yearly deficits are likely to continue. Although the problem continues, it is not nearly as serious as it was prior to 1993.

The three major laws passed between 1974 and 1992 to cure the federal budget crisis were (1) the Gramm-Rudman-Hollings Act (also called the Balanced Budget Act of 1985), (2) a revised Gramm-Rudman-Hollings Act in 1987, and (3) a Budget Enforcement Act of 1990. The provisions of each law were complex and ineffective. The first two were based on establishing deficit reduction targets for specific fiscal years. The third law sets targets within categories. Each law left major loopholes such as funding the bail-out of the savings-and-loan industry failures, which incurred major funding deficits. The 1980s federal budget failures has meant the collapse of budget regularity, the encouragement of deceitful accounting practices, a premium on gimmicks that produce short-term improvement but do not ease the structural problem, strained relationships between the president and the Congress, lessening the effective leadership of the president, congressional congestion and frustration, overloading the ability of the political leaders to reach an effective solution, crowding out other important national concerns, and insufficient resources to respond to emerging issues and priorities. Since 1993, the situation has improved with considerable stress placed on "reinventing government" by Vice President Gore, cutting back on many programs, and raising taxes, especially user fees after 1994.

State and Local Challenges

Unlike the federal situation, state and local governments are passing balanced budgets, but they are also under pressure as some budgets are being passed late and budget gimmicks are being employed to help deal with their budget challenges. When recessions exist, they place serious strain on state and local budget processes. Nevertheless, state and local governments are meeting the fundamental challenge of budgeting, which is making those important budget decisions within the context of balancing revenues and expenditures. At all levels, but especially in medium-sized and small governments, more professional expertise is needed to improve forecasting, capital financing, financial management, and use performance measures. Even today, many local governments do not have program budgets and use performance measures to judge program effectiveness and efficiency. Although the situation has improved, many budget and financial management staffs are not able to conduct sophisticated analyses, thus significantly limiting their professionalism.

The professional challenges of budgeting and financial management are significant, as demonstrated by the illustrations in this book. However, budgeting is an activity that can be done with a minimum of professionalism. Thus, state and local governments can "get by" if they achieve yearly balanced budgets. Unfortunately, the loser in "getting by" is government, the image of government, and the taxpayer, who receives fewer and poorer services for the tax dollar. A good budget and finance office will not solve all of government's problems, but more services and a higher quality of performance should be the results of such an office. If forecasting is improved, then idle cash will produce more revenue, and disruptive financial emergency controls need not be used. If capital financing practices are good, then less interest will be paid on the government debt, and more capital improvements will be possible for the same tax dollar. If creative financial management of enterprise funds is used, governments will have more revenue available at a time when taxpayers are hostile to tax increases. If budget and financial offices can make more effective use of rapidly improving computer technology, then time-consuming, routine "numbers crunching" can be replaced with more sophisticated analyses designed to improve the quality of government management. The professional challenges are exciting, but they will not be confronted and conquered easily. The highest levels of professionalism will be required.

The Government Finance Officer's Association (GFOA) has developed a local budget awards program, which is having an impact on the quality of budgeting in local government. Governments voluntarily submit their annual budget document to the GFOA. They send them to GFOA member reviewers who use evaluation criteria adopted by the GFOA. If the government's budget document is given a passing grade, then the government budget office will get an award from GFOA, which the local government normally places in next year's budget document. The process has been sufficiently rigorous and the comments constructive enough to influence the profession. This peer-group review process is upgrading the local budget processes.

REVIEW QUESTIONS

1. The roots of the executive/legislative struggle go back as far as 1215, but the struggle greatly influences how budgeting is done in the United States today. Explain those roots and how that struggle helps us understand modern budgeting. In what ways do we see that struggle taking place in modern budgeting?
2. Compare and contrast the rationalist approaches to budgeting (for example, PPB, MBO, and ZBB) with the incrementalist approaches. Explain how the role of analysis varies—if it does—in each approach.
3. Compare and contrast line-item budgeting, program budgeting, and performance budgeting.
4. Explain the 1974 congressional budget reforms. What was meant to be accomplished, and what means were devised to accomplish those ends?
5. The current federal budget process is said to be inadequate. Why? What reforms could help resolve the identified problems?
6. The professional challenges of state and local budgeting are significant. What are those challenges? What should be done by professionals to meet those challenges?

REFERENCES

Advisory Commission on Intergovernmental Relations. *ACIR State Legislative Program*, vol. 4. *Fiscal and Personnel Management.* Washington, D.C.: Government Printing Office, November 1975.

ALYANDARY-ALEXANDER, MAND (ed.). *Analysis for Planning, Programming and Budgeting: Proceedings of the Social Cost-Effectiveness Symposium.* Washington, D.C.: Washington Operation Research Council, 1968.

ASPIN, LES. "The Defense Budget and Foreign Policy: The Role of Congress," *Daedalus* (Summer 1975), 155–74.

BAKKER, OEGE. *The Budget Cycle in Public Finance in the United States.* The Hague: W. P. Van Stockum, 1953.

BARTIZAL, JOHN R. *Budget Principle and Procedure.* Englewood Cliffs, N.J.: Prentice Hall, 1942.

BEAUMONT, ENID. "The New York Case from a Public Administration Perspective," *The Bureaucrats*, 5, 1 (April 1976), 101–12.

BEKER, JEROME. "Measuring Cost Effectiveness in Human Services," *Canadian Welfare*, 51, 1 (January/February 1975), 5–6.

BENSON, GEORGE, et al. (eds.). *The American Property Tax: Its History, Administration and Economic Impact.* Claremont, Calif.: Institute for Studies in Federalism, Claremont Men's College, 1965.

BLACK, GUY. "Externalities and Structure in PPB," *Public Administration Review*, 31, 6 (November/December 1971), 637–43.

BREAK, GEORGE F. *Agenda for Local Tax Reform.* Berkeley, Calif.: Institute of Government Studies, University of California, 1970.

BRUNDAGE, PERCIVAL HACK. *The Bureau of the Budget.* New York: Holt, Rinehart & Winston, 1970.

BUCK, A. E. "Performance Budgeting for the Federal Government," *Tax Review* (July 1949).

CAIDEN, NAOMI. "The Myth of the Annual Budget," *Public Administration Review*, 42, 6 (November/December 1982), 516–23.

FISHER, LOUIS. "Annual Authorizations: Durable Roadblocks to Biennial Budgeting," *Public Budgeting and Finance*, 3, 1 (Spring 1983), 23–40.

FLEISCHMAN, RICHARD K., and R. PENNY MARQUETTE. "The Origins of Public Budgeting: Municipal Reformers During the Progressive Era," *Public Budgeting and Finance*, 6, 1 (Spring 1986), 71–77.

GOOD, DAVID. "Envelope Budgeting: The Canadian Experience." Paper prepared for the 1983 Annual American Society for Public Administration National Conference, New York, April 17, 1983.

GRAFTON, CARL, and ANNE PERMALOFF. "Budget Reforms in Perspective" in *Handbook on Public Budgeting and Financial Management*, Jack Rabin, and Thomas D. Lynch, ed., New York: Marcel Dekker, 1983.

HARTMAN, ROBERT W. "Congress and Budget-Making," *Political Science Quarterly*, 97, 3 (Fall 1982), 381–402.

HOWARD, JAMES A. "Government Economic Projections: A Comparison Between CBO and OMB Forecasts," *Public Budgeting and Finance*, 7,3 (Autumn 1987), 14–25.

LELOUP, LANCE T. "After the Blitz: Reagan and the Congressional Budget Process." Paper presented at the Southern Political Science Association Meeting, Memphis, Tenn., November 5–7, 1981.

LEWIS, C. W. "History of Federal Budgeting and Financial Management from the Constitution to the Beginning of the Modern Era," *Public Budgeting and Financial Management*, 1, 2 (1989), 193–214.

LYNCH, THOMAS D. *Federal Budget and Financial Management Reform*. Westport, Conn.: Quorum Books, 1991.

PYHRR, PETER A. *Zero-Base Budgeting: A Practical Management Tool for Evaluating Expenses*. New York: John Wiley & Sons, 1973.

RABIN, JACK, and THOMAS D. LYNCH (eds.) *Handbook on Budgeting and Financial Management*. New York: Marcel Dekker, 1983.

RUBIN, IRENE S. "Budgeting For Our Times: Target Base Budgeting," *Public Budgeting and Finance*, 11, 3 (Spring 1991), 5–14.

SCHICK, ALLEN. *The Capacity to Budget*. Washington, D.C.: The Urban Institute Press, 1990.

———"Manual on the Federal Budget Process." Washington, D.C.: U.S. Congressional Research Service, December 24, 1991.

SMITH, LINDA. "The Congressional Budget Process: Why It Worked This Time." *The Bureaucrat*. Vol. 6, No. 1, Spring 1977. pp. 88–111.

WENZ, THOMAS W., and ANN P. NOLAN. "Budgeting for the Future: Target Base Budgeting," *Public Budgeting and Finance*, 2, 2 (Summer 1982), 88–91.

3

BUDGET BEHAVIOR

Public budgeting is done by human beings, and one can understand a great deal about budgeting by examining the factors that influence human behavior within this special context. This chapter first examines how the key actors in the budget process interact. The next major topic is an in-depth examination of the agency budget office and the perspectives associated with the office. The final major topic is a careful examination of the strategies associated with the game of budgeting. This chapter examines:

1. the political influence patterns among the key actors in the budget process;
2. means commonly used to cultivate an active clientele;
3. the duties of an agency budget office;
4. the perspective of a budget officer and typical behavioral patterns;
5. four common philosophic attitudes of budget officers toward the budget process;
6. explanation of how confidence in the budget officer is developed;
7. the significance of program results in budgeting;
8. the preparation process for hearings;
9. the review setting;
10. spender's strategies;
11. cutter's strategies;
12. strategies to support new programs; and
13. some important cautions in public budgeting.

POLITICS AND PERSPECTIVE

Four Institutional Roles

Public budgeting can be understood in terms of four institutional roles. Each has a definable behavior. Exhibit 3–1 shows the interrelationship among the groups.

EXHIBIT 3–1 Interrelationships of Institutional Roles in Public Budgeting

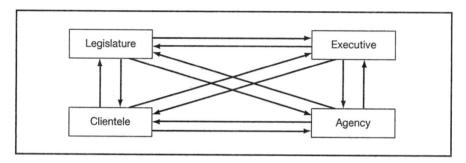

The four institutional roles are the *agency*, the *executive*, the *legislature*, and the *clientele*. Two other groups, the courts and the media, are significant, but are not discussed here because their influence patterns are unusual. Discussion of their influence is outside the scope of this text. The agency is the institution with the responsibility for managing the programs and preparing the initial budget. The executive is loosely defined here to mean the chief executive, his or her staff, and the central budget office. (The department, of which the agency is a part, plays an odd role, sometimes acting as an extension of the executive but often acting as a superagency, depending on the stage of the budget process.) The legislature is the legislative branch of government, such as the Congress in the federal government. The clientele is a group affected by the agency's programs and it takes an active interest in the agency's policy.

The double lines in Exhibit 3–1 represent several two-way influence patterns. The agency influences the executive through its budget request and the executive's budget decision is one form of executive influence on the agency. The executive influences the legislature through its executive budget requests, and the passage of laws is one form of influence upon the executive. The agency's programs by definition affect its clientele. Clientele groups are well known for their lobbying (influencing) activity on legislators, but they also lobby and influence the chief executive and the agency. Less well known is that legislatures and executives can influence clientele groups directly. To make matters more complex, an influence pattern may involve more than two groups. For example, a clientele group influences Congress on appropriation legislation which ultimately becomes law, and then the agency is influenced by the language of that appropriation legislation.

A case study involving the U.S. Maritime Administration illustrates the influence patterns. In the Nixon administration, there was a strong desire at the highest levels in the U.S. Office of Management and Budget to phase out the operating and shipbuilding subsidies at an accelerated rate. The OMB required the Maritime Administration to launch an analytical study of exactly how this was to be accomplished. Somehow, Mrs. Sullivan, who headed the House Appropriations subcommittee, discovered the OMB study. She was extremely upset that the OMB wished to change policy clearly established in the law and phoned OMB Director Mayo. The substance of that conversation was not recorded, but the director withdrew the request for the study. This series of events illustrates the influence of the central budget office on an agency as well as the strength of a single legislator on a central budget office.

Clientele influence on agencies is not fully appreciated. In *Policy Analysis for Public Policymaking*, this author presented several case studies involving the budget process in the U.S. Department of Transportation. In February 1970, the Office of Management and Budget called for a special analytical study by the Urban Mass Transportation Administration of that agency's policy guidance for capital grants reflected in the published *Information to Applicants*. In time, the study and a revised *Information to Applicants* was prepared. Before it became official, a letter was formally sent (as required by OMB Circular A-85) to inform state and local government associations of the proposed new guidelines. The Circular A–85 standard OMB guidance requires an agency-to-clientele interrelationship prior to the time that the final government policy becomes effective.

In this instance, representatives of the transit industry and the cities were taken by surprise. They took strong exception to the "unrealistic data demands and planning analyses" that would be imposed. They felt that the DOT committed a breach of faith because there was no informal consultation prior to sending the official notification. They reacted by developing a counterstrategy—they met with agency officials and tried to soften the most undesirable aspects of the new selection criteria. The agency officials felt that they came close to the clientele's feeling while keeping within the strict OMB policy prescriptives. This case illustrates the infrequently documented influence of a clientele group on an agency.

Legislative groups and chief executives can influence clientele groups directly. The most noticed such influence is at the large conventions of these groups when high-ranking legislators or executives address the members. Less publicized meetings occur when legislative and executive officials request cooperation or seek lobbying support for key legislation.

"End runs" and finesses do occur in this complex four-way relationship. For example, an agency can influence its clientele group by pointing out the implications of existing proposed policy. The clientele group can then go to either the legislature or the executive to kill the proposed policy. A more complex situation would be when the agency has to proceed with some action (for example, conserve energy) which its clientele group may find distasteful. The agency might be able to counter likely pressure by having the chief executive lobby the clientele group and the legislature. This would strengthen the chances of success for the agency by minimizing clientele resistance.

In the budget process, the agency-to-clientele-to-legislature triangular relationship is a common pattern. The more sophisticated clientele groups recognize that the size of the budget and the individual programs are significant. In many cases, an informal communication network exists between the agency and the clientele group. Any formal, publicly available information is monitored, analyzed, and communicated to clientele members. Sometimes active campaigns are launched to build a strong lobbying presence for particular budget issues of importance to the clientele.

State and local patterns normally are not as complex as those found on the federal level. However, large state and local governments have patterns more similar to the federal level. The seriousness of lobbying and clientele groups, not surprisingly, relates to the amount of money or the potential amount of money involved; thus, large governments with large programs tend to have the active clientele groups. In medium-sized and small governments, clientele groups can and do act less formally. Clientele interests are handled as nonpaid, part-time activities via simple phone calls and meetings. Often, on-the-record views are expressed in public hearings; or, possibly, even a demonstration or media event might be organized. Highly emotional confrontations are rare on budget issues, but they do occur.

Each aspect—the agency, executive, legislature, and clientele—has a separate institutional role. Each perceives itself as a separate group, although individual exceptions can be cited—for example, an agency political appointee may identify solely with the chief executive. Also, each group can be further subdivided, and subdivisions may come into conflict and threaten to harm the larger group. For example, the Maritime Administration is composed of maritime unions and operators. When they work together they are surprisingly powerful for their respective sizes, but the alliance can and does break down on specific issues. In the Congress, the substantive and appropriation committees sometimes are in conflict. In the executive, two staff agencies such as the White House staff and the Office of Management and Budget can also be in conflict on issues, but in the executive branch, the chief executive can arbitrate internal disputes more easily than in the legislative branch.

Role Objectives and Enemies

The agency and its leadership almost always have pride or a sense that its programs are worthwhile. The career employee recognizes that his or her job and income are associated with the agency's objectives. In some instances, an almost missionary zeal and self-identification with the agency can exist among the top agency leadership. In other instances, the zeal may be only a belief that what the agency does is a worthwhile function. Rarely do top agency leaders disagree with the mission or the fundamental value of the agency and its programs.

Another factor to consider is the budget process itself. The agency is always placed in the position of requesting and defending. Reviewers are always doubting the agency and demanding facts and better arguments. Not surprisingly, agency executives often find themselves defending the agency when it comes under attack. The president, governors, and mayors sometimes act surprised when their agency appointees argue the agency position.

Given the dual elements of self-worth and role demands, chief executives should be more surprised if their appointees don't speak for their agencies. Given those circumstances, issues are viewed from the perspective of the agency's mission and the people in the organization. Does a change further or detract from the agency's mission? Will the people in the organization benefit from or lose because of a change? Programs are justified with these questions well in mind. Lee Sigelman (1986) examined survey data of high-ranking state administrators covering 1964, 1968, 1974, and 1978. Sigelman concluded that their support for truly major agency expansion does not appear to be extremely widespread. He noted even a substantial number called for little or no agency expansion. In other words, agency administrators do request and defend their budgets but that does not mean that they necessarily pursue a budget-maximizing strategy. Some may act out of self-interest, defined in terms of salary, perquisites, reputation, power, and patronage. However, the facts show that motivations are much more complex than deliberate, single-minded pursuit of self-interest.

The chief executive plays a different role. The executive wishes to economize, cut requests, and coordinate programs. There is an arm's length relationship between the executive and the agency leadership in spite of the fact that agency political appointees serve at the pleasure of the executive. The executive must maintain the option of saying "no" to an agency request. Requests must be reviewed carefully and cuts are necessary for purposes of economy and better allocation of resources around the executive branch. When the executive decision is reached, the chief executive expects that the agency will formally support the executive decision even though the agency may not perceive the decision to be in its own best interest. Discipline is maintained in several ways: formal statements are cleared by the executive's staff, budget requests must follow the executive's budget and allowance letter, the political influence of the chief executive is significant, and the agency head can be fired.

Another factor for state and local government agency heads to consider is that their chief executives can sometimes veto or reallocate items in line-item budgets. These powers vary greatly from one government to the next, but some chief executives can unilaterally reconstruct the council-approved budget using the line-item veto. The only limit on the power is the likely political resistance the chief executive would receive from the legislature or city council. When chief executives wield this type of power, agency officials would be hesitant to challenge or try to circumvent them.

The legislature (sometimes called council, board, or commission) plays an entirely different role. It is the people's elected deliberative body, normally composed of well-intended, intelligent individuals. However, on budget matters, the legislature is often confronted with confusing information and little time to make decisions. At the federal level and in some large state and local governments, the legislatures may even dominate the policy-making process, but this is not often the situation. Normally, legislatures are not the initiators, but rather play a more reactive role. Attention is given more to pet projects and issues of local popular concern rather than to a unified, comprehensive approach to the budget.

The clientele members are interested in how an agency's program affects them. They meet and discuss in conferences the significance of existing legislation, the chief executive's attitudes toward programs, and the policies of the agency. Sometimes the clientele works as a whole, but often various subgroups act, with some coordination among the groups. Clientele groups vary, with success often depending on clientele leadership, the stakes involved, the organizational network, the dedication of the members, the issue, and the strategies and tactics employed.

The paths of clientele influence vary. Often a special agency-clientele relationship occurs because an unofficial policy of job rotation exists. For example, a former lobbyist or key member of a clientele group can be and often is appointed to a high-level government position which is important to the clientele group. Sometimes clientele groups support the winning president or congressman. This also can lead to a cordial climate. Lobbying is the standard path of influence. Also formal and informal relationships can exist between the agency and the clientele, as illustrated in the UMTA and Maritime case examples cited earlier.

Agencies and clientele groups can have anticlientele groups. For example, consumer groups can oppose the manufacturing interests and government regulating bodies. In recent years, more groups from right-to-left political spectrum—Nader, environment, antinuclear, and so on—have become active. These groups are often significant.

Who the "good and bad guys" are depends on values, issues, and perspectives. For some agencies, there is a pattern in which various actors tend to be allies on most issues. This need not be the situation. From the agency's point of view, the executive may be the stumbling block on an issue and the essential ally on yet another issue. From the clientele's viewpoint, the agency may be an enemy causing useless red tape or a vital agency necessary for the survival of the clientele members. Each situation must be examined separately. Rarely does a uniform and consistent pattern exist over time, with one set of actors who are always friends and another set who are always enemies. The patterns evolve and change; thus, the actors must adapt to a dynamic environment.

Cultivation of an Active Clientele

For most government agencies, there is no problem identifying a clientele group. Highway departments are well aware of their clientele. The Veterans' Administration hears from its clientele. However, some agencies cannot easily identify clientele groups. For example, the United States Information Agency does not serve people in this country. What group is its clientele? The U.S. Bureau of Prisons does not have an active clientele group. In such cases, the nature of the organization or its mission precludes a clientele group; thus, the agency is handicapped in the pluralist style of American government.

The most obvious way to cultivate a clientele is to carry out the agency's programs, but some strategy is involved in building a supportive clientele. In the first place, the clientele members should understand and appreciate the full extent of the benefits they receive from the agency's programs. In the second place, most legislatures represent the whole population, so a breadth of clientele members across the nation, state, or city is best if the clientele wishes to lobby the legislature. Third, some clientele members may be in a better position to aid the agency, such as a group in the House Appropriations Committee chairperson's home district. Finally, mute clientele members are not that useful, so they must be encouraged to be active politically.

Strategies of both expanding and concentrating the clientele are used. An agency can take care to provide grants or assistance across the country or build a balanced set of programs which appeal to several specific sectors of society. Agencies have their public information officers explain the programs, and attendance at clientele conferences is considered very important. Some clientele members can be acquired by changing or adding attractive services for that group. For example, in an area where senior citizens are well organized, the parks department is wise to have programs for the elderly. Often the intensity of support is important, so the program may be altered to be sure to benefit a particularly influential group.

The clientele must be heard by the legislature and the executive. In some instances, the clientele members are poorly organized or not adept in dealing with American democratic institutions. Congressmen, senators, and legislators often assume that if they do not hear from supporters, no one cares. Given the need to cut, the tendency is to cut where no one cares enough to complain. Legislators do consider themselves to be guardians of the treasury, but they do not like the uncomfortable feeling they get when cuts return to haunt them at the next election. Even saying "no" to an impassioned plea is not pleasant. An agency rarely advocates lobbying the legislature, but its officers can explain the significance of lobbying and stress that the small budget is a problem which can be corrected by the legislature.

Sometimes agencies structure subunits to attract clientele. For example, the agency is broad-based but effective lobbying is done by narrow focus groups. The agency can appeal to those narrow groups. For example, the National Institute of Health uses subunits focused on specific diseases that correspond to the active health clientele groups. The result is a strong set of clientele groups. The hazard in this approach is that a glamorous subunit can lessen support for the other units.

Another approach is the creation of an advisory committee. Even the most conservative group of advisors tends to advocate the desirability of the agency's program. This can lead to increased and more effective clientele support.

Agency Budget Office

The place for developing and orchestrating the budget process is the agency budget office. The duties of such offices vary, as they sometimes include the accounting function and an analytical/planning unit. There are some common duties which describe what an agency budget office does. The following is an excellent list of duties from one agency budget office—the Budget Division of ACTION in the federal government:[1]

1. In conjunction with the appropriate operating officials, develops budget estimates for programs and offices, conducts budget reviews, and recommends budget allocations.
2. In conjunction with appropriate operating officials, develops, presents, and justifies ACTION's budget submission to the Office of Management and Budget and to the Congress, including financial and personnel exhibits, budget narrative material, and budget back-up data. Prepares Agency witnesses for hearings before the Office of Management and Budget and the Congress.
3. Recommends budget priorities as the result of Office of Management and Budget and Congressional budget guidance for use within the Agency.
4. Prepares apportionments, allotments, and maintains overall control of Agency financial resources and position allocations.
5. Issues operating budgets with position and average grade allocations to all offices, regions, and posts, and ensures budget execution with legislative authority and limitations.
6. Conducts budget reviews and analyses during the fiscal year and recommends reprogramming actions and other funding adjustments.
7. Recommends and implements budgetary procedures, budget controls, and reporting systems and makes recommendations regarding the financial aspects of the management information system to improve financial management within the Agency.
8. Works with appropriate operating officials to coordinate the budget with Agency plans, objectives, and programs.
9. Acts as the Agency's primary point of contact with other governmental agencies on budget matters.

Exhibit 3–2 illustrates the variety of activities of budget execution responsibilities and the complex interrelationships which commonly exist among people performing budget responsibilities.

Perspective of the Budget Officer

Much of the work of the budget officer is repetitive. Exhibits 3–2 and 3–3 point out the yearly routine. The budget process has an established pattern, and after a few years the substantive issues of the agency also take on a familiar pattern. Budgeting is largely repetitive and the filling out of reports tends to make the work mechanical.

[1]Budget Execution Responsibilities, ACTION, 1975.

EXHIBIT 3–2 Functions, Responsibilities, and Interrelationships of Budget Execution Personnel

FUNCTIONS	OFFICIALS: DIRECTOR/ DEPUTY	ASSISTANT DIRECTOR FOR OPP	BUDGET DIRECTOR	ASSISTANT DIRECTOR FOR A&F	ALLOTMENT HOLDER	INTERMEDIATE BUDGET HOLDER (10 REGIONS; OFFICE)	OPERATING BUDGET MANAGER
Apportionment request	Responsibility delegated to OPP	Submits request to GMB	Prepares request from sum of allotments; monitors	Receive info copy of apportionment; monitor for pos. viol.			
Continuing resolution	Concur with GC interpretation		Coordinates activity; issues instructions				
Treasury warrant request			Prepares request	Request to Treasury			
Allotment issuance	Reviews, approves	Issues allotments	Prepares allotment from sum of operating budgets	Receive info. copy of allot.; monitor for pos. violation	Receive allotment; monitor		
Operating budget issuance			Directs; issues jointly; monitors		Review and approve budgets; jointly issue	Review and approve subordinate budget request	Recommend operating budget totals
Reapportionment	Request to the OMB	Concurs in request	Prepares request with back-up				
Allotment reprogramming	Final approval in cases of question	Approves reprogramming	Recommends; prepares documents		Request reprogramming		
Operating budget reprogramming			Reviews requests; concurs in all decisions	Insures account reporting compatible with format	Review request; approve if operating group budgets change	Review; approve if operating group budget totals unchanged	Request reprogramming

	1	2	3	4	5	6
Estimation of receipts/reimbursements		Prepares; estimates; monitors				
Allotment management	Concurs	Monitors		Manage within budget totals and restrict		Manage within budget atotals and restrictions
Operating budget management		Monitors				
Quarterly review	Approves new budget allocations	Directs review; recommends new allocation		Prepare data; recommend new levels	Recommend new levels for operating group	Recommend change in operating budget
Year-end review	Approves new budget allocation	Directs review; recommends changes		Recommend changes	Recommend changes	Recommend changes
Violation reports	Receive report; report to president and Congress		Complete review of open obligations Instigate report to director with evidence			
Personnel and average grade ceiling	Reviews and approves allocation to 10 major offices	Develops/reviews allocation to 10 major offices	Recommends allocations to operating units	Recommend intermediate level totals	Recommend allocations to operating units within operating groups	
Review of past-year performance		Analyzes; prepares report				
Preparation of status of funds report		Provides budget input to reports	Generate reports and distribute			

Source: Budget Execution Responsibilities, ACTION, 1975.

The budget officer sees the world in terms of dollars, accuracy, and legality. The agency and its activities must always be translated into money. Budget officers will discuss new and old ideas, but eventually they ask, "What does this mean in terms of money?" Accuracy is essential. As will be discussed later, having the confidence of others is quite useful to the budget officer, and confidence is not increased by making mistakes, especially in simple math. Care must be taken to establish procedures that double-check tables, ensure that final typing is error-free, and verify the accuracy of stated facts. Legality is also a concern. If money is spent for reasons not permitted by law, then the budget officer may go to jail. There are few agency-level decisions about which the budget officer does not know, and often the law fixes responsibility for agency action on the agency head and budget officer. Wisdom dictates that the budget officer must be sure of the legality of questionable matters in order to avoid later problems.

Deadlines are the guiding force for a budget officer. Sometimes they seem impossible, and often they are crucial. A common situation is to see a budget officer working late at night or on the weekends in order to meet some deadline. If a deadline is missed, then someone—usually the agency head—will be upset. More significantly, the agency may have lost an important opportunity or handicapped itself in a decision-making situation. Timeliness can mean even the survival of the agency's program. On the other hand, some deadlines are foolish and the wiser person will take the extra time to do a better job because timeliness is not significant. The decision to ignore a deadline should be based on a knowledge of how and when the information will be utilized.

The budget can be used to minimize or surface disagreements. The budget officer is an artist who realizes that a budget can be presented in many ways in spite of the requirements of format. For political or internal management reasons, specific issues may best be hidden or minimized. This can be done by placing the issue within a larger, more dominant subject. In many situations, surfacing disagreement is a much better strategy. An issue can be surfaced by presenting it with some prominence in the budget document. This forces decision makers to deal with the problem and try to resolve it. In many instances, minimizing or surfacing a disagreement is mandated by outside forces, such as a major media story on the subject, which cannot be ignored. In some instances, these decisions are made by the budget officer; thus, his or her political and management judgment is important.

Deadlines and other pressures force the budget officer to use the satificing approach to many decision-making situations. When someone is demanding a budget submission, and the timeliness of that submission is important, then the budget officer may be pleased to find even a satisfactory answer. Budgeting is done under pressure, and the budget officer must do the best that he or she can in the time available. Searching for ideal answers on all occasions is not compatible with budgeting.

EXHIBIT 3–3 Flowchart of Budget Division of ACTION

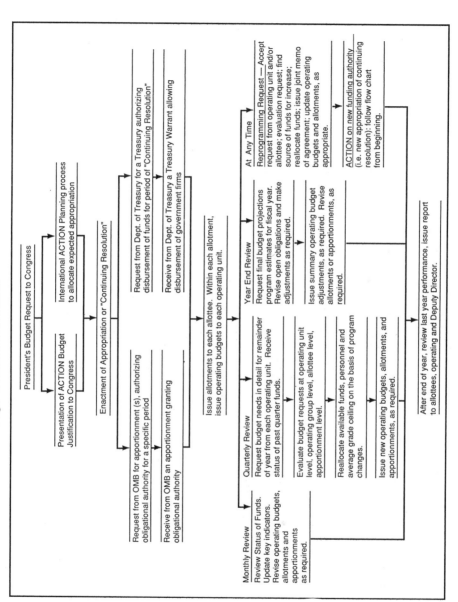

President's Budget Request to Congress

Presentation of ACTION Budget Justification to Congress

International ACTION Planning process to allocate expected appropriation

Enactment of Appropriation or "Continuing Resolution"

Request from OMB for apportionment (s), authorizing obligational authority for a specific period

Receive from OMB an apportionment granting obligational authority

Request from Dept. of Treasury for a Treasury authorizing disbursement of funds for period of "Continuing Resolution"

Receive from Dept. of Treasury a Treasury Warrant allowing disbursement of government firms

Issue allotments to each allottee. Within each allotment, issue operating budgets to each operating unit.

Monthly Review
Review Status of Funds. Update key indicators. Revise operating budgets, allotments and apportionments as required.

Quarterly Review
Request budget needs in detail for remainder of year from each operating unit. Receive status of past quarter funds.

Evaluate budget requests at operating unit level, operating group level, allottee level, apportionment level.

Reallocate available funds, personnel and average grade ceiling on the basis of program changes.

Issue new operating budgets, allotments, and apportionments, as required.

Year End Review
Request final budget projections program estimates for fiscal year. Revise open obligations and make adjustments as required.

Issue summary operating budget adjustments, as required. Revise allotments or apportionments, as required.

At Any Time
Reprogramming Request — Accept request from operating unit and/or allottee; evaluation request; find source of funds for increase; reallocate funds; issue joint memo of agreement; update operating budgets and allotments, as appropriate.

ACTION on new funding authority (i.e. new appropriation of continuing resolution): follow flow chart from beginning.

After end of year, review last year performance, issue report to allottees, operating and Deputy Director.

Agency Budget Behavior

As explained earlier in this chapter, loyalty to an agency is a common behavioral phenomenon. This loyalty is similar to that found in professional athletes. When they work for a team, loyalty to the team is given. Budget officers believe in their agency's mission and feel that their role is important for the well-being of the agency. Blind loyalty does not exist because program weaknesses are well-known. A more balanced loyalty prevails that recognizes faults but believes the program essentially is or can be sound.

Individuals working in a public agency take pride in their work. This can lead to the desire to expand the projects and programs. Budget reviewers are often frustrated by agency desires to expand programs, but such expansion tendencies are positive indicators of the health of the program's management. Agencies should not be criticized for being enthusiastic. Reviewers should applaud positive attitudes while recognizing the reviewers' role may call for them to disapprove expansion.

Budgeting's political context often supersedes apparent rationality. What might appear to be the best solution is not necessarily the best position for the agency to take. Recall that agencies exist in a context of powerful interacting forces. When a person is sailing, the best sailing course may be directly toward the ultimate objective. Sometimes tacking into the wind is necessary because of the force of the opposing wind. In public administration, the budget strategy may not be to advocate or oppose a position directly, but to wait for the clientele or legislature to react to circumstances. Judgment is essential.

Often there is some flexibility in budgeting as a result of what some call gimmicks. How to employ those gimmicks is another important talent. For example, the timing of obligation and disbursements can be significant, and this timing can be controlled by the budget officer. Another trick is that a given expense item can be assigned to one of two programs. This choice permits some often needed flexibility. Gimmicks exist because some discretion exists and a budget officer can use that discretion to ease the burden of managing the program. Skillful budget officers are aware of the available discretionary decisions and use them to ease the problems of public management.

Public budgeting requires decision makers. Even decisions not to act represent policy choices. If a budget reviewer delays a program or project for another year, that is a decision which often has important implications. Decisions may be based on sound reasoning, but they do affect people. Decision makers must be able to live with criticism because budget decisions often generate strong arguments. Also, decisions are often made on meager information, thus contributing to the possibility of self-doubt in the minds of public budget officers. If the budget officer cannot deal emotionally with criticism and doubt, then he or she should consider a different type of work. Doubt and criticism are a part of public budgeting.

Public budgeting requires the highest professional characteristics. Later in this chapter, the importance of confidence in the budget officer will be explained.

Confidence is established through professionalism. Honesty and integrity are essential professional characteristics. This does not mean that the budget officer does not prepare the *strongest case possible* for a program, but it does mean that "possible" includes avoiding lies and misrepresentations. No one faults a budget officer for being sensitive to shifting political causes (for example, environment, energy, inflation, unemployment) and framing budget justifications to take advantage of those shifting but temporarily persuasive rationales. This political sensitivity comes together with accuracy, legality, honesty, integrity, and other factors to constitute a professional.

One unfortunate characteristic of some budget officers is arrogance. This characteristic exists more in budget reviewers found in units like the department budget offices and the U.S. Office of Management and Budget (OMB). Lord Acton once stated that power corrupts and absolute power corrupts absolutely. Even budget officers and budget analysts possess some power because of the nature of their job; a few are corrupted, but many more become intoxicated. They know they have power, and they let others know it with their arrogance. For example, young OMB budget examiners may be mild-mannered before they start working for the OMB, but once on the job they can visit the "field" and act in a cavalier, flippant, or even bossy manner to people with much higher civil service rank and longer experience. Such behavior is not wise professionally because it often leads to a needless lack of cooperation from the agency, thus making the examiner's job that much more difficult.

Budget officers are almost always career civil servants who work quite closely with politically appointed agency or department heads. This close rapport is sometimes influenced by the unusual position agency heads must face. Often they are expected to give their allegiance exclusively to the chief executive but the role of agency head strongly induces a loyalty to the agency. In some instances, these two loyalties are in conflict, thus presenting an agency head with an extremely difficult emotional dilemma. When such situations arise, the budget officer will become quite aware of the dilemma because the agency head's handling of that dilemma will influence the budget process. Understanding the dilemma is helpful, but there are no easy answers to this type of situation.

Public budgeting is an activity which requires responsible people. In the federal government, this responsibility is dramatized. If a budget officer over-obligates or permits an amount to be spent in excess of that apportioned by the OMB, then a legal violation has occurred which can result in his or her being fired, fined, or sentenced to jail. Exhibit 3–4 is the quote from the Anti-deficiency Act which details the action required when violations occur. A fine or jail sentence results from willful violations. Such violations are rare.

Good professionals love the game. They find it challenging and exciting. They love being important and having responsibility. They love the need to work under pressure and yet deliver quality work. They love knowing all the complexities of budgeting and being able to use their skills. They love the intrigue and excitement of both politics and public management.

EXHIBIT 3–4   Anti-deficiency Act (Section 3527 of Revised Statutes, as amended)

Actions required when violations occur.

1. *Administrative discipline; fines; or imprisonment.* In addition to any penalty of liability under other law, any officer or employee of the United States who shall violate subsections (a), (b), or (h) of this section shall be subjected to appropriate administrative discipline, including, when circumstances warrant, suspension from duty without pay or removal from office; and any officer or employee of the United States who shall knowingly and willfully violate subsections (a), (b), or (h) of this section shall, upon conviction, be fined not more than $5,000 or imprisoned for not more than two years, or both.

2. *Reports to President or Congress.* In the case of a violation of subsections (a), (b), or (h) of this section by an officer or employee of an agency, or of the District of Columbia, the head of the agency concerned or the Commissioner of the District of Columbia, shall immediately report to the President, through the Director of the Office of Management and Budget, and to the Congress all pertinent facts together with a statement of the action taken thereon.

A 1991 survey by Katherine Willoughby of ten Southern state budget offices helps us understand what guides budget officer behavior. She focused on state government budget analysts and discovered that they took their decision-making cues primarily from gubernatorial direction, agency efficiency, and changes in workload data if spending plans were being reviewed. Less important were the influence of the agency head and the legislative agenda. Of least importance were the acquisitiveness of the agency head and public support for the program. She noted that the fiscal stability of the state and the age of the analysts were also factors in influencing their decisions.

Sydney Duncombe and Richard Kenney (1987), who examined how budget officials in five states defined agency budget success, concluded that it is a complex, multidimensional concept that goes beyond maximizing state appropriations. They found most budget professionals were "satisficers" and not "maximizers." Aaron Wildavsky (1964) correctly concluded that budget strategies and objectives were contingent upon climate and circumstance. In Exhibit 3–5, note that perceptions varied significantly among agency officials, executive budget staff, and legislative budget staff. Budget reviewers believe agencies defined success in terms of protecting programs and "winning the budget influence game." Agencies view good relations as a significantly higher measure of their budget success than do their executive and legislative opponents.

EXHIBIT 3–5   Importance of Selected Budget Success Measures As Seen by
Budget Officials (% Reporting "Very Important")

Measures of Budget Success	AGENCY OFFICIALS (N=50) RANK %		EXECUTIVE BUDGET STAFF (N=25) RANK %		LEGISLATIVE BUDGET STAFF (N=25) RANK %	
1. Whether good relationships were maintained with the legislative budget staff	1	60	5	28	7	24
2. Whether good relationships were maintained with the governor and budget staff	2	58	5	28	5	28
3. Whether the agency was able to protect existing programs from being cut below the amount needed to continue at the existing level	3	54	2	48	1	44
4. Whether the agency had to lay off staff this year	4	53	4	36	2	32
5. Percent of agency budget request funded by the leg.	5	35	3	40	7	24
6. Percent of agency budget request funded by the gov.	6	34	1	52	9	20
7. Whether the agency was able to fund new programs this year	7	24	10	16	2	32
8. Percent increase in approp. above current year	8	14	7	20	2	32
9. Percent increase in approp. over a 4-year period	9	12	8	8	5	28
10. Whether the agency was able to spend its entire approp.	9	12	8	8	10	0

Source: Sydney Duncombe and Richard Kinney, "Agency Budget Success: How It Is Defined By Budget Officials In Five Western States." *Public Budgeting and Finance*, Volume 7, 1, (Spring 1987), pp. 24–37.

Four Views

In Chapter 1, decision-making models and their importance were explained. People working in budgeting are often influenced by these normative theories, and four ideal types can be used to describe typical reactions to those normative theories. The four ideal types are *the true rational believer, the pure reactive person, the budget-wise person* (the cynic), and *the wise budget person.*

The True Rational Believer. With the influence of PPB, there are people working in public budgeting who believe strongly that decision making related to public budgeting should use the rational approach. If decisions don't follow that approach, then they consider the decision highly questionable and in error due to lack of professionalism or the unfortunate intrusion of politics into proper decision making. They try to ensure that as many decisions as possible, especially significant decisions, should follow the rational approach: (1) set goals and objectives, (2) define alternatives, (3) analyze alternatives, and (4) select the best decision or make the recommendation.

Such faith in the normative decision-making theory called the rational approach leads to unfortunate consequences in public budgeting. Many public organizations have vague multiple and sometimes mutually conflicting goals and objectives. Articulating specific goals and objectives may be impossible, but analysis may still be useful for decision making. If analysis is limited to the rational approach, then analysis cannot be conducted. This is an unnecessary constraint applied to circumstances in which analysis could be useful. Thus the decision maker is handicapped unnecessarily. Another problem with the rational model is that it implies no limits exist to the defining of alternatives and the analysis of alternatives. As is pointed out in this author's book, *Policy Analysis in Public Policymaking*, some individuals will proceed to spend large sums of money on analysis when the end results will be as useful as a much more limited analytical effort. Those individuals are motivated by the rational model to pursue the alternatives and examine them exhaustively. Another problem with the rational model is that its believers don't appreciate the importance of feedback in analysis; thus helpful feedback can be ignored.

A more subtle problem of the rational model is the inherent assumption that there is one overall perspective. Recall the fable earlier cited involving several blind men and an elephant. The storyteller stresses how each blind man examines a different segment of the elephant and proceeds to argue with the other blind men over the nature of the beast. The ironical thrust to the story is that all parties including the storyteller were inherently limited by their perspective. Any object or series of events can be described in an infinite number of ways, and there is no one description, contrary to what the storyteller assumed. The rational model leads us to make the same mistake as the storyteller. One is wiser to recognize that there are only shared perceptions of felt needs, which can be translated into formulations of problems and objectives. Unfortunately, the common use of the rational model does not encourage such sophistication.

The Pure Reactive Person. In contrast to the true rational believer is the pure reactive budget person. This type of person acts in a stimulus-response pattern. The budget calendar and the requests govern this type of person. Little thought is given to shaping events or somehow making a difference through the reactor's product. The job is merely a task to be done as defined in the job description or by the demands of the job. Decision-making models mean little to this type of person.

However, the political-administrative dichotomy is used as the justification for his or her mechanical response. Such a person believes that political decisions should be left to the political appointee and that civil servants should merely respond to the wishes of the political appointees.

The hazard of this approach is that mindless or potentially foolish mistakes are not avoided. The budget person has a unique vantage point and can often understand both the political actors' viewpoints as well as the workings of government. By merely reacting, the government loses the important insight of the budget expert; thus, more errors are likely to occur. An aggressive, outspoken budget staff can improve government greatly, but reactive staff will permit policy makers to make unnecessary—often significant—errors. Most policy makers recognize the value of an aggressive and outspoken—rather than a reactive—budget staff.

The Budget-Wise Person. These people are aware of all the forms and tables but discount them almost completely because the government's decisions are all political. They are often cynical about life in general and stress the public nature of "public administration." Sometimes they can cite dramatic examples of gross politically inspired decision making, sometimes involving corruption and often involving vote trading. Such decision making then does preclude effective public management. This type of person stresses that such decision making is inevitable and that all that a budget staff can do is react and watch events unfold. In some government settings, the cynic is right; but in many others, the political actors in the political process are influenced by well prepared budget justifications, and professional budgeting does translate into effective public management. If a cynical view dominates where professional budgeting could make a difference, then a valuable opportunity for more effective government is lost.

The Wise Budget Person. People of this type recognize that politics is sometimes of overriding importance. They also believe that analysis has its limitations but can often help greatly in decision-making situations. Professional public budgeting can be extremely significant to the way government is managed. We hope that this text will help more people be wise budget persons.

Develop Confidence

Having the confidence of the budget reviewers, especially the appropriations committees, is extremely important to the budget officer. If confidence does not exist, any reviewer can ask hard questions and force the agency to justify every detail. If the appropriations committees lack confidence, they can write into the appropriation bill or committee report very specific special conditions, thus tying the hands of the agency and making program administration a nightmare. If confidence is established, the budget reviews are less difficult, and greater administrative latitude is provided for public management discretion.

There is a natural tendency on the part of the reviewers to place confidence in budget officers because some facts and management judgment must be accepted on faith. The sheer complexity of the budget plus the lack of time to review budgets means that not everything can be reviewed in depth. Priorities of reviewers' efforts in examining are decided upon with the more questionable or politically sensitive topics receiving the greatest attention. Budget reviewers would like to trust the expertise of the best budget officer because valuable budget reviewer time can be saved. Thus, a budget officer is wise to establish a reputation as being highly professional.

The ideal model of a highly professional budget person is used by reviewers to "rate" budget officers. The criteria vary, but a fairly accurate picture can be painted of the type of person most likely to be trusted. Such a person is

1. a master of detail;
2. hard working;
3. concise;
4. frank;
5. self-effacing and devoted to the work;
6. tight with the taxpayer's money;
7. capable of recognizing a political necessity when it is present; and
8. conscientious about keeping key reviewers (for example, members of Congress) informed of sensitive changes in policy or important developments.

Budget officers find that a reputation of playing it straight is wise. Lying, covering up, and being tricky are highly undesirable characteristics for the career civil servant. Memories can be long among top reviewing staffs. If reviewers, especially appropriations committees, feel that they have been mis-led, strong punitive actions can be taken, such as tying the agency into administrative knots with special appropriation language. On the other hand, a positive reputation can even mean securing emergency or supplemental funds on the basis of skimpy hearings: that is, getting funds almost entirely on the integrity of the budget officer.

Reputations are enhanced with professional friendship. A close personal relationship with budget reviewers, such as the agency's congressional subcommittee staff, can ease tensions. Years of outstanding service are even more significant than friendships because such experience often builds a sense of integrity and trust which constitutes "professional friendships." In many cases, these professional friendships are built on shared work experiences and service together in professional associations.

One of the characteristics associated with building confidence is being capable of recognizing political "necessity." However, judgment can differ on the question of "necessity." Some accommodation to favors and pet projects does occur, but such practices can move from the unusual to the expected. When this occurs, effective public management cannot be carried out. Part of building confidence is being able to turn down political actors so that requests are not considered a "political necessity." Techniques for pleasant turn-downs include the following:

1. "My hands are tied"—other factors may exist, such as an executive mandate which precludes the favor.
2. "Maybe in the future"—the favor may be granted, but the timing is simply not wise then.
3. "But look at the other positive actions we have taken"—stress that other decisions were in their favor or to their liking, and appeal to the notion that one should only expect to win a "fair share" of the time.
4. "It cannot be done"—economic, technical, or other reasons can be cited why the request is either impossible or extremely unwise to fulfill.

Other strategies can be employed to minimize granting favors. Action on the favor can be delayed. If they are truly serious, the political actors will pursue until they get action. Delay thus acts as a filter for the true "necessities." A parallel strategy is to give in on the most intensely sought favors and pet projects. Intensity can also be measured by means used to bring pressure upon the agency. Regardless of how intensity is shown, the strategy is to give in on the intense favors and resist on the less intense favors and pet projects.

Strategies and techniques can help, but in a few cases the consequences must be faced. Sometimes budget officers must face a no-win situation due to their professional or personal ethics or the need to support persons in the bureaucracy such as the agency head. In some instances, the situation can be mitigated by allowing one political actor (for example, a member of Congress) to do battle with another political actor (for example, a political appointee or the media); but such a ploy can result in making two enemies and losing rather than gaining their confidence. In other situations, the budget officer may merely have to use time to heal relationships or hope that key actors don't blame the budget officer but blame the deed. The consequence may be severe, but sometimes one's professional integrity requires action which, ironically, can harm one's professional reputation.

There is no developed method for establishing confidence. All that can be done is to be aware of the techniques and strategies available, to observe successful budget officers, and to use careful judgment. No one approach is useful for all budget reviewers or all situations. Each set of circumstances must be considered separately before action is taken.

Results

Confidence in a government program often rests upon demonstrated results. Results are significant because the public and political leaders anticipate that some benefits will be evident from government programs.

There is an important distinction between an activity accomplishing its purpose and people feeling that they are being served. Politically, the latter is more significant. Often the distinction is only theoretical because accomplishment translates to the people realizing their lives have been enhanced, but this need not be the case. The people—the agency's potential clientele—may be unaware of the importance of the program, may have come to take it for granted, or may feel that the program is not important. Earlier in this chapter, the significance of the clientele in the political process was noted. If the potential clientele members are not active supporters of the program, then the program may very well fail, given the normal political competition for funding support.

For an agency, serving an appreciative clientele is ideal. The best kind of result is one that provides services to a large and strategically placed appreciative clientele. The best type of clientele is one that brings its satisfaction to the attention of decision makers, such as the appropriations committees and the president. Not all agencies are blessed with such a happy harmony of circumstances, so attempts must be made to develop alternative means to build and maintain the essential support of key decision makers.

If an agency does not enjoy overwhelming public support, a persuasive case can be made with tangible accomplishments. In the budget justification process, emphasis is placed on the accomplishments of the program. The criteria used to judge success are sometimes the subject of debate, and sometimes semantic confusion is used to rationalize odd criteria for success. In such circumstances, the merits of the accomplishments are less persuasive. Nevertheless, the citation of accomplishment is normally highly useful in any budget justification.

If the listing of results is not sufficiently impressive, the agency can extend an invitation to the decision makers or anyone likely to influence the decision makers (for example, the media) to visit the agency. Budget reviewers and other influential people are shown the need (for example, the poor being helped), the activity (for example, the production of a missile), or heroic efforts by an overworked staff (for example, emergency room care at a hospital). Often this technique is extremely useful. The U.S. space program used this approach quite successfully to maintain high public interest in its efforts. However, there are significant risks. The reviewers may not be impressed, and this can translate into lower budgets rather than increased or sustained budget support.

A hazard of visits and other attempts to make highly complex programs more understandable is the problem of explanation. Most political decision makers are not experts, so explanations and visits must be simplified to communicate the essential message without technical verbiage. If they are too simple, then the complex nature of the challenge is not understood, and the level of funding seems unwarranted. If they are too complex, then the reviewer questions the clarity of the management direction, and, again, the level of funding is reduced, or the program is cut entirely. Selecting the exact visit format and explanation for complex programs can indeed be a challenge.

A hazard of demonstrating tangible accomplishment is that the program may be praised and then cut because the program objectives have been met. Government programs are designed to meet a problem, and success may mean the problem ceases to exist. If that occurs, the program should cease to exist. The irony is that losing one's job seems like a punishment rather than a reward.

Some government programs are disadvantaged by not having tangible accomplishments that they can demonstrate. For example, unless the civil defense program is called on in an emergency, the civil defense agency cannot point to any tangible accomplishment. Another example is the International Communications Agency, which broadcasts propaganda overseas. How does one deal with such programs when tangible results cannot be shown? There are several ploys that can be used:

1. "Our program is priceless"—argue that results are not evident, but pose the question: What if the program did not exist? If we did not have civil defense, what cost would there be in human lives if disaster occurred?
2. "Results of our program cannot be measured"—argue that a demonstration of results is simply not possible given the nature of the program. This may be a truthful argument, but it will not be very persuasive.
3. "Results will be evident in the future"—argue that results are not evident now because the program is new or the program's results are only evident when an emergency occurs. This is a more appealing argument, but skeptics can say that an emergency is the wrong time to find out that the program does not work.
4. "Figures show"—argue facts and figures show results in spite of the fact that they really are not relevant. This is a foolish ploy, given the potential loss of confidence that could result.
5. "In this complex situation, the figures confirm"—argue by ignoring the questionable cause-effect relationships within a multiple causal situation. This is a reasonable ploy, but care must be taken in the wording so that the statements are positive but not false. Extreme claims which cannot be tested should be avoided.
6. "Please notice that we reviewed more than a thousand applicants"—argue by focusing not on results but on the procedures and process measures of the organization. The critical observant reviewer can always ask, "So what?" but making a display of facts and figures is better than saying nothing because the information does demonstrate that some activity did take place.
7. "You must appreciate that we cannot prove the relationship of this education to later achievement, but we know such a relationship exists" —argue that faith establishes the relationship between the program and the desired benefits in society. If the subject is something that is taken for granted, then such an argument might be successful.

Preparing for Hearings

Hearings often are important in building confidence in a program and program officials. In some situations, hearings only serve to brief decision makers or to create a record to be used to convince others. However, hearings can and often do affect decision makers, given the competing pressures on their time and the inadequate preparation they give to the review of budget material. Hearings are particularly important in establishing confidence. Program officials who cannot answer or who answer questions poorly create an impression that those running the organization do not really understand what they are doing.

Rehearsals for budget hearings are essential. The number of hearings vary by agency and government, but four hearings on the budget alone are the minimum number in the federal government. As noted in an earlier chapter, rehearsing or holding mock hearings, is a standard practice. Agency administrators play the role of key reviewers such as the appropriations committee chairperson. Tough questions are anticipated and answered before the hearing in order to avoid later difficulties. Mock hearings are an excellent device to expose weak justifications, to build effective agency coordination in handling questions, and to appreciate the perspective of the reviewer. Mock hearings also help the budget officer decide what subjects should be discussed and stressed in the traditional opening statement.

The key to preparing for budget hearings is to do sufficient research to avoid or minimize surprises in the hearing. A surprise usually makes the administrator appear to be ignorant and can rattle him or her to the point of answering all the remaining questions poorly. A diligent search of past hearings and statements often indicates what the reviewers consider important. Also a review of the program itself and reactions to the program are essential in framing the tough questions. Often the rapport of the budget officer with others, such as people in the central budget office, can be a vital resource for intelligence.

Briefing books for hearings are useful. Normally, they include only the tough or standard questions and answers which are anticipated. They may include a brief discussion on the perspectives of each reviewer, but such information is often common knowledge. Also such descriptions can fall into the wrong hands, leading to unnecessary embarrassment.

Questions in a hearing come from a variety of sources, including the reviewer (for example, a senator), staff, clientele, and even the agency itself. Questions are sometimes planted, with entire lists of questions supplied by the agency. Sometimes the planted questions are the most difficult, so that the agency can go on record on a subject in the best possible manner. Planted questions rarely occur at the department and OMB hearings, but they are common in the Congress, where friendly legislators wish to aid a program. In some instances, the rapport between staffs is so close that the effect is the same as planted questions.

Presentations at hearings tend to create a portrait of the agency leadership in the minds of the reviewers. Hearings are an opportunity to paint a self-portrait of credibility and generate a favorable mood toward the agency. The leadership can take on such mantles as protector-of-the-public safety, man-of-science, statesman, guardian-of-the-environment, and so on. Effective hearing presentations tend to ward off unpleasant and time-consuming probes of an agency.

The best way to make a positive impression at a hearing is to know the budget. There is no adequate substitute for being knowledgeable, but knowledge can be coupled with a good, organized presentation. Normally, presentations and answers that are brief and to the point but that offer an opportunity to go into more depth on follow-up questions are most effective. Care can be taken to give the impression that important subjects are not being slighted. An administrator can be forgiven for not knowing a detail, and, in fact, such data are often supplied for the record after the hearing. Administrators are sometimes not forgiven for not knowing the answers to questions involving management direction. Questions—even on detail—often can be anticipated and answered or transmitted at the time of the hearing, Such action is extremely impressive and builds confidence.

Hearings are a game with certain taboos. Agency officials recognize that they have two masters—the legislature and the executive—but agency officials cannot challenge the chief executive's budget even though they may wish for more support. However, everyone present at the hearing can tell if the officials mean otherwise. This communication is achieved by:

1. exhibiting a marked lack of enthusiasm;
2. being too enthusiastic to be credible;
3. refusing to answer questions by protesting loyalty to the chief executive; and
4. yielding to sharp-pointed questioning.

These taboos are significant. If the central budget office or the department feels the agency is not adhering to the established executive branch policy, then the agency head and other political appointees can be fired. "Speaking against the administration" can be taken extremely seriously; but in a few instances the central budget office or department may not wish the agency to resist legislative desires to increase the budget over executive branch requests as a political strategy. Each situation must be judged separately.

Another taboo is that the agency should not admit yielding to clientele pressure. The agency is accountable to all the people; thus yielding to one clientele is an admission of favoritism. It also admits that pressure can be successful. Instead, language is carefully phrased to indicate the agency wishes to receive advice from citizens and does act upon suggestions which have intrinsic value; the agency does respond to sound advice but the decision is made only on the merits of the advice. Pressure is not influential according to this taboo and should not be admitted to openly.

STRATEGIES

Reviewers versus Reviewed

The budget game requires advocates and reviewers. The agency is the advocate, but clientele groups and sometimes even legislators can also be called advocates. The reviewers are the department officials, the central budget office (for example, the OMB), the House appropriations subcommittee, and the Senate appropriations subcommittee. As the budget moves through the budget cycle, reviewers change roles and become advocates. For example, after the central budget office has reviewed the budget requests and final executive branch decisions are made, then that former reviewer is an advocate to the legislative appropriations subcommittees. The primary advocate, however, is always the agency. If the game is played well, there always exists an arm's length relationship between advocate and reviewer. Each plays the role with caution, care, and an awareness of the natural tendencies associated with each role. A requirement for a good game is that each party know the rules and strategy. Ideally, the game should be played by professionals. An uneven game results in unreasonable cuts or unreasonably high budgets. Both results are undesirable.

One budget strategy failure illustrates the gamesmanship. Occasionally, an agency will resubmit the previous year's budget with the only change being the fiscal years mentioned in the text. When this occurs, the reviewers question the budget request because intervening variables since last year must cause some program changes. The possibility of an *identical* budget request approaches zero because administrative environments always change. A distinct likelihood exists that another reviewer may have ordered the agency to use the same budget level as the previous year's budget, but to use the *identical* budget request seems to imply lack of adaptability to changing conditions. Part of the game is to at least give the appearance of managing the program, and this is not done by using last year's budget.

Budget requests are rarely approved intact, and reviewers normally reduce (cut) the request. There are several common rationales given for cutting budgets:

1. a climate of opinion existed that was against spending;
2. strong views by influential decision makers necessitated the cut;
3. spending on your program became a political football; and
4. there was an overriding need to balance the budget.

The reason cited may address the management capability or fundamental objectives of the agency's program. However, such statements are more difficult to rationalize against the superior expertise of the agency on those topics. The reasons cited above are less subject to dispute and appeal, thus they are more likely to be cited.

Some ironies can exist with budget cutting. An agency may wish to have a certain program cut or may even cut its own program. For example, maybe the agency leadership lost faith in a program, internal discipline called for cuts, or higher priorities in some programs meant cuts in other programs. Interestingly, cuts can stimulate mobilization of the agency clientele, thus eventually resulting in even higher budgets than would have occurred without those earlier cuts.

Another phenomenon that can occur is intralegislative conflict. One obvious area of conflict is between the two chambers (House and Senate). Conference committees are intended to resolve such disputes, but strategies can be used so that one chamber's position dominates. For example, the Senate may raise the total in order to achieve the desired amount through compromise. Another tactic is to have a chamber pass a resolution supporting its conferees, thus permitting them to cite the solidarity and intensity of feelings in their arguments. Conference committees are often unpredictable and most agencies would prefer to avoid this uncertainty unless one chamber cuts their requests significantly. A less obvious area of conflict is between the substantive committee and the appropriations committee. In some instances, the agency can be the innocent victim of such disputes.

Spenders' Strategies

There are game strategies that an agency can apply in seeking to get its budget requests approved. This section explains the various strategies that are commonly used, but does not attempt to comment in depth upon how, when, and in what way the strategies should be applied to maximize their effectiveness. Such matters require judgment based on each separate budget situation.

There are some fairly common, safe strategies that are employed. Budget requests are often padded because the agency wishes to be able to meet unanticipated contingencies and to compensate for the fact that reviewers often cut requests almost automatically. Obvious or nondefensible "padding" can lead to an important loss of confidence, but "extras" can normally be easily defended. A related strategy is always to ask for more. This demonstrates an aggressive agency that has a strong belief in its mission. The increase may not be merited, but the reviewers are forced to address the increase and may forget to argue the possibility of a program level decrease. In connection with this strategy, the agency is careful to spend or obligate all the current year's funds. If there is any surplus, the reviewer may argue that the agency's current funding is more than adequate and there is no need for additional money. Another safe strategy is to alter the written or oral budget presentations as much as possible to highlight the best aspects of the agency's program and minimize the worst aspects.

Budgeting is a complex activity. "Sleight-of-hand" tricks do exist and they can be part of a budget strategy. For example, numbers in budgets are rounded often to the nearest hundred thousand or even million. For some small but politically important budget items, the practice of rounding can be an advantage. Another "trick" is to recast the budget into different categories than those used in the previous year. The redone categories can be utilized to focus attention on or away from programs, depending upon the budget's strategic purposes. Also, redone categories inhibit longitudinal analysis and this may be an advantage to the agency. In addition, there are a variety of back-door spending devices: one of them is no-year funds. One sleight-of-hand technique is to use unobligated appropriations or disobligated appropriations (that is, funds previously obligated but for which obligation was subsequently withdrawn, often because of nonuse by grantees) to finance projects beyond the apparent level of budget-year appropriations. For example, let us say that an agency has $15 million left over from last year's budget and also has $20 million disobligated from previous years. This $35 million technically should be deducted from the budget request, but normally the subtraction is not cited or is poorly cited by the agency.

Another sleight-of-hand trick is the fund transfer. An agency can often transfer money from one account to another. By using several transfers among several funds, illusions can be created about the money that was obligated. This unprofessional trick can be used also to defraud the government or mislead reviewing groups such as prospective bond buyers. Careful accounting can uncover such abuses, but such work is detailed and time consuming.

Most spender strategies are direct and simple. The agency merely points out that the tasks it performs have expanded and more money is needed to fund the program. Another strategy is to point out the backlog of requests or tasks. The argument is then made that an increase is needed to eliminate the backlog and that a cut would increase the size of the backlog. A third strategy or argument is to appeal to a national standard by showing that the agency can meet the standard with a given level of budget support. This strategy is used often by highly professional groups (for example, medical and educational).

Sometimes the strategy is to argue with economic concepts. A program activity may involve a fee, such as an entrance fee or license. The agency argues that a given budget level would attract more people to the activity, thus increasing the revenue from the activity. The increased revenue might be larger than the expenses in the budget. A more complex argument is that an increased budget for a program like a subsidy would increase the operation and payroll size. The argument is made that because of the multiplier effect of the subsidy the government would recover more in additional taxes (for example, income tax) than was paid out for the subsidy. Another argument is that an increased budget would permit greater productivity as a result of a better cost average per unit or the use of the extra money to purchase labor-saving devices.

Other arguments are predicated more on emotion. The agency argues that the revenue of the government has grown and that the agency should receive a fair share of the growth. A bolder strategy is to argue that a high-level commitment exists on the project and that there is no option but to fund the program. A less bold but equally emotional strategy is to plead that the program is "squeezed to the bone" and that a certain funding level is essential for meaningful program operation.

In many situations, the agency wishes to start a new program, but the newness is masked. Once funded, a "foot-in-the-door wedge" or "camel's nose under the tent" has been established. This precedent greatly helps the agency convince reviewers, because the standard for new programs tends to be harsher than the standard for existing programs. The agency will often argue that the money does not represent a new initiative but rather a continuation of old programs. This may be quite true literally, but the new dimension may constitute an entirely new, major emphasis, which, logically, should be considered a new program. However, such treatment would bias the reviewers against the effort.

Spenders' strategies can constitute a high political risk for the agency and agency officials. One strategy is to react to a request for cuts by suggesting cuts be taken first on projects that enjoy strong political support. By cutting the "sacred cows" or popular programs, the cutter is placed in a politically difficult position and may withdraw the request to cut the program. The risk for the agency head is that the chief executive may be offended by the use of this strategy and fire the political appointee. A second strategy is to shift the blame. The agency points out that if the full requested amount is not funded, then certain specific activities will not be undertaken. The agency makes it clear to the reviewer that the responsibility for not funding the activity will be placed on the reviewer. In some situations, reviewers are sobered by such responsibility and the related political implications; thus, they act favorably on the budget request. A third strategy is to argue that a cut is irresponsible and that the project must be funded at the requested level or not funded at all. This is a sound argument for many projects because there is a lower limit at which the project cannot be sustained as viable. The risk in such an argument is that the reviewer may indeed decide to cut the whole project.

Another high-risk strategy is to spend fast in order to be short of funds. The agency deliberately spends the money at a fast rate and then goes back to the reviewers for supplemental appropriations. This strategy is employed infrequently but it does occur, especially when the agency is asked to absorb large cuts. This is an extremely high-risk strategy because of the likelihood that the top agency officials will be considered to be irresponsible and poor managers. Firing of top officials is often a result of the use of such strategies.

Cutters' Strategies

Just as there are game strategies for an agency, there are strategies for the reviewing groups. Some strategies are safe and fairly standard. Other strategies are essentially counterstrategies to be used against spenders' arguments and ploys. The discussion here, as in the previous section, is addressed to explaining the strategies and not to an in-depth treatment of their application in a variety of contingencies.

The safe approaches include reducing increases, questioning hidden "revenues," cutting less visible items, and employing delay. The political support for existing programs can be quite strong, and the pressure for increases may be strong also. However, the exact size of the increase is almost always open to discussion and cuts in the increases are easier to sustain. Another safe approach is to investigate and try to isolate "hidden" revenue, such as the use of the previous fiscal year's appropriations or the use of existing government property rather than the purchase of new property. Normally, some savings can be found with this approach and few can fault the results. Another approach is to cut the less visible or less politically supported items. This approach should be employed with some discretion because such "saving" may be false economy. For example, the replacement program for a city water pipe system can be deferred, but the wiser policy is probably a yearly systematic program. Delay is a particularly easily applied strategy. Whenever another study is conducted or delays are caused for other reasons, the result is that the item is not included in the budget. This is one of the most successful cutter's strategies, because all that needs to be done to justify a delaying study is to raise a question.

Several fairly standard arguments and ploys exist. One is always to cut something. If no cuts are made, the credible power of the reviewer is questioned. Also, the reviewers are aware that the spenders have a natural tendency to include items that they could do without. Thus, cuts will eliminate those "frills." A second approach is to argue that initial allocations are unnecessary. If nothing starts, then budget expansion is diminished. A third approach is to defer or reject projects on the grounds that initial dollars cannot be spent correctly by the end of the fiscal year. New programs really experience difficulty in staffing themselves; thus they rarely can do a decent job in the first year. By arguing that a program will not do a decent job in the first year, each year the cutter can prevent the program from coming into existence. A fourth approach is never to allow a precedent to be established. Precedents lead to continued budget requests. An effective ploy is to argue that there is only so much money and that some is available for program increases. The question is then asked: Whose turn is it? This focuses the debate away from the amount and gets the various units to argue against each other. A sophisticated ploy to be used in a few circumstances is to eliminate interagency competition, which tends to be more expensive due to the expansive nature of competition itself in the public sector.

The cutter need not accept or live with strategies employed by the spender. Counterstrategies do exist. If the agency says the increase is "so small," the counter is to argue that no item is too small to eliminate or to suggest that such small items can be absorbed without a budget increase. If the agency argues that they should have a fair share of the growth, the cutter can ask what is "fair" and never accept any definition. Another counterstrategy is to challenge work load data. Often such data are collected poorly and can be challenged easily on methodological grounds. Normally, the cutter can argue that productivity increases—for a number of reasons, such as a worker's becoming more experienced at a new job (that is, learning curve)—should mean that increases or even decreases are appropriate in a given program.

One spender's strategy is to place the blame on the cutter for the cuts, but that blame need not be accepted. The cutter can force the agency officials to say what they believe should be cut first. If the spender is likely to put forth political sacred cows for cutting, the cutter can anticipate and neutralize the strategy by insisting that the agency must suggest items to be cut but stipulating which items cannot be considered as candidates for cutting.

Cutters normally have the advantage because they need only question and the spender has the burden of proof. The strongest asset the spender has is expertise, and care must be taken to maintain the expert's credibility. Spenders can employ strategies but most of them must be executed with an aura of expertise.

Since 1980, an important phenomena in state and local governments has been cutback management. Those experiencing the need to cut programs rarely appreciate the phenomena is not only common during times of recession but the cutback steps taken are usually about the same in all cutback situations. Such cuts cannot be avoided because revenues prove inadequate and the constitutions of almost all states require balanced budgets. Although there may be some desire to use selective cuts, political pressures normally result in first cutting the least painful such as unfilled positions, deferrable capital items, and maintenance projects. Next, the government halts raises and considers across-the-board reductions with selective exemptions from those reductions. Although reserves are wise to use—especially to compensate for forecasting error possibilities—typically, reserves go very quickly in periods of recession. Politically and psychologically, an across-the-board approach provides an egalitarian appeal that is easier to accept than targeted reductions. From a management point of view, targeted cuts are often wise as they provide an excellent way to enhance productivity, but political and psychological reasons may prevent such cuts.

In the 1980s and the early 1990s, fiscal crises of state and local governments were widespread. For example, in 1991, over 38 states had major budget shortfalls. The 1990–91 economic recession had more significant effect on state and local government than the previous 1970s and 1980s recessions. Governments responded with a combination of largely ad hoc tax and user fee increases, program cuts, government restructuring, "passing the buck" to other governments, and reducing their employment. Exhibit 3–6 presents the most common state government cutback strategies employed, according to a 1991 survey done by Marvin Druker and Betty Robinson (1993). They reported that the constraints on the implementing of those strategies were:

- concern for service level;
- need to comply with mandates;
- legislative restriction;
- union contracts;
- civil service rules; and
- court-ordered restrictions.

EXHIBIT 3–6   Cutback Strategies

STRATEGIES	NUMBER OF STATES
Reducing the Number of Workers	
Freeze on filling vacancies	34
Early retirement	18
Voluntary (temporary) leave	15
Mandatory furloughs	12
Reduced hours	10
Job sharing	5
Increasing work week	1
Layoffs	13
Reducing the Costs of Employees	
Deferred pay increase	18
Reducing costs of benefits	6
Shutdown of state operations	3
Pay cuts	2
Lag payrolls	2
Reorganizing State Workforce	7

Source: Marvin Druker and Betty Robinson, "State's Responses to Budget Shortfalls: Cutback Management Techniques." In Thomas D. Lynch and Lawrence Martin (eds.), *Handbook of Comparative Public Budgeting and Financial Management*. New York: Marcel Dekker, 1993. p. 195.

Municipal fiscal stress strategies reported by Gary Mattson (1989) were grouped into cutback adoption, privatization, and revenue enhancing. Cutback strategies include wage freezes, hiring freezes, layoffs, capital budget deferrals, and across the board cuts. Of these, layoffs are the least popular strategy. Privatization strategies include contracting out, load shedding, and coproduction/volunteer. Of these, load shedding is the least popular strategy. Revenue enhancing includes greater use of user fees and local tax options. The latter is least popular.

New Programs

The previous strategies are for normal, day-to-day budget situations. New programs require extraordinary efforts on the part of the spenders. Often new programs are established in reaction to a crisis or to what some consider to be a crisis. Such crises rarely are manufactured, but groups do take advantage of crises to establish new programs or to radically increase existing programs. The political climate in a crisis is such that political forces concur that the need is obvious and the debate centers on the "solutions." But even that debate is different because the political climate calls for a solution, and delay is an unacceptable condition. Standards are lowered, and the key is effectiveness. Efficiency becomes a less significant topic. In such an environment, agencies have a much greater opportunity to get viable ideas accepted, and new or radical increases in programs do occur.

Agency or clientele advertising and salesmanship can sometimes result in the creation of new programs. Dramatic names or labels such as *Mission 66* or *Headstart* can be significant in capturing enough popular attention. Good presentations are necessary. A well-organized effort can start new programs, but the presence of anticlientele groups (even small groups) can be fatal to such efforts. Rarely are advertising and salesmanship adequate by themselves. Normally they must be linked to a cause of the day (for example, the environment, pollution, national defense, inflation, unemployment). Ironically, overselling sometimes can be dysfunctional because the new program can become so popular that the agency's other programs suffer. Advertising and salesmanship should not be underrated, but the times and places are more significant in the beginning of most new programs.

Cautions

Unlike a parlor game, the budget game has serious consequences. Spenders' and cutters' strategies are used, and sometimes one side or the other plays the game poorly. This is unfortunate because the budget process is usually best served when both sides play the game well. One particularly serious game fault is when the agency leadership forgets that the agency is a *public* agency designed to serve *all* the people. True, the clientele is only part of the public, and most of the agency's dealings need only concern the clientele, but circumstances do exist in which the public nature of an agency prohibits continuous, harmonious relations with the clientele group (for example, a coal company dealing with the Interior Department on a strip mining question). Public agencies can be captured by their clientele.

The mood of the times often is much more important than given strategies of spenders or cutters. Such moods change, and they create a significant climate that favors, disfavors, or is neutral to specific programs. Government officials are sensitive to current events and recognize that those events are much like the weather for the farmer. The weather is very important, and the farmer can do some things to mitigate the bad effects of weather, but it is still a largely uncontrolled governing force. Some political storms must be accepted as either a favorable or an unfavorable reality by government officials.

One last caution is noted. If the mood of the times becomes favorable to a program, and the reviewers become converts to the mission of an agency, the agency will discover that its new, expected role, according to the reviewers, is to think and act very big. The meaning of "big" depends on the size of the government and the dimensions of the problem. If the agency does not think in expansive terms, then criticisms, such as being overly concerned about "petty economies," are likely to occur. Such role expectations are sometimes difficult to comprehend, given the normal budget process, but the agency must accommodate to the expected role or be subject to remarkably unpleasant political pressure.

REVIEW QUESTIONS

1. What political influence patterns exist in the federal government in terms of budgeting? Why are they important to understand?
2. Why is it important for an agency to cultivate a clientele? How is that done? What problems and cautions are important to understand?
3. What are the typical duties of an agency budget officer? What views and behaviors should be anticipated?
4. What is the agency budget officer's perspective? Contrast that to the executive and legislative perspective.
5. Why are confidence, results, and hearings important? Explain how confidence can be enhanced. How can one prepare for hearings?
6. What strategies can be used by advocates of spending and by reviewers critical of spending?

REFERENCES

ANTHONY, ROBERT. "Closing the Loop Between Planning and Performance," *Public Administration Review* (May/June 1971).
ANTON, THOMAS J. *The Politics of State Expenditure in Illinois*. Urbana: University of Illinois Press, 1966.
AXELROD, DONALD. "Post-Burkhead: The State of the Art or Science of Budgeting," *Public Administration Review* (November/December 1973).
DRUKER, MARVIN and BETTY ROBINSON. "States' Responses to Budget Shortfalls: Cutback Management Techniques." In Thomas D. Lynch and Lawrence Martin (eds.), *Handbook of Comparative Public Budgeting and Financial Management*. New York: Marcel Dekker, 1993, pp. 189–204.

DUNCOMBE, SYDNEY AND RICHARD KINNEY. "Cutbacks—Idaho Style," *Public Budgeting and Finance*, 4, 2 (Summer 1984), 87–98.

———. "Agency Budget Success: How It Is Defined By Budget Officials In Five Western States," *Public Budgeting and Finance*, 7, 1 (Spring 1987), 24–37.

LYNCH, THOMAS D. *Policy Analysis in Public Policymaking.* Lexington, Mass.: Lexington Books, 1975.

MATTSON, GARY A. "How Iowa's Small Towns Cope with Financial Retrenchment," *Small Town*, March–April, 1989, 18–24.

PARKER, STEVE. "Budgeting as an Expression of Power." In Jack Rabin and Thomas D. Lynch (eds.), *Handbook on Public Budgeting and Financial Management.* New York: Marcel Dekker, 1983.

SIGELMAN, LEE. "The Bureaucrat As Budget Maximizer: An Assumption Examined," *Public Budgeting and Finance*, 6, 1 (Spring 1986), 50–59.

WILDAVSKY, AARON. *The Politics of the Budgeting Process.* Boston: Little, Brown, 1964.

WILLOUGHBY, KATHERINE G. "Patterns of Behavior: Factors Influencing the Spending Judgments of Public Budgeters." In Thomas D. Lynch and Lawrence Martin (eds.), *Handbook of Comparative Public Budgeting and Financial Management.* New York: Marcel Dekker, 1993, 103–132.

4

BUDGET FORMATS
AND PREPARATION

This chapter addresses the topics of budget formats, building the budget, budget reviews, and legislative adoption. It covers:

1. why budget formats are significant;
2. the various budget formats and how they apply to general policy, budget balancing, and the improvement of government management;
3. the role and work of the central budget office in initiating the process of building the budget;
4. the central role and tasks of the agency in preparing the budget;
5. the importance of the steps associated with executive and legislative reviews of the budget;
6. the use of executive budget bearings in the review process;
7. the ingredients and preparation of the executive budget document;
8. the congressional budget timetable;
9. the legislature's deliberative process on the budget; and
10. the formats used in legislative adoptions of budgets.

BUDGET FORMAT

The Important Means

Formats are important and procedures are not neutral. The *means* of budgeting affect the *ends* of budgeting. How? Decision makers tend to think about what is put in front of them. Thus, budget classifications tend to define reality for budget makers and reviewers by channeling their attention and thought to specific areas. To illustrate this point, Edward A. Lehan in *Simplified Governmental Budgeting* (1982) asked his readers to examine two exhibits similar to Exhibit 4–1 and Exhibit 4–2 and to prepare simple follow-up questions.

EXHIBIT 4–1   A Line–Item Format

CODE ENFORCEMENT	BUDGET
Personal Service	$60,238
Contractual Service	7,863
Supplies	1,376
Total	$69,477

The line-item format focuses thinking and discussion on things to be bought and tempts officials to alter expenditure patterns in ways largely unrelated to policy issues on service levels.

EXHIBIT 4–2   A Program Format

CODE ENFORCEMENT	BUDGET
Plan examination	$12,331
Inspection	40,339
Education	15,529
Total	$68,199

A third format—performance budgeting—is illustrated in Exhibit 4–3. Note how the reader's mind tends to be directed toward questions of efficiency.

EXHIBIT 4–3   A Performance Budget Format

CODE ENFORCEMENT	ITEMS	BUDGET	UNIT COST
Plan examinations	744	$12,331	$16.57
Inspections	19,371	40,339	2.08
Education (graduates or trainees)	12,333	15,526	1.26
Total		$68,196	

Typical questions:
1. Are there any inefficiencies?
2. Can we lower unit cost? How?
3. Why is the unit cost of plan examination so high?

Which budget format (line-item, program, performance, PPB, ZBB, TBB) is the best? Given that the format does influence the decision-making focus, the selection of a format depends on the desired decision-making environment. What mind-set do you wish to create? The three major concerns of a budget officer are (1) to raise the level of debate, (2) to ensure that policy control is maintained, and (3) to improve the quality of management in the government. Given these objectives, the choice of format can still vary substantially, depending on the political and managerial context.

Fortunately, the three objectives of a budget office can be met not only by the recommended budget but also by the operating budget, the capital budget, other budget office documents, and meetings. Thus, some flexibility exists in the means to accomplish the objectives. However, in this chapter, only the format of the recommended budget will be addressed. In an excellent book, *Effective Budgetary Presentations: The Cutting Edge* compiled by Girard Miller (1982), the Government Finance Officers Association (GFOA) presented examples of the common components of local government budgets. These components are the budget cover, table of contents, organization charts, transmittal letter, financial summaries, goals and objectives, divider pages, revenues, departmental and activity budgets, program budget summaries, performance measurements, enterprise and internal service funds, capital outlay, special analyses, accompanying documents, reader's guides, budgetary procedures, budget preparation instructions, and legislative adoption. Students are encouraged to review this unique collection of samples to understand some of the format possibilities available to a budget office.

In summary, each format channels thought differently. Line-item budgeting tends to take decision makers away from policy issues and focus attention on expenditure savings. Program budgeting tends to focus attention on policy differences and on choices among policy options. Performance budgeting places the focus on questions of efficiency rather than of effectiveness.

In a 1986 survey of 750 local government budget practitioners drawn from the active membership roster of the Government Finance Officers Association, Daniel E. O'Toole and Brian Stipak asked what type of budget format their jurisdiction uses, used five years ago, and expects to use five years from the survey. The formats cited were line-item, performance, program, zero-base/ target-base, and hybrid. The line-item format predominated with 83 percent either using it exclusively (58 percent) or in a hybrid arrangement (25 percent). However, the survey showed a trend away from the exclusive reliance on the line-item format toward a hybrid format. The line-item format use declined from 75 percent to 58 percent, and is predicted to be 35 percent in the future.

Distinguished Budgets

In 1984, the Government Finance Officers' Association established an annual Awards for Distinguished Budget Presentations. The procedures followed in the awards program are similar to those in the GFOA Certificate of Conformance in

Financial Reporting program. Interested local governments send their last annual budget, supporting material, and an entry fee to the GFOA. Each budget is reviewed by at least three GFOA member reviewers, using evaluation criteria that stress the budget as a policy document, an operations guide, a financial plan, and a communication device. The GFOA recognizes the budget as a policy-setting instrument and wishes to make sure that policy making is explicit. The criteria call for general government and specific unit statements of policy, which can be in the form of goals and objectives, mission statements, or strategies. Any change in policy since the last annual budget should be explained in the budget document. Ideally, the rationale for the policy as well as the policy implementation and monitoring process should be explained. In addition, the criteria demand that the budget development process, including its later amendments, should be explained in the budget document itself.

The GFOA realizes that the budget is also an important operational guide during the current year to all the units in government. Thus, clarity of purpose in terms useful to bureaucratic units is imperative. Budget programs and line-items must be tied to the government's organizational units. The criteria call for stating the work force of each unit in terms of the organization chart and presenting the information for both the current and budget years. The criteria also expect the capital spending decisions to be explained in terms of their effects on daily operations and operating expenditures. In addition, specific objectives, performance targets, and important deadlines of department heads should also be included in the budget. The budget must provide a means to measure and permit accountability for performance or lack of performance in government.

The GFOA recognizes that the technical relationship of financial structure to the operations of government must be defined in the budget. Thus, the following technical topics must be explained in the budget, but in a manner understandable to the lay reader:

1. the major revenue sources;
2. the bases for forecasting, including predictions of events or factors that will influence forecasts;
3. the organization of funds used by the government;
4. the end-of-the-year projections of financial conditions;
5. a capital financing element (a separate capital budget is possible for larger governments);
6. a consolidated picture of operations and financial activity;
7. the debt management issues; and
8. the accountability basis used by the government.

To the GFOA, communication to the public is extremely important. The image of government is often not positive. Part of the problem is that the public does not understand what government does for them. Given that the budget is normally the single best comprehensive presentation on what a government is going to do with its tax resources, the GFOA believes care must be taken to communicate those policies in a manner in which the general public can understand government's programs, policies, and financial needs. To accomplish the goal of better communication, the GFOA criteria call for the following:

1. availability to the public of the draft budget primer to its adoption by the government decision makers;
2. clear summary information on the budget, covering topics of interest so that the media and the public can understand key points such as the size of programs, the revenue sources, and the policy changes of concern to the public; and
3. normal communication devices, which aid in understanding large complex sets of information; including a budget message, a table of contents, a glossary of terms, an identification of the basic units in the budget, charts and graphs with narrative explanations, key assumptions used in preparing the budget, a cross-index, and supplemental information, including statistical tables.

The evaluation criteria define "a good budget document" and largely implies what is a good budget process. The criteria are not predicated on any particular approach, such as ZBB, but they do encourage the use of program categories and performance measures. The criteria do reflect some definite normative guidance on what the GFOA considers important in a budget document.

The award program for Distinguished Budget Presentations is taken quite seriously by the GFOA and local governments. Of the first eighty-one governments submitting their budgets for review, fifty-one (63 percent) received the award. Given that governments are not required to participate and few truly unprofessional governments would participate, the rate of failure is significant. The first city to receive an "especially notable" award was Dayton, Ohio. Those governments that have received a budget award from the GFOA are justifiably proud of their professional achievement. Not only is the budget award program defining "good budgeting," it also serves as an important stimulant for improving the quality of local government budgeting in general.

Robert C. Rickards examined Texas cities and counties using the GFOA budget criteria. He used two reviewers and they looked at sixty-nine cities and eighty-six counties in Texas. They applied the GFOA criteria and concluded that Texas cities on average had "acceptable" budget documents but Texas counties had "very weak" presentations. Improvements are not likely to come from longer budget presentations but from more targeted efforts. Some common improvements are providing a glossary of terms, specifying the presentation's accounting basis, explaining the budget process and amendment procedure, discussing capital spending impacts and debt management issues, and furnishing draft budgets to the public. The biggest shortcoming was the readability of the budget presentations with many of them resembling accounting tables unintelligible to anyone except the persons preparing them. Beyond such common sense recommendations, the author noted that budget presentations could be improved by emulating good budget presentations and following the professional recommendations that exist in the literature.

Ends Defining Means

From a format design perspective, the desired ends should influence what format or formats should be used. A tendency of budget presenters is to use a standard approach for all programs, and this is desirable because it permits comparisons. Nevertheless, various programs do deserve individual presentations in order to highlight the most useful information for decision-making purposes. Format designers should decide first on the general format and then on extra information useful for specific programs.

Three common concerns should be weighed when deciding on format:

1. How can decision makers be helped to deal with *general policy*, matters?
2. How should the *budget* be *balanced*?
3. How can decisions of policy makers be used to *improve* the *quality of government management*?

Four common difficulties associated with helping elected decision makers formulate policy are (1) trying to get elected officials to focus on the major policy issues rather than insignificant and time-consuming issues that make relatively little difference to the future of the community, (2) fostering a decision-making environment in which counterproductive political tensions are reduced so that important and timely policy can be made, (3) sensitizing decision makers to the future-year implications of their decisions, and (4) achieving an awareness that budget decisions do relate to specific government actions which affect individuals and society. The first difficulty is commonly handled with program budgeting and formalized budget approaches such as PPB and ZBB. The latter is especially useful as a means to inform novice political executives of the policy implications of budget decisions. The second difficulty, according to one noted author, Aaron Wildavsky, can be handled well by line-item budgeting, which permits more face-saving because it focuses attention on relatively unemotional subjects such as salaries, travel, and supplies. The third difficulty is handled by requiring revenue and expenditure forecasts to be made possibly five or more years beyond the BY. Requiring a financial program schedule is also an appropriate procedural way to meet this concern. The fourth difficulty is resolved by having program budgets include performance measures that show the products or services produced by government programs as well as their impact on individuals and society.

Dealing with the challenge of balanced budgets commonly requires (1) getting both policy makers and government agencies to accept the existence resource constraints, (2) helping policy makers justify to the public the need for more government resources (that is, higher property taxes), and (3) shifting political pressure from the more controversial revenue sources to the more acceptable revenue sources. The first type of situation is best suited for a TBB approach, which assumes a given revenue level and works from that assumption. Ideally, with TBB, budget decisions beyond the arbitrarily established limit simply should not be considered. The limitation of such an approach is that government problems are not limited by arbitrarily established revenue limits. The second situation occurs when policy makers decide that more taxes are needed, but the public is not yet supportive of that policy position. Budgets can be constructed to stress the need, how government action can resolve that need, and the necessity for more money if that need is to be resolved. Program budgeting is particularly useful if it is combined with appropriate measures of program services and social needs.

The third situation is more complex. Governments receive their revenues from various sources, of which some are more politically sensitive at various times than others. One way to help deal with that political reality is to minimize pressure on the politically sensitive revenue sources by shifting as much cost as possible to less sensitive revenue sources. For example, if property tax is a hot political issue, then user-fee revenues can be increased as much as possible to cover expenses. The budget format can show, for each expense item, the source of revenue. This would permit the probing inquiry that would seek to shift the burden to the least politically sensitive revenue source.

Striving to improve government management usually includes (1) stressing efficiency and productivity in government management, (2) establishing top level control procedures in order to ensure that policy is carried out and that fraud and abuse are minimized, (3) establishing proper review practices to minimize overhead costs, (4) stopping unnecessary end-of-the-year purchases, and (5) improving management through better use of new technology and development of professionals and other employees. The first concern is normally addressed with performance budgeting or, more commonly, separate ad hoc productivity studies, internal audits, and the hiring of more program reviewers. Edward A. Lehan advocates a format (see Chapter 5) which includes marginal analysis and allows decision makers to consider the optimum funding level that will result in the greatest productivity. Exhibit 4–4 is an example of a performance budget developed by Edward A. Lehan for the government of Jamaica. The second concern can be addressed in the operating budget by using a line-item format that assigns dollars to specific units. Another strategy often employed is to increase audit and inspector general staffs. The third concern is associated with a greater organizational sophistication. Formats that include overhead comparative and longitudinal cost data focus attention on that concern and are helpful. The fourth concern can be addressed by good accounting practices. Accounting data illustrating the problem can be included in the budget or in a special analysis accompanying the budget. The fifth concern can be spotlighted in the budget by a narrative that discusses plans for the use of new technology and how staff will be developed. First-priority use of new funds can be singled out for upgrading technology, which should result in productivity improvements. Professional development (that is, training) can be included as one of the fringe benefits of employment and made less vulnerable to normal line-item budget cuts.

In summary, one can choose among budget formats in order to better highlight particular concerns. Such highlighting will not necessarily guarantee specific decisions, but it will channel thought.

EXHIBIT 4-4 Jamaica Budget/1986-87

Problem Definition and Goal. The estimated 1986-87 workload totals 5,100 analyses. This projection embraces 2,000 pharmaceutical investigations, 1,800 toxicological reports, 300 analyses of food and 1,340 investigations related to customs and excise duties.

Although the workload increased by 23% in 1985-86, and is expected to rise again in 1986-87, the potential demand for analyses is estimated to be far higher, perhaps as high as 12,000 annually. Indeed, in 1974-75, when the Lab was able to respond more promptly to requests, it produced over 12,000 analyses. As will be pointed out, more intensive use of the Lab can significantly reduce unit costs.

In addition to *accuracy*, Lab effectiveness and efficiency depends on *speed*. Progressively declining over the years, the Lab's responsiveness, measured by proportion of analyses done "on-time," is estimated at 30% for 1986-87, given existing staffing and equipment.

In 1986-87, recognizing the constraints of existing equipment, but assuming full staffing, the Lab aims to deliver 1,530 analyses on time, or 30% of its total project workload.

ANALYTICAL WORKLOAD	1984-85	1985-86	1986-87
Backlog April 1	59	84	100
Requested Analyses	4,000	4,500	5,020
Tests Completed "On-time"	3,975	4,484	1,530
Tests Completed "Over-due"			} 3,570
Backlog March 31	84	100	20

Target Population. Lab services are used by hospitals and health clinics (652,000 patient contacts), the Courts Custom and Excise Revenue Officers, 8 pharmaceutical manufacturers and private individuals, labs and food processors.

MINISTRY OF HEALTH GOVERNMENT CHEMIST

EXPENDITURES (000's)	1986-87 BUDGET	1985-86 REVISED	1985-86 APPROVED	1984-85 ACTUAL
Analytical Services	874	502	722	429
FINANCING PLAN				
Service Charges	127	3	NA	3
Taxation	747	499	722	426
Revenue	874	502	722	429
PERFORMANCE DATA				
Analyses	5,100	4,884	NA	3,975
Paid Hours	74,880		NA	
Hours/Analysis	14.7		NA	
Cost/Analysis	$ 144		NA	
On-time Delivery Ratio	30%			

*Reflects a $734,000 operating budget

EXHIBIT 4–4 (continued)

EXPENDITURE ANALYSIS	CODE	INPUT FACTOR	INPUT UNITS	UNIT PRICE	1986–87 BUDGET	1985–86 REVISED	1985–86 APPROVED	1984–85 ACTUAL
Personal Emoluments	01	Staff Hours	74,880	7.28	545	382	417	333
Travel Expenses	02	Vehicles	4	4,500	22	12	20	13
Supplies and Materials	03	Various Factors	NA	NA	45	9	40	21
Public Utilities	06	Various Factors	NA	NA	53	64	50	53
Operating & Mainte-nance	07	Various Factors	NA	NA	5	10	5	9
Subscriptions	08	Reference Documents	18	3,555	64	25	40	—
Equipment	14	Units	2	70,000	140	—	150	—
					874	502	722	429

Source: Adapted from the 1986–87 Jamaica Budget.

BUILDING THE BUDGET

Program Financial Schedule

On a quarterly basis, each department and agency can be required to transmit a program financial schedule to the central budget office. This now fairly common budget requirement provides useful information to the budget office. On a quarterly basis, the central budget office can better forecast expenditure needs. The schedule categorizes the program by activity, method of finance, and fiscal year. Schedules commonly forecast five years beyond the budget year and include output measures associated with the desirable appropriation levels. The schedules are also divided into obligations and expenditures, thus providing useful information to economists and analysts concerned with the government's cash flow. Thus, the data can be used to estimate likely expenditure demands. This is useful data in preparing the budget call and issuing executive guidance on budget preparation.

These forecasts should not be viewed as extremely accurate, but merely as an indication of likely financial patterns, given existing policy. In each quarter, policy can change and other factors can evolve, making periodic updating essential. The program financial schedule is particularly significant prior to the development of the central budget office's budget call. The total of the schedules equals a reasonably high estimate of what all the departments and agencies will request. This intelligence is useful in framing budget office guidance for building the budget.

Budget Call

Budget Coordination. Exhibit 4–5 presents a slightly modified budget calendar used by the city of Los Angeles. The calendar is important to the building of the budget because it establishes essential deadlines. Preparing a budget is a complex undertaking involving the whole government. Coordination is achieved by first deciding who must do what when. This is decided in the calendar. The budget calendar milestones of a local government include:

1. distribution of instructions and forms;
2. preparation of revenue estimates;
3. return of completed budget request forms;
4. completion of review and preliminary preparation work assigned to the central budget agency;
5. completion of executive review and executive determination of final budget content;
6. submission of the budget to the legislative body;
7. completion of budget hearings;
8. preliminary legislative determination of the content of the appropriation ordinance or budget to be approved;
9. final action by the legislative body;
10. executive approval or veto of the adopted budget and legislative action;
11. completion of administrative actions, if any, needed to finalize budget appropriations; and
12. beginning of fiscal year.

EXHIBIT 4-5   Budget Calendar, Los Angeles

DATE	ACTION TO BE COMPLETED
January 2	Mayor's Budget Policy letter requesting department heads to submit proposed work programs and budget estimates for ensuing fiscal year. Necessary forms and revisions to budget manual are transmitted with that letter.
February 1	City administrative officer approves staff budget assignments, which are thereafter distributed to the staff.
February 15	Current-level work programs and budget estimates received from department heads.
March 1	Service betterment budget estimates, if any, received from department heads.
April 10	City administrative officer reviews tentative Capital Improvement Expenditure Program and, upon approval, transmits it to the Public Works Priority Committee by April 10.
April 10	City administrative officer submits annual salary recommendations to City Council by April 10.
April 10-30	Hearings conducted by the Public Works Priority Committee to determine final priority of capital projects to be included in Capital Improvement Expenditure Program for ensuing year.
April 10-17	Preliminary budget hearings held by city administrative officer and budget coordinator with the assistant budget coordinator and staff analyst for each department.
April 18-28	City administrative officer assisted by budget coordinator conducts departmental budget hearings with each department head, at which time the staff analysts' recommendations for that department budget are presented and department head is given an opportunity to express his viewpoint.
May 1	Final date for submission by city controller of the official estimates of revenue from all sources (other than general property taxes).
May 1	City administrative officer submits the official estimate of revenue from general property taxes.
May 1-5	Mayor, assisted by city administrative officer, conducts budget conferences with each department head. Attended by Council members, press, and taxpayer groups.
May 5-12	Final budget decisions made by mayor assisted by city administrative officer.
May 12-31	Budget printed under supervision of city administrative officer.
June 1[1]	Mayor submits proposed budget to City Council.
June 1-20	Council considers mayor's veto of any item and may override mayor's veto by two-thirds vote.
June 20-25[1]	Mayor considers any modifications made by City Council and may veto such changes.
June 25-28[1]	Council considers mayor's veto of any item and may override mayor's veto by two-thirds vote.
July 1[1]	Beginning of fiscal year—budget takes effect.

[1]Charter requirement.

Once the preliminary estimates of expenditures and budget calendar have been prepared, the central budget office can proceed with preparing for the budget call. The call gives guidance to all the departments and agencies on how to go about preparing the budget. In many governments, including the federal government, much of the guidance is standardized and established in official bulletins and circulars such as OMB Circular A–11. Agency budget officials need only refer to the established procedures and report forms. In addition to the standard operating procedures, each year special guidance is issued in the form of a "policy" letter, "allowance" letter, an executive policy message, or a statement on the budget. The "policy" letter is used in the federal government to convey executive guidance and budget ceilings. The "allowance" letter comes later to inform federal agencies and departments of presidential or OMB decisions after the executive review process.

Budget Guidance. The executive policy message or statement on the budget at the state and local level requests budget information and establishes guidance. For example, the policy may be one of "hold-the-line" retrenchment, or expansion. Also, programs and activities to be emphasized or deemphasized are announced. Common subjects discussed in municipal statements include:

1. mandated increases, such as pension payments, salary increments, and debt service;
2. raise or change in taxes;
3. request to hold the line or identify inadequate services requiring expanded effort;
4. plea for economy;
5. explanation of local economic trends influencing the budget; and
6. explanation of who must provide what information and when it is due (the budget calendar).

The detailed explanation call may be in the form of a budget instructions booklet, which provides guidance to the agencies and departments. The booklet contains:

1. the preliminary statement of executive budget policy;
2. the table of contents, including listing of forms;
3. the budget calendar;
4. general instructions; and
5. specific instructions for each form, including a sample form.

Budget office follow-through is essential. The instructions must be sent to the chief departmental officials. Each level of government will repackage the instructions and reissue them to lower levels. Eventually, the program managers receive the information requests. Meetings are useful at all levels to clarify and avoid possible confusion. Special care should be taken to explain any changes in the procedures. Every official involved should understand the current financial status and likely trends, including personnel pay trends. Emphasis must always be given to the need for accurate, prompt, and uniform replies. The types of forms required are explained in Municipal Finance Officers Association publications cited in this chapter's references.

The budget call always asks for a statement of government functions, activities, and work programs, or some narrative explaining what services are to be received for the tax dollar. The general instructions asking for this budget explanation normally stress the desirability of brevity, clarity, and comprehensiveness. The explanation should reflect any program changes and even emphasize those changes. Each level in the executive branch uses the information, with the central budget and department levels focusing on having a complete inventory of government activities keyed to specific units assigned to functions and activities. The descriptive detail is greater at the unit and agency level.

Agency Call. Exhibit 4–6 is a sample agency call for estimates used in past federal budget training manuals. The call draws attention to the executive policy and the required forms to be used in the agency. For example the call might note that the agency is still operating under a continuing resolution for the current year, and cite how to handle particularly sensitive information. The call states who should prepare the information (that is, assistant directors and division heads) and when the information is due (for example, August 20). Note that only twenty days are allowed to compile the information. Tight deadlines do occur in budgeting. If zero-base budgeting were used, the instructions would require alternative decision packages and priority rankings.

EXHIBIT 4–6 Agency Call for Estimates (Sample)

August 1, 19PY

MEMORANDUM TO ASSIST DIRECTORS AND DIVISION HEADS

Subject: *Instructions for Preparation of the Budget Estimates for FY 19BY*

The 19BY budget submission to the Office of Management and Budget (OMB) will conform generally to the program and activity structure used for the 19CY budget estimate. The overall budget estimate will be prepared to reflect policy and program decisions that resulted from budget meetings held by the Director on the 19BY budget.

For purposes of the presentation to the OMB, descriptive materials for the various programs should be brief statements covering the points outlined in the following format. It is expected that the submission to the Congress will be a more detailed budget.

Since no appropriation has been approved for the Agency for 19CY, the program estimates for that fiscal year will be the same as in the 19CY Budget to the Congress. Under item "C." of the instructions, supplementary data is being requested for the preparation of staff salary estimates and travel and other administrative expenses that are spread among the activities shown in the Salaries and Expenses appropriation.

Estimates and drafts of the justification material must be received by the Budget Office by August 20.

Comptroller

Source: Resource Conservation Agency, Washington, D.C. 20550.

Preparing a budget at the agency level is a difficult task. The material must be assembled from the units and the budget figures, in particular, must conform to agency policy set down by the agency head. Personnel statistics and cost information is normally calculated by the budget office to compute the salaries and expense portion of the budget. If the agency has field units, the process is more complex because more groups are involved. Extreme accuracy and consistency are important because their absence denotes sloppy preparation and poor management.

The format of the agency budget requests varies greatly depending upon which budget reform happens to be in vogue. The format can be a detailed line-item presentation that permits greater control over the bureaucracy, a program budget that stresses policy issues and their budget implications, a performance budget that relates input to program accomplishments, a zero base budget that focuses on marginal value and prioritization, or an incremental budget that stresses changes from past policy decisions. The format selected is important, but a more important factor is the quality of professionalism devoted to preparing and reviewing the budget. Good professionalism calls for in-depth understanding of the agency and the related budget implications. How this is done is explained in Chapter 6. Too often the format is established by some budget reform movement instead of being tailored to the type of programs administered by the agency as well as to the needs of the central budget office.

BUDGET REVIEWS

Once the agency prepares the budget, the review process begins in the executive and legislative branches. The agency first meets with the department officials. They conduct a complete examination of the budget request, often including budget hearings. Departmental budget decisions are made and the agency budget request is revised based on department level decisions. Normally, the department recommends cuts but is a more friendly reviewer than the central budget office. The latter unit next reviews the agency or compiled departmental budget. Recommendations are made by the central budget office to the chief executive and sometimes departmental officials make direct last-minute appeals to the chief executive. Finally, the chief executive's budget is released.

Executive Budget Hearings

Normally, the agency submits its budget to the reviewing party, who carefully analyzes the submission. Chapter 5 describes how program and budget analyses can be conducted. After the initial analysis of the submission and any other available material, the reviewing party, such as the department budget office, is prepared to seek additional information. Often this is done by formal written questions to the agency on specific inquiries and sometimes more informal inquiries are made. The reviewers—budget examiners—prepare an analysis of the material and prepare background material for a hearing. Hearings need not be held but they enable the budget officer and the executive to obtain a better understanding of an agency's request and reasons supporting that request.

Agencies also prepare for hearings. The depth of preparation varies but the agency is wise to prepare carefully. Anticipated questions from the reviewers can be developed, and responses can be written and studied by the agency's representatives. A plan of action or strategy can be prepared, keeping in mind the factors discussed in the chapter on budget behavior.

The hearing itself is semiformal, with testimony rarely transcribed. The chief executive of the department should chair the meeting to ask questions and understand the budget request. The principal budget officer is present and plays an active role. Often questions are prepared for the chief executive to facilitate the process. The agency presents a statement and questions follow or the review is handled entirely with questions and answers. Regardless of the style used, the agency should explain its program, especially any program changes. The questioners should probe for elaborations on vague points as well as potential political or management problems. The hearing is only for information purposes and this forum is inappropriate for tentative or final decisions because more deliberation is necessary.

After the hearing is completed, the budget analysts carefully review their notes and reconsider the submission and other material. Guidance from the departmental chief executive is also reviewed. Often the reviewers may ask some additional questions by phone or in writing. The departmental budget office then prepares its final analysis and recommendations.

The departmental chief executive is then briefed on the budget. The briefing depends upon the management style of the chief executives. Some delegate the entire responsibility to the budget office, and others review the requests in detail. Normally, the pressure of time on the chief executive prevents long, detailed reviews of requests. A set of briefing information usually includes:

1. summary of agency requests;
2. recommendations of budget office;
3. summary of the past year's chief executive's ideas relative to the budget;
4. added suggestions by the budget office;
5. preliminary budget (balanced for state and local government); and
6. summary of policy issues.

A similar process exists at the gubernatorial or presidential level of government. This review takes place after the departmental reviews.

Executive Budget Document

Budget Message.   Budgets sent to legislatures and city councils are almost always accompanied by a budget message. The contents vary depending upon the political situation. Normally, the message includes a discussion of the financial condition of the government and a commentary on the current year operating budget, such as "the current budget is and will continue to be balanced." Revenue highlights are mentioned, including revenue estimates, new revenue sources, and prospects on increased or new taxes. The government is usually put into perspective by citing major trends in finance, population changes, income level shifts, and so on. The principal elements of the proposed expenditures are explained, including the rationale for any major program changes. Sensitive topics like "mandatory" increases as well as pay and fringe-benefit policy are mentioned. Problem areas not addressed by the proposed budget are cited, often with an explanation for that omission. At the local level, the message could also explain the relationship between the operating and capital budgeting. The message summarizes the highlights of the budget and blunts political criticism if possible.

Budget Summary.   A summary of the budget is essential. It should present consolidated summaries of revenues and appropriations. At the federal level, various economics-related information is presented. At the local level, the comparative statement of resources includes:

1. cash surplus at the end of the first prior year;
2. estimated receipts for the current year;
3. anticipated expenditures during the current year;
4. estimated cash surplus at the end of the current year;
5. anticipated income during the budget year;
6. proposed expenditures during the budget year; and
7. projected cash surplus at the end of the budget year.

Additional information can be included in the local budget summary. A statement on the tax rate and the assessed valuation of the property, including amount of land, improvements, and exemptions, is often included. A statement on other revenue sources is useful. The statement of appropriations by organization unit can be included. Finally, a summary of appropriation to various activities can be mentioned.

Budget Detail.   After the summary material, the detailed revenue and expenditure estimates are presented. The revenue estimates are grouped by funds and presented by comparing the budget-year estimates with those of the prior year and current year. Appropriate footnotes are added to explain tax rates, tax base, and nonrecurring bumps or valleys in the estimates. All assumptions used in preparing the revenue estimates are explained. The detailed expenditure estimates often include:

1. a narrative explanation of the functions of each department, suborganization unit, and activity, as well as a separate section for comments on the major changes proposed in each activity;
2. a listing by department and suborganization unit of the objects of expenditure and by activity with an identification of proposed resource changes;
3. a listing by position title for each unit and activity as well as any proposed changes; and
4. an identification of the work load volume being undertaken in conjunction with each activity.

The executive budget document is often considered to be the budget even though the legislature may make some changes. In some jurisdictions, the budget is the final document passed and approved by the legislature. Regardless of the stress given the executive budget document, it is extremely influential in the decision-making process. The document is the chief executive's plan. Any modification must be done with the awareness that any changes cannot be simply additions or deletions. Even in the federal government, additions to the budget raise the question of either "Where is the extra money going to come from?" or "What programs are going to be cut?" If deletions are suggested, the easier but still difficult question raised is either "Where is the extra money going to be spent?" or "What taxes should be cut?" These are not simple questions, and the executive budget becomes the point of departure for legislative consideration of the budget.

Congressional Budget Timetable

Budget Milestones. In the earlier discussion of the budget calendar, there are target dates set for legislative action on the budget. For many governments, the executive may be considered presumptuous to state target dates for the legislatures because of the separation of powers concept. In spite of that attitude, most budget people can estimate fairly accurately what the target dates are in the legislative budget process. Often the legislative body will state its own targets in its rules. The one forcing deadline is the beginning of the new fiscal year, by which, everyone agrees, the budget should be adopted. The other deadlines fall between the time when the legislature receives the chief executive's budget and the beginning of the fiscal year.

In the federal government, the congressional deadlines were set by the 1974 Budget Act. These critical targets, coupled with serious prodding by the budget committees, encourage the Congress to pass timely appropriation legislation, avoiding the pre-1974 practice of passing appropriation legislation three to six months into the current year. Both the targets and the active pushing of the budget committees are essential. The targets set a standard. Budget committees use social and political pressure to achieve responsible congressional action.

The seriousness of not passing timely appropriations is often overlooked. If no appropriation legislation is passed, then the government cannot pay its employees or anyone else. Government operations cease to exist because no one has the authority to spend money. If a decision has not been reached on appropriations prior to the beginning of the new fiscal year, then a legislative body passes a continuing resolution, which normally says that the government can continue to obligate and spend at last year's budget levels. The wording of the continuing resolution could also say the government can proceed at the lower of either last year's budget or the approved version of the House or Senate bill. The wording is normally framed to permit spending at the lowest amount the legislature is likely to pass. Managing a program under a continuing resolution is no significant problem unless the final legislation provides the manager with significantly less or more money than the continuing resolution. If less money is provided, the entire program may have to stop. If more money is provided, the program may have to obligate money recklessly in order to use it during the remainder of the fiscal year. Either situation is bad public management that can be compounded by repeated yearly use of the continuing resolution, as has happened with Congress.

Congressional Budget Timetable.   The congressional budget deliberative process starts with the presidential submission of the Current Services Budget. This budget alerts the Congress, especially the Congressional Budget Office, the budget committees, and the appropriation committees, that they should be anticipating specific revenue, expenditure, and debt levels unless current policy is changed. The Current Services Budget also provides a baseline of comparison to the later presidential budget.

The presidential budget, with the Current Services Budget, is sent to the Congress fifteen days after Congress convenes in the new calendar year (for example, January 20). The budget normally follows the State of the Union address to Congress by about one week. Presidents usually address Congress with a specific budget message that is more detailed and specific than the earlier State of the Union speech. The budget messages vary in content with a president's style, but the earlier discussion follows a common pattern, with the exception that more emphasis is often placed on the national economy.

By February 1, the Congressional Budget Office must send its annual report to the budget committees. This report analyzes the economy, the Current Services Budget, and the president's budget. Alternative levels of spending are suggested. Interestingly, the original legislation called for an April 1 submission, but the CBO realized this did not give the budget committees sufficient time to digest the CBO report, so the date was changed by mutual consent.

By March 15, the various committees, such as appropriation committees, must submit their respective reports to the budget committees. These are tentative financial guesses by the committees regarding amounts for revenues, expenditures, and debt. The committees use the CBO report, the president's budget, and the detailed back-up information supplied by the agencies to help them arrive at reasonable budget estimates.

One month later, on April 15, each budget committee reports its recommended budget resolution. This resolution represents the difficult compromise on the entire budget: the revenues, expenditures, and debt, as well as targets for each committee important to the budget process. One month later, on May 15, each chamber votes on its own resolution. An inability to reach a decision would destroy the process. Opposition can come from the conservatives (for spending too much money) and from the liberals for spending too little money. The resolutions need not be the same in each chamber. May 15 is also the deadline for reporting all authorization bills. The Congress doesn't want unanticipated expenses resulting from authorization legislation, so this deadline is essential.

Seven days after Labor Day in September, final action on appropriation bills is required. This gives the appropriation committees several months to hold their hearings and make their difficult decisions.

By September 15, final action on the second budget resolution is required. This permits last-minute changes that might be due to intervening circumstances since the first resolution was passed. Often, there may be no difference between the first and second resolution, but an opportunity for flexibility has been provided. By September 25, all final actions on budget reconciliation should be passed, thus providing a uniform consolidated congressional budget in each chamber.

The remaining days in September are used to resolve differences between chambers, pass the legislation, permit a presidential veto, and reconcile or override the veto. All this can be done if there is perfect cooperation among the chambers and the president. If not, then delays will result, and a continuing resolution may be necessary because the federal fiscal year begins on October 1.

Legislative Considerations

At all levels of government, legislative bodies consider budgets and budget supporting material. This information is the key to proper legislative understanding of government operations. The considerations and the subsequent legislation permit the legislative oversight activity to exist. The purse strings are important. If weaknesses are identified, legislators can retailor policy often with their redrafted budget. The budget consideration in legislatures is a much more open process than the executive review. Thus legislative budget hearings serve as a forum for better community understanding of government as well as a device to permit citizens to express their views on budget matters.

The time needed for legislative consideration of the budget varies with the size of government. Committees must have time to study the budget and related information, conduct hearings with public officials and possibly with interested citizens, discuss policy internally, and finally enact the legislation. Normally, sixty days is a reasonable time for smaller local governments.

Legislative organization to deal with the budgets also depends largely the size of government. Larger governments should have standing committees with highly competent professional staff support. Committees and staffs can be organized on a partisan or a nonpartisan basis. Given the complexity of government and budgeting, more of the smaller states and local governments should hire professionally trained and experienced public administrators. Exhibit 4–7 presents an illustrative page from a legislative analyst's review of a budget request. The reader will notice how a good analyst can focus attention on the items that should concern the legislator.

The hearing is the standard method used to gather information and focus on potential problems of concern to the legislature. Often these problems are isolated through careful staff program and budget analysis. The legislative hearing is conducted differently from the executive hearing. With legislative hearings, a transcript is often maintained, and there are more coequal questioners of the agency personnel. Some legislators are friendly and others are hostile. Just as in the executive hearings, the agency is wise to prepare for the hearings with briefing books, to plan strategies and tactics, and to have rehearsals. The hearings are usually scheduled more at the convenience of the legislative committee than of the agency. Follow-up questions are common, as in executive hearings. Decisions are not made at hearings, but rather at closed door "mark-up" sessions.

If public participation is part of the hearing, then the committee normally takes care to give due notice of the time and place of the meeting. Failure to give due notice or to notify all the likely interested "publics" can result in heated public criticism.

The legislatures normally have the power to modify the executive's budget, but that is not always the case in local government. Even if the power exists, modifications are difficult because all components of the budget are interdependent. If one figure is adjusted upward, another figure must be cut if the budget is to balance. Exhibit 4–8 illustrates one city council's modifications.

The adoption of the budget can vary in terms of detail. Appropriations should be itemized by department in order to fix responsibility. Some argue that they should be itemized by major object classification and others by program or activity. There is no one correct way. Object classification is good for greater control, especially when there is a low threshold of trust afforded the government's middle- and lower-level managers. Program classifications are good for situations which need management flexibility to operate effectively and efficiently. Detailed line-item budgets are extremely inflexible. Necessary taxes and a formal resolution on the final official revenue estimate accompany or are passed at the same time as the budget.

EXHIBIT 4–7   Legislative Analyst's Review Sheet, Department of Hospitals and Institutions, 1993 Budget Request

NEWARK CITY HOSPITAL

The 1993 Budget request of $6,469,185.00 for the Newark City Hospital shows an increase of $229,131.67 over 1992 Operations, as follows:

1993 Budget Appropriations	$6,453,424.00	1993 Request	$6,469,185.00
1992 Emergencies	115,149.96		
	$6,568,573.96		
Less Cancellations	328,520.63		
Net 1992 Operations	$6,240,053.33	1992 Operations	6,240,053.33
		Increase	$ 229,131.67

The request for 1,270 employees is 25 less than the 1,295 in 1992.

PAGE NO.	LINE NO.	
4		There were 29,669 less patient days In 1992 than in 1991, resulting from a drop in admissions from 18,760 in 1991, to 15,460 in 1992, a net drop of 3,300.
5		The average day's stay per patient dropped from 9.5 to 9.1. The average daily admissions dropped from 60.9 in 1991 to 56.4 in 1992, a net drop of 4.5 admissions. The average daily census of patients in the hospital dropped from 575.6 in 1991 to 549.9 in 1992, a drop of 25.7 in 1992.
6	1 & 2	What is the status of the Medical Director and the Assistant Medical Director?
6	3	Will the Comptroller's position be filled? Is the present incumbent Joseph Rubino to remain on the hospital payroll?
10	12A	Has this position been filled?
19	37	Is this position going to remain in the hospital?
25		New employee, Director of Surgery. In accordance with policy followed in similar cases the appropriation for this employee will be deleted because there is no valid ordinance supporting it. The appropriation will be made after adoption of the ordinance and before final adoption of the budget by amending the approved budget.
41	103A	Bernice Lippe replaced the Director of Nurses on January 14, 1993 at the minimum salary of $37,500.00. Her salary as Assistant Director of Nursing Education on Page 112 was $36,460. One pay should be deleted from the Directorof Nurses' appropriation and one pay remaining in the Assistant Director of, Nursing Educations's line on page 112.

EXHIBIT 4–8 Schedule Setting Forth Changes Made by City Council in City Manager's Original Estimate of 1990–91 Budget

	MANAGER'S ESTIMATE	REVISED AMOUNT
Office of City Manager Reason for change—Reduced cost of annual report, reduction of .5 man year administrative analyst. Add cost of salary increase.	$146,135	$ 138,246
Secretary-Treasurer Reason for change—Add cost of salary increase.	166,844	169,484
Accounting Reason for change—Delete one accountant position. Add cost of salary increase.	77,686	74,751
Data Processing Reason for change—Add cost of salary increase.	179,470	181,303
Purchasing Reason for change—Add cost of salary increase.	30,867	31,539
Tax Reason for change—Add cost of salary increase.	400,390	408,861
Legal Reason for change—Add cost of salary increase.	99,472	101,636
Retirement Administrator Reason for change—Add cost of salary increase.	22,731	23,043
Personnel and Civil Service Reason for change—Add cost of salary increase. Add cost of salary and wage survey.	29,703	50,349

LEGISLATIVE ADOPTION[1]

The ultimate budget is the legislative adoption version, which can be several appropriation laws (the federal government's approach), one massive, complex appropriation law (used by many states), or a relatively brief text (used by some local governments). Sometimes the budget submitted to the legislative body includes the recommended act or ordinance.

[1]Much of the material in this section comes from Girard Miller (compiler), *Effective Budgetary Presentations: The Cutting Edge*. Chicago: Government Officers Finance Association, 1982.

Often budget ordinances are complex because of state legal requirements. In some jurisdictions, the resolution includes tax rates, purchasing authority, personnel action authorizations, and transfer procedures. Some use broad legislative grants of authority, and others have extensive line-item detail for each government unit.

The ordinance:

1. acknowledges receipt of an executive budget from the county manager;
2. recounts earlier publication and a public hearing;
3. summarizes appropriation by fund and category;
4. estimates revenue;
5. levies property taxes;
6. authorizes administrative transfers of appropriations within a fund; and
7. approves and reapproves funds for ongoing capital improvements.

REVIEW QUESTIONS

1. Explain how budget formats channel thought. Explain how formats can direct thought to and highlight general policy matters, budget-balancing issues, and improvement of the quality of government management.
2. Why are the program financial schedule and budget calendar important preliminary steps to the budget call?
3. What budget instructions are important in building a budget? Why?
4. Contrast executive and legislative hearings.
5. Why is the central budget office "powerful"?
6. What information should be in an executive budget? Why?
7. Explain the significance of the congressional budget timetable.
8. Contrast the virtues of a simple versus a comprehensive budget ordinance or law.

REFERENCES

ARONSON, J. RICHARD, and ELI SCHWARTZ (eds.). *Management Policies in Local Government Finance*. Washington, D.C.: International City Management Association, 1975.

BURKHEAD, JESSE. *Governmental Budgeting*. New York: Wiley, 1956.

FISHER, LOUIS. *Presidential Spending Power*. Princeton, N.J.: Princeton University Press, 1975.

GRIZZLE, GLORIA A. "Does Budget Format Really Govern The Actions of Budgetmakers?" *Public Budgeting and Finance*, 6, 1 (Spring 1986), 60–70.

JASPER, HERBERT N. "A Congressional Budget: Will It Work This Time?" *The Bureaucrat*, 3, 4 (January 1975), 429–443.

LEHAN, EDWARD A. *Simplified Governmental Budgeting*. Chicago: Municipal Finance Officers Association, 1982.

MILLER, GIRARD (compiler). *Effective Budgetary Presentations: The Cutting Edge*. Chicago: Municipal Finance Officers Association, 1982.

MOAK, LENNOX L., and KATHRYN W. KILLIAN. *Operating Budget Manual*. Chicago: Municipal Finance Officers Association, 1963.

Municipal Performance Report 1, 4 (August 1974).

O'TOOLE, DANIEL E., and BRIAN STIPAK. "Patterns and Trends in Budget Format Innovation Among Local Governments," *Public Budgeting and Financial Management*, 4, 2 (1992), 287–310.

RICKARDS, ROBERT C. "City and County Budget Presentations in Texas: The Current State of the Art." *Public Budgeting and Finance*, 10, 2 (Summer 1990) 72–87.

SMITH, LINDA L. "The Congressional Budget Process—Why It Worked This Time," *The Bureaucrat*, 6, 1 (1977), 88–111.

U.S. Civil Service Commission, Bureau of Training, The Management Science Training Center. *Budget Formulation*, 1976.

WILDAVSKY, AARON. *The Politics of the Budgetary Process*. Boston: Little Brown, 1964.

5

ANALYSIS APPLIED TO BUDGETING

Budgeting requires analysis, and this chapter introduces a wide variety of analytical techniques useful in public budgeting. It is not a how-to-do-it chapter; rather, it shows how significant types of analysis relate to budgeting. The first section focuses on the theoretical foundation on which analysis can be applied in the public sector. The following sections describe the difficulties associated with applying the theory, describe useful elementary analysis, explain the important analytical tool called *crosswalk*, focus on revenue and expenditure forecasting, explain productivity analysis, and explain benefit-cost analysis. At the completion of this chapter, the reader should know:

1. a theoretically useful model that is consistent with the context of a democratic society;
2. application difficulties associated with the model;
3. simple analytical techniques that help us understand key relationships;
4. the three common approaches to revenue forecasting as well as the basics of econometrics;
5. expenditure forecasting approaches, including bargaining, unit cost, and time-series methods;
6. how an econometric model can be useful in expenditure forecasting and simulation;
7. the basics of productivity analysis, underlying productivity through regression analysis, and how to strengthen budget requests;
8. the difference between benefit-cost and cost-effectiveness analysis;
9. the fundamental concepts associated with benefit-cost analysis; and
10. the analytical limitations to the benefit-cost technique.

THEORETICAL FOUNDATION

A Budget System Approach and Accountability

The Budget System Approach (Exhibit 5–1), developed by this author but similar to a model developed by Herbert Simon, is based on the assumed desirability of accountability in the public sector as well as an assumed chain of cause-and-effect within the system. The cause-and-effect chain runs from *input* (for example, money, expertise, policy direction), to *process* (that is, the performance of administrative activities), to *outputs* (that is, the products and services produced by the unit), and finally to *outcomes* (that is, the impacts on individuals and society). Between the beginning of the chain and the end—and especially between outputs and outcomes—intervening variables from the political, economic, and social environment are likely to exist. Nevertheless, this theory assumes that the input eventually and necessarily causes the outcomes, even though that cause may not be sufficient to produce the effect itself.

EXHIBIT 5–1 Budget System Approach

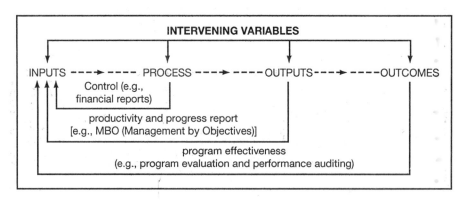

Accountability is theoretically made possible by recognizing that the chain of cause and effect can be monitored through three feedback mechanisms—control, productivity and progress reporting, and program effectiveness—as well as reactions from the intervening variables, including lobbying from clientele groups and media news stories about the impact of the program on the public. The more formal feedback mechanisms permit policy makers and management to know what process as well as program outputs and outcomes actually exist, so they can be compared to intended process, outputs, and outcomes. Thus, policy makers and managers can be expected to be aware of and be accountable for the results of their decisions and their performance. According to J. D. Stewart, accountability consists of the following five distinct levels or steps on a ladder: policy, program, performance, process, and legality. The Budget System Model lends itself to this view of accountability. According to the Government Accounting Standards Board (GASB), accountability is the paramount objective of government financial reporting.

The Budget System Approach can be used in a democratic or authoritarian society. In a democratic society, policy differences among various leaders and peoples are a primary and institutionally accepted aspect of policy making. Social values compete in an ongoing (and, one hopes, nonviolent) conflict over the nation's policy. The theory does not assume there is one correct government solution or best set of values. It *does* assume that the conflict in political values does not necessarily give consistent and clear guidance to government program managers and that logically consistent government policy will not necessarily be selected. Given that democratic reality, the theory expects that normally the persons supplying information will communicate salient data, which permits policy makers to confront and deal intelligently with their multiple-valued electorate. To be useful in this theory, program output measures, in particular, should be understood and defined in the political context of the government and the larger society it serves.

Public budgeting is a phenomenon that exists at the nexus of policy making and management. The chain of cause and effect within the system links policy and management. In government, the assumption is made that its programs do and even should influence individuals and society. In addition, increases and decreases in government programs will make an important impact on individuals and society. Budgeting, in part, is the allocation of resources based upon decisions, but implicit in each such decision is a process to carry out that allocation. Management cannot be separated totally from policy because the means to carry out the policy does influence eventual outcomes. This theory assumes that there is a chain of cause and effect, or, at least, policy makers believe such a chain exists.

The Budget System Approach helps decision makers and budget analysts who are preparing information in support of decision makers. Two important concerns of budget analysis are program effectiveness and efficiency. Insight on the first is achieved by looking at program outcomes and the ratio of input to outcome. Insight on the latter is achieved by examining the process and the ratio of input to output, with consideration given to providing the same or similar level of work with fewer resources. The role of the budget analyst in the budget office is not to make policy but to raise the level of debate among the policy makers so that they can focus on the truly significant policy and related management questions. Thus, the budget office should facilitate accountability and encourage more intelligent decisions about the allocation of government resources.

As noted in Exhibit 5–2, there is greater use of program information associated with analysis in the budgetary process in the past two decades. According to unique survey research done by Robert D. Lee, Jr. (1993), an increase in the use of performance measures, particularly, took place in state government in the early 1970s. However, the use of program information remained static, and, in the case of future year projections, it increased in the late 1980s. Nevertheless, research on the state of Georgia indicates that the development of valid and reliable evaluation measures may occur, but their use in actual budget decision making on a systematic basis does not yet exist in that state. At both the agency and central budget office levels in Georgia, Thomas Lauth (1985) reported that performance measures were not taken into account during budget preparation and review largely because top officials did not use that information in their decision-making processes.

EXHIBIT 5–2   Program Information in State Budget Documents (percent)

	1970	1975	1980	1985	1990
Effectiveness measures included					
Most agencies	2	24	28	26	24
Some agencies	27	40	43	49	41
None	71	36	30	26	35
Productivity measure included					
Most agencies	8	26	28	24	33
Some agencies	37	48	49	52	44
None	55	26	23	24	24
Future-year effectiveness measures included					
Yes	2	18	19	13	26
No	98	82	81	88	74
Future-year productivity measures included					
Yes	8	20	19	18	37
No	92	80	81	83	63

Source: Robert D. Lee, Jr., "The Use of Program Information and Analysis in State Budgeting: Trends of Two Decades." In Thomas D. Lynch and Lawrence Martin (eds.), *Handbook of Comparative Public Budgeting and Financial Management*. New York: Marcel Dekker, 1993, p. 173.

As noted earlier in Chapter 2, people in an agency must believe that the reform (that is, performance measures) is used seriously by key decision makers in government before the reform influences organizational behavior beyond meeting requirements. To the extent it occurs, performance measures will be significant in government management and decision making as indicated by Professor Lee's research. Exhibit 5–3 shows that top state executive and legislative decision makers do use effectiveness and productivity analyses.

EXHIBIT 5–3 Use of Analysis in State Budgeting (percent)

	1970	1975	1980	1985	1990
Central budget office assists depts. regarding program analyses					
Substantial	4	21	10	7	9
Some	38	50	56	68	75
Practically none	58	29	33	24	17
Executive budget decisions based on effectiveness analysis					
Substantial	15	20	11	21	26
Some	23	59	70	64	64
Rarely	62	20	20	14	11
Executive budget decisions based on productivity analysis					
Substantial	19	27	21	29	45
Some	32	54	64	67	55
Rarely	49	19	15	5	0
Legislative decisions based on effectiveness analysis					
Substantial	25	20	12	12	9
Some	19	48	66	73	74
Rarely	56	32	22	15	17
Legislative decisions based on productivity analysis					
Substantial	19	20	10	15	13
Some	25	32	56	76	81
Rarely	56	48	34	10	6

Source: Robert D. Lee, Jr., "The Use of Program Information and Analysis in State Budgeting: Trends of Two Decades." In Thomas D. Lynch and Lawrence Martin (eds.), *Handbook of Comparative Public Budgeting and Financial Management*. New York: Marcel Dekker, 1993, pp. 175 and 178.

Program Impact Theory

The focus in budget examination is on understanding existing and planned management strategy as well as on program effectiveness. Regardless of the approach (for example, PPB, ZBB, or TBB) to budget preparation, a common theoretical framework exists, which assumes a cause-and-effect relationship between the program's inputs and its ultimate impacts on society or the environment. The examiner (also called the budget analyst) assumes that such a relationship can and should exist, and then attempts to discover if the actual or intended approach to managing the program can and is likely to lead to the intended program outputs and outcomes. And, the examiner wants those results accomplished with the greatest program effectiveness consistent with the political values of the policy makers.

Almost all government programs are intended to affect society or individuals in some way or the necessary legislation would not have been passed. Often, the desired impacts on society are vague and even internally contradictory, but there almost always is some purpose behind each law and government program. There is an assumed cause-and-effect relationship: The government program is intended to produce an effect on society. This assumption is central to much of the analysis useful in budgeting. Often, budget analysts try to determine if a resource request and even the program itself is worthwhile, given the results of that program.

The burden of proving the worth of a program and a specific resource request is placed on the agency. The agency must justify the budget to the department, the executive, and the legislative body. Often those involved act as if absolute proof exists that a given program is worthwhile. Unfortunately, those holding such a view are not sensitive to the philosopher Descartes, who held that absolute proof for any subject other than one's own existence (*Cogito, ergo sum.*) is not possible; therefore, we must use other criteria in evaluating it.

In public administration, the criterion of "necessary but not sufficient cause" is normally the best. For example, if the ultimate desired effect is to reduce the crime rate, holding the police force responsible for that effect may seem reasonable until one realizes that poor police work is not the only reason for the existence of crime. Good police work may be necessary, but it alone is not sufficient to reach a low crime rate. Too often analysts and decision makers apply the harsher "necessary and sufficient" criterion in judging the worth of government programs. This unfortunate conceptual mistake merely leads to false expectations and frustrated administrators and citizens.

Conceptually, an analyst should be able to develop a program impact theory. Given a set of resources and the conditions in society, a government program can produce outputs which, in turn, will lead to outcomes. The resources, in part, are reflected in the budget request. The outputs are the achieved objectives of management. Those objectives provide guidance to the lower officials and administrators in the bureaucracy. The outcomes are the achieved objectives one cites in program evaluations. Those impacts or outcomes are what higher-level decision makers should view in judging the government program.

The program impact theory is the heart of any good budget justification. The person justifying the budget should be arguing that the agency will achieve the legally stated desired effects (that is, the law's purpose) on society or individuals if the agency is given the requested resources. The program impact theory should be the conceptual means to relate the resource requests to the stated end results caused in society.

If the desired end results do not occur, then two types of failure are possible: (1) the agency did not do its job correctly, or (2) the theory was incorrect. If the agency conceptually separated outputs and outcomes correctly and gathered the necessary data, then the type of failure can be determined. If the objectives of management were met, then one type of failure can be eliminated. This permits proper focus on theoretical failure, which is the responsibility of the highest-level decision makers for using poor theory, or of the academic community for not developing adequate theories. Once the failure is identified, then attention can be focused on discarding faulty theories and developing more useful theoretical understandings. This identification of failure is particularly significant and helps us understand the relationship of social science research and the needs of higher-level administrators.

Data measures are critical because the assumption is made that each key portion of the model (for example, input, process, output, and outcome) can be accurately described. Data measures for input tend to be easy to define because line-item budget detail or aggregate numbers representing money and positions almost always exist. Data measures for process normally are not difficult to acquire and not critically needed for most budget analyses. Output data measures are obtained by asking what the unit produces in terms of products or services. For most units and programs, isolating data measures is not difficult, but the information may not be collected on a routine basis. Outcome data measures are often very difficult to obtain, as government units normally do not routinely record the individual and societal impacts of their programs.

Deciding what data measures to use is not an easy task. Normally, the best process to follow is to reason backward while focusing on a specific unit and program. The question "What impact does this particular program have on the organization (if the program is administered by a service unit to an organization) or on society (if the program directly affects society)?" should be asked. Then the analyst should seek specific means to measure that impact. Next, the analyst should identify the program outputs by seeking to understand exactly what the unit does or produces that causes those previously identified program outcomes. Data measures of output should give an accurate picture of what takes place. Outputs are defined and are relevant only in the context of program outcomes. The process stage can be omitted, but it does permit a more in-depth analysis, which helps postulate recommended efficiency improvements. The last stage in reasoning backwards is the input. What input contributes to and affects the process, output, and outcome? Input that does not contribute to output and outcome is not needed.

The use of performance measures has been recommended since at least the turn of the century, with reform groups such as the Hoover Commission arguing for performance budgeting. In the 1990s, an increasing interest in performance measures in the United States has built on the Government Finance Officer's Association stress on performance measures, increased use of measures by the better managed cities, the research on performance measures by the Urban Institute and others, and its stress by the chief financial officers and the General Accounting Office at the federal level. The Governmental Accounting Standards Board (GASB) was established by professional organizations to improve state and local government accounting standards. One of its projects is to explore requiring the use of performance measures as part of the normal accounting process in state and local government. There is a reasonable chance that the use of such measures may become required in the future for those governments that wish to be certified as using acceptable accounting practices.

The GASB defines three broad categories of performance measures, or Service Effort, and Accomplishment (SEA): service effort, service accomplishment, and effort to accomplishment. The SEA categories are as follows:

1. Measurement of effort (called input here)
   a. Measures of financial resources
   b. Measures of nonfinancial resources
      (1.) Personnel
      (2.) Other
2. Measurement of accomplishment
   a. Output measures
      (1.) Service or product quantity
      (2.) Quantity of a service or product that meets a certain quality requirement
   b. Outcome measures
3. Measurement that relate effort to accomplishment
   a. Effort to Output—efficiency
   b. Effort to Outcome—effectiveness

APPLICATION DIFFICULTIES

The application of a theoretical model in public administration can be difficult, but the difficulties can be anticipated. Commonly, analysts and line officials using the model will (1) mix up outputs, outcomes, process, and data measures; (2) confuse the types of appropriate output measures; (3) not understand how to apply the concept to staff and service units; and (4) not fully appreciate that an inability to determine outcome and output measures may indicate program nonperformance.

Mix-Up

The most common mistake, when applying this model, is to mix up the model elements and measures. For example, an agency may insist on using descriptive measures that explain its administrative process. Those measures often indicate work effort (for example, ten hours to write the report) or ratio of staff to clients (for example, student/teacher ratio of 30 to 1). There is nothing wrong with such measures per se, but program output and outcome measures must also be determined, and each measure should be correctly defined. Questions addressed to program effectiveness cannot be answered with process data alone.

Another mix-up is the confusion of outcomes and outputs. In fact, the two are often used interchangeably. This is an unfortunate mistake, as it leads to improper use of analysis. Proper identification of model components makes it possible to determine program effectiveness and efficiency. The best way to avoid such confusion is to address program outcome first and reason backward to program outputs.

Types of Output Measures

Public administrators are sometimes unaware that program outputs, especially services, consist of two types that should be treated differently. The first type is the result of a project with a defined end-product or service. Constructing a building or writing a report are examples of that output type. The second type reflects a desire to provide ongoing services or products within some defined limits of acceptability. As long as the service is done correctly within those limits, then the output is judged satisfactory. Failure or less than satisfactory service is defined by the number of occasions that the level of service falls outside the ideal limits.

A common mistake is to be unaware of how best to define the second type of output. Administrators will judge a license bureau by the number of licenses issued rather than the percent of licenses issued within an acceptable waiting time. The quality of output is not considered, and important managerial considerations are ignored. End products or services are counted, but the program output quality is overlooked.

Staff and Service Units

When first introduced to the model, individuals tend to focus on units that are the primary service producers within the government. As they start to apply the model, they discover staff units (for example, budget offices) and service units even within line departments (for example, bus maintenance). They become confused about how to apply the concept in situations in which staff and service units do not have a direct impact on citizens and society.

The best approach is to work backward from outcomes. If the analyst or manager is focusing on a bus maintenance unit in public transit, the first point to understand is that the overall unit outcome is to improve the movement of people along traffic routes and permit the mobility of the transportation disadvantage. How does the maintenance unit contribute to that overall transit outcome? The answer is the unit's outcome—for example, keeping a percentage of the bus fleet in operation at all times. Since public transit program output is measured in terms of ridership, the next question should focus on how the actual work or work products of the bus maintenance unit contribute to ridership. For example, the unit preventatively maintains ten buses each week. That would be one of the unit's program outputs.

For many professionals, the question of how to handle a staff unit like a budget office is confusing. The first point to understand is that the role of a staff unit is to service the government so that it can work effectively. For example, a budget unit should (1) help raise the level of debate for policy makers so that they are more likely to make better decisions, (2) monitor budget execution so that the policy of the duly constituted decision makers is followed unless a conscious decision is made not to follow that policy, and (3) promote and foster better public management within the government. Specific data measures can be developed for each program output and outcome. The second point is that outcomes should be understood as a function of the program outputs. For example, program outputs such as the annual budget document and various reports are not sufficient program outcome measures per se. The outputs should be judged in terms of their contribution to program outcome, such as raising the level of policy debate. The budget execution system should be judged in terms of its success in getting government units to follow policy. Various ad hoc reports and studies should be judged in terms of their impact on improving public management or raising the level of policy debate. Thus, budget office output must be understood in terms of its positive contribution to the office's outcomes.

Nonperformance Option

Sometimes program outputs and outcomes are unsuccessfully defined. The potential reasons for failure include the professional inadequacy of the budget analyst and insufficient cooperation from an agency that refuses to define necessary data measures. Perfect measures are often inappropriate for use because of the time it takes to collect those measures or because of high costs in collecting the data. Therefore, trading off the quality of the measure against the effort to collect it is a common professional challenge. An unacceptable situation occurs when top agency personnel fail to make a reasonable attempt to resolve trade-off problems. In such cases, budget office leadership must be apprised of the situation and must decide whether to attempt to force the agency to develop the desired output and outcome measures. Not all such battles can be won; the budget office must decide if that particular battle should be fought and when it should be fought. Normally, government executive leadership is willing to support the budget office leadership on such matters, as it is in the best interest of executive leadership to have such information.

A possible reason why program outcomes and outputs cannot be defined is that the agency may not be performing any useful service. Often when an agency is particularly uncooperative in defining outcomes and outputs the behavior is simply a defensive attempt to cover up poor management. That possibility must always be appreciated by the budget office and top management. Care must be taken that other explanations are eliminated because charges of agency cover-up are likely to evoke attacks on the professional competency of the budget analyst by the program manager. If problems of this type are possible, budget office leadership should involve top management assistance as soon as possible so that an intelligent approach can be taken to deal with this type of defensive behavior.

DATA MEASURE CONSTRAINTS

The application of this model is always dependent on the constraints associated with the use of data measures. To use this model properly, an understanding of quantitative techniques and research methods is necessary. For example, some measures used will apply only to an ordinal data scale, and the uninformed will misapply analytical techniques meant to be used for only ratio data scales. For the most sophisticated use of analysis, the best scale is ratio, but that is often impractical or impossible given the character of the problem and data.

The best measures to use are uniform in nature and contain a high number of units of output for which one assumes the same level of quality in each unit of output. For example, the water and sewer systems measure their output in gallons of water or sewerage processed at an acceptable level of quality. Measures of this type permit the use of the most powerful analytical techniques. Unfortunately, not all program outputs are susceptible to this ideal type of measure. For example, a planning unit's outputs are not useful for budget analytical purposes if these outputs are merely considered to be updated comprehensive plans. The usefulness of those plans must be judged using some type of ordinal or even interval scale.

A common ploy by agency officials is to use measures which are ratios between ideal and actual performance. For example, animal control agencies might compare the number of strays to actual captured dogs. Normally, the ratio shows that the program is doing reasonably well, but the impression is given that more resources (input) would improve the ratio. The problem with such ratios is that the ideal is often a highly questionable figure, and the ratio may not be measuring the true outcomes and outputs. If the stray dog problem is defined as the existence of stray dogs, then the measure of dogs captured may be quite correct. If the dog problem is more accurately described as strays in inappropriate areas, then outcomes should be defined differently. Maybe the solution to the dog problem should really be defined as capturing strays within a given time after a complaint has been registered. If so, again, the animal control unit outputs should be restated to indicate how many dogs are not captured within acceptable time constraints. Notice that occasionally the outcome and output can be identical or almost identical for operational purposes.

Although perfect program outcomes and outputs may be found, there is the problem of selecting one or more data measures. In some circumstances, the data measures selected could be more expensive to acquire than the cost of the programs they are to measure. Obviously, practical trade-offs must be made in deciding if added clarity in the budget decision-making process is worth the added cost of the data measure.

Another problem with data measures is that they can react with and influence negatively the workings of a program. For example, the knowledge that data is used by decision makers can encourage some managers to distort the data or engage in defensive behavior which avoids facing up to and resolving managerial problems. The negative energy which can be created by data measures must be understood and countered to the extent possible.

One tactic is to use nonreactive measures. For example, worn tile in front of a museum exhibit indicates popularity. Normally, nonreactive measures are easily available and often inexpensive to acquire. Another advantage is that their apparent lack of connection with key program events means that monitoring them will not affect the measurement instrument itself. The problems with nonreactive measures are that they can be isolated only by a creative imagination and that their positive relationship with program outcomes and outputs is not often perfect. Nevertheless, good nonreactive measures should be used when practical.

ELEMENTARY ANALYSIS

Defining Relationships

Most analysis used in budgeting is not complex. *Trend charts, scatter diagrams, simple regression analysis, marginal cost analysis, discounting to present value,* and *Kraemer's Chi Square* are all relatively simple analytical techniques. Often relationships involving budget requests, final budgets, year-end estimates of current expenses, and actual performance are important. If relationships can be established, then the budget analyst's job is made easier. Normally, relationships are best described using a conventional scale, but sometimes a logarithmic scale or index numbers can be employed to better highlight the significance of the data. One common relationship is to show a given variable as it changes over time. If a trend is apparent, then long-term forecasting is made easier and future consequences become more predictable.

In many situations, the relationship between two variables is more difficult to determine. One approach is to place the two variables on two axes, as illustrated in Exhibit 5–4. The analyst then places dots representing each simultaneous occurrence of the two variables. The result is a *scatter diagram* that may indicate a relationship between the two variables. Exhibit 5–4 shows such a relationship for a car between maintenance cost and miles driven. The line is a *simple regression analysis* defining that relationship.

EXHIBIT 5–4   Illustration of Statistical Analysis

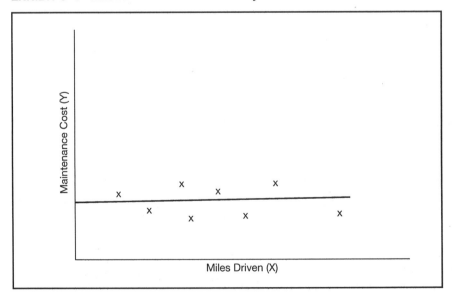

Marginal Cost and Discounting

Another useful technique is *marginal cost analysis*. The initial cost of a government program is often expensive, while further effort leads to lower unit costs. This means that in many circumstances the analyst should understand that marginal costs are lower. This might prove to be highly significant. For example, if an agency is asking for a proportionate increase in funding, the analyst might question this request because marginal costs should not increase proportionately.

In order to perform marginal cost analysis, the data must be separated into one-time *fixed costs* and *recurring costs*. Common one-time fixed costs include research, project planning, engineering, tests, evaluations, land purchases, facility construction, equipment, and initial training. Common recurring costs include personnel expenses, employee benefits, maintenance, direct contributions to people, payments for services, and overall and replacement training. The fixed costs remain the same, but the recurring costs increase with added units. Thus, as the units increase, the unit cost decreases. These data can be plotted on a simple chart or described in simple statistical expressions.

Another technique is *discounting to present value*. A dollar received or spent in the future is not equivalent to a dollar received or spent today. Therefore, adjustments should be made if comparisons are to be made. The technique is similar to the statistical concept used to compute compound interest at the bank. This technique is useful when comparisons must be made, but the two subjects must not occur during the same time period or involve different financing methods.

Fred A. Kramer (1976) has cited a simple but common situation to illustrate the use of this analytical technique. A city must choose between contracting with a private garbage collector for $65,000 per year or having city employees do it. The latter option would require a $40,000 truck and a $55,000 yearly operating expense. Without discounting, the best option is apparently to let the city employees collect the garbage. With them, the cost is $315,000 over the five years of the truck's life. With a private contractor, the cost is $325,000. Using city workers would apparently save the city $10,000 per year over the five-year period in operating expenses. However, with discounting, the best option is the private contractor. The following shows the important arithmetic:

SAVINGS IN THE YEAR	× 8% DISCOUNT FACTOR	= PRESENT VALUE
1	$10,000	.926	$ 9,260
2	10,000	.857	8,570
3	10,000	.794	7,940
4	10,000	.735	7,350
5	10,000	.681	6,810
Total Present Value of Annual Savings=			$39,930

In the example, the private contract is the best buy because the total present value of annual savings is less than the $40,000 capital investment. If city employees were used, the city would pay $40,000 for a truck but save a total of $50,000 over five years. The application of discounting to the yearly savings lets us realize that the true savings are not $50,000, but $39,930, because the value of money over time must be considered. Thus, discounting shows us that the options are nearly equal, but the contracting option saves the city $70.

Caution must be stressed in using the discount technique. Numbers have a way of seeming so final and clear. Realistically, the ingredients in the question should be carefully weighed in terms of their sensitive character. An output of a program is sensitive when the results can be altered by minor changes in a variable. If the analysis is highly sensitive, then any recommendations made on the basis of the analysis should be questioned because the technique does not warrant the implied certitude. This technique can be abused by changing the annual returns or savings, the life of the asset, the amount of the investment, the discount rate, or the annual returns in the earlier years. This does not mean the technique should not be used, but it should be used with a complete understanding of the possible distortions.

CROSSWALKS

Conceptual Bridge

One of the most useful analytical tools for the budget examiner is the *crosswalk*. It is a simple matrix table relating different categories. It serves as a conceptual bridge between two organizational means to describe and control agency activities. By constructing several bridges, the examiner can explore various organizational perspectives on what should be done and what is done as well as check important interrelations. Some of the more common categories that can be crosswalked are:

1. programs, projects, activities, tasks;
2. uniform object classifications;
3. appropriation structure;
4. major organizational units;
5. objectives used in connection with management-by-objectives or program evaluations; and
6. funds (including grants-in-aid) used in government accounting.

A very useful crosswalk is between the program and the uniform object classification (also called line-item). In many sophisticated budget offices, both program and line-item categories are used. In order to maintain consistency, the crosswalk is a valuable tool because it shows the interrelationship of the two ways of looking at the budget. In addition, a careful examination of the crosswalk helps to isolate potential problems, such as inadequate resources for some line-items in some programs.

Another useful crosswalk is between fund and line-item. Often an agency can draw upon several funds in its daily operations. Thus, a given line-item expense may be associated with two or more funds. The crosswalk is a display of information that can help the manager decide which fund to charge for a given line-item. By looking at a cumulative crosswalk of expenses in an organization, a budget analyst can see if the funds were used together in a meaningful way and more intelligently judge the budget request in a given fund for the next year.

The appropriation-to-unit crosswalk is also useful. Sometimes a legislature provides funds that are used by several organizational units. A tool to keep track of which unit is responsible for each portion of the money is the crosswalk. Without such a tool, lower-management responsibility is unclear and judging management performance becomes more difficult.

In the federal government, the program-and-authorization crosswalk is very useful at the agency level. In the executive branch, budgets are prepared using the program concept. In the legislative branch, budgets are justified and discussed in terms of legal authorization language. Thus, the agency budget official must use both the program concept of program and legal authorization in justifying and defending requests for funds. As a means to translate more easily and ensure a consistency between executive and legislative information, the crosswalk is a valuable tool.

An unused but potentially significant crosswalk is between the MBO objectives and the program structure or appropriation structure. MBO can be an extremely useful public management technique, but often it is applied without reference to the budget. This is foolish; how can one reasonably expect objectives to be met without also establishing that necessary resources are available to conduct the program? The two should not be treated in isolation, but they are by many agencies. If they are treated separately, this indicates strongly a lack of coordination of management direction within the agency because both MBO and the budget are tools to achieve management direction.

If the agency has activities that fulfill more than one objective at a time, then a program-evaluation objective—program-structure crosswalk—is treated somewhat differently from the other crosswalks. Normally, each matrix square states dollar amounts representing mutually exclusive activities. This permits the crosswalk to be validated for internal consistency by merely checking if the horizontal and vertical summary columns are equal. In the case of evaluation objectives, dollar amounts can be counted more than once if they fulfill more than one purpose. For example, a given activity may increase safety and reduce energy consumption (for example, enforcing the 55-mile-per-hour speed limit). Thus, the crosswalk matrix squares would show the dollar amount (maybe even the name of the activity) under two different vertical categories. This type of double counting can also exist with a crosswalk using MBO objectives.

Determining Consistency

The budget examiner can ask to see various crosswalks for the reasons suggested above. Essentially, crosswalks help the examiner determine if the agency has internally consistent management direction and control capability to ensure the integrity of that direction. If the agency does not act with one management direction, the crosswalks expose that problem. If the agency cannot provide crosswalks, this suggests poor management. It is possible for the agency to manage its affairs well without using crosswalks, but it should be able to construct them if there is a consistent management direction. If crosswalks cannot be constructed or if the ones provided show inconsistent management policy, then the budget examiner can probe further to isolate the exact nature and reasons for the internal management inconsistency.

Crosswalks can also be used to check for external consistency of management direction with past publicly announced positions and orders of higher authorities. A set of crosswalks is among the best evidence of the exact management policies of an agency. Those policies may not be consistent with the agency's past policies or positions articulated to the public or policy directives from higher authorities. If the budget examiner happens to have the crosswalks from past budgets, then they can be compared with the most recent crosswalks. In this manner, policy shifts can be isolated. Budget examiners can also determine if the policy direction from the crosswalks matches public positions and policy established by higher authorities. If there is inconsistency, then further probing may be warranted to determine the reason for the inconsistency.

REVENUE FORECASTING

Three Approaches

Revenue forecasting calls for a separate treatment of each revenue source. The standard approach is, first, to determine the patterns associated with each revenue source. Next, the base must be determined and then the forecast is made based on assumptions and the determined pattern. Forecasting is merely a sophisticated form of guessing that depends on good data and good judgment, often refined through experience. The techniques of forecasting range from the simple to the complex, but all should be used with the principle of conservatism in mind (that is, underestimating revenue and overestimating expenditures).

Notwithstanding this accepted advice, governments do not always use that principle. In a study by William Earle Klay and Gloria A. Grizzle (1986) of state government forecasts of sales tax receipts, they discovered a slight tendency on the average to overstate revenue.

Information is important to revenue forecasting, and certain background information should be retained. This includes copies of legislation, legal history, administration factors concerning the tax, or any change in charts showing changes in the tax rate over time and the monthly yield, with an explanation of any abnormal change in the trend line; and data on any significant variables that affect the revenue yield.

The three revenue forecasting approaches are *qualitative, time series*, and *causal analysis*. Qualitative (also called judgmental) approaches are, in essence, based solely or primarily on human judgment, but math can be involved. William Earle Klay (1983) of Florida State University surveyed the revenue forecasting practices of all fifty states and found that thirty used panels, interagency work committees, or conferences in their revenue forecasts. Normally, economists constituted these "expert" groups of forecasters, but occasionally politicians were included. Expert judgment is best used when key revenue elements are highly variable, no history exists, or revenues are strongly influenced by political considerations (for example, intergovernmental transfers).

The *time series* approaches (for example, trend analysis) are based on data that have been collected over time and can be shown chronologically on graphs. One such approach involves using the last completed year as a basis for the revenue estimate (in France, this method is called "rule of penultimate year"), assuming that there is growth in the economy and related revenue sources. Another simple technique—*the method of averages*—is to average the revenue generated over the last three to five years. Again, the assumption is made that there is a growth trend in the tax source, rather than a decline or an uneven tax yield. A more sophisticated method involves using moving averages and attributing greater weight to more recent revenue yields. A still more sophisticated method is the Box-Jenkins method, which will be described later in the expenditure forecasting section. Normally, the trends are shown on arithmetic graphs, but some analysts prefer semilogarithmic graphs because they reveal rates of change in tax yields more clearly.

When using time series techniques, the forecaster is especially interested in the nature of seasonal fluctuations that occur within a year, the nature of multiyear cycles, and the nature of any possible long-run trends that might underlie the seasonal and cyclical fluctuations. The major weakness of this approach is that economic turning points are not easily identified. Trend analysis should be used to forecast revenue items that are not highly variable and that (1) amount to minor percentages of the budget or (2) are not dependent on economic or political considerations.

Causal methods deal not with the history of a single variable but with the historical interrelationship between two or more variables. One or more predictor variables forecasts tax yield directly or indirectly by first forecasting the future tax base. For example, multiplying the estimate of the average tax to be collected per taxpayer by an estimate of the number of taxpayers results in a forecast of income tax revenue. Various survey techniques can be used to determine these two predictor variable estimates. Some communities use a payroll tax. To forecast the revenue, they estimate the area payroll and tax rate and multiply them. A variation is to calculate the tax rate by occupational groups. A third method is first to determine the interrelationship between personal income and leading economic indicators and then to use the leading indicators to determine personal income. The tax yield is determined from the personal income. For sales taxes, the area or state sales are forecasted, and the tax yield is calculated from that level of sales.

These causal forecasting methods are predicated on selecting the correct predictor variables, defining their interrelationship to tax yield correctly and, finally, collecting accurate data. An added advantage to these methods is that they can help policy makers reflect on various "what if" options for taxes and other policies so that they can better gauge the implications of their policy choices. Drawbacks to these methods include the need to collect extensive accurate data, the cost of developing causal models, and high computer costs. Fortunately, computer costs are decreasing. If revenues are strongly influenced by changing economic conditions, causal models (for example, econometrics) are especially useful.

Accuracy in revenue forecasting is important, especially when the forecast predicts more money than is actually received by a government that must have a balanced budget. The results are painful government midyear adjustments that result in frozen positions, elimination of travel and other easily cut costs, and, finally, payless "paydays." If forecasts result, embarrassingly, in unpredicted surpluses, then the government, faces the politically difficult task of explaining tax rates that appear to be unnecessarily high.

Econometric Forecasts

Econometric forecasts are complex causal analyses that have many causal variables and are often computer-dependent. The age of econometrics began in the 1930s with Jan Tinbergen, a Dutch economist. He developed a number of equations to represent the workings of his nation's economy. In America, the use of econometrics by state governments has mostly occurred since 1978, with few local governments using the technique today (some exceptions are New Orleans, Dallas, Winston-Salem, and Mobile). The basic equation is $Y = f(X)$, with Y the dependent variable, affected by the independent, explanatory, predictor variable X. The statement merely says that Y is somehow dependent on (is a function of) the value of X. To develop a revenue forecasting model, the following are essential:

- a data history or time series for all variables;
- a set of mathematical expressions that best explains the past relationships among the variables; and
- a means of identifying the future values which one or more of the explanatory variables will assume.

Causal models may consist of a single regression equation or several regression equations. Exhibit 5–5 presents the revenue forecasting methodologies used for the Ohio general fund in 1984–1987. Semoon Chang used a single regression equation for his econometric model for Mobile's sales tax receipts. At the other extreme, Florida's state estimates made use of 123 regression equations. Many analysts rely on popular national econometric models such as those provided by Chase Econometrics, Data Resources, Inc., and Wharton Econometric Forecasting Associates. Worthy of note is an observation by John Peterson formerly of the Government Finance Officers Association (1979): "As a general rule, sophisticated models have been ignored by practitioners in the past. After their construction and initial operation by consultants, they have sometimes ended up gathering dust on the shelf." This method involves statistics, and unless staff can explain statistical concepts so that officials can understand them, informed official judgment may be impossible. To use this technique, the following statistical concepts should be understood:

1. R squared coefficient of determination, which shows the proportion of variation in the dependent variable attributable to variation in the independent variables;
2. the T test of relationship with a particular independent variable;
3. the F test, concerning the significance of the equation as a whole;
4. the Durbin-Watson statistic, which is an indicator of whether serial correlation exists, thereby suggesting that important information has been omitted;
5. the standard error of estimate; and
6. the mean absolute percentage of error.

EXHIBIT 5–5   Revenue Forecasting Methodologies for Selected Ohio General Fund Taxes

SOURCE	% OF TOTAL RECEIPTS	METHOD	VARIABLES
Personal Income Tax	37	Simulation Model	Growth in Personal Income
Non-Auto Sales Tax	27	Regression Analysis	Disposable Income & Industrial Production Index
Corporate Franchise	9	Regression Analysis	U.S. Corporate Profits Before Taxes and Industrial Products Index
Public Utilities	8	Time Series for Each Utility	Various
Auto Sales Tax	7	Regression Analysis	Personal Consumption Expenditures for Motor Vehicles & Ind. Products Index
All Other	12	Times Series/CPI Index	Various

Source: William J. Shkurti. "A User's Guide To State Revenue Forecasting," *Public Budgeting and Finance*, 10, 1 (Spring 1990), p. 84.

Forecasting Practices

Research reported by John Forrester in 1993 indicates the use of the various types of revenue forecasting techniques in American cities. The most common combination of techniques were expert and other, trend and other, and deterministic and other. His findings are presented in Exhibit 5–6. Jane McCollough and Howard Frank reported on a survey of municipal governments in 1992. They found the most used revenue forecasting techniques were judgmental (75.9 percent), trend-line (48.6 percent), and moving averages (36.2 percent). Techniques reported as not used were Box-Jenkins (97.6 percent), classical decomposition (91.0 percent), exponential smoothing (91.0 percent), and econometric (80 percent).

EXHIBIT 5–6   Use of Revenue Forecasting Techniques (n = 108) (percent)

FORECASTING TECHNIQUES	TAXES			FEES & CHARGES	REVENUES FROM	
	PROPERTY	SALES	UTILITY		STATE	FEDERAL
None	2.8	18.5	25.0	3.7	5.6	18.5
Expert	5.6	2.8	5.0	10.7	15.7	25.9
Trend	12.0	14.8	17.6	11.1	10.2	6.5
Deterministic	9.3	0.9	2.8	4.6	7.4	7.4
Econometric	3.7	11.1	5.6	2.8	3.7	1.9
Expert and Other	42.6	31.5	25.0	43.5	29.6	21.3
Trend and Other	47.2	37.0	30.6	50.9	35.2	20.4
Determ. and Other	34.3	18.5	19.4	32.4	14.8	9.3
Econ. and Other	17.6	14.1	16.7	24.1	12.0	8.3
State Forec. & Ot.	6.5	10.2	6.5	4.6	16.7	1.9

Source: John P. Forrester, "Use of Revenue Forecasting Techniques." In Thomas D. Lynch and Lawrence Martin (eds.), *Handbook of Comparative Public Budgeting and Financial Management.* New York: Marcel Dekker, 1993, p. 154.

Empirical information indicates that revenue forecasting at the state and local level is not accurate. In a 1985 study, the Public Policy Institute of New York documented the revenue forecasting practices of thirty-two states responding to their survey. It reported that the accuracy of state revenue estimates varied between +15 and -25 percent, with a variance of +/- 2 to 5 percent most common. In the 1986 study of state sales tax forecast accuracy by William Earle Klay and Gloria A. Grizzle, they discovered one state underestimated by 31.6 percent and another overestimated by 40.6 percent. Exhibit 5–7 presents Irene S. Rubin's (1987) findings on the accuracy of revenue forecasting in Illinois. She surveyed 102 cities and found that accuracy (defined as +/- 2 percent) varied from a high of 61.6 percent for property taxes to a low of 16 percent for property tax replacement (a small transfer payment from the state). Interestingly, utility taxes were overestimated 57.8 percent of the time. Rubin asked why there were misestimates, and she concluded the fiscal stress was the most important predictor of revenue bias. She said, "When both tax effort and revenue stress are high, there is a tendency to overestimate; when both are low, there is more of a tendency to underestimate." The type of local government was not a good predictor of misestimates.

EXHIBIT 5–7   Accuracy of Revenue Estimates

SOURCE	NO. OF CITIES	% UNDER	% ACCURATE	% OVER
Property	112	18.8	61.6	19.6
Sales	118	47.5	31.4	21.1
Income	118	39.0	26.3	34.7
Utility	45	22.2	20.0	57.8
Property Tax Replacement	100	76.0	16.0	8.0
Motor Vehicle	114	54.4	29.8	15.8
Revenue Sharing	108	32.4	34.3	33.3

Source: Based on an Illinois Revenue Survey, 1987, cited in Irene S. Rubin, "Estimated and Actual Urban Revenues: Exploring the Gap," *Public Budgeting and Finance*, 7, 4 (Winter 1987), pp. 83–94.

Measuring historic accuracy of revenue forecasts within a jurisdiction is simply a matter of contrasting forecasts with actual receipts. Once these comparisons are made, the analyst can determine where forecasting improvements are needed. Normally, large inaccuracies in small revenue items are not significant because often such inaccuracies tend to cancel each other out in the aggregate. Serious problems occur when there are modest errors in large revenue items because they can mean significant revenue shortfalls. Normally, the further away the forecast from the forecasted event, the more likely there will be a forecast error; thus, forecasters prefer late forecasts whenever possible. William J. Shkurti (1990) suggests that good revenue forecasting is associated with reasonable economic assumptions, sound estimating techniques, constructive use of alternative forecasts, a system of monitoring, revision and evaluation, and a clear and complete presentation. At the state level, a variety of revenue forecasting practices exist, including the use of single executive agency forecasts, the use of council of outside economic advisors, and consensus forecasting.

Sometimes revenue estimates are inaccurate because of political interference. For example, Maine's Republican Governor John R. McKernan Jr. faced a serious campaign challenge in his second term. As reported in a December 1991 issue of *Governing* magazine, (Shanahan, 1991) Steven Gold of the nonpartisan Center for the Study of the States said the Maine governor "would have lessened his chances of re-election if he had been honest." Instead, Gold says McKernan made "gargantuan revenue estimates, told the voters, 'We're all right, Jack,' and right after the election, Maine had to enact draconian budget cuts." The same article cites another

politically inspired poor forecasting by Massachusetts Governor William R. Weld
and quotes Florida's James Zingale, "Politicians are inclined to disguise problems
in the hope that they'll go away." Nonetheless, often many forecasting errors are of
a technical nature. Forecasting can be improved by more detailed data, more timely
information, more sophisticated use of computers, and sometimes by making it
harder for elected officials to politicize the numbers.

In order to cushion the negative possibilities of estimating revenue short,
governments create contingency reserve funds. Even if the government has good
revenue forecasting practices, statistical error margins make the use of such reserves
a reliable means to ensure a continuous flow of public service without resorting to
disruptive schemes. No single formula exists to decide the optimum level of such
reserves, and in periods of fiscal stress, the maintenance of any reserves becomes
politically very difficult. The optimum size of the reserve should be related to the
likely statistical error margin, which often indicates a 5 percent reserve is best.

EXPENDITURE FORECASTING

Bargaining and Unit Cost Approaches

The burden for estimating expenditures normally rests on the agency, but the
techniques are often similar to those of revenue forecasting. In some situations, a
bargaining approach is used in which the agency's estimate of its optimum program
is tempered by the economic and political climate, including budget call instructions. (Agency estimates can be based on detailed work plans involving months of
preparation or upon quick judgments involving a few minutes.) The central budget
office reviews the request, refining, cutting, and adding to the judgment of the
agency, with the possible participation of political executive and legislative officials. The final adopted expenditures represent the collective judgment of dozens
of officials and staff.

Another set of expenditure forecasting techniques is based on accounting
information that uses unit cost data. This method is similar to *fiscal impact analysis,*
which calculates the municipal costs of proposed local real estate developments by
using per capita cost multipliers, the average cost of providing a certain level or
standard of service, and other simple calculations. The three major steps in the unit
cost approach are: (1) choosing a level of analysis, (2) analyzing units and unit costs,
and (3) making necessary assumptions and calculations.

In selecting the level of analysis, budget analysts will often use the object
code level, but subcode or function levels can be used. An example of subcode level
use is found in Arlington County, Virginia, which records each employee's anniversary date, wage rate, grade, longevity increase (if any), fringe benefit costs, and
other data. Using this information, the computer does an annual projection of the
wages and fringe costs for each employee, and aggregates these costs into the
desired object codes, divisional units, departments, and funds. An example of
function-department level use is found in Syracuse, New York, where expenditures

by department are broken down into labor, nonlabor, fringe, and miscellaneous expenditures. These relatively gross aggregates are assembled for a jurisdiction forecast.

The second step of analysis of units and unit costs is done by examining past and current units and unit costs, such as the gallons of heating fuel charged to object code 306 of the Building Management Department. A more sophisticated version would be to multiply the unit cost by the price index when one is calculating specific future year forecasts.

The third step is to include assumptions for future years and then simply to multiply. For example, in the heating fuel situation, assume that 50,000 gallons are to be consumed in the BY at a cost of $2 per gallon; 50,000 multiplied by $2 equals $100,000, to be budgeted in object code 306 of the Building Management Department. The result is an annual or multiyear forecast for a particular expenditure which can be aggregated to arrive at a total expenditure forecast.

Time Series Methods

Many agencies use an *incremental* or *trend-line* approach in expenditure forecasting. Historical data defines the trend line, which shows the expenditure pattern over time. The slope of the line is the rate of change. The formula for a line is $Y = a + bX$ where Y is the dependent variable, X is the independent variable, and b is the slope of the line. The trend line establishes a historical pattern, and the forecaster need only take the next time period (for example, BY) and read up to the trend line and over to the expenditure level. In Exhibit 5–8, this approach shows that the expenditure forecast for the BY is $50,000. Judgment is used to determine any appropriate deviation from the trend based upon factors likely to cause unusual change.

EXHIBIT 5–8   Trend -Line Forecast

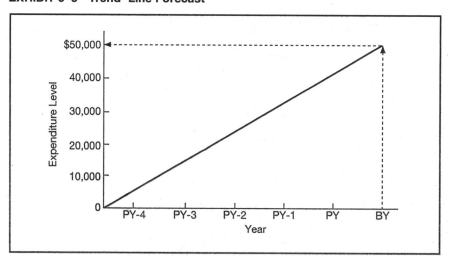

Two other time series methods are *moving averages* and *exponential smoothing*. In moving averages, one adds up the expenditures in past time periods and averages them. The assumption is that averaging the values will minimize data randomness and seasonality. Thus, the more data points used, the smoother the forecast. The limitations of the method are as follows: (1) it depends on sufficient data observations, thus it is not useful for new programs; (2) it is only useful for short-term forecasts involving one to three time periods; and (3) it is unable to forecast a change in the basic trend. In exponential smoothing, one uses the last forecast value and the estimated *alpha factor weight* of any value between 0 to 1 (for example, 0.1, 0.5, 0.9) and takes the difference between the forecast value for the most recent time period and the actual value realized. For example, $5,000 was spent in the CY and $4,500 in PY. To calculate the BY with an 0.8 alpha factor, we calculate $5,000 + 0.3 ($4,500–$5,000), which yields a BY forecast of $4,850. If the forecaster expects little data randomness, then a small alpha factor would be used; conversely, much data randomness would make a high alpha appropriate. The major value of this technique over moving averages is that fewer data points are needed and recent rapid trend changes are better reflected. The inherent disadvantage of the technique is the necessity for arbitrary assignment of an alpha factor.

A third time series technique is *adaptive filtering*. The four steps of the technique are as follows: (1) a forecast is developed by taking a weighted average of the previous observations, (2) the forecast and actual value realized are compared and errors calculated, (3) the weights in the weighted average are adjusted to minimize calculated error, and (4) the new set of weights is applied to forecast the subsequent period. The process is repeated as new actual data become known. This technique requires many calculations and is normally done with a computer. The technique is particularly useful when a great deal of historical data is available and those data exhibit considerable randomness.

A fourth emerging technique is *autoregressive moving averages* (ARMA), of which there are two types: *autoregressive models* and *moving average models*. Autoregressive models (AR) assume that future values are linear combinations of past values. Moving average models (MA) assume that future values are linear combinations of past errors. Autoregressive models use past data on the dependent variable at various time intervals to develop the forecast. Moving average models seek to eliminate the randomness of data by dropping a past observation as a new one becomes available. Box-Jenkins techniques are used to select and test ARMA models. ARMA techniques tend to produce very good one- to three-year forecasts. The techniques are very complex, but advances in computer software have eliminated many time and cost problems.

The Box-Jenkins method is a systematic elimination procedure to identify the most appropriate ARMA model and determine the appropriate forecasting model. First, the model is identified by means of various statistical tests and judgmental evaluations. Second, a trial-and-error approach using statistical estimation techniques is employed to determine the data array with the smallest mean square error. Third, after an adequate model is constructed, a forecasting equation is derived that reflects the data through the current period. A bonus of this technique is that it not only forecasts, but it does so with delineated limits of reliability.

Expenditure Econometric Model

Various expenditures are largely predicated on factors that lend themselves to econometric models. For example, at the state level, social service expenditures are directly related to the state economy, and education and criminal justice expenditures are related to state demographics and economic factors. Models can be used that not only predict likely expenditures but also help policy makers understand the most sensitive factors that influence each functional activity.

One such example is the Massachusetts Welfare Model developed by Data Resources, Inc. That model is used for short-term forecasts and sensitivity analyses of eligibles, case load, and expenditures in various welfare assistance categories. The model contains: (1) earnings distribution of the state and individuals; (2) an estimation routine for calculating Aid to Families with Dependent Children (AFDC) and General Relief (GR) eligibles from a combination of welfare policy standards and state demographic parameters applied to the earnings distributions for families and unrelated individuals; (3) econometric equations explaining eligibles' rate of participation in AFDC and GR, by sex and family status; (4) econometric equations explaining average expenditures per case in AFDC and GR; (5) identities deriving AFDC and GR case loads by a combination of items 2 and 3; and (6) identities deriving AFDC and GR total expenditures by a combination of items 4 and 5. The model uses 77 variables, including economic, welfare policy, and endogenous variables, as well as welfare eligibles definitions, rates of participation, miscellaneous inputs, and numerous simultaneous econometric equations. A similar multivariate forecast model was developed by the state of Washington with a fourteen-month average prediction error of only .42 percent (2 percent is considered excellent).

The model is used both for forecasting and *simulation* ("what if" analysis). It forecasts welfare eligibles, case load, and expenditures by program. It forecasts the earnings distributions of families and individuals. It simulates the impact on eligibles, case load, and expenditures of alternative U.S. and state economic scenarios. It simulates the impact on welfare case load of changes in the unemployment compensation program. And, finally, it simulates the impact on eligibles, case load, and expenditures of alternative welfare policies such as (1) cost-of-living increases, (2) a change in the income deduction for work-related expenses, (3) a change in the assistance tables reflecting new budget levels by family size and living arrangements, and (4) a change in federal statutes.

In forecasting, the model works in several steps. First, the U.S. and state economic data are used to derive family earnings distributions and to determine persons eligible for welfare. Next, welfare participation rates are calculated, using such factors as work availability and wage opportunities (normally, if the economy has worsened, welfare benefits and participation are higher). Welfare case load and total projected welfare expenditures are calculated. Finally, administrative costs are determined.

In simulations, the model works with "what if" scenarios. For example, "What if 5 percent federal eligibility regulations are changed to exclude persons with any income?" The model calculates the changes and predicts the mean monthly case load and other factors.

PRODUCTIVITY ANALYSIS

Productivity

Productivity is a measure of efficiency usually expressed as the ratio of the quantity of output to the quantity of input used in the production of that output. Commonly, productivity focuses on output per man-hour of change or changes in cost per unit of output. It does not measure the work completed versus the work needed to be completed.

The concept of productivity is often misunderstood. It is falsely tied to harder physical work, when it is in fact tied to doing the work with less effort but still increasing output. This is normally done by better work procedures, better use of machines, or better worker attitude toward the job. In quantifying productivity, the mistake is made of using outcomes (benefits to individuals and society) instead of outputs (products of the program). There are normally too many intervening variables between outcomes and outputs to permit a meaningful usage of outcomes. Another conceptual confusion is that an increase in productivity may reflect a cost reduction, but a cost reduction is not always a result of an increase in productivity. Other reasons for cost reduction can exist, such as a simple budget cut. However, too often we do equate productivity with cost reduction.

A study on productivity in the federal government was conducted in the mid-1970s, and its findings on the reasons for increases in productivity are enlightening. A commonly cited reason for a productivity increase was an increase in the work load, thus allowing the agency to lower its unit cost. Fixed and variable costs explain how productive advantages can result from increased work loads. In other cases, productivity increased because of improved training, increased and better use of job evaluations, greater upward mobility, or the use of a career ladder to develop the work force. In some instances, greater productivity was due to automation and the use of new labor-saving equipment.

Although productivity is a simple concept, there are not simple uniform answers for increasing productivity. Each situation must be examined separately. The federal study illustrates this point by saying the greater productivity resulted from (1) improved morale resulting from job redesign and enrichment, and (2) reorganization and work simplification. The study seems to say that making a job more complex and making a job simpler both result in greater productivity. This apparent contradiction can be resolved by understanding the human factor related to the job situation. For some people, the job is too complex and beyond their abilities. The answer is work simplification. For some people, the job is too simple and their boredom leads to poor work habits. The answer is job enrichment, such as rotation or a larger range of responsibilities. Sound increased productivity recommendations must be based on a knowledge of management science as well as human behavior. Exhibit 5–9 is a useful checklist developed by the National Center for Productivity and Quality of Work Life (1978).

The same federal study also cited some common reasons for declines in productivity. Increased product complexity cannot always be factored out of the measurements, and that complexity can mean less productivity. For example, increased environmental, safety, and legal requirements mean added work steps, equipment, or additional features. This may be in the public interest, but one of the disadvantages is increased production costs, thus a loss in productivity. Another reason for the loss of productivity is a steady and sharp decline in workload that is not matched by staff reductions. Either human compassion or labor agreements can mean lower productivity, but, again, other practical reasons supersede the desire for efficiency. A more common reason for a decline is, ironically, the installation of a new or automated system. For a period of time during the installation, both the automated and old system must be operated, thus decreasing productivity until the old system is phased out. These reasons are significant and suggest the complex issues which prevent us from always achieving increased productivity.

Simple Regression Analysis

The basic assumption of *regression analysis* is that change in the dependent variable Y is related to change in the independent variable X, either positively or negatively. In regression analysis, the independent variable need not necessarily cause the dependent variable, but a relationship does exist that may be causal in nature. Simple regression analysis uses a straight line $Y = a + bX$ to describe the relationship. The slope b is the regression coefficient and measures the change in Y given one unit of change in X. The constant a represents the distance between the point where the regression line intercepts the Y axis and the origin. In order to draw the regression line, the *method of least squares* is used. This type of analysis assumes a normal probability distribution for the observations and assumes that the error values are independent of each other (that is, no autocorrelation exists).

Exhibit 5–10, Exhibit 5–11, and Exhibit 5–12 show a simple linear regression for neighborhood libraries in an urban county. The independent variable X is the full-time-equivalent circulation staff working at each library unit. There is an assumed relationship between circulation staff size and actual books in circulation during the CY. Exhibit 5–11 and Exhibit 5–12 state the input and output data and show how the least squares method is used to determine the line on Exhibit 5–10. Note that the line fits or explains the various actual data observations, which are coded library values.

EXHIBIT 5–9   What Do You Know About Your Productivity?

The following set of questions can be used as a self-audit to determine what your organization is doing and what your organization may need to do to make programs more productive.

1. IS THE EFFICIENCY OF STAFF PERSONNEL MEASURED?

Are critical outputs identified for each program?
Are work counts and time-utilization records maintained for these critical outputs?
Are unit times developed for the outputs? Are trend data available for the unit times?
Is unit cost information available?
Are efficiency data reported periodically to management?
Are unit times compared among regions?
Are they compared with other organizations doing similar work in or out of government?

2. ARE PERFORMANCE STANDARDS SET FOR CRITICAL PROGRAM OUTPUTS?

Are time standards used?
What percentage of the work is covered by standards?
Are performance reports regularly prepared and distributed to persons responsible for performance?
Are standards used by supervisors of day-to-day operations to plan and schedule work?
Are the standards used in planning and budgeting?

3. IS PROGRAM EFFECTIVENESS MEASURED?

Are performance indicators available that address program effectiveness?
Do performance indicators include the target population, the level of service, and the desired impact?
Are measurable goals tied to indicators of program effectiveness?

4. IS THE QUALITY OF WORK PROPERLY CONTROLLED?

Are error and timeliness data maintained and reported on a regular basis? Are quality standards used?
Is quality of performance measured and reported on a regular basis?

5. IS OVERALL PRODUCTIVITY PERFORMANCE MEASURED?

Are measures used that combine effectiveness and efficiency by relating to results?
Are cost-effectiveness measures used?
Are the major cost elements identified for each program and are costs determined?

6. ARE METHODS AND PROCEDURES ANALYZED FREQUENTLY?

Are your managers currently aware of what others are doing in operations similar to yours?
Are mechanization and new technology continually reviewed for possible application to your operation?
Are staff specialists asked to make improvement studies?
Do supervisors and employees make suggestions on improving operational details?

7. ARE EMPLOYEES MOTIVATED TO PERFORM AT A SATISFACTORY LEVEL?

Are employees told how well they perform?
Are merit increases and awards tied to performance?
Are "quality of working life" motivational techniques used?

Source: National Center for Productivity and Quality of Work Life, *Improving Productivity: A Self-Audit and Guide.* Washington, D.C.: National Center for Productivity and Quality of Work Life, 1978, pp. 10–11, 13.

EXHIBIT 5–10   Book Circulation

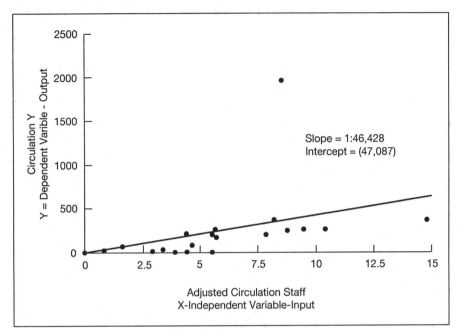

How does this type of analysis assist in the budget process? Essentially, the Book Circulastion regression line is the CY average productivity curve for the library system. Libraries to the left and above the line are more productive; hence, an examination can be undertaken to see what they are doing right. Of course, an examination can also be addressed to the least productive units. Another useful feature of this analysis is that any requested additional FTE circulation staff of a unit should generate, ideally, the normal productivity output. Budget analysts can query, "Will the library indeed generate the desired circulation, or will productivity be lowered if that additional staff is added?" Regression analysis can be useful in determining and fostering greater productivity.

Multiple regression is considered more useful than simple regression analysis because more independent variables can be used. Thus, it should yield a more accurate fit when compared to actual data. Normally, however, the number of variables should be kept to a minimum (for example, four).

Productivity and Budgeting

Agencies can strengthen their budget requests by citing productivity measures. Reviewing authorities normally more readily accept cost estimates based on data involving productivity. Those requests are more impressive and help establish agency credibility. Exhibit 5–13 is extracted from the 1975 U.S. Budget Appendix. It illustrates how hard facts strengthen the agency's justification of its budget even

EXHIBITS 5–11 and 5–12   Productivity for Libraries—Circulation Staff (Input): Circulation (Output)

LIBRARY OUTLETS	INPUT	OUTPUT	INPUT X	OUTPUT Y	x × y	x × x
BM	4.5	233170	4.50	233170	10429265	20.25
CP	2	62222	2	62222	124444	4
CR	3	2939	3	2939	8817	9
CC	4	4929	4	4929	19716	16
CS	10.7	238127	10.70	238127	2547958.90	114.49
D	3.6	25615	3.60	25615	92214	12.96
D/CC	0	0	0	0	0	0
DR	5.6	203404	5.60	203404	1139062.40	31.36
ER	8.3	406135	8.30	406135	3370920.50	68.89
H	9.7	236389	9.70	236389	2292973.30	94.09
HW	8.6	2048727	8.60	2048727	17619052.20	73.96
LL	8.7	227368	8.70	227368	1978101.60	75.69
LH	4.8	63214	4.80	63214	303427.20	23.04
M	8.8	234892	8.80	234892	2067049.60	77.44
MR	1	45184	1	45184	45184	1
MZ	4.5	7449	4.50	7449	33520.50	20.25
NL	4.7	55722	4.70	55722	261893.40	22.09
PP	1	50406	1	50406	50406	1
RL	5.7	137722	5.70	137722	785015.40	32.49
RI	5.5	5229	5.50	5129	28209.50	30.25
SR	14.7	355862	14.70	355862	5231171.40	216.09
SI	7.8	165386	7.80	165386	1290010.80	60.84
TM	5.7	277234	5.70	277234	1580233.80	32.49
Total	132.90	3243225	132.90	5087225	41918646.50	1037.67
Average	6.04	147419.32	5.78	221183.70		
Slope	46,427.57					
Intercept	-47,086.94					

$$b = \frac{n \sum x_i y_i - (\sum x_i) (\sum y_i)}{n \sum x_i^2 - (\sum x_i)^2}$$

$$b = \frac{6468219.11}{234.83} = 46,427.57$$

$y = bx + c$
$c = y - bx$
$c = 221,183.70 - (46,427.57)(5.78)$
$c = -47,167.65$

Note: Due to computer rounding, this number is 25.04 higher than these summary numbers indicate.

in an agency such as the Mediation and Conciliation Service. Exhibit 5–14 illustrates how productivity measures can be melded into a budget justification document. The most helpful data and measures are the following:

1. productivity indices that relate end products produced to manpower or cost measures;
2. unit cost ratios that relate work performed to all or a part of the cost of performing the work;
3. work measuring ratios which relate work performed to manpower needs in carrying out the work;
4. program or work load data that show trends in the program work; and
5. statistical data, such as regression analysis, that relate experience data to manpower.

EXHIBIT 5–13   Selected Illustration of a Presentation of Output Data in the 1975 Budget Appendix Federal Mediation and Conciliation Service Salaries and Expenses

The Service, under Title II of the Labor Management Relations Act of 1947, assists labor and management in mediation and prevention of disputes affecting industries engaged in interstate commerce and defense production, other than rail and air transportation, whenever in its judgment such disputes threaten to cause a substantial interruption of commerce. Under the authority of Executive Order 11491 of October 29, 1969, as amended by Executive Order 11616, dated August 26, 1971, the Service also makes its mediation and conciliation facilities available to Federal agencies and organizations representing Federal employees in the resolution of negotiation disputes.

1. *Mediation Service.* During 1973, dispute notices and other notifications affecting 117,884 employers were received by the Service. Cases totaling 21,745 were assigned for mediation, and 21,032 mediation assignments were closed during the year. About 89% of the mediation assignments closed which required the services of mediators were settled without work stoppages. A total of 26,973 mediation conferences were conducted by mediators during 1973. The workload shown above includes assignments closed in both the private and public sectors. Cases in process at the end of 1973 totaled 5,449; this is the normal carryover of open cases from month to month, with seasonal fluctuations. The following chart shows a five-year comparison of workload data:

DISPUTE WORKLOAD DATA

	1969	1970	1971	1972	1973
Cases in process at the beginning of the year	5,260	5,113	5,020	4,889	4,736
Mediation assignments	21,839	19,769	21,727	19,308	21,745
Mediation assignments closed	21,986	19,862	21,858	19,461	21,032
Cases in process at end of year	5,113	5,020	4,889	4,736	5,449
Mediation conferences conducted	31,605	30,334	32,293	29,223	26,973

Source: Extracted from p. 878 of the 1975 Budget Appendix

EXHIBIT 5–14   Illustration of Selected Agency Productivity Trends; The Defense Supply Agency

Since the activation of DSA, constant management attention to the basic goal of maximum efficiency has produced significant operating economies. In the early years of DSA, 1962–1966, increased productivity was realized through manpower reductions as numerous organizational and procedural improvements were effected. However, it was not until FY 1967 that a formal output and productivity evaluation system was installed. Since that time, overall output per man-year has increased almost 30 percent.

Chart I depicts the composite productivity trend for the agency from FY 1967 through FY 1973. The index shown was derived from the basic data which constituted DSA's input to the Government-wide productivity project. Improvement has averaged about 5 percent per year for the past six years. DSA currently employs about 52,000 military and civilian personnel in performing its assigned mission. Had the increase in productivity reflected on this chart not been realized, today's job would require about 10,000 more personnel than are currently employed.

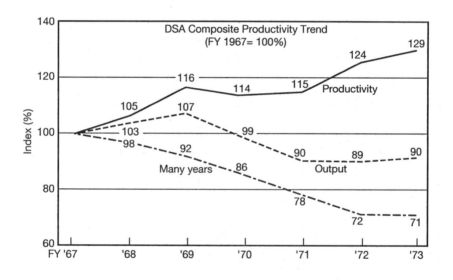

Source: Adapted from pp. 35–36 of the Joint Financial Management Improvement Program, "Report on Federal Productivity, Volume II: Productivity Case Studies," June 1974.

In a 1988 survey of American local governments, Glen Hahn Cope investigated the relationship of performance or productivity measures to improved productivity. Seventy percent of her respondents reported that the information developed for and used in the budget process was used for other management purposes in their government. Fifty-nine percent reported that the management and budget information was used to increase the jurisdictions' productivity. She also asked if the respondents thought that improvements in the budget process could actually improve their organization's productivity. Seventy-seven percent said yes. Cope concluded that budgetary information is not only useful for management purposes but it also contributes specially to improved local government productivity beyond its use in budgetary decision making.

THE BENEFIT-COST CONCEPT

Concept: What and Why

Benefit-cost analysis is based on the rather simple belief that projects should be judged on the basis of project cost versus project benefits. At best, benefit-cost analysis is a guide for investment decision. It can help decision makers decide if specific expenditures should be undertaken, if the scale of the project is appropriate, and what the optimum project size should be. Some treat benefit-cost analysis as a framework for a general theory of government investment.

Cost-effectiveness is sometimes confused with benefit-cost analysis, but there are advantages to maintaining the distinction. Cost-effectiveness assumes benefits and does not compare them with cost as in benefit-cost analysis. In cost-effectiveness analysis, the analyst wishes to determine the least costly means to achieve the objective. Frequently, all methods of analysis using inputs, alternatives, and outputs mean cost-effectiveness analysis, including benefit-cost. However, cost-effectiveness can often be the more effective analytical technique, and blurring the distinction between the techniques tends to blind practitioners to the comparative advantages of the techniques. Both have their advantages, but often cost-effectiveness can be used where benefit-cost is a meaningless technique.

The sophisticated benefit-cost analysis is useful. It can establish a framework for reasonably consistent and uniform project evaluations at the staff level. This can lead to added discipline in the political process because weak projects will appear inferior, thus making their funding difficult in an open political setting. The technique is most useful when the choice set is narrow and the decision involves economic alternative investments. The technique draws increasing criticism when intangibles and complex social values are present in the analysis. Value perspectives such as reallocation of wealth are not addressed well with benefit-cost analysis.

Benefit-cost analysis involves defining a *choice set, analytical constraint measurements*, and a *choice model*. Analysis must be made manageable so that work can be done within a reasonable time frame. Thus, parameters or range of projects must be established. Analytical constraints (for example, legal, political, distributional, financial, and physical) must be understood, stated, and either treated as side considerations of the analysis or included in the analytical objective functions. Benefit-cost analysis involves measurements; therefore, all the challenges and analytical limitations of data apply to benefit-cost analysis. Those challenges and limitations must be understood or serious analytical mistakes will be made and decision makers will be given misleading advice. A full treatment of this topic is beyond the scope of this text, but it is covered in books concerning research methods. The choice model is the means used to relate the estimated costs and benefits. It is the formula. The model (formula) is used to decide how the measures will be incorporated into the overall analysis.

Procedures

The procedures of benefit-cost analysis involve defining the *objective functions, benefits*, and *costs* as well as calculating present value. The objective functions specify without weighing the ultimate values used in the analysis. Examples include increasing national income, aggregate consumption, supply of foreign exchange, and employment. The functions must be quantifiable, or they cannot be treated in the analysis. Benefits are defined normally as the present value of the contributions in relationship to the objective function. Costs are sometimes defined in terms of reducing the objective function. They are also the present value of the resources that are employed and are valued as opportunity costs as a consequence of implementing the project.

The calculations in benefit-cost analysis are complex, owing to several factors. Both benefits and costs must be measured over time in order to permit a broad view of project impacts, especially economic consequences. Benefits are measured by the market price of the project outputs or the price consumers are willing to pay. Costs are measured by the monetary outlays necessary to undertake the investment. Both occur over time. Unlike the private sector, *externalities* (that is, project effects on others that occur because of the project's existence—such as downstream pollution from a plant) are calculated into public sector benefit-cost analysis. Also, opportunity costs are valued because full employment and scarce resources are assumed to exist. This means that some worthwhile choices are foregone once the decision is made to undertake the project, and this is a project cost. If the assumption is incorrect (for example, if full employment does not exist), then costs should be revised downward).

Alternative Choice Models

The decision on projects is often made by ranking alternative projects. The ranking depends on the choice model (formula) used. The various models do not give the analyst the same results. The four models are the following:

Benefit-cost	Based on discounted present value
Benefit/cost	Ratio of present value of benefits and costs
Rate of return or marginal investment	Discount rate that puts the benefits and efficiency costs at equilibrium
Payout period	Number of years of benefit needed so that the benefit equals the cost

Each model has its inherent bias. The benefit-cost model biases the decision in favor of large projects because of the manner in which the figures are calculated. Any deductions from benefits rather than adding to costs would affect ratios and thus would affect the benefit/cost model. If benefits or costs do not occur evenly over time, this may not be computed properly in mathematical models unless special provisions permit this unevenness.

Virtually all practitioners prefer the benefit-cost (discounted present value) model. It focuses on explicit treatment of budgetary and other constraints as well as project indivisibility and interdependencies. This model forces the separate treatment of those matters without confusing them with the determination of the proper discount rate. Also, calculation of present value is not a behind-the-scenes adjustment because it must be treated openly in the analysis.

Benefit-Cost Ingredients

A purpose of this chapter is not to explain how benefit-cost analysis is done but rather to stress the sophisticated analytical nature of the technique as well as the inherent limitations of the technique. Too many professionals advocate and even use the technique without understanding its true analytical sophistication. It is a worthwhile technique, and it should be studied by those interested in public budgeting. However, the first step is to recognize the complex nature of this type of analysis and to be especially sensitive to its limitations.

The remainder of this section examines key factors associated with benefit-cost analysis. Stress is placed on the limitations and cautions which should be associated with this technique. This stress is meant to sensitize the reader to the analytical problems associated with the technique. A full explanation of how to apply the technique is beyond the scope of this text, and readers are encouraged to learn more about this and other analytical techniques in further study.

Benefits and Estimation

Benefits are classified as *primary, secondary*, and *intangible*. Primary benefits are the values of goods or services resulting from project conditions. They are included in the analysis. Common examples are additional crops due to land irrigation and annual savings in flood damages. Associated costs (for example, seed for irrigated land) are subtracted from primary benefits. Secondary benefits either stem from or are induced by the project, but do not directly result from the project. Their inclusion as benefits is subject to controversy. Intangibles are nondollar-value benefits (for example, aesthetic quality of the landscape) which, by definition, cannot be included in the benefit-cost calculations.

What gets counted as "benefits" is important. Therefore, if the major benefits are intangibles, then the analysis often loses much of its worth. Also, if the major benefits are secondary, the inclusion of them is controversial and the resulting analytical conclusions would be subject to a complex debate involving the technique more than the project. The purpose of analysis is to aid decision makers, and the result of using controversial techniques is to confuse further the decision-making process.

Benefit-cost analysis is almost always used prior to the project's existence; therefore, costs and benefits are estimated over the projected life of the project. Cost estimates include construction engineering, relocation of households, erosion, and third-party effects. Benefits are harder to estimate, especially if they do not occur evenly over time. Decisions must be made on when to stop counting, what not to count, how to count, and how to aggregate benefits. These decisions may greatly affect the analysis; therefore, controversial decisions may lead to controversial analytical conclusions.

One commonly voiced concern is how to handle costs that have already been made (that is, *sunk costs*). This is not a controversial subject because they are treated almost uniformly as not relevant to the project cost and are not calculated. Sunk costs may be of significant political concern, but they are not added into the project cost.

Discount Rate

The most controversial ingredient of benefit-cost analysis is the *discount rate*. The controversy centers not on its proper role in the analysis, but on how it should be determined. It is significant because a higher rate means that fewer projects will be justified, especially if they have costs accumulating over a long period of time. The rationale for a discount rate is that the resources used in a particular project could have been invested elsewhere to yield future resources larger than the amount invested; therefore, this should be taken into consideration in the analysis.

Several approaches to determining discount rates are advocated. One says that a discount rate should have a bias toward present goods over future goods, whereas another argues for giving higher value to future goods. Others argue opportunity cost should be based on equivalent private investments, whereas still others say external effects should be added and subtracted from those private opportunity costs. The debate is endless, and most analysts end up by using an arbitrary interest cost of federal funds in a certain period to select a rate.

If the projects analyzed are similar in size and duration, then the rate used is not significant as long as the same approach is used for all projects. If not, then the analytical results become controversial.

Externalities, Risk, and Other Considerations

Externalities are included in benefit-cost analysis, but they are difficult to determine. *Technological externalities* involve the physical input-output relationship of other producing units. *Pecuniary externalities* involve the influences of the project on the prices of other producing units. For example, a public recreation facility may affect demand on, and thus the price of, nearby private facilities. Measurement of externalities is treacherous. Ideally, only "important externalities" are included in the analysis. Interestingly, the influence on the local wage rate is normally not included as "important." Controversy can easily surround the inclusion of externalities as well as the measurement of them.

Often benefits and costs involve *risk* and *uncertainty*. Risk can be described by a probability function normally based on experience. Uncertainty, in its purest meaning, is not subject to probability determination. This means that risk can be included in the analysis, but uncertainty cannot be included. Methods of calculating risk and uncertainty vary. Some methods establish a higher permissible rate than 1.0. Some use a higher rate of discount, and some rationalize the arbitrary benefit stream cutoff by referring to risk and uncertainty. An analyst can deal with risk by including a probability function in an already complex formula, but uncertainty by definition must be treated arbitrarily. Such treatment leads to controversy over the analytical results.

Two other considerations illustrate the complexity of this technique. As was pointed out, sometimes private opportunity costs are used to determine public project opportunity costs. The danger is that private market costs are higher owing to the different tax statuses and costs of financing. Another consideration is that user charges may not be independent of the benefit measures. User charges will restrict use, thus benefits will he reduced. Benefit-cost analysis requires a great deal of thought and care. If that professional treatment is not afforded, then embarrassing controversy can develop over the quality of the analysis.

Benefit-cost analysis is biased toward values associated with money. It does not work well with projects concerning social equality, and the poor tend to be discriminated against with this technique. For example, the value of life is often computed in terms of earning power, thus an airplane passenger is treated as worth more than a bus rider. Values such as equality of opportunity cannot be treated well with this technique. If the project involves such values, then the use of the benefit-cost technique itself will be controversial.

REVIEW QUESTIONS

1. Explain the budget system model, its consistency with democratic theory, and the importance of data measures.
2. Explain the various application difficulties associated with using the budget system model.
3. Compare and contrast a scatter diagram, marginal costs, and discounting. In what ways is each a useful analytical technique in budgeting?
4. Explain the significance of a crosswalk as an analytical tool. What would be crosswalked and why?
5. Compare and contrast qualitative, time series, and causal analysis approaches to revenue forecasting. Explain why good forecasting is important to government.
6. Compare and contrast the various approaches to expenditure forecasting.
7. Misunderstanding the productivity concept can lead to what types of difficulties? What are some of the most common reasons for government not to increase productivity? Why are there no simple uniform answers to the question of how to increase productivity?
8. Explain how regression analysis can help one achieve greater productivity.
9. Compare and contrast benefit-cost and cost-effectiveness analyses.

10. Explain why benefit-cost is a sophisticated and difficult technique to apply. Explain how benefit-cost analysis can be abused as a technique. How can benefit-cost analysis be counterproductive to decision making?

REFERENCES

BAHL, ROY, and LARRY SCHROEDER. "The Role of Multi-Year Forecasting In The Annual Budgeting Process For Local Governments," *Public Budgeting and Finance,* 4, 1 (Spring 1984), 3–13.

BURKHEAD, JESSE, and JERRY MINER. *Public Expenditure.* Chicago: Aldine, 1971.

Committee for Economic Development. *Improving Productivity in State and Local Government.* New York: Committee for Economic Development, March 1976.

COPE, G. H. "Walking the Fiscal Tightrope: Local Government Budgeting and Fiscal Stress," *International Journal of Public Administration,* 15, 5 (1992), 1097–1120.

DAVIES, THOMAS R., and JAMES A. ZINGALE. "Advanced Software for Revenue Forecasting: What to Consider Before Investing in Technology." Paper prepared for the 1983 American Society for Public Administration National Conference, New York, April 17, 1983.

FORRESTER, JOHN P. "Use of Revenue Forecasting Techniques." In Thomas D. Lynch and Lawrence Martin (eds.), *Handbook of Comparative Public Budgeting and Financial Management.* New York: Marcel Dekker, 1993, 149–167.

FOUNTAIN, JAMES R. "Governmental Accounting: Where Is It Heading," *Public Budgeting and Finance.* 7, 4 (Winter 1987), 95–103.

HATRY, HARRY R. "Overview of Modern Program Analysis Characteristics and Techniques: Modern Program Analysis—Hero or Villain?" Washington, D.C.: Urban Institute, 1969.

———, LOUIS BLAIR, DONALD FISK, and WAYNE KIMMEL. *Program Analysis for State and Local Governments.* Washington, D.C.: Urban Institute, 1976.

ISAAC, STEPHEN, in collaboration with William B. Michael. *Handbook in Research and Evaluation.* San Diego, Calif.: Edits Publishers, 1971.

KLAY, WILLIAM EARLE. "Revenue Forecasting: An Administrative Perspective." In Jack Rabin and Thomas D. Lynch (eds.), *Handbook on Public Budgeting and Financial Management.* New York: Marcel Dekker, 1983.

KLAY, WILLIAM EARLE, and GLORIA A. GRIZZLE. "Revenue Forecasting in the States: New Dimensions of Budgetary Forecasting." Paper delivered to the American Society for Public Administration at Anaheim, Calif., April 14, 1986.

KRAMER, FRED A. "The Discounting to Present Value Technique as a Decision Tool," *Special Bulletin 1976E* (November 24, 1976).

LAUTH, THOMAS P. "Performance Evaluation in the Georgia Budgetary Process," *Public Budgeting and Finance.* 5, 1 (Spring 1985), 67–82.

LEE, ROBERT D. Jr. "The Use of Program Information and Analysis in State Budgeting: Trends of Two Decades." In Thomas D. Lynch and Lawrence Martin (eds.), *Handbook of Comparative Public Budgeting and Financial Management.* New York: Marcel Dekker, 1993, 169–188.

McCOLLOUGH, JANE, and HOWARD FRANK. "Incentives For Forecasting Reform Among Local Finance Officers," *Public Budgeting and Financial Management.* 4, 4 (1992), 407–29.

MOAK, LENNOX L., and KATHRYN W. KILLIAN. *Operating Budget Manual.* Chicago: Municipal Finance Officers Association, 1963.

National Center for Productivity and Quality of Work Life. *Improving Productivity: A Self-Audit and Guide.* Washington, D.C.: National Center for Productivity and Quality of Worklife, 1978, pp. 10–11, 13.

PETERSON, J. E. "State and Local Fiscal Forecasting." In *Resources in Review.* Chicago: Government Finance Officers Association, 1979, p.16.

PLOTNICK, ROBERT D., and RUSSELL M. LIDMAN. "Forecasting Welfare Caseloads: A Tool To Improve Budgeting," *Public Budgeting and Finance.* 7, 3 (Autumn 1987), 70–81.

ROSS, JOHN P., and JESSE BURKHEAD. *Productivity in the Local Government Sector.* Lexington, Mass.: Heath, 1974.

RUBIN, IRENE S. "Estimated and Actual Urban Revenues: Exploring the Gap," *Public Budgeting and Finance.* 7, 4 (Winter 1987), 83–94.

SHANAHAN, EILEEN. "Cracks in the Crystal Ball," *Governing,* December 1991, 29–32.

SHKURTI, WILLIAM J. "A User's Guide to State Revenue Forecasting," *Public Budgeting and Finance,* 10, 1 (Spring 1990), 79–94.

STEWART, J. D. "The Role of Information in Public Accountability," In Tony Hopwood and Cyril R. Tomkins (eds.) *Issues in Public Accounting.* Oxford, Great Britain: Philip Allan, 1984, 14–15.

TOULMIN, LLEWELLYN M., and GLENDAL E. WRIGHT. "Expenditure Forecasting." In Jack Rabin and Thomas D. Lynch (eds.), *Handbook on Public Budgeting and Financial Management.* New York: Marcel Dekker, 1983.

Urban Institute and International City Management Association. *Measuring the Effectiveness of Basic Municipal Services.* Washington, D.C.: International City Management Association, February 1974.

U.S. Joint Financial Management Improvement Program. *Productivity Programs in the Federal Government.* Washington, D.C.: U.S. Joint Financial Management Improvement Program, July 1976.

VASCHE, JON DAVID, and BRAD WILLIAMS. "Optimal Governmental Budgeting Contingency Funds," *Public Budgeting and Finance,* 7, 1 (Spring 1987), 66–82.

WRIGHT, CHESTER, and MICHAEL D. TATE. *Economics and Systems Analysis: Introduction for Public Managers.* Reading, Mass.: Addison-Wesley, 1973.

6

ANALYTICAL
PROCESSES

In public budgeting, there are five analytical processes that are designed to help professionals deal more intelligently with their policy and administrative challenges. Each one—*program analysis, budget examination, process analysis, program evaluation*, and *auditing*—is briefly described here, but greater attention is given to budget examination and process analysis due to their central importance to public budgeting. The reports produced from each process should be viewed as normally useful input to better budgets. Program analysis looks *de novo* at the policy implications of programmatic budget decisions. Budget examination is the primary analytical process that actually produces the budget. Process analysis is a careful focus on the management process itself so that improvements can be identified. Program evaluation looks backward and helps the budget examiner decide if the program was effective or sufficiently effective to justify the requested money in the BY. Auditing is also reflective in character and helps the budget examiner focus on questions of both effectiveness and efficiency. The chapter will explain:

1. the approach essential for useful program analysis;
2. how budget examination can be undertaken using the various concepts and techniques explained in the text;
3. a useful approach to look closely at the process and identify process improvements;
4. the basics of program evaluation; and
5. the essentials of auditing, especially the types of information that can be forthcoming from a "good" program audit.

PROGRAM ANALYSIS

In program analysis—sometimes called policy analysis—the focus is on considering the new policy options that are implicit in the budget. Such analyses are often highly quantitative in character, but that need not be true. There are elements common to all program analyses, regardless of their character. A frequent complaint of high-level executive officials is that they really could not get the agencies to provide the information necessary to judge budget requests. Often this is more an admission of professional incompetency than a commentary on the budget process. If a reasonable effort, as explained here, is put into budget examining by competent professionals, then the central review staff will be in a position to make reasoned judgments based on agency requests and alternative policy options. Good program analysis should isolate sensitive policy questions and identify the likely implications of the various viable policy options within the limitations of the data and the analytical technique used.

Selecting Issues

Selection of potential issues can proceed systematically. What are the unsettled influential issues that determine program direction and emphasis? What issues are being raised by key influential people in the legislature, executive, clientele, media, and judicial settings? What are the apparent policy dilemmas facing the agency? The analysts can use these questions to develop a reasonable list of potential issues for analysis. Normally program issues are abundant. The usual problem is not to find issues but to select the best issues for program review purposes. The Urban Institute has developed the following criteria for selecting issues for analysis:

Importance of an Issue

1. Is there a decision to be made by the government? Can the analysis significantly influence the adoption of various alternatives?
2. Does the issue involve large costs or major consequences for services?
3. Is there substantial room for improving program performance?

Feasibility of Analysis

4. Can the problem be handled by program analysis?
5. Is there time for the analysis to be done before the key decisions must be made?
6. Are personnel and funds available to do the analysis?
7. Do sufficient data exist to undertake the analysis, and can needed data be gathered within the time available?

The first consideration is the importance of the issue. As suggested by the previous criteria, the potential significance of an analysis of the issue, the consequence, and the potential for improvement should be considered. If no one will use an analysis of an issue, then proceeding with the analysis is certainly foolish. Given a lack of time to perform analysis, the analyst is normally wise to concentrate on the big issue, especially if notable improvements are possible.

The next consideration is the feasibility of analysis. Many problems do not lend themselves to program analysis or the time available is so brief that useful analysis cannot be conducted prior to the time the key decisions are made. Personnel, funding, or data limitations may exist which preclude analysis. Each of these factors must be assessed honestly before work on program analysis begins or the effort may be worthless.

Exhibit 6–1 presents some illustrations of the issues that might be subject to program analysis.

Issue Assessment

Once the issues have been defined, a preliminary assessment can be made before an in-depth analysis is conducted. In most situations, an agency suggests issues, and the central budget office decides which issues to investigate. Those issues may or may not be the ones suggested by the agency. The involvement of the central budget office is wise as it helps to ensure the significance of the report once it is written, but the lack of a preliminary assessment of the issues is not wise. In far too many analytical situations, reports have been commissioned without a proper appreciation of what was requested. The instructions requesting the study may have been too vague or misleading. Another possibility is that further thought will reveal that there is no real need for an analysis, thus saving thousands or even millions of dollars. Preliminary assessments are extremely useful.

The issue assessment is a written presentation that identifies and describes the major features of a significant issue facing the government. The assessment is only a few pages long, but it clearly sets out the ingredients that would be considered in a major issue study. According to Harry P. Hatry of the Urban Institute (1976), the outline or major subjects in an issue assessment are as follows:

1. *The Problem.* What is the problem and its causes? Identify specific groups (e.g., the poor) affected. How are they affected? Identify characteristics of the group. How large and significant is the problem now? What are the likely future dimensions of the problem?

2. *Objectives and Evaluation Criteria.* Define the fundamental purposes and benefits of the program. Identify the evaluation criteria by which progress toward the program objectives should be judged.

3. *Current Activities and Agencies Involved.* Identify all relevant groups involved in attempting to deal with the problem. Identify what each group is doing, including costs and impacts. Activities, costs, and benefits should be projected into the future.

4. *Other Significant Factors.* Cite the other major factors, including political realities, that affect the problem. Identify unusual resources, timing limitations, or other factors of significance.

EXHIBIT 6–1   Illustrative Issues for Program Analysis

LAW ENFORCEMENT

1. What is the most effective way of distributing limited police forces by time of day, day of week, and geographical location?
2. What types of police units (foot patrol, one- or two-officer police cars, special task forces, canine corps units, or others) should be used, and in what mix?
3. What types of equipment (considering both current and new technologies) should be used for weaponry, for communications, and for transportation?
4. How can the judicial process be improved to provide more expeditious service, keep potentially dangerous persons from running loose, and at the same time protect the rights of the innocent?
5. How can criminal detention institutions be improved to maximize the probability of rehabilitation, while remaining a deterrent to further crime?

FIRE PROTECTION

1. Where should fire stations be located, and how many are needed?
2. How should fire-fighting units be deployed, and how large should units be?
3. What types of equipment should be used for communications, transportation, and fire fighting?
4. Are there fire-prevention activities, such as inspection of potential fire hazards or school educational programs, that can be used effectively?

HEALTH AND SOCIAL SERVICES

1. What mix of treatment programs should do the most to meet the needs of the expected mix of clients?
2. What prevention programs are desirable for the groups that seem most likely to suffer particular ailments?

HOUSING

1. To what extent can housing-code enforcement programs be used to decrease the number of families living in substandard housing? Will such programs have an adverse effect on the overall supply of low-income housing in the community?
2. What is the appropriate mix of code enforcement with other housing programs to make housing in the community adequate?
3. What is the best mix of housing rehabilitation, housing maintenance, and new construction to improve the quantity and quality of housing?

EMPLOYMENT

1. What relative support should be given to training and employment programs that serve different client groups?
2. What should be the mix among outreach programs, training programs, job-finding and matching programs, antidiscrimination programs, and postemployment follow-up programs?

WASTE

1. How should waste be collected and disposed of, given alternative visual, air, water, and pollution standards?
2. What specific equipment and routings should be used?

(continued)

EXHIBIT 6–1 (*continued*)

RECREATION AND LEISURE

1. What type, location, and size of recreation facilities should be provided for those desiring them?
2. How should recreation facilities be divided among summer and winter, daytime and nighttime, and indoor and outdoor activities?
3. What, and how many, special summer programs should be made available for out-of-school youths?
4. What charges, if any, should be made to users, considering such factors *as* differential usage and ability to pay?
5. *Alternatives.* Describe alternative programs designed to meet the problem and the major characteristics of each.
6. *Recommendations for Follow-up.* Making choices among alternatives is inappropriate because, by definition, this work is only an assessment. Recommendations can be made on the next administrative step (for example, full-scale analysis). What is the best timing for and scope of the needed follow-up analysis? Should the analysis be a quick response or an in-depth study? Frank descriptions of analytical difficulties should be cited. What major data problems exist? How should they be dealt with under the circumstances?

Source: Harry Hatry, Louis Blair, Donald Fisk, and Wayne Kimmel, *Program Analysis for State and Local Government.* Washington D.C.: The Urban Institute, 1976, p. 11.

The assessment serves as the basis for deciding to request a special analytical study and for framing instructions for the study.

Commentary on Analysis

The conduct of analysis largely depends upon the subject *to* be analyzed, the context of the study, and the techniques used. Each of these subjects is outside the scope of this chapter and can be studied properly under the heading of microeconomics, operations research, systems analysis, and statistics. Chapter 5 discusses some elementary analytical concepts useful in budgeting as well as in explaining benefit-cost analysis.

There are ten factors—five technical and five bureaucratic—that particularly influence the results of analysis. Those factors are the following:

1. study size;
2. study timing;
3. methodological adequacy;
4. consideration of implementation;
5. nature of problem studied;
6. decision-maker interest;
7. implementor's participation;
8. single-agency issue;
9. proposed changes in funding; and
10. immediate decision needed.

There are five factors that appear to be more significant than the others. The three most significant "technical" factors are study timing (that is, studies were well timed so that study findings were available at key decision points); consideration of implementation (that is, studies included an explicit consideration of political and administrative issues that might affect implementation of study findings); and nature of problem studied (that is, studies focused on well-defined problems rather than on broad or open-ended ones). The two most significant "bureaucratic" factors are immediate decision needed (that is, issues that could not be deferred by policy makers); and decision-maker interest (that is, issues in which decision makers had shown clear interest).

In program analysis, care must be taken to avoid four common mistakes that occur as a result of an unrealistic desire to analyze for the sake of analysis. One mistake can be labeled "search under the lamp." A well-known story tells of the man who was searching at night for his lost watch, under a street light. A friend comes by and offers to aid in the search. The friend asks where the man lost the watch, and the man replies that the watch was lost half a block up the street. The friend then asks why the man is searching next to the street lamp. The man answers that the light is much better under the street light. In policy analysis situations, analysts often will concentrate their investigation on those aspects that are easy to measure and downplay the aspects difficult to measure. Thus they are looking under the street lamp instead of "up the street" where the watch was lost.

Another common mistake is to become fascinated by technique. An intellectual challenge for an analyst is to use and develop more sophisticated analytical—often mathematical—techniques. The normal desire is to select issues that require complex techniques or use more complex techniques when simpler ones would be adequate. Analysts should address the analytical problems and not techniques, otherwise there is means-ends confusion.

A third mistake is to delay reports and even policy decisions so that analyses can be performed for their own sake. Analysts can be consumed with interest in the analytical question, much as some people are consumed by crossword puzzles, mysteries, and good books. This consuming interest can overwhelm the original reason for the analysis. As was pointed out earlier, report timeliness is critical, and sometimes analytical purity must be sacrificed for timeliness.

The fourth mistake is to overanalyze. In some situations, a good analyst quietly thinking for a few hours may produce results equal to or better than an army of survey researchers. We automatically tend to use certain well-known approaches to analysis without appreciating their limitations and the tolerance for error implicit in the issue being studied. The advantage of the issue assessment mentioned earlier is to avoid such a mistake.

A final commentary on analysis is that there may be only "poor" solutions to problems. This commentary may seem obvious, but this realization is often difficult for decision makers to accept. If a program analysis is conducted and only "poor" solutions are cited, the decision maker can conclude either that solutions are indeed "poor" or that the analysis was bad. Thus, the analyst can be placed in an awkward position. The only professionally acceptable course of action is to be sure that no desirable answers exist and to explain this fact properly in the analyst's report.

Presentations of Results: Some Prescriptions

A common failure of program analysis is poor presentation of study results. The work itself may be excellent, but the presentation is inadequate.

The first advice on presenting results is to review them carefully before they are distributed. The pressure of meeting a deadline and the distasteful chore of proofing combine to discourage proper review of papers before they are distributed. These final checks are essential if embarrassing mistakes or insensitive political statements are to be avoided.

Report findings should be in writing. Oral reports are useful, but they should supplement or summarize written reports. Written reports provide the essential record, which is often useful even years after a report was prepared.

Care must be taken to prepare compact, clear summaries. The summary is normally the first important portion of the report that is read—the other material may never be read. Long, vague summaries are counterproductive, as they discourage use of the report.

In most program analysis reports, two or three options are discussed. If only one option were discussed, then the credibility of the report would be questioned. Many options only tend to confuse matters. Two or three options are adequate normally to illustrate the varieties of solutions. If the range of solutions is broad, the presentation of only two or three options is done to illustrate the types of solutions.

Studies must set out limitations and assumptions. Professional standards alone require such candor. On a more practical level, professional reputation and confidence are enhanced by frank, honest reports. A decision maker may not like the qualifications, but if something goes wrong, the analyst is protected by that candor. Also, the decision makers are apprised fully of the risks inherent in their decisions.

Studies should discuss potential windfalls and pitfalls related to the issue. *Windfalls* are collateral benefits resulting from actions and decisions. *Pitfalls* are collateral hazards or disadvantages. Both can be overlooked easily in the analyses and by decision makers. The potential for oversight is the reason why this material should be in the report.

The studies should contain simple graphics where possible to communicate major findings and conclusions. Most readers will benefit from both written and graphic explanations. Graphics should not stand alone—reference should be made to them in the text. Complex graphics should be avoided because readers may not be able to understand them.

Clarity requires that jargon be avoided. If a special vocabulary is well known and used, then such jargon (for example, "piggyback containers," "subsystem") can be used. Jargon is the shorthand means of communication. However, most program analysis reports are meant for managers and other decision makers unschooled in the jargon; thus, it only makes the paper difficult to read.

Reports and studies should be written for the decision makers. Authors of reports and studies should know who are the intended and likely users of their work. What are the backgrounds, knowledge, and biases of the report and study users? If the users have extensive technical knowledge, then authors should use that fact in preparing the report. If the user has strong biases and the report finding runs counter to those biases, then greater care should be taken to explain and fully document the findings.

From the public budgeting perspective, one of the most obvious failures in the presentation of program analysis results is the omission of an explanation of how the recommendations should be translated to operational management direction. People working in budgeting are interested in policy debates and analysis, but their lives involve operational decisions. Study findings and recommendations must be translated to the operational before they can be treated as something more than a possibility. Exactly in what ways should the current program be changed? What specifically are the present and future budget implications? These questions should be addressed in the program analysis reports and studies if they are to be meaningful to the budget process.

Role of the Chief Executive

The product of program analysis is meant for decision makers, especially chief executives. If there is support from the chief executive and that person uses the products of program analysis, then there is a reasonable chance that program analysis will be significant in the government decision-making process. On the other hand, without top-level support and use, program analysis as an activity is worthless. Detailed top-level involvement is not needed, but the following types of involvement are essential. According to the Urban Institute (Hatry 1976), officials should:

1. participate actively in the selection of program and policy issues for analysis;
2. assign responsibility for the analysis to a unit of the organization that can conduct the study objectively;
3. ensure that participation and cooperation are obtained from relevant agencies;
4. provide adequate staff to meet a timely reporting schedule;
5. insist that the objectives, evaluation criteria, client groups, and program alternatives considered in the analysis include those of prime importance;
6. have a work schedule prepared and monitored periodically; and
7. review results and, if findings seem valid, see that they are used.

BUDGET EXAMINATION

An important activity in the budget process is budget examination, which uses other forms of analysis and specific analyses to review agency budget requests and make staff recommendations to legislative and executive political leaders. This section explains how budget analysts can perform sophisticated budget examination within the context of democratic government, complex technology, and current analytical techniques.

Information Sources

Reviewers are not limited to the agency budget submission in forming their analysis and conclusions. Information can be obtained from the budget submissions, hearings, reports that may be available, other information such as newspaper stories, and answers to specific questions prior to and after budget hearings. The most important information source is normally the agency budget request because it directly addresses the information needs of the budget reviewer. Hearings are also a valuable information source, as they can be used to focus on specific inquiries. Hearings permit direct oral interchange between the agency and the reviewers. Reviewers should also make use of any available reports, such as special analytical studies and program evaluation reports. This type of information often is not organized well for budget analysis purposes, but studies and reports do provide useful insight and suggest areas of fruitful inquiry. Other information sources, such as national media reports and books, can also be extremely helpful in framing inquiries.

Specific questions by reviewers and answers by agency officials are valuable to budget reviewers. These questions and answers can occur before and after hearings. They can be oral or written depending upon the reviewers' request. The major limiting factor is time. Rarely are questions asked prior to budget submissions because the submissions may contain the answers. If there is a short time interval between the submission and the hearing, then written questions and answers may be impossible—normally at least five working days are needed to develop answers, have them approved by top agency personnel, and have them typed and transmitted. If there is an equally short time interval between the hearing and the central budget office decision on the budget, then, again, written questions may not be possible. Time pressures dictate that the answers must not require new analysis but use existing information.

The key to an outstanding budget review is for the reviewer to gain the necessary program information and insight. No one source of information is adequate, and many inquiries can be tailored for the situation. The advocate wishes to anticipate inquiries so that confidence in the agency budget personnel can be enhanced. Both the examiner and the analyst preparing the submission have in common a set of information. One wishes to know the information and the other should be ready to supply the information. What can a good budget examiner look for and what should a good agency budget analyst be able to provide?

Code of Ethics

Ethical considerations are significant and do tend to be overlooked until a crisis occurs. Improper conduct can mean fraud, impotent and frustrated policy, inefficiency, counterproductive management practices, and an inability on the part of the professional to develop professionally. In 1989, Thomas P. Menson surveyed the National Association of State Budget Officers (NASBO) to identify their opinions on what ethical issues were most important in budgeting. Thirty-five states responded. Seventeen identified not having impartiality, including outright collusion, and fifteen identified conflict of interest as important ethical issues to them. Other issues noted less frequently were accuracy, gubernatorial loyalty, confidentiality, fairness, objectivity, honesty, compliance with codes and statutes, integrity, credibility, quality of work, and responsiveness.

Both the American Society for Public Administration (ASPA) and the Government Finance Officers Association (GFOA) have codes of ethics. Exhibit 6–2 displays the GFOA Code of Professional Ethics.

EXHIBIT 6–2   GFOA Code of Professional Ethics

The Government Finance Officers Association of the United States and Canada is a professional organization of public officials united to enhance and promote the professional management of governmental financial resources by identifying, developing and advancing fiscal strategies, policies and practices for the public benefit.

To further these objectives, all government finance officers are enjoined to adhere to legal, moral and professional standards of conduct in the fulfillment of their professional responsibilities. Standards of professional conduct as set forth in this code are promulgated in order to enhance the performance of all persons engaged in public finance.

I.   Personal Standards

Governmental finance officers shall demonstrate and be dedicated to the highest ideals of honor and integrity in all public and personal relationships to merit the respect, trust and confidence of governing officials, other public officials, employees, and of the public.

- They shall devote their time, skills and energies to their office both independently and in cooperation with other professionals.
- They shall abide by approved professional practices and recommended standards.

II.   Responsibility as Public Officials

Government finance officers shall recognize and be accountable for their responsibilities as officials in the public sector.

- They shall be sensitive and responsive to the rights of the public and its changing needs.
- They shall strive to provide the highest quality of performance and counsel.
- They shall exercise prudence and integrity in the management of funds in their custody and in all financial transactions.
- They shall uphold both the letter and the spirit of the constitution, legislation and regulations governing their actions and report violation of the law to the appropriate authorities.

III.   Professional Development

Government finance officers shall be responsible for maintaining their own competence, for enhancing the competence of their colleagues, and for providing encouragement to those seeking to enter the field of government finance. Finance officers shall promote excellence in the public service.

(continued)

EXHIBIT 6–2 (*continued*)

IV. Professional Integrity–Information

Government finance officers shall demonstrate professional integrity in the issuance and management of information.

- They shall not knowingly sign, subscribe to, or permit the issuance of any statement or report which contains any misstatement or which omits any material fact.
- They shall prepare and present statements and financial information pursuant of applicable law and general accepted practices and guidelines.
- They shall respect and protect privileged information to which they have access by virtue of their office.
- They shall be sensitive and responsive to inquiries from the public and the media, within the framework of state or local government policy.

V. Professional Integrity–Relationships

Government finance officers shall act with honor, integrity and virtue in all professional relationships.

- They shall exhibit loyalty and trust in the affairs and interest of the government they serve, within the confines of this Code of Ethics.
- They shall not knowingly be a party to or condone any illegal or improper activity.
- They shall respect the rights, responsibilities and integrity of their colleagues and other public officials with whom they work and associate.
- They shall manage all matters of personnel within the scope of their authority so that fairness and impartiality govern their decisions.
- They shall promote equal employment opportunities, and in doing so, oppose any discrimination, harassment or other unfair practices.

VI. Conflict of Interest

Government finance officers shall actively avoid the appearance of or the fact of conflicting interest.

- They shall discharge their duties without favor and shall refrain from engaging in any outside matters of financial or personal interest incompatible with the impartial and objective performance of their duties.
- They shall not, directly or indirectly, seek or accept personal gain which would influence, or appear to influence, the conduct of their official duties.
- They shall not use public property or resources for personal or political gain.

Source: Government Finance Officer's Association, *Code of Professional Ethics*. Chicago: GFOA, 1988.

Ethical considerations are significant and do tend to be overlooked until a crisis occurs. The code of ethics which follows is part of the handbook for budget analysts in the state of Florida, and its purpose is to guide the professional conduct of state budget analysts. The role of budget examiners and the proper carrying out of their responsibilities is critical to a successful budget process. Improper conduct can mean fraud, impotent and frustrated policy, inefficiency, counterproductive management practices, and an inability on the part of the examiners to develop and grow as professionals and as members of an organization.

The following code of ethics and its implications should guide professional conduct.

EXHIBIT 6–3   State of Florida Code of Ethics

1. *No gifts or favors may be accepted by a budget analyst beyond minor social courtesies which have little or no significant value.* This first ethical principle is obviously intended to prevent corruption and improper influence on analysts by actors in the political process. It is critical (1) if objectivity, as well as the confidence of others in that objectivity, is to be maintained; and (2) if the policy issues are to be determined through the democratic process. As stated, it does not require the analyst's total separation from influencing factors, but such a separation is not inconsistent with this principle. Some budget offices do require total separation because of the importance of the analyst's being free from the possibility of any improper influence.

2. *The role of the analyst does not extend to independent action which establishes government policy.* Analysts are expected to gather information, analyze it, and recommend policy with appropriate supporting data and documentation. Their purpose is to raise the level of debate associated with policy making, not to make policy. Budget analysts are staff functionaries whose job is to help the true policy makers—the elected officials and their appointees. They are called on to provide useful information to help the political decision makers arrive at more enlightened decisions. Often, examiners judge their success by how much they shaped policy rather than by their role in creating an environment in which more enlightened decisions are more likely to occur. As long as the budget analyst is part of a political system in which overriding policy is established by elected officials, the examiner should view his or her role as advisory. If the examiner's advice is not taken, no professional failure occurred unless his or her presentation of that information tended to inhibit enlightened decision making.

3. *Examiners must maintain their objectivity, which includes presenting all aspects of issues fairly and excludes advocating an agency's position for any purpose other than to clarify the issues.* Being emotionally committed to the agencies under review is one of the hazards of budget examination. Analysts must avoid becoming staff advocates of agency requests; instead, they must remain detached so that they can critically examine budget requests. This presents a staffing dilemma for budget offices. On the one hand, examiners must be involved with a line agency long enough to know the complexities of that agency; on the other hand, examiners must not be coopted, which does tend to occur over time. There is no simple way to deal with this ethical principle, but it is important that the spirit of the principle be respected.

4. *Every attempt must be made to ensure that managerial decisions are made by the proper line officials.* Managers must make their own decisions, whereas analysts must be free to comment on those decisions and to facilitate a more thoughtful decision-making process.

5. *Analysts must avoid acting in an arrogant manner to anyone, including other government officials.* Analysts may have their own strong opinions, but these opinions must be kept under control. Sensitivity and respect for feelings must be shown to all individuals who are part of the budget process. Examiners are staff advisors and not managers of line government units. A professional problem stemming from the examiner's unique access to high officials and role as overseer of the budget process is a tendency to substitute his or her own decisions for those of the line manager. Sometimes the examiner will arrogantly demand information on some policy change from the line manager. Sometimes a line manager, as a ploy to escape responsibility, will ask the staff budget to make managerial decisions (e.g., whether to buy or lease equipment). In either situation, the examiner must recall that his or her responsibility is primarily advisory and he should maintain a cordial working relationship with the line manager.

6. *In framing recommendations and in dealing with the bureaucracy, the examiner must make every effort to foster and improve the quality of government management.* Recommendations and accompanying information should be sensitive not only to policy considerations but also to the managerial environment needed to accomplish that policy.

(continued)

EXHIBIT 6–3 (*continued*)

7. *The professional development and growth of the examiners is important.* Budget analysts must continually strive to understand the substantive policy and management issues associated with the units being examined. Analysts must also strive to improve their budget examination skills and knowledge so that better work can be performed. Improved government quality does not occur automatically and improvement usually comes only after a struggle. Given other policy and management concerns, budget analysts can easily overlook or fail to emphasize the improvement of government management as a continuing priority. Ironically, examiners are in a unique position to foster and encourage those improvements. For example, funds for professional development tend to be ignored rather than treated as one of the fringe benefits associated with employment for a progressive organization. The budget analysts should insure that such matters are not overlooked. Professional development also applies to the examiner. The tendency is to become involved in the daily tasks and neglect one's own professional development. Thus, this ethical principle calls upon analysts to recognize the importance of their own professional growth and to pursue it by means of formal education, training, and professional conferences.

Source: Thomas C. Foss and Thomas D. Suttberry, eds. *State Budgeting in Florida: A Handbook for Budget Analysts.* Tallahassee: Florida State University, Public Managers Training and Advisory Service, 1983.

Services Performed

Results of services performed are important. The budget examiner determines the services or types of services that are anticipated from the planned budget. Historical information can be used to illustrate the type of service likely to be provided as well as to establish the reliability of the agency to perform as planned. The budget submission often indicates objectives and states likely products of the agency. The examiner looks beyond specific outputs and tries to ascertain the likely impacts on society and individuals directly and indirectly due to the program. And, unanticipated good and bad effects are considered. It is helpful if the information is available in the budget request. If not, the information may be available in speeches or program evaluation reports.

The agency normally has an excellent explanation of its likely outputs. Any budget is a plan requiring forecasting, so every budget must be tentative, since there is no guarantee the events will evolve as planned. This is accepted; if something else were said, the budget examiner would question the realism of the agency. The character of the explanation of output and projected benefits depends on whether the program is *demand-responsive* or *directed*. Demand responsive programs react to individuals and groups that meet the agency's general criteria of need and seek assistance. In contrast, directed programs are established to fulfill a specific need and are managed directly by government. Demand-responsive programs are grants-in-aid and direct benefit (for example, food stamps) programs. In demand-responsive programs, the government cannot control the rate or type of demand; thus, it is conditioned by outside factors. In directed programs, the government has a high degree of control over exactly what it will do.

Budget examiners can probe direct programs for the management plan of the agency. The agency normally has a detailed plan of how it will use its resources to achieve specific outputs. It should have a definite fix on the likely benefits and spillover effects of the program. The examiner's role is first to make sure such a plan exists, and second, to see that the plan has a reasonable chance of being successful. The plan and management should be flexible enough to meet likely contingencies.

Budget examiners handle demand-responsive programs differently. Budget examiners probe these programs in terms of anticipated demands and likely outputs and benefits. Agency management should have excellent forecasts of likely demand. The agency should have prepared an analysis of various likely funding scenarios and estimated the likely outputs and benefits of each scenario. To the extent that the agency can control its ability to meet the program demand, the agency should be able to explain what it can do and the significance of its action in terms of the scenarios and resulting outputs and benefits. If the agency cannot provide these explanations, then its ability to manage the requested funds properly can be strongly questioned.

If the budget examiner ever sees vagueness in the information provided, this can serve as a red flag to the examiner. Vague subjects can be isolated carefully because vagueness indicates possibly serious managerial problems. If agency management does not know how to deal with a situation or if there is serious internal conflict, then agency budget officers must be vague about those situations in the budget request because the uncertainty cannot, by definition, be resolved. Good budget officers may be able to minimize the problem but they cannot abide the use of a vague answer. Budget examiners can probe carefully the exact reason for the vagueness. The explanation may be merely a poor presentation rather than management difficulties. If the vagueness is isolated early enough, questions and hearings can be used to determine the exact nature of the problem. This probing requires skill; but unless the agency budget officer directly lies, the budget examiner can isolate the problem, given enough time. Even in the rare cases in which the agency personnel lie, a skillful examiner can normally isolate the problem because logical consistency is difficult for liars to maintain.

Program Inputs and Outputs

The budget examiner should determine key input, process, and output measures. These concepts are explained in more depth in Chapter 5. Briefly, there are measures that tend to be more useful than others. These indicators show the resources going into the program, what activities are taking place, and the results attributable to the program. These measures are used for comparative and trend-analysis purposes. By performing elementary analysis, the budget examiner can determine questionable program budget requests and poor management practices and can identify important changes in the program's environment that are not correctly reflected in the budget request.

Exhibit 6–4 is a checklist used by the city of Los Angeles to review performance reports. Notice how the budget examiner is sensitive to the interrelationship of input, process, and outputs. The examiner maintains a questioning, arm's length relationship with the agency.

EXHIBIT 6–4   Checklist for Review of Performance Reports

GENERAL

1. Check total gross man-hours for department with the combined total standard hours plus paid overtime hours as shown for each pay period on the IBM Personnel Audit Reports of the Controller (on file in Budget Administration Division).

PERSONNEL

2. Have any new activities or sub-activities been added over those shown in original work program?
3. If so, how many positions are being used? Cost estimate?
4. Are any previous activities or sub-activities eliminated or curtailed?
5. If so, how many positions which were included in last year's work program have been eliminated? Cost estimate?
6. Net increase or decrease in cost as result of additions and deletions?
7. Are there any special projects on which work was performed on a one-time basis only?
8. If so, what sub-activities were affected and how many man-hours were devoted to such special projects?
9. How does the actual number of personnel utilized compare with the number of authorized positions?

MAN-HOURS

10. Where both net man-hours and gross man-hours are reported, what is the percentage of net total to gross total? Are there any sub-activities which have lower percentages than the overall average percentage? Which are they and how much variation from average is there? What are the causes? (Vacations, sick leave, other absences?)
11. How does actual work performed compare with the estimate for each sub-activity?
12. Has there been an increase or decrease in the number of personnel actually utilized over last month's figures?

MAN-HOURS PER UNIT

13. How does the gross man-hours per unit for each sub-activity compare with last month's figures?
14. How does the net man-hours per unit for each sub-activity compare with last month's figures?
15. What is the reason for any increase or decrease?
16. In sub-activities where work performed and work unit are comparable, what is the variation between gross man-hours per unit for such sub-activities?
17. What is the variation between net man-hours per unit for such sub-activities?

OVERALL APPRAISAL

18. Based on the above analysis, could any employees have been transferred temporarily during slack periods?
19. If so, how many and in what classes of positions?

(continued)

EXHIBIT 6–4 (*continued*)

20. Based on the previous analysis, were any additional employees required to handle peak loads?
21. If so, how many and in what classes of positions?
22. Were there any backlogs of work resulting from lack of sufficient personnel?
23. If so, how much?
24. What class of personnel and how many employees would be required to eliminate backlogs?
25. Are backlogs the result of seasonal variations? Of improper scheduling of vacations? Of greater than normal absences due to sickness? Of unfilled positions? If the latter, what is the recruitment situation?
26. At the end of each quarter, determine what percentage of last year's annual program has been completed for each sub-activity.
27. Will the remaining portion of the annual program be completed by the end of the current fiscal year if that rate of progress is maintained?
28. Will more or less personnel be required in each sub-activity to complete annual program?
29. If so, how many and in what classes of positions?

Source: Los Angeles, California, City Administrator's Office.

The budget examiner can also check the accuracy of tables and data supplied by the agency. Exhaustive checks are not necessary, but any uncommon results, important statistics, and common places where errors occur can always be checked. Tables can be checked by observing if there is proper internal consistency among tables. Often totals of summary columns can be checked against other summary columns for internal consistency. Simple arithmetic errors do occur even in the most important budget requests. Commonly errors occur when incorrect pay rate scales are used or when personnel are placed in the wrong classification.

Budget examiners can review carefully the money requested and can be sensitive to hidden revenue sources or "sleight-of-hand" tricks. This is a conventional spender's strategy, and the diligent reviewer can determine when such a strategy is being used. The examiner must be well versed in back-door spending techniques and must know if any of them can be used by the agency. The examiner can profit from the use of accounting reports. Use of fund transfer, lag time among administrative reservations, obligations, expenditures, and closing of accounts can be significant in determining hidden revenue. Other types of hidden revenue or improper expenditure estimates require considerable knowledge of the programs, but examiners can sometimes find such savings. For example, possibly the program can use existing government facilities rather than rent or lease new property. Another possibility is an interagency or intergovernmental cooperative management agreement, which would allow savings as a result of economy of scale.

For the budget examiner, detailed tables from agencies isolate personnel by grade, type, unit, and status (permanent, temporary, part- or full-time). A critical resource is always personnel. Does the agency have too many or too few personnel for the assigned task? Maybe the agency has enough people, but they are of the wrong grade or type, or are poorly distributed among the units. Two common problems occur when an agency overexpands its highest ranks and fails to reallocate its personnel once a major task has been accomplished. Examiners cannot address such questions without detailed information on personnel. Another problem occurs when the personnel hired are not properly trained to handle upgraded and more complex work requirements. Judgments in this area must be predicated on a knowledge of the personnel as well as of the new challenges facing the agency. Budget examiners can often profit by comparing the agency's overhead and direct costs. A common mistake in bureaucracies is to allow *overhead* (that is, those people and costs that serve to make the agency operate) to grow at the expense of *direct costs* (that is, those people and costs that perform the activities directly associated with the agency's mission). Examples of overhead are personnel, legal, housekeeping, and budget activities. The proper size of overhead and even the definition of overhead are topics subject to debate. Ideally, overhead should be large enough to facilitate agency effectiveness and efficiency. In some situations, the overhead activities can grow to a point where agency effectiveness and efficiency are actually decreased. The budget examiner can examine the facts and determine if overhead is becoming excessive.

The data can be used to identify relationships between program demands and workload. For example, there tends to be a positive identifiable relationship between the population under the age of 25 in an area and the number of parole officers needed. If such relationships can be verified, then the examiner is in a much better position to judge the budget request.

Trends on program inputs and outputs are valuable information for the budget examiner. For example, if resources have been increasing and outputs decreasing, then serious questions must be raised concerning the efficiency and possibly even effectiveness of the program. What are the causes underlying trends and deviations from the apparent natural trend? Does there appear to be any positive or negative relationship between and among trends? For example, does salt tend to be more effective than sand in alleviating snow conditions? This answer can lead to suggestions resulting in the use of cheaper substances while maintaining the same level of service to the public.

Comparative data on program inputs and outputs are also valuable information. What do comparable cities spend for the same type of services? What levels of output do they achieve? What explains the differences? Can those positive advantages be achieved in the budget examiner's city?

Emphasis and Change

Whether the budget request is presented in incremental or zero-base format, the budget examiner needs information on yearly budget emphases and changes in emphases from prior years. Decision makers wish to know how much stress is being placed on a given program relative to other program efforts. Balance is a political consideration, thus it is useful information for decision makers. They also wish to know if the agency is shifting its policy from previous years. This can best be determined by comparing the budget request with previous budget requests and actual obligation/expenditure patterns.

Budgets can be categorized into various logical subdivisions. A single categorization is probably inadequate for the variety of analytical needs of the budget examiner. One categorization should reflect the major agency tasks, projects, and continuing activities. Another categorization may be necessary to relate the inputs (for example, dollars requested) to agency goals and intended benefits. However, often one categorization may be sufficient for both purposes if the agency is not handicapped by multiple inconsistent objectives. A categorization using line-item information is normally not useful because various purposes can lie behind the use of the same items of expenditure.

Categorizations can provide comparative information over several fiscal years. Dollars requested and possible specific inputs and outputs can be presented in terms of the prior year, actual current year estimates, budget-year estimates, and possibly budget-year-plus-five estimates. Such a display of data permits comparative analyses by fiscal year. Thus, program increases and decreases over time can be isolated.

Complex programs, involving contracts extending beyond the budget year, can be misleading in terms of increases and decreases. Obligations can be made for continuing, expanding, or starting programs. The decrease or increase in a given fiscal year only gives useful information on the rate of obligation, and says nothing about the use of the money. The categorization in such programs should indicate the changes in the funding level of programs divided into subcategories of continuing and expanded programs. And, any new programs can be identified as such. As noted in Chapter 3, the spender's strategy calls for the use of flexible definitions by the spender. The budget examiner can understand the nature of each program so that definitions and categorizations can be challenged.

The previous categorization and related work are all designed to help the budget examiner identify emphases and shifts. What programs, projects, activities, or tasks are receiving greatest stress? This is judged in the context of the available resource, the maximum effort that could be given, and the relative emphases among the programs. Each is important in judging "emphasis." What programs, projects, activities, or tasks are receiving increased or decreased support? To answer that question fully, the budget examiner discovers whether changes are addressed to existing or new programs. Also, the examiner relates the change to program outputs, including anticipated benefits or harm to society and individuals. This analysis helps answer the follow-up question: Is the change worth it? Budget examiners seek *hard data* and get *written responses* to this type of inquiry in order to avoid later misunderstandings between the examiner and agency officials.

Program and financial plans (PFP) are required periodically (quarterly or semiannually). They are summary tables of the budget, categorized by major programs and activities. In the federal government, the PFP includes both obligations and disbursements; however, obligations are normally sufficient for state and local government purposes. The information covers the past year, current year, budget year, and budget-year-plus-five.

The PFP should be analyzed by the examiner for patterns reflecting policy and consistency with previously established management policy. The PFP should reflect any changes in policy, and it is particularly useful prior to the budget call to forecast possible agency requests. Quick comparisons against past PFPs can be made to see if an evolution in policy is occurring. If changes are not occurring, the agency should be questioned, because agency policy is rarely constant and lack of change reflects a neglect to update the PFP. The PFP is an advance warning, and the examiner can encourage the agency to use the PFP in that manner.

Responsiveness

A major concern of a budget analyst is to be sensitive to the concerns of elected political leaders and appointees and insure that existing programs are carrying out established policy. In gathering information and examining programs and their issues, budget analysts seek useful data that reflect upon the policy matters significant to the legislators. Budget examiners should identify all major policy concerns in their area that pertinent political officials would wish to understand in terms of their budget decisions. Examiners should try to identify desired new programs, changes in existing programs, and desired analyst follow-through on programs and projects considered important legislatively.

Even in unusual years when tax receipts are particularly high, few funds are available for all desired improvements in existing programs and new programs. Resources for new and improved programs are normally small, but that does not mean that new programs should automatically be disregarded. Improved programs are prime candidates for funding if:

1. they result in unit-cost savings in those programs where growth is inevitable (use unit-cost analysis and marginal-cost analysis);
2. the improved program can be an alternative to other current programs (use cost-effectiveness analysis);
3. the improvements can generate benefits in the area economy over the cost of the program (use benefit-cost analysis); or
4. a case is made that intended political outcomes are significant in terms of the values of pertinent political officials.

New programs are prime candidates for funding if:

1. they are mandated by current law to begin in the BY; or
2. a cost-effective alternative exists to current programs (use cost-effectiveness analysis).

If the above conditions exist, the budget examiner should bring them to the attention of the political appointee when new or improved programs are being considered. An examination should identify the likely program outcomes, the groups positively and negatively affected, and the effect on those groups. This is particularly true of new or improved programs; political officials should be apprised of the implications of such programs so that they can take intelligent positions on them. In addition, examiners should be able to explain the theoretical linkages between direct budget amounts and government action, services and products produced, and program outcomes on society and individuals.

Analysts must be convinced such linkages exist, and any doubts should be shared with pertinent political officials. The desired outputs should lead to the desired outcomes in the BY and specified years beyond the BY. Programs should be reviewed for timeliness, appropriateness, and necessity. The desired inputs and planned management activities should lead to the desired outputs in the BY and beyond. This requires the examiners to be sure each program is funded at least at the minimum level for viable operations. This is done by defining the minimum useful output level and by being sure the input level (for example, salaries, expenses, and equipment) can produce that desired output level.

Examiners review current programs to determine outmoded, nonproductive, duplicative, overlapping, or very low priority programs or parts of programs. When this occurs, examiners should fully document and carefully justify recommendations because agency opposition is likely. If required, statutory, ordinance, or regulation revisions should also be recommended and all costs, including staff, should be deleted. Cost-effectiveness analysis might be especially useful here.

Effectiveness and Efficiency

A major concern of budget examination is program effectiveness and efficiency. The budget analyst's focus should be on the adequacy of the planned management processes to ensure that the programs will be managed correctly. The examiner should be confident that intended outputs and outcomes will be achieved. The best evidence for this is the agency's established track record of achievement. Beyond that, the budget analyst should be confident that administrative or outside factors will not prevent the intended outputs and outcomes from occurring. Such confidence is normally acquired by site inspections and inquiries to agency officials to see if they have anticipated properly the likely administrative and outside factors that could interfere. Examiners should review programs for documented workload change. Was there unavoidable growth in workload that cannot be absorbed? Conversely, workload decreases should be noted. In both situations, adjustments in staffing, expenditures, and other resources should be considered. Unit cost and marginal cost analyses might be particularly useful. Input to output ratios (productivity measures) are very useful and can be of interest to political officials. Marginal analysis is particularly helpful in determining the optimal input level for the most effective program operation.

Normally, maximum use should be made of nongeneral revenue sources rather than the general fund. Examiners should examine user fees, grants, trust funds, and internal service funds to be sure that they cover the maximum amount of expenses permitted in order to take pressure off the general fund. Unit cost analysis is useful in determining proper user-fee charges. At the state and local levels, analysts should seek full justification from former or reduced federally funded programs.

A common failure of government agencies is not to aggressively recruit and develop employees, especially professional employees. Specific sums of money should be earmarked for professional development, including education, training, and professional conferences. Care should be taken to document carefully how the professional development improves employees. Politically inappropriate travel must be carefully avoided.

Interagency staff harmony and interagency and intraagency cooperation can achieve efficiencies. Examiners should determine if agencies' support processes (for example, budget, personnel, general services) work in harmony and provide consistent management direction and control. This can be done by site visit or by questioning agency personnel.

In this day of rapidly advancing technology, analysts should be sure that each agency is taking advantage of modern technology to improve the quality of government services and achieve greater efficiencies. Examiners should determine the type of program—for example, capital purchase or leasing—that can be used to improve program output and efficiency.

Exploring Private Options

If a public activity can be transferred to the private sector, then taxes are potentially less and another source of taxes can be created. Therefore, one task of a budget examiner is to explore the possibility for policy makers of using private approaches for the delivery of public services. The following actions can be taken sometimes to involve the private sector in public programs in a useful way:

1. contracting out;
2. giving franchises;
3. giving grants and subsidies to help someone else do the job;
4. providing vouchers;
5. substituting volunteers for government employees;
6. encouraging self-help and do-it-yourself efforts;
7. altering regulations or tax policy;
8. encouraging private agencies to take over an activity;
9. otherwise reducing demand for services, through marketing;
10. obtaining temporary help from private firms;
11. using fees and charges to adjust demand; and
12. forming joint public-private ventures.

Each of the above actions has consequences for both service levels and costs. If demand for government services can be reduced, then costs can be cut. Altering regulations or tax policy as well as increasing fees can reduce demand for government services. Another means to lower demand is to confront the problem directly by a variety of marketing techniques. People can be encouraged to alter their behavior in constructive ways. For example, public education programs can be used to discourage unnecessary calls for ambulances, to encourage water conservation, to encourage the use of car pools, to reduce smoking, to dial "911" for emergency calls, and so on.

Sometimes the public services can be maintained but at a lower cost. For example, contracting out a service (for example, garbage collection) to a private company can sometimes reduce taxpayer cost and still maintain service levels. Labor costs are usually a large cost item in government. If tasks can be done by volunteers, then cost savings can be significant. Another device is to get a temporary loan of help from a private firm. Hiring a permanent expert is more expensive than getting temporary assistance for a short period of time.

Another desirable consequence of private sector involvement is to reduce government service by transferring part of the demand to the private sector. One way to do this is for a local government to award a franchise to a private firm to provide service within a certain geographical area. This is often done with ambulance and mass-transit service. A second approach is to provide a grant or subsidy to the private sector to have them provide a specific service. This approach is used sometimes by local government for social welfare services such as child care, assistance to the homeless, and so on. A third approach is to use vouchers. This is sometimes done for medical services. Instead of providing a hospital for the poor, government provides vouchers to poor citizens needing hospital services. They, in turn, can select their own hospital. A fourth approach is to encourage self-help. The government encourages individuals or groups, such as neighborhood associations, to undertake activities for their own benefit. Examples are the programs of Alcoholics Anonymous and neighborhood clean-up campaigns.

An excellent means to raise more money and take the burden off the major tax source is to apply or increase user fees. If that policy is adopted, there should be some means, such as a voucher policy, to deal with the question of economic equity when low-income people may be excluded from public services. Vouchers have the added advantage, in some circumstances, of often improving the quality and responsiveness of services to the public. If the service is publicly provided, the economy of scale or public pressure may result in minimum staff resources being used for an important purpose. If the service is privately provided with a voucher service, then the voucher user can take advantage of a much wider range of units that offer the needed service. The major problem with a voucher system is that an illegal secondary market (that is, a black market) in resold vouchers can easily exist. This allows voucher holders to sell them and not receive the services contemplated by public policy. If care is not taken, voucher systems can easily be corrupted.

Forecasting

Budgeting is always future-oriented, and predicting the future is important in terms of both revenues and expenditures (see Chapter 5). Normally, a government has many revenue sources, of which the largest are usually forecasted by a central authority such as the chief state economist or county budget office. The smaller revenue sources tend to concern specific departments and are forecasted by them. Analysts should verify department forecast accuracy by comparing past forecasts and actual money received. In addition, the examiner should verify agency expenditure forecasts by checking past-year accounting reports, developing comparative cost data, and checking to avoid improper inventory build-up. For demand-responsive programs, analysts should normally use marginal utility analysis; but for one-time projects, analysts should review cost estimates, especially in relationship to construction time assumptions. Careful examination of Program Evaluation and Review Technique (PERT) time and PERT costs can be particularly useful in determining the reasonableness of the expenditure forecast. Care should be taken to review prior-year nonrecurring expenditure summaries in order to ensure that CY projects and programs do not extend improperly into the BY. Care should also be taken to identify actual and potential nonplanned cost escalations.

An interesting approach to government forecasting is called "consensus forecasting" by the state of Florida. The legislature's Division of Economic and Demographic Research prepares revenue forecasts, recommends formula budgeting, and prepares expenditure forecast models for state's programs. In doing this, the unit uses a remarkably large database, extensive computer capability, and complex economic models. Economic data are acquired from major national economic forecasting organizations and are added to the unique data collected from state sources. In addition, data are gathered on state education, criminal justice, and social services. All these combine into the Florida database and are used with an econometric model containing 123 simultaneous equations. The result is a Florida economic forecast that is critical in developing forecasts for state revenues, education expenditures, criminal justice expenditures, and social service expenditures. The data are also used to develop education, criminal justice, and social service formula budgets. Whenever possible, analysts should seek comparative program data. Often, other public or private agencies are doing something similar to the agency being examined. By contrasting input, process, output, and outcome data, the analyst is in a much better position to judge forecasting accuracy. If another agency in a comparable government is doing the same thing for less money, that fact is helpful.

A common mistake made by examiners is not to demand and receive an accurate analysis of future-year operating expenditure implications of large capital and nonrecurring cost projects. Building a new facility is one consideration, but maintaining it properly is yet another matter. Budget examiners should seek such analyses, and fiscal implications should be explained carefully to the political decision makers.

Politically Sensitive Subjects

Both political and professional officials discover that there are sensitive management practices in which error can lead to serious political or managerial consequences. Examiners should identify those areas, check on the frequency of errors in those areas, and be sure that existing control procedures are adequate. Budget analysts should identify any occurrences of politically or managerially embarrassing or illegal actions, especially in such sensitive areas as travel (with special stress on out-of-state travel), energy use, authorized positions, capital outlays, consulting, and mainframe computers. An analysis of such matters should isolate inadequate control procedures and determine if existing or planned control procedures create a counterproductive management hardship on line officials.

Two expense items normally should be zero-base and fully documented. Temporary employment and consulting are not meant to be a regular personnel expense, but that can occur. Careful attention should be paid to ensure that this line-item category is not being abused. Data processing is not only an expensive line-item category, but one that should be watched carefully. Early decisions tend to commit management to certain future hardware and software decisions. However, given the extreme rate of technological advancement, care must be taken to ensure that proper decisions are being made and reviewed each year.

Detailed Budget Examination

Detailed budget examination involves looking carefully at (1) salaries, benefits, and temporary employee expenses; (2) price-level increases for expenditures; and (3) operating, capital outlays, and trust fund schedules. Normally, across-the-board cost-of-living expenses are calculated separately by the central budget office. Agencies are commonly asked to continue CY annual rates for authorized positions, modified for any appropriate productivity improvements. Budget analysts normally use agency information to calculate lapsed salaries rather than use an overall lapse factor. Care should be taken to examine vacancy rates as well as salary funds that have been transferred or have reverted to other line categories. Commonly, new positions are assumed to be at minimum current pay rates, with all necessary benefits included; benefits are calculated as percentages of the salary base. Examiners should confirm the rates and calculations. Budget analysts may find matrix algebra to be extremely useful in making these adjustments.

In calculating current program expenses, examiners normally start with CY levels and adjust them for program reductions and modifications. Care should be taken not to drop the input to levels below which desired output becomes impossible. Deductions from current estimated expenditures should include nonrecurring and nonessential items, nonessential inventory build-ups, and expenses for deleted or lapsed current positions. In normal years, inflation increases are allowed at the wholesale price index level, but these may not be at a flat percentage. If one or more categories dominate the expenses, price increases for those categories should be treated separately. If unusual price changes occur in significant items (for example, insurance, telephone, travel), they should be calculated separately. Data processing expenses also must be reviewed carefully. Budget analysts should balance user unit costs against the data center's information. Examiners should use a general services schedule for rental space and the current market rate for private space. Rates can be unnecessarily high due to choice location or unnecessary colocation requests.

Budget analysts should be sure that each equipment item is justified. State or local contract prices should be used and additional equipment requests should be fully documented and verified. Equipment replacement should be done by means of standard rules unless specifically requested with full documentation. Examiners should be sure that inventory levels and practices are justified. Often governments use general and specific guidelines for commonly purchased items. These guidelines should be used in judging equipment requests.

Special attention should be given to grant and trust programs. Normally, policy makers prefer not to replace federal cuts with general revenue funds unless the basic intent of a necessary program is seriously jeopardized. State and local governments prefer funding "in kind" rather than "cash matching." Budget analysts should ensure that jointly funded programs maximize federal and trust (for example, user fee) receipts as well as leave justifiable ending balances. All calculations that produce beginning and ending balances, including trust fund investments, should be carefully examined. Normally, small working capital amounts are allowed to cover cash flow requirements.

Automation

The budget preparation process can be automated, and various activities in that process are commonly automated. For example, revenue forecasting and preparation of budget allocation formulas are often automated. The former activity often involves a great deal of data, and the latter involves not only large data sets, but also "what if" types of analysis using those data sets. Some jurisdictions use computers to "roll up" the data from the lowest units to higher levels of aggregation. A few jurisdictions have a comprehensive automated budget preparation process. Normally, the weakest aspect of the system relates not to computers, but to failure to acquire good performance (output or outcome) measures.

Regardless of the scope of automation, the keys to understanding automation are to use systems theory and to think backwards from the products of the automated system. A simple input-process-output system model is central to automation. One defines the products and then designs the process and inputs to get the desired outputs (products). In budget preparation, the most important output can be the appropriation act. However, it can be the revenue estimate report. Hardware (that is, the computer and related equipment) and software (that is, the instructions to the computer on how to manipulate the data) should be defined in relationship to the desired output reports. The input reports are the means to get the necessary data into the computer.

Automation can mean that "data crunching," consideration of "what if" possibilities, preparation of complex multiple consistent crosswalks, and even performance of various types of analysis can be done more accurately and faster with a computer. It permits much more sophisticated analysis and higher-quality budgeting. Automation also means a new set of complexities, including frustration when massive data sets are "lost" and computer breakdowns occur. Increasingly, automation will be more common as hardware becomes less expensive and more useful software is developed.

The microcomputer has particular relevance to the budget process and the electronic spreadsheet is especially significant software. Given the many tables employed in budgeting, commonly used tools are the multiple column and row light-green paper, plus the calculator. The electronic spreadsheet is the modern replacement for those tools. The grandfather of the electronic spreadsheet is the VisiCalc® program which was conceived in 1978 by Daniel Bricklin and Robert Frankston. The VisiCalc program produces spreadsheets of 63 columns or more by 254 rows. However, the advantages go much beyond a very big sheet of data. The sheet is organized with letter labels for columns and number labels for rows. Thus, one can identify each cell of this very large matrix (for example, A24, G2, M150, AA50). One of the strengths of the electronic version is that the user can use a formula to derive the answer for each cell and the formula can be stated with other cells as variables in the formula. Thus, a cell's value can be calculated by entering 7 + 13 or entering "add cell B24 (with a value of 7) to cell G177 (with a 13 value in it)." This permits use of complex interrelations of data, which we commonly need for analysis and accounting. Analytical problems, such as purchasing decisions, often use sets of data arrayed by columns and rows. Thus, they are well suited for the electronic spreadsheet. Some analytical tools, such as the crosswalk, are ideally suited.

The major frustration with light-green ledger paper is the reality that mistakes are made, new ideas require major changes, and "what-if" analyses are often needed. The results are many erasures and versions of the first spreadsheet. The power of the electronic spreadsheet is the ease of making modifications. Rows and columns can be added even in the middle of the spreadsheet. Any data changes are automatically recalculated, saving time and eliminating mistakes. Thus, errors can be changed quickly and new ideas can be added easily. The most dramatic strength is that "what-if" analysis becomes dramatically easier. Instead of preparing new sheets and running the calculator on all the new numbers, the user merely finds the cells that contain the key variables, and makes the changes. Automatically and within seconds, all the numbers are recalculated. Some electronic spreadsheets, such as Lotus 1-2-3®, can take a set of cells and convert them into graph, pie, and bar charts. More advanced software permits the user to link electronic spreadsheets. For example, in budgeting, let us assume we have a spreadsheet for each unit of government. In order to prepare aggregate information, some of the most important numbers must be "rolled-up" to the department and government level. This can be done by linking spreadsheets so that the entire set of spreadsheets can be updated when we enter changes in the unit's spreadsheet.

Microcomputers are a big hit in budgeting and financial management. Exhibit 6–5 shows their positive influence on managerial concerns. There have been improvements in the areas of employee satisfaction, decision-making, the mainte-

nance of schedules, and the meeting of budget limits. Exhibit 6–6 shows the
remarkable effect on productivity in various tasks. Notice the improvements in
budgeting, cash management, financial modeling, and forecasting. Clearly, the
microcomputer is radically changing the manner in which public budgeting and
financial management is done.

EXHIBIT 6–5 Microcomputer and Managerial Concerns

CONCERNS	VERY POSITIVE	POSITIVE	NO CHANGE	NEGA-TIVE	VERY NEGA-TIVE
Employee Satisfaction	23.9%	56.1%	18.6%	1.1%	.3%
Worker Health	2.0	7.1	89.8	.6	.6
Employee Communications	4.5	29.4	65.0	.6	.6
Job Reductions	4.2	13.2	79.4	2.5	.6
Loss of Management Control	2.4	10.1	84.6	1.7	1.1
Security of Information	3.9	17.9	73.1	4.5	.6
Quality of Decision	17.9	59.4	22.1	.3	.3
Maintenance of Schedules	14.1	45.4	40.0	.3	.3
Meeting Budget Limits	10.2	31.8	56.8	.6	.5

Source: John W. Ostrowski, Ella P. Gardner, and Magda H. Motawi, "Microcomputers in Public
Finance Organizations: A Survey of Uses and Trends," *Government Finance Review*, February
1986, p. 26. Used by permission.

EXHIBIT 6–6 Productivity and the Microcomputer

TASK	SUBSTANTIAL INCREASE %	MODERATE INCREASE %	NO CHANGE %	DECREASE %
Accounting	44.9	41.9	12.1	1.0
Billing	35.3	39.7	23.5	1.5
Budgeting	51.2	41.8	5.5	1.6
Cash Management	50.0	39.4	10.1	.5
Financial Modeling	51.8	39.1	9.1	0.0
Forecasting	51.0	42.5	6.5	0.0
Inventory	34.7	39.6	24.8	1.0
Payroll	34.0	35.1	27.8	3.1

Source: John W. Ostrowski, Ella P. Gardner, and Magda H. Motawi, "Microcomputers in Public
Finance Organizations: A Survey of Uses and Trends," *Government Finance Review*, February
1986, p. 27. Used by permission.

In a May 1986 survey, Stanley B. Botner determined the extent, nature, and
impact of microcomputers in the fifty state central budget offices. His results are
reported in Exhibit 6–7. It shows extensive use of microcomputers and continuing
mainframe use.

Exhibit 6–7   Data Processing Support

FUNCTION	MICRO NO.OF STATES %		MAINFRAME NO.OF STATES %		COMBINATION NO.OF STATES %		NONE NO.OF STATES %	
Prep. budget worksheet	11	22.9	13	27.1	23	47.9	1	2.1
Rev. forecast.	16	33.3	5	10.4	25	52.1	2	4.2
Exp. forecast.	9	18.8	7	14.6	24	50.0	8	16.7
Dev. budget inc. budgetary alter.	9	18.8	14	29.2	22	45.8	3	6.3
Appro. bill tracking	16	33.3	19	39.6	10	20.8	3	6.3
Control of exp.	2	4.2	30	62.5	12	25.0	4	8.3
Budget reports	6	12.5	15	31.3	25	52.1	2	4.2
Special projects and studies	24	50.0	2	4.2	19	39.6	3	6.3
Program analysis prior to enact.	21	43.8	4	8.3	8	16.7	15	31.3
Program evalu.	16	33.3	5	10.4	9	18.8	18	37.5
Productivity analysis	18	37.5	2	4.2	7	14.6	21	43.8

N=48

Source: Stanley B. Botner, "Utilization and Impact of Microcomputers in State Central Budget Offices," Public Budgeting and Finance, 7, 3 (Autumn 1987), p. 101.

PROCESS ANALYSIS

Focus

The purpose of process analysis, in the context of public budgeting, is to help the line managers and the budget analyst understand the existing bureaucratic process between organization input and output. It is not an attempt to define the optimal process that will most effectively use available resources, although a by-product might be that determination. It does seek to determine if the existing process is an effective use of resources and to identify idle or poorly used resources.

This subtle stress in process analysis for public budgeting can be overlooked. When examining a budget, the analyst is seeking insight that will help higher-level decision makers and foster improved management within the organization. The budget analyst must always appreciate that a staff function is being performed and that the line-unit supervisor is responsible for managing his or her unit. The analyst is only an aid to the manager and other higher-level managers and policy makers in the government. Thus, process analysis in the context of budget examination is not striving necessarily to find the optimal process as that task is really the responsibility of the line manager. Instead, process analysis here is used only to help others make reasonable judgments on the effectiveness of the existing process and the quality of management in that unit.

Steps

The steps in process analysis are as follows:

1. define programs within the organizational divisions of the government;
2. define the minimum level of service for each program; and
3. develop a flow chart for the process of each program.

Defining programs and minimum levels of service are difficult professional challenges. In order to foster greater managerial accountability, programs normally should be defined within specific lowest-level organizational units in a government. The defined programs should be the major sets of activities in an organizational unit that produces specific projects and services. If programs cut across organizational units, then both managerial and fiscal accountability are much more difficult to establish and maintain. A major problem in defining sets that are identified as programs and sometimes forcing such "fits" is that it may discourage needed managerial cooperation. Nevertheless, defining programs is very useful and helpful managerially for most administrative situations.

The problem of defining a program's "minimum level of service" is often a difficult challenge. "Minimum level of service," as notably used in ZBB, is the lowest amount of resources needed to conduct the program as a viable administrative undertaking. The professional challenge for the budget analyst is that line managers nearly always consider their present level minimum, and they tend to refuse to consider the possibility of lesser amounts than what they are currently using. The best approach to take is to define with the manager the existing inputs and outputs. Then, the analyst starts posing "what if 5 percent less, 10 percent, and so on" situations to seek clarification of what would happen to the outputs. Next, the analyst should attempt to determine the impact of those smaller outputs upon the program outcomes. This may become a problem because some managers have difficulty conceptualizing their program and program outcomes. Normally, some reasonable minimum level of service becomes apparent after some discussions.

Flow charting the process of each program involves identifying, first, what activities take place in the unit, and, second, who does what aspect of each activity. The latter should include an estimate of the percentage of time in a work week devoted to each activity by each person or class of employees in the unit. Flow charting gets the line manager away from broad superlatives about the virtues of programs and focuses on exactly what the unit does. The first document presents the unit's activities; normally, this is best defined by stating the trigger actions within the unit (for example, a phone call from a client) and charting what follows until the unit produces a specific service or product. The chart, which can be done in several ways, should show the relationship of the steps to each other. The chart shows the activities done on a day-in and day-out basis (see Exhibits 6–8 and 6–9). The second document identifies who does what activity, the payload and position description of each person, and the percentage of time on each activity (see Exhibits 6–10 and 6–11).

EXHIBIT 6–8   Daily Activities

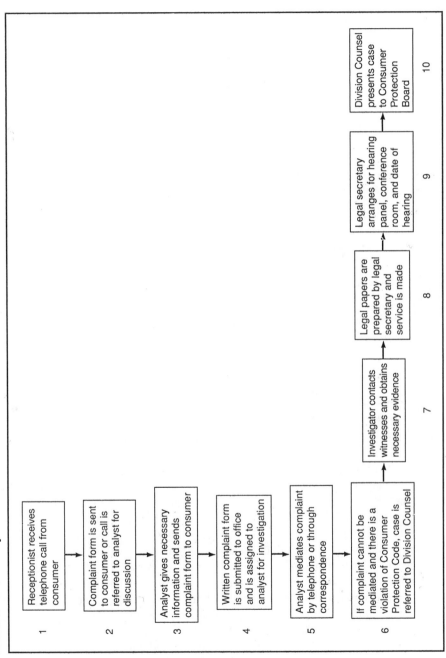

1. Receptionist receives telephone call from consumer

2. Complaint form is sent to consumer or call is referred to analyst for discussion

3. Analyst gives necessary information and sends complaint form to consumer

4. Written complaint form is submitted to office and is assigned to analyst for investigation

5. Analyst mediates complaint by telephone or through correspondence

6. If complaint cannot be mediated and there is a violation of Consumer Protection Code, case is referred to Division Counsel

7. Investigator contacts witnesses and obtains necessary evidence

8. Legal papers are prepared by legal secretary and service is made

9. Legal secretary arranges for hearing panel, conference room, and date of hearing

10. Division Counsel presents case to Consumer Protection Board

Source: Broward County, Florida, 1983.

EXHIBIT 6–9   Daily Veteran's Office Activities

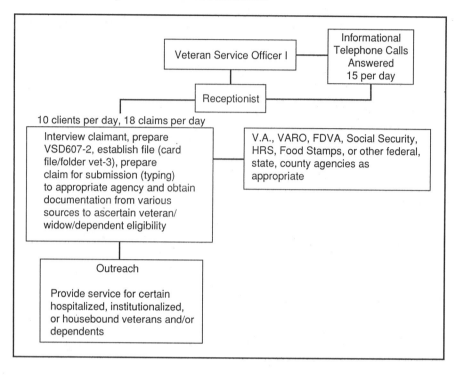

Source: Broward County, Florida, 1983.

   The limitations of process analysis for the budget analyst are primarily those of time and organization size. The budget calendar forces the budget analyst to work within a finite time frame. Thus, normally the necessary time is not available to do this time-consuming analysis. Priority of the analyst's time is decided by the current politically hot or managerially sensitive units. Depending on the nature of the political or managerial concerns and the budget offices' appropriate role, those factors will determine which programs should or should not be analyzed by the budget analyst.

   Organizational size is a limitation because the technique is most effective with small units (less than twenty persons). For larger organizations, techniques such as regression analysis of specific inputs and outputs are effective. For example, in a large decentralized urban library system, a regression analysis (see Chapter 5) was used which related input (that is, full-time positions used in circulation) to output (that is, books circulated by specific branch libraries). A scatter diagram was used and a linear regression line was drawn. The line represented the system's productivity for the book circulation program. Deviations identified successful and unsuccessful "program management" and permitted longitudinal and comparative data analyses. The process-analysis tool should be used, in connection with the regression analysis, to determine the most and least successful units.

EXHIBIT 6–10   Staff Analysis

Section Supervision:	1 Assistant Director <u>1</u> Secretary - I Total 2
North Network:	4 Family Counselor I 2 Family Counselor II 1 Family Counselor III 1 Network Supervisor 1 Secretary - I
Central Network:	3 Family Counselor I 2 Family Counselor II 1 Family Counselor III 1 Network Supervisor 1 Secretary - I
South Network:	3 Family Counselor I 1 Family Counselor II 1 Family Counselor III 1 Network Supervisor <u>1</u> Secretary - I Total 24 + 1 psychologist = 25 employees
Child Care Program:	1 Child Development Specialist I 4 Child Development Specialist II 1 Program Supervisor (C.D.S. III) <u>1</u> Secretary - I Total 7
Directed Job Search:	1 Special Projects Coordinator <u>1</u> Secretary - I Total 2 SECTION TOTAL: 36

Average client service per direct-service employee = 643 clients, which provides only 2.7 hours per client per employee, based on a (1) one-time service frequency. Average client is seen eight (8) sessions (8 hours of direct services, plus required indirect services).

Source: Broward County, Florida, 1983.

EXHIBIT 6–11   Performance Time Analysis

This analysis reflects performance on a monthly basis. The "available" hours are calculated by multiplying 37.5 x 4, which equals 150 available working hours.

STAFF:	Family Counselor II - 5 employees.	
Screening:	Attendance is required because of therapeutic knowledge Average screening time is 2 hours per week Average time per month:	8 hours

(*continued*)

EXHIBIT 6–11 (*continued*)

Counseling Services:	Individual and family counseling with a caseload of 38 cases	
	Average time required per session:	1 hour
	Average time estimated per month (some clients require additional time if family is in critical state or has several members)	80 hours
	Average time estimated per month in recording/ case documentation (3 hours per week): entry in case file per session is required	
Group Counseling:	These are not youth groups as facilitated by Family Counselor I; these groups are multi- problem family groups whose children are acting out with evidenced delinquency.	
	Average number of groups per quarter is 4	
	Average number of hours estimated per month:	32 hours
	Average recording time per month:	1 hour
Special Community Assignments:	Respond to communities who need assistance in developing youth programs and preventing local juvenile crime. Communities request speakers and parent/community groups request a one-time parenting skills or problem solving workshop.	
	Average number of engagements, workshops; meetings attended per month is at 3 hours per session.	2
	Average number of hours per month:	6 hours
Support Services:	Attend case staffings at school, attend in-house staffings (attendance required).	
	Participate in case consultations with psy- chologist.	12 hours
	(Average staffing attended = 4 per month; average length of staffing is 2 hours)	
Crisis Counseling:	Provide immediate intervention to walk-in clients.	
	Average walk-ins for crisis counseling is 15 clients per month.	
	Average counseling session in crisis counseling is 2 hours	30 hours
	Total # of workload hours required vs.	181 hours
	Total # of work hours available	150 hours

This difference in hours required and hours available has made it necessary for us to minimize assistance to community groups. It has further reduced the quality in case documentation and has required some clients to be placed on every-other-week and sometimes monthly service cycle. Our involvement in multiproblem family groups has already been reduced. This continued cutback will result in less effective results of diverting youth from the juvenile justice system.

Source: Broward County, Florida, 1983.

The limitations of time and organization size are largely mitigated by a patient budget office. The constraint of a fiscal budget year is limiting that period, but over time, the entire government can be examined carefully using process analysis. Any information acquired but not used in one set of budget decisions can be used in subsequent budget decisions. Even the limitation of organizational size can be overcome. A regression analysis can be used to isolate the best and the worst. With that insight, process analysis can be targeted and, thus, used more effectively. If in a large organization, the necessary data is not available to do the desired regression analysis, a patient budget office will seek to develop the necessary data and then to use it.

Advantages

The advantages of process analysis are that it provides a useful snapshot in time that (1) helps us to understand the inner workings of an organization, (2) identifies ineffective use of resources, and (3) leads to management improvements. The snapshot in time is analytically important because it permits both longitudinal and comparative analyses. Line managers are often not trained in public administration. Thus, process analysis provides them and the budget analyst with a significantly heightened awareness of the activities that take place in a program and the role of each employee in those activities. Often, prior to that analysis, the line manager was not even aware of those facts and their implications on his or her role as a manager. Managers are often surprised by what they find. This analysis particularly and immediately identifies weak and strong programs. Weak managers cannot provide necessary information, whereas strong managers normally overwhelm the analyst with relevant information. Process analysis also helps mediocre programs as it permits their managers to understand the internal processes more logically.

Process analysis helps identify ineffective use of resources (inputs). For example, a government's youth services activity in a large urban county had been trimmed back over the years, and its administrative management section with higher-priced positions was quite large. A process analysis showed that the organization was top-heavy with too many leaders and not enough workers. In another program in that same county, a process analysis identified activities that were being done by regular personnel that could be done just as effectively by unpaid volunteers.

Process analysis contributes significantly to management improvement because it:

1. helps line managers understand management and the need to justify their resource requests;
2. fosters a sensitivity to the importance of and the meaning of productivity;
3. helps identify weak management;
4. helps identify managers who need management training;
5. identifies managers who have taken their organization away from policy-determined objectives; and
6. trains managers in techniques that can help them manage their own programs.

Line managers are not normally educated in public administration, and they have no exposure to public management except for what they experience or deduce from their own values and attitudes. Budgets and the need to justify them are a new side of life as are other day-to-day management activities. In smaller governments, central budget offices may have prepared budgets for unit managers without their involvement. Process analysis treats unit managers not as children on an allowance, but, rather, as adults who must justify their resource requests and manage those resources correctly once they are received.

Process analysis, coupled with budget examination, fosters a unit management sensitivity for the meaning and importance of productivity. Managers are asked to think in terms of input and output relationships. That type of thinking may not be present in a line manager, but is required by process analysis. It must be learned by the managers, or process analysis cannot be done intelligently.

Weak managers are frustrated by process analysis because they cannot justify or even explain what they do with their resources. Budget analysts normally must spend a great deal more time working with weak managers. In one situation in a local government, a unit withdrew its $1.5 million request for added resources when upper levels of management in the division realized that the program manager could not explain how the additional monies would improve the program. A useful byproduct is that specific and general managerial training needs become more apparent with process analysis. If a manager has difficulty understanding "input," "output," and how to flow-chart activities, specific education or training should be provided for that person. If managers cannot understand the essential concepts, then, wherever possible, they should be counseled regarding their career development and encouraged to move into areas more suited for their talents.

Another management plus of process analysis coupled with budget examination is the identification of organizational units that have deviated from their intended function. For example, a local government provided a mobile social service van on location in poor neighborhoods. On examination of the unit's process, the real services provided by two professional social workers were voter registration and a check of pulse rates. Obviously, the unit had abandoned its stated purpose, and professional social workers were being misused. Providing voter registration service is not inappropriate, but costs for such services should be reflected correctly in the voter registration section of the budget or policy makers are being misled.

The final above-cited advantage of process analysis is training line managers in useful managerial and analytical techniques. Line managers are exposed to and learn to appreciate the techniques. For example, the urban library's management was impressed with the earlier cited use of regression analysis in the library circulation activity. They are now using the technique in other library programs.

Context Is Important

The previous discussion may leave the false impression that successful process analysis application is merely a central budget office decision. Top-level management should strongly support the whole concept and demand line-management cooperation. Organizational resistance is difficult to overcome without that type of support. In a period of tight or declining budgets, one can often find more serious and useful cooperation and desire, especially from higher-level officials.

Another possible misunderstanding is that there is some cookbook set of approaches that can be applied uniformly from jurisdiction to jurisdiction. Although this chapter suggests what can be done, the actual doing must be tailored to the unique situation of each jurisdiction. A creative approach to professionalism is needed to adapt the concepts and techniques to new situations. Normally, the biggest practical problem inhibiting process analysis is a lack of adequate data. A proactive solution for a central budget office is to support budget requests for data collection as long as the data collected can also be useful for budget purposes.

Needed Interpersonal Skills

A working assumption of a budget analyst should be that the analyst is part of a team attempting to provide the desired levels of service at the lowest cost. To the extent possible, the analyst strives to have the line managers use the same assumption. For this mind-setting process to be most effective, top-level officials must articulate this perspective and promote that attitude with their policies, decisions, and actions. The analyst should extend the mind set so that line managers become a part of the "we" and "team."

To work properly as a "team player," the analyst should strive to appreciate and understand the manager's perspective. The difficult character of the job and the commitment to public service must be understood emotionally as well as intellectually. Analysts should strive to appreciate how the manager feels when employees must be cut and to understand the difficult challenge of supervising employees who continue to work for long periods after they have received termination notices. Budget analysts must attempt to make the line manager's tasks easier whenever possible.

A proactive posture is best. The analyst and line manager should recognize that they can contribute positively to better policy making and better management of the organization. They should not be merely passive or reactive. In fact, one of the distinctive characteristics of most successful top-level line managers is being proactive, especially in the budget process. Reactive managers tend to be the weak managers.

Another useful working assumption is that every organization, regardless of size, can have its funds cut to some extent without loss of service. The challenge for the budget analyst is to discover "how." The challenge for the line manager is to take the existing resources and maximize output levels. Thus, tension can and does exist between the two organizational actors, but it can be constructive. The analyst should decide carefully how to approach dealing with specific line managers in order to create the necessary mind-set and get the needed information. The line manager should decide how to respond to those data requests so that effective program management can be achieved at minimum overall commitments of the line personnel.

Honesty

Budget analysts must earn their reputation for being honest and cooperative with line managers. Being doctrinaire and having a know-it-all personality can poison a useful professional relationship. Constructive cooperation is essential. Analysts must appreciate that the line manager's budget is much like their own paycheck. Managers are sensitive to any changes affecting their unit's budget. Analysts must strive to achieve a trust relationship in which both parties appreciate the other's perspective. Such relationships take time to develop, thus a wise office policy is to have budget analysts assigned to the same units for at least two years.

The following simple practices can be very useful in establishing professional line manager/analyst relationships:

1. Phone calls and other messages should be returned promptly.
2. When possible, the analyst should strive to attend line manager's internal group meetings as well as to read their reports and studies.
3. Normally, an analyst knows more about top-level developments than does the line manager. A simple sharing of information can thus be quite useful to the manager and help in establishing the desired rapport.
4. An analyst should often go the extra step of initiating the news-sharing rather than waiting for specific inquiries.
5. Nothing should be printed in the budget document without the line manager's knowledge. Agreement is not always possible, but the manager should not feel that the analyst is acting unilaterally.
6. If there are any dollar or word changes, the line manager should be notified. Again, surprises should be avoided.
7. If the budget analyst does make a mistake, such mistakes should be freely, quickly, and openly acknowledged. To do otherwise, can deepen any feelings of distrust and unfortunately contribute to a conspiracy explanation of events.

Obviously, there can and should be exceptions to these "proverbs." However, if the spirit of them is followed, the working relationship between the analyst and the line manager should be good.

Cooptation

One concern in budget offices is that the relationship can become so strong between the analyst and the line manager that cooptation takes place. Analysts must be able to scrutinize but not be overly tolerant of managerial mistakes. Cooptation problems can be avoided if analysts are given new division assignments every two to three years. In fact, in order to avoid boredom, better analysts will seek rotations. One interesting phenomenon is the subtle and sometimes not-so-subtle different ways that line managers treat their ex-budget analysts once the relationship has changed.

PROGRAM EVALUATION

Program evaluation focuses on program outcomes (the impacts of government programs on individuals and society) and essentially deals with the question of program effectiveness. As a way to conduct inquiries, it is very much influenced by logical positivism or what is commonly called the scientific method. Most evaluators believe that evaluation is first and foremost an application of rigorous scientific procedure to reach reliable and valid conclusions on the impact of programs. Program outputs are considered independent variables, and program outcomes are considered dependent variables. For example, to evaluate a new vaccine, one could use an experimental design that calls for measurements to be taken before and after the vaccine is used. Two groups would be part of the experimental design, but only one would get the vaccine. The research design is graphically explained as follows:

experimental group $\qquad O_1 \times O_2$
control group $\qquad O_1 \quad O_2$

Conclusions on the causal effectiveness of the vaccine would be made by comparing first the "before" and "after" observations and then the difference between the observations of the experimental and control groups. There should be significantly less disease in the vaccine group. One of the problems with such a research design is that withholding treatment from the control group is wrong ethically since the patients in the control group are not informed that they have received a placebo rather than the vaccine; but without a control group the evaluators cannot be certain of their conclusions. The "solution" to evaluative problems when better research designs cannot be used is to apply quasi-experimental designs. They do not allow one to reach definitive conclusions on program effectiveness, but they are better than no design at all.

The typical evaluation question is: "To what extent is the program succeeding in reaching its goals?" The steps in evaluation consist of the following:

1. find out the program's goals;
2. translate the goals into measurable indicators of goal achievement (desired outcomes);
3. collect the data on the indicators for those who participate in the program and control group; and
4. compare the data on the experimental and control groups with the desired program outcomes.

Commonly, identifying "measurable indicators of goal achievement" is very difficult, and such efforts result in anything but the desired characteristics of clarity, specificity, measurability, and behaviorally oriented data, leaving the evaluator in no position to determine if the desired program outcomes were accomplished. The challenge for evaluators is to counter that natural tendency. They can do that by investigating the program, specifying reasonable goals, and seeking confirmation. Sometimes, they use elaborate, consensus-building exercises. Despite the difficulty, most approaches to program evaluation require the evaluator to develop some definition of program goals.

The next step is developing the measures, a process which is sometimes called instrumentation. The process is "modeled" by identifying attributes and describing the program outputs and outcomes as well as interim steps between them. The Urban Institute publication, *How Effective Are Your Community Services*, provides a detailed list of useful attributes and measures of government services. Measures selected can deal with attitudes, work behavior, services, turnover, budgets, changes in the environment, and so on. Measures can focus on people and deal with values, attitudes, knowledge, and skills. They can focus on institutions and deal with responsiveness. Normally, evaluators attempt to conceptualize the entire chain of cause and effect from acquisition of dollars to fund the program to ultimate program outcomes. In addition, possible intervening variables are isolated. The ultimate purpose is to be able to assert as definitive a conclusion as possible about the program's effectiveness.

The budget is a comprehensive framework to make government decisions and is a source of potentially reliable information on what government is doing and how well it is being done. Logically, the two should be interrelated but often there is little connection. Program evaluation arose in the 1960s as a broad-based institutionalized application of social and physical science research methods addressed to decision-relevant public program and policies. Notwithstanding reforms like PPB, MBO, and ZBB, there was relatively little stress on seeking to enhance the impact of program evaluations on budget decision making. Commonly, at the federal level, major budget decisions are not made on the basis of analysis, but, rather, on the basis of deeply held philosophical views.

There are impediments to the use of program evaluation by budget decision makers. One is organizational separation. The evaluation activity is commonly not done in the same unit as the budget. This creates communication difficulties and often unhealthy competition and conflict. A second impediment is the conflicting perceptions of time. Budget decisions are made in a highly rigid annual cycle, whereas evaluation is done in terms of when the question is being examined and the availability of resources to address the question. Evaluators rarely can predict the time required to complete their tasks, and, often, slippages of months and years occur in order to achieve acceptable evaluation products. That regard for time may be essential for evaluators, but it is not practical for time-sensitive budget decision makers. A third impediment is the conflicting intellectual frameworks. Budgeters are faced with many difficult decisions that often preclude consideration of long-term issues that need not be addressed in the very near future. Evaluators tend to be researchers seeking answers to larger issues that often involve methodologies that do not reflect either timely or pragmatic realities of the political decision-making process.

As Harry Havens of the U.S. General Accounting Office argues, an integrated policy development process should include a multiyear budget and policy review effort. Such a process should involve a jointly developed system for monitoring key indicators of efficiency and effectiveness as well as discrete studies on major policy issues timed around specific public policy decision points. The one-year budget formulation process that ignores program evaluation tends to focus on the simple, quick fixes rather than on carefully developed and necessarily complex long-term strategy.

Eleanor Chelimsky argues that if evaluators are to build their work into the budget process, the following three problem areas need to be confronted:

- development of evaluation findings which can be applied to specific program decisions in the budgetary process;
- development of an acceptable relationship between evaluation and budgetary time frames and schedules; and
- establishment of a dialogue between budgeters and evaluators.

AUDITING

Purpose of Auditing

Auditing is a vital activity. Its most important function is to validate the correct operation of the accounting system. This includes verifying the accuracy of inventories and existing equipment; determining that proper legal authority exists to perform current government activities; checking the adequacy of internal control practices and procedures; uncovering fraud; and isolating waste and mismanagement. Political accountability and democracy become largely meaningless unless the general public and the political leadership have a reasonably effective means to validate the correct operation of the accounting system and to establish that democratically established policy is being followed. A 1983 news story about a rash of mysterious fires in Nigeria illustrates the central importance of auditing. The fires not only destroyed several buildings, including a thirty-seven-story building as distinctive to the Lagos skyline as the twin World Trade Center skyscrapers are to New York's, but also derailed an investigation into government corruption. They occurred in buildings housing departmental accounting records, and they seem to have been set to cover up embezzlement, provoking violent antigovernment protests by university students. Such acts of arson are not limited to places outside the United States.

Beyond being an essential safeguard of government accountability, auditing is also important in establishing credibility and in improving government management. It provides independent judgments of the manner in which public officials carry out their responsibilities as well as of the credibility and lawfulness of their financial statements. This is particularly important to investors when they are deciding to buy a government's notes and bonds. Auditing improves efficiency and economy by examining and reporting on government procedures, operations, and management policies. Auditing helps decision makers improve effectiveness by evaluating whether a program was carried forward as planned, met its program objectives, and produced desirable changes.

Two common varieties of audits are the pre- and post-audits. *Pre-audits* are done before obligations are made. In many states, the elected auditor performs essentially pre-audit functions. Pre-audits focus upon determining legality and examining vouchers. The depth and detail of a pre-audit vary, but the importance of independence is always present. The disadvantages associated with pre-audits are that they:

1. reduce the level of responsibility;
2. lead to red tape;
3. foster interagency friction; and
4. are costly.

The *post-audit* is the more common form of auditing. It also should be done by an independent group. It can focus on verifying documents, checking transactions and procedures, or examining administrative effectiveness and efficiency. Post-auditing is not a closing of accounts. However, sometimes accounts cannot be closed without an audit.

Audits can be conducted within an agency. If that is done, the audit should be independent and focus on evaluating legality of actions and effectiveness of administrative controls. Such audits commonly:

1. review compliance with and appraise performance under policies, plans, and procedures established by management for carrying out its responsibilities;
2. examine financial transactions;
3. test the reliability and usefulness of accounting and other financial and program data produced in the agency;
4. review the effectiveness with which the agency's resources are utilized; and
5. examine the effectiveness of safeguards provided to prevent or minimize waste or loss of agency assets.

Internal versus External Audits

Internal audits can be distinguished from *internal inspections*. The latter are designed to confirm that policy, procedures, and reporting are being carried out correctly. They are addressed to employees who are responsible for carrying out particular operations such as meat inspection, food-stamp applicant screening, and unemployment insurance interviews. Internal auditing addresses broader concerns of legality, effectiveness, and efficiency.

External audits are similar to internal audits, but they are done by independent agencies. A typical external audit examines accounts, checks on the accuracy of recorded transactions and inventories, does on-site review of stocks, verifies physical existence of equipment, and reviews operating procedures and regulations. The congressional audit agency for the U.S. federal government is the General Accounting Office (GAO). This agency reports directly and is responsible to the Congress. By law, an agency must respond to GAO reports, forcing it to comment on the problems raised by GAO and encouraging a statement of how the agency will resolve the problems. The GAO investigates fraud, waste, and mismanagement. Its audits often focus on delegation of responsibility, policy direction (including program evaluation), budget and accounting practices, and the adequacy of internal controls, including internal auditing. Legislative audits are commonly post-audits; thus, the group appropriating the money often makes the final check on its expenditures.

Whether done internally or externally, audits are intended to increase government accountability. The desire for accountability is rooted in the American distrust of authority. In 325 B.C., Aristotle said: "Some officials handle large sums of public money; it is therefore necessary to have other officials to receive and examine the accounts. These inspectors must administer no funds themselves. Different cities call them examiners, auditors, scrutinizers and public advocates." (Mosher, 1979) In 1777 the American Continental Congress created the inspector general of the army to find possible abuses in General Washington's army. During the Carter administration, the Inspector General Act of 1978 was passed, and it was strengthened in the Reagan administration to fight government fraud, waste, and abuse.

Auditing Principles

Governmental auditing principles have been established by the American Institute of Certified Public Accountants (AICPA), a nonprofit professional association, and the U.S. General Accounting Office (GAO). In addition, the National Council of Governmental Accounting (NCGA) has issued standards drawn from the AICPA auditing standards. The publications *Audits of State and Local Governmental Units* by AICPA and *Standards for Audit of Governmental Organizations, Programs, Activities and Functions* contain the accepted auditing standards. Exhibit 6–12 gives the GAO audit standards which serve to guide both accountants and auditors. Stress is placed on assuring legal compliance and complete disclosure of government financial positions and operations. Legal provisions take priority over accounting principles, and accounting systems are to provide budgetary operational control. The auditing standards adopt the fund accounting concepts; value fixed assets at their original cost; do not use depreciation in fund accounts; adopt the modified accrual method for the major funds and for other funds such as enterprise and trust; call for revenues to be classified by fund and source and expenditures to be classified by fund, function, organizational unit, character, and object class; assert that common terminology and classifications should be used; and specify that periodic and annual comprehensive financial reports be prepared, with the latter showing all government funds and financial operations.

EXHIBIT 6–12   GAO Audit Guide Outline

I. Questions on the General Standards
  1. Audit Scope
     a. Statutory Provisions
     b. Fulfillment of Responsibilities
     c. Audit Planning
  2. Staff Qualifications
     a. Education
     b. Professional Achievements
     c. Training Program
     d. Staff Appraisal System
     e. Use of Consultants
  3. Independence
     a. Head of Audit Organization
     b. Organizational Independence
     c. Audit Freedom
     d. Availability of Audit Reports
     e. Conflicts of Interest
     f. Selection of External Auditors
  4. Due Professional Care
     a. Organization and Responsibility
     b. Policies
     c. Planning System
     d. Quality Control System
II. Questions on the Examination and Evaluation Standards
  1. Audit Planning
     a. Preliminary Planning
     b. Audit Program
  2. Staff Supervision
     a. Clearly Defined Responsibilities
     b. Audit Program
  3. Compliance with Statutory and Regulatory Requirements
  4. Evidence and Auditing Procedures
  5. Evaluation of Internal Control
  6. Financial and Compliance Audits—General
  7. Audits of Economy and Efficiency Matters
  8. Audits of Program Results
  9. Workpapers
  10. Exit Conference
III. Questions on the Reporting Standards
  1. Form and Distribution
     a. Form
     b. Distribution
  2. Timeliness
  3. Content
     a. Clarity and Conciseness
     b. Objectivity and Constructive Tone
     c. Scope
     d. Adequacy of Support and Persuasiveness
     e. Recommendations
  4. Financial Reports

Auditing procedures are spelled out in the AICPA and GAO publications so that specific questions are uniformly asked and the role of the auditor is clearly defined. The two keys to understanding auditing are professionalism and documentation. The guide stresses the importance of an independent, highly educated adult staff that systematically and carefully reviews the financial and related managerial facts in the audited unit. Audit workpapers are critical. For example, they must show the following:

1. that the audit staff obtained an understanding of the audited entity before determining specific audit tests and procedures;
2. that the audit staff followed up on findings;
3. that the following were considered:
   a. internal control evaluation results,
   b. completion and accomplishment of audit objectives,
   c. consideration of matters related to audit objectives, and
   d. conformance with standards;
4. that the audit program was followed;
5. workpapers show sufficient data and support findings and conclusions; and
6. that the auditor's time was budgeted and recorded.

The workpapers serve as the basis for the audit findings and recommendations. In well-prepared workpapers, the above and other considerations are reflected so that any problems are completely documented. Focus is placed on determining the adequacy of internal control, compliance with statutory and regulatory requirements, adequacy of accounting system, existence of economy and efficient conduct, and program effectiveness. An audit includes not only a report of findings and recommendations but also an exit conference in which auditors explain their conclusions.

USE OF ANALYTICAL PROCESSES

Based on a 1988 survey of 181 U.S. cities, with 129 responding, Stanley B. Botner determined the use of analytical processes patterns related to public budgeting in American cities. He contrasted his findings with the 1982 study of Poister and McGowan. Botner concluded there was an increase in the use of program budgeting in large cities, a decrease in the use of both ZZB and MBO, a sharp increase in management information systems, and an increase in performance monitoring. Exhibit 6–13 presents Botner's 1988 findings. The high use of program budgeting, management information systems, performance monitoring, program analysis, forward-year projections, and budgeting of revenues and expenditures affirm the importance of analysis in modern budgeting. Botner asked the respondents in large municipalities what the major trends in budgeting during 1978 to 1988 were. Eighty-one percent responded as follows:

- declining intergovernmental revenues and searches for alternative revenue sources;
- meteoric rise of computerization;
- increased emphasis on performance and productivity;
- projections of revenues and expenditures;
- program budgeting;
- strategic planning;
- concentration on efficiency; and
- increased emphasis on control and accountability.

EXHIBIT 6–13   Large-City Use of Analytical Tools and Processes

ANALYTICAL TOOLS AND PROCESSES	(N = 129) NUMBER OF CITIES USING	PERCENT OF CITIES USING
Program Budgeting	95	74
Zero-Based Budgeting	21	16
Management By Objectives	55	43
Computerized Mgt. Inf. System	95	74
Performance Measurement	89	69
Productivity Improvement Methods		
Quality Circles	34	26
Other	22	17
Program Analysis	93	72
Program Evaluation	67	52
Projection of Revenues and Exp.	111	86
Forward-Year Budgeting of		
Revenues and Expenditures	58	45

Source: Stanley B. Botne, "Trends and Developments In Budgeting and Financial Management in Large Cities of the United States," *Public Budgeting and Finance*, 9, 3 (Autumn 1989), p. 38.

REVIEW QUESTIONS

1. Explain how one goes about developing a useful list of major program issues and then selects from that list. Explain the usefulness of an issue assessment and what should be considered in such an assessment.
2. What factors influence an analysis? Why is the chief executive particularly significant? What type of chief executive support is important?
3. Explain some of the common mistakes made in the analysis and presentation of analytical results.
4. What is the rationale behind ethical codes in general and the one described in this chapter in particular?
5. How does a budget examiner isolate services performed? Why is this important? What key program input, process, and outputs should be especially examined? How does a budget examiner identify program emphasis and change?

6. From a budget examiner's perspective, how does one attempt to achieve responsiveness to duly elected political leaders? What concerns are commonly significant?
7. What does one examine in order to help establish economy and efficiency in government?
8. Explain how a budget analyst should use forecasts in his or her budget examination.
9. What types of queries are common in a detailed budget examination?
10. How does one go about automating a budget examination process?
11. Explain how to do process analysis. Why are context, interpersonal skills, and honesty important in process analysis?
12. What is the focus of program evaluation and how does research design relate to that concern? What challenges do program evaluators face?
13. What is accomplished in auditing? What are the types of audits?
14. Explain the relationship between accounting and auditing. Explain auditing procedures, especially their purpose.

REFERENCES

ADAIR, JOHN J. REX SIMMONS. "From Voucher Auditing To Junkyard Dogs: The Evolution of Federal Inspectors General," *Public Budgeting and Finance*, 8, 2 (Summer 1988), 91–100.

BOTNER, STANLEY B. "Trends and Developments In Budgeting and Financial Management in Large Cities of the United States," *Public Budgeting and Finance*, 9, 3 (Autumn 1989), 37–42.

BOTNER, STANLEY B. "Utilization and Impact of Microcomputers in State Central Budget Offices," *Public Budgeting and Finance*, 7, 3 (Autumn 1987), 99–108.

BRYAN, MARVIN. "Business Forecasting," *PC Magazine* (August 1986), pp. 211–234.

CHELIMSKY, ELEANOR. *Using Evaluation in the Budget-Making Process*. Washington, D.C.: U.S. General Accounting Office, 1982.

FOSS, THOMAS C., and THOMAS D. SUTTBERRY (eds.). *State Budgeting in Florida: A Handbook for Budget Analysts*. Tallahassee: Florida State University, Public Managers Training and Advisory Service, 1983.

GOODNOW, FRANK J. "The Limits of Budgetary Control." In *Proceedings of the American Political Science Association*. Baltimore, Md., 1983.

HATRY, HARRY P. *A Review of Private Approaches for Delivery of Public Services*. Washington, D.C.: Urban Institute, 1983.

HATRY, HARRY, LOUIS H. BLAIR, DONALD M. FISH, JOHN M. GREINER, JOHN R. HALL,JR., and PHILLIP S. SCHAENMAN. *How Effective Are Your Community Services?* Washington D.C.: The Heban Institute, 1977 and 1992.

HATRY, HARRY P., LOUIS BLAIR, DONALD FISK, and WAYNE KIMMEL. Program Analysis for State and Local Government. Washington, D.C., Urban Institute, 1976, p. 11.

HAVENS, HARRY. "Integrating Evaluation and Budgeting," *Public Budgeting and Finance*, 3, 2 (Summer 1983), 102–113.

LINDBLOM, CHARLES E. *The Policy Making Process*, 2nd ed. Englewood Cliffs, N.J.: Prentice Hall, 1980.

LYNCH, THOMAS D., and SHERRY A. "Practical Tools For Budget Examination." Paper for the Southeastern Regional Conference of the American Society for Public Administration. Tallahassee, Fla., October 1983.

McCaffery, Jerry. "MBO and the Federal Budgetary Process," *Public Administration Review*, 36, 1 (January/February 1976), 33–39.

Menson, Thomas P. "Ethics and State Budgeting," *Public Budgeting and Finance*, 10, 1 (Spring 1990), 95–108.

Miller, Ernest G. "Implementing PPBS: Problems and Prospects," *Public Administration Review*, 23, 5 (September/October 1969).

Moak, Lennox L., and Kathryn W. Killian. *Operating Budget Manual*. Chicago: Municipal Finance Officers Association, 1963.

Mosher, Frederick C. *The GAO: The Quest for Accountability in American Government*. Boulder, Colo.: Westview Press, 1979, p. 131.

Ostrowski, John W., Ella P. Gardner, and Magda H. Motawi. "Microcomputers in Public Finance Organizations: A Survey of Uses and Trends," *Government Finance Review* (February 1986), 23–29.

Rousmaniere, Peter F. (ed.). *Local Government Auditing*. New York: Council on Municipal Performance, 1979.

Schwartz, Eli. "The Cost of Capital and Investment Criteria in the Public Sector," *Journal of Finance*, 25 (March 1970), 135–42.

Scott, Claudia Devita. *Forecasting Local Government Spending*. Washington, D.C.: Urban Institute, 1972.

Spencer, Bruce P. "Technical Issues in Allocation Formula Design," *Public Administration Review*, 42, 6 (November/December 1982), 524–29.

Thai, Khi V. "Government Financial Reporting and Auditing." In Jack Rabin and Thomas D. Lynch (eds.), *Handbook on Public Budgeting and Financial Management*. New York: Marcel Dekker, 1983.

Wachs, Martin. "Ethical Dilemmas in Forecasting for Public Policy," *Public Administration Review*, 42, 6 (November/December 1982), 562–67.

Weiss, Carol H. *Evaluation Research*. Englewood Cliffs, N.J.: Prentice Hall, 1972.

Wildavsky, Aaron. *The Politics of the Budgetary Process*. Boston: Little, Brown, 1964, 1984.

7

OPERATING BUDGETS
AND ACCOUNTING

The actual execution of the budget and fund management are not as politically and behaviorally oriented as the budget formulation phase, but they are complex and important. Control is the most significant emphasis in budget execution because both the executive and legislative officials demand that the agency follow the established policy set down in the budget. A significant concern is the correct use of idle cash due to the lag between collecting taxes and spending money. Idle cash can be invested, thus earning extra revenue for the government.

This chapter also discusses the fundamentals of government accounting. Stress is placed on explaining those accounting and auditing concepts that are particularly useful to public budgeting. A large section of the chapter is devoted to describing an elementary set of accounting reports that greatly aid the public budget process. Topics covered in this chapter include:

1. how responsibilities can be fixed on key officials and why that designation is helpful in ensuring proper control;
2. budget execution suggestions that reflect an appreciation of common management problems;
3. factors and pitfalls that should be weighed in developing the operating budget;
4. current-year adjustment and policy reinterpretations;
5. administrative reservations, allotments, *and* other budget concepts;
6. expenditure controls;
7. cash internal control;
8. management information systems;

9. significance and procedures for cash management;
10. techniques used to determine proper cash and security positions;
11. basics of investment in marketable securities; and
12. the fundamental definitions, beliefs, and norms of government

DESIGNING CONTROL

Fixing Responsibility

If control is to be established, careful consideration must go into designing procedures and fixing responsibility. One of the most effective ways to achieve control is to associate a specific program or programs with an office. Only the person holding that office has the power to obligate or control expenditures. Care is taken to avoid having more than one person authorizing obligations for the program; thus, errors or fraud can be traced to the responsible person. If responsibility is split, then mistakes are more difficult to correct and legal actions are more difficult to pursue.

The Federal Anti-Deficiency Act is designed to focus responsibility. The director of the Office of Management and Budget must apportion appropriated money and other funds into specific amounts available for portions of the fiscal year for particular legally sanctioned projects or activities. The appropriation and funds are apportioned to the agencies. Two officers are given special responsibilities. The agency head is responsible for obligations and the integrity of the budget control system. The agency budget officer is responsible for ensuring the money is not overobligated. The Anti-Deficiency Act states that a person knowingly and willfully violating the apportionments can be fined and imprisoned. If the person violates the apportionments without knowledge, then that mistake subjects the person to administrative discipline such as a reprimand, suspension from duty without pay, or removal from office. This Act fixes responsibility quite clearly, and it has been an effective device.

Budget Execution

Budget execution depends on top-level support. Top management must recognize the importance of proper budget execution and support the budget office. No procedures can work unless top management uses them. If the agency head is willing to overspend the budget or refuses to insist that useful budget forms be followed, then budget execution will be chaotic and lack control. The agency head need not develop the procedures or take an active role, but that agency head must support the budget officer who does develop the procedures. Ideally, the agency head would understand public budgeting sufficiently to demand proper budget execution, but that is not essential to the budget officer who is highly competent. If the agency head supports the budget officer, then budget execution can work effectively. The operating managers in the organization must also support the budget system. They must understand the system in terms of how it affects them and what they must do in support of it. Ideally, they should understand the larger context of the system and public budgeting in general so that problems and requests can be anticipated. If operating managers do not support the system, then reports and other needs are not timely or are incorrect, thus causing embarrassment and possibly even causing administrative hardships.

Budget execution also depends on a qualified budget staff and a positive attitude toward the concept of public trust. If the budget staff is unaware of the needs of budget execution, then serious management problems are likely to occur. If there are insufficient people on the staff, then they will be overwhelmed, thus forcing them to concentrate on major problems and allowing some routine matters to become major problems. Many employees, especially top management and budget office employees, have a sense of public trust. If they view their jobs as the means to further private interests, then the possibility of corruption is increased. In addition, employees should be concerned with economy and efficiency. The first concern should be program effectiveness, but economy and efficiency are important if the government is to get maximum use for its tax dollar. Also budget behavior tends to foster a maximum spending approach, and an economy-efficiency ethic is necessary to overcome this natural tendency in budgeting.

A budget execution system should be established that gives direction to agency activities and permits continuous and current reviews to determine if planned objectives are being met. One approach is to link an operating budget with management objectives using the management-by-objectives method (MBO). If this is done, each agency unit is asked to develop objectives and progress reports. A crosswalk (explained in Chapter 5) is used to link objectives and the operating budget. The operating budget should be keyed to the major line units in the organization in such a way that specific programs, objectives, and dollar amounts are related to line organizational units.

In order to work smoothly as an organization and to avoid intercommunication difficulties, established procedures are needed to change work plans, schedules, and use of funds. Those procedures should be designed to ensure all factors are considered and all key people in and outside the organization are notified of the decision in a timely manner. Circumstances do arise where procedures must be short-circuited; but if the procedures are designed properly, short-circuiting of procedures will be infrequent. The design of procedures is always a difficult task, and care must be taken to make them as simple and effective as possible.

To fix responsibility, formal authorization is given each official who will order the spending of money. The authorization is reviewed to be sure such delegations of authority are permissible under the law. The authorization is written carefully so that any later confusion and misunderstandings about the authorization are eliminated. Allotments and operating budgets can be coordinated with the formal authorizations so that officials know how much money they must deal with as well as any other guidance necessarily associated with the dollar amounts.

The accounting and related record systems can be designed to serve prescribed budgetary needs. Accounting is described in more depth later in this chapter. Briefly, the budget execution activity is carried out in a larger context than accounting, but the actual recording of transactions should be done so that analysis can compare actual practice with planned practice as defined in the budget. This comparison is essential if the analyst is to know if the policy was carried out.

Once the budget execution system has been designed, there are three helpful operational considerations. First, if possible, performance standards—maybe in connection with management-by-objectives—can be established in connection with the operating budget. This would aid greatly in productivity studies and performance budgeting. Performance measures are considered a part of the government accounting process. Second, the nature of the unit's activity often does not lend itself to performance standards; but if it does, advanced planning linking performance estimates with available funding levels is also a useful management method. Third, regardless of the type of government activity, financial obligations can be scheduled in advance to achieve a desired rate of expenditure and avoid a final month deficit.

Thomas J. Kane, Jr. (1984) surveyed large city budget directors and he found the most important budget execution function was making sure the budget stayed in balance throughout the fiscal year. Seventy-seven percent listed that function as a major concern. In comparison, fulfilling the legislative programmatic intent ranked second and was listed as a concern but not a major one. Interestingly, avoiding scandal by ensuring funds are spent is properly ranked a distant third.

Another concern in budget execution is to develop a system that monitors considerations such as legality, propriety, and economy. In some governments, the legality and economy issues are monitored by means of pre-audits. The advantages of catching these errors must be considered against the complex, expensive procedures added to government operation. In many grant-in-aid programs, an elaborate procedure to check legality, propriety, economy, equal opportunity, and environmental quality is probably justifiable. If the program is a routine daily operation such as street maintenance, then an elaborate clearance procedure would be foolish. In those circumstances, management judgment would be needed to seek special advice on matters like environmental issues when unusual conditions warrant such advice. The use of special clearance procedures can be institutionalized if the issue becomes common; thus, overall time and effort can be saved by checking the matter before obligations are made.

In developing and using a budget execution system, several factors are weighed carefully. Must the operating budget be prepared under unusual legislative appropriation conditions, or is a revision (for example, supplemental appropriation) likely? Is a continuing resolution in effect? What size and structure is the organization (for example, field, regions, area offices)? What type of financial concepts (these are explored later in this chapter) are appropriate to use in the context of the organization? What are the sources of funds and how is that important to the budget execution system? What financial, quantified work unit data, personnel, and manpower measures should be collected, and how? How should personnel ceilings and personnel restrictions be enforced or reflected in the budget execution system? What should be the frequency, level, and coordination means for budget execution reporting? Each of these questions must be considered and answered in the context of the work environment. Each answer can help budget officials better design and operate the budget execution system. Follow-up is essential. Frequent and regular reports are needed to check on work progress, objectives yet unaccomplished, and the status of the various funds (funds are explained in the chapter on accounting). If a problem or question arises from the reports, then prompt, regular, and careful follow-up is needed or the problems and questions tend to be forgotten until they become major problems. An organized system of audits and inspections must be established to verify and supplement the reporting system. If audits and inspections do not exist, then fraud, cheating, or merely poor operational practices are more difficult to isolate before they become a widespread problem.

Pitfalls to Avoid

An operating budget can:

1. become unmanageable to top, middle, and first-line managers if it is not carefully designed for each level of management;
2. be too complex and detailed for management and thus become cumbersome or useless;
3. be too late or too inaccurate for decision-making purposes;
4. be out of synchronization with the accounting system;
5. be out of touch with the rest of the budget process; and
6. be ignored by top management, thus guaranteeing its ultimate failure.

Some of these major pitfalls were discussed in the previous section, but they should be stressed again. Designing an operating budget requires careful attention. For example, the budget and accounting offices involve various people who are trained differently. Each group views its needs separately, and, often, the operating budget system is developed or becomes nonsynchronized with the accounting system. Care must be taken to avoid this natural tendency.

An operating budget must serve all levels of budgeting. The tendency is to be too demanding of the first-line managers and thus make their tasks even more complex. Care can be taken to understand the needs and burdens placed on each level of management. However, the operating budget must provide information in a timely manner, especially to top management, and it should provide essential information for other phases in the budget cycle.

If the operating budget is ignored by top management, then the whole process is likely to be a failure. The key person in the agency is the head, and that person has the power to make exceptions to the operating budget. This power is essential in order to provide managerial flexibility to adapt to unusual circumstances which can and do arise. If that power is abused by frequent needless exceptions, then the discipline of the operating budget breaks down and advantages of the procedures are lost. An equally serious matter is when the agency head does not even create a budget execution system or does not update the system. The agency cannot be protected from bad management when it occurs at the highest levels.

Current-Year Adjustments

Regardless of how well a budget is planned, adjustments are made in the current year. Sometimes the adjustments involve transferring funds from one fund or appropriation to another. Sometimes the adjustment involves new appropriations and the legislature must pass supplemental appropriations. The reasons for changes vary from poor management to unanticipated events (for example, heavy snowfalls) to political strategies (for example, legislative approval is more likely in a supplemental request). In many state and local governments, the law requires almost all changes to be approved by the legislature. In some local governments, the executive branch has greater latitude and does make changes unilaterally to such an extent that the changed operating budget is significantly different from the legislatively approved budget.

Normally, changes are small and appropriations are written broadly enough so that legislative approval is not needed. If significant changes do occur and new legislation is not needed, the agency is still wise to inform the legislature of the change. Otherwise, a poor relationship can develop between the agency and its appropriation committees.

Flexibility in budget execution tends to exist in six ways: object classification, the appropriation structure, contingency appropriations, emergency provisions, transfer authority, and reprogramming authority. Many governments do not use statutory prohibitions precluding agencies from realigning funds among object classification. Such tight control may exist within the executive branch, and sometimes tighter control exists on certain types of objects such as money used for travel. At the federal level, flexibility extends sometimes to when the funds are spent if the funds are not appropriated on a one-year basis. According to Bernard T. Pitsvada (1983), about 53.5 percent of the FY 1983 federal budget was structured to allow one-year appropriations to be extended. Another method used to provide added flexibility during the current year are contingency appropriations (for example, disaster relief) and emergency provisions. The latter permits an agency to transfer funds to deal with emergencies after any earmarked fund purposes are met. Laws are also written to permit agencies sometimes to transfer funds from one appropriation account to another to meet needs unforeseen when the budget was passed. Agencies rarely invoke their transfer authority at the federal level without the prior approval of Congress. Reprogramming relates to realignment of funds within an appropriation for other than budgeted purposes. Reprogramming is normally done with the informal approval of the interested congressional committees.

Often transfer of appropriations occurs when functions are transferred to other agencies. The sums do not change, but a different person is given control of the funds. This often occurs in government reorganizations.

Requests for budget adjustments are rigorously reviewed, except when functions are transferred. Budget adjustments should be rare or both the executive and the legislature will spend most of their time reconsidering most of their decisions. Such requests should involve an emergency. Also, supplements are not consistent with uniform budget considerations, which weigh all budget demands at the same time. Exhibit 7–1 illustrates a request form for budget adjustments. Answers are needed to the following questions:

1. Was the item in the original budget requested?
2. Is the money for a recurring or nonrecurring expenditure?
3. What type of adjustment is requested?
4. What is the account number, title, and amount of adjustment?
5. What is the related unencumbered balance (explained later in this chapter)?
6. What is the reason for the request?

BUDGET CONCEPTS AND REPORTS

Allotments and Budget Concepts

After the money has been appropriated by the legislature and apportioned by the central budget office to the agency, then the agency has control over the funds and agency budget controls are used. The primary control is the *allotment*. It provides authority from the agency head to the operating officials to incur obligations within prescribed amounts for a specific period of time. The allotments must be consistent with appropriations and apportionments. Allotments and operating budgets can be melded because the operating budget fulfills the function of an allotment and more. Allotments can be made using organizational units, activities, geography, or object classification as the categories, depending on management needs. Allotments are normally made at the highest practical operating level in order to focus managerial responsibility. The level depends on the amount of authority delegated in the particular organization.

Allotments can be designed to complement the management structure of the agency and the problems faced by the agency. Normally, allotments are quite specific on highly sensitive controllable object classifications such as travel. Often the agency must cut current-year funds severely, and the controllable items receive the burden of such decisions. Thus, the controllable items must be "controlled" through the use of specific allotments. And, allotments often are subdivided in terms of "targets," "allowances," "work plans," "financial plans," or other categories, depending on the management devices used by the agency. The categories and names of categories are not significant as long as management control and delegation of responsibility are facilitated. Exhibit 7–2 is an example of an initial allocation and allotment schedule used in a city government.

The use of budget terminology is not uniform; but regardless of the terms used, the concepts are important to understand. Thus far, authorization, appropria-

EXHIBIT 7–1 Request Form for Budget Adjustments

DEPARTMENT: CODE#: _____ NAME: _____
SUB-ORGANIZATION UNIT: CODE#: _____ NAME: _____
ACTIVITY: CODE#: _____ NAME: _____

1. Item was ____ was not ____
   included it the department's
   original budget request

2. Type of Expenditure
   Recurring ____
   Non-recurring ____

3. Type of Adjustment
   ____ Inter-Classif. Transfer
   ____ Inter-Divisional Transfer
   ____ An Allocated Reserve Transfer
   ____ Supplemental Appropriation

The Budget Adjustment Requested will Require the Following Revisions:

4. From:

5. For Accounting Dept. Use Only

Account No.	Account Title	Amount	Unencumbered Bal. Before Adjustment	Unencumbered Bal. After Adjustment
	CROSS TOTALS			

6. To:			
TOTAL TO BE ADJUSTED TO ABOVE			

7. Reasons for Adjustment Request: (Set forth reasons the adjustment is required, the factors involved in arriving at costs, and the status of the account from which transfer is made.)

Approval Requested by:_____ Date:_____

Approved as to Availability of Funds by the Central Accounting Office:

_____

Approved by Budget Officer:_____ Date:_____
Approved by Chief Executive:_____ Date:_____
Approved by President of Counsil:_____ Date:_____

Source: Lennox L. Moak and Kathryn W. Killian, *Operating Budget Manual.* Chicago: Municipal Finance Officers Association, 1963, p. 311. Used by permission.

EXHIBIT 7-2 Schedule of Initial Allocations, 1963 General Fund Appropriations (000 Omitted)

Appropriation Title Account Code	PERSONAL SERVICES 100 CLASS		PURCHASE OF SERVICES 200 CLASS		MATERIALS AND SUPPLIES 300 CLASS		EQUIPMENT 400 CLASS		OTHER CLASSES		TOTAL ALLOCATION
	Allocation	Allotment Reserve	Class	Amount	Class	Amount	Class	Amount	Class	Amount	
Streets											
Administration	$ 394	$ 313	200	$ 7	300	$ 6	400	$ 2			$ 409
Highways	2,265	1,932	200	28	300	55	400	9	500	$ 6	2,872
			261.61	46	305.05	69	405.05	24			
					307.07	74	411.11	31			
					314.14	36	428.28	100			
					315.15	96					
					328.28	33					
Sanitation	12,462	9,877	200	7	300	59	400	39			15,807
			205.05	1,000	305.05	82	428.28	1,080			
			211.11	31	310.10	29					
			260.60	111	311.11	66					
					314.14	33					
					315.15	519					
					316.16	41					
					318.18	43					
					323.23	38					
					328.28	168					
Survey and Design	1,308	1,403	200	13	300	28	400	20			1,429
			250.50	60							

222

Department											
Traffic Engineering	984	770	200	8	300	37	400	8			1,549
					305.05	189	410.10	108			
					310.10	139	428.28	46			
					316.16	30					
Street Lighting	349	277	200	1	300	12	400	13			3,859
			220.20	2,653	305.05	26	428.28	21			
			260.60	688	310.10	97					
TOTAL	$17,762	$14,232		$4,652		$2,005		$1,501		$6	$25,926
Public Welfare Administration & Social Services	$690	$534	200	13	300	8	400	2	505.05	$495	$9,402
			290.90	8,194							
Surplus Foods Distribution Program	171	132	200	11	300	10					540
			210.10	38							
			285.85	310							
Children's Reception Center	131	101	200	1	300	23	400	1			155
Child Welfare Center	413	320	200	13	300	32	400	3			498
					313.13	36					
Youth Conservation Services	421	329	200	26	300	10	400	3	505.05	120	734
			250.50	143	313.13	12					
						1					
TOTAL	$ 1,826	$ 1,416		$ 8,748		$ 131		$ 9		$615	$11,329

Source: Philadelphia, Pennsylvania, Budget Bureau.

tion, apportionment, and allotment have been explained. These terms are used uniformly. Each represents a different hurdle that must be passed before money is actually spent. Other useful concepts (labels based on common usage) along the way to spending the funds are *administrative reservation, obligation, accrued expenditure*, and *outlay* or *disbursement*. To this list should be added *inventory* and *cost*, even though they occur after money has been spent.

Administrative reservation means setting aside some funds for a specific purpose. This technique is commonly used by agencies that grant money, but it can be used by other groups that have a lag between deciding who should receive the money and drafting the legal obligating documents. Some certitude is needed as to the availability of funds, and the administrative reservation provides that assurance. In a few instances, the legal obligating documents cannot be written. Thus, the possibility exists that funds will not be forthcoming in spite of the administrative reservation. The lag between reservation and obligation can be only a matter of minutes or it can be several weeks, depending on administrative circumstances and requirements.

Expenditure Controls

Expenditure controls are techniques that help to ensure that expenditures are made only in the amounts and for the purposes specified in the appropriation act. There are two types of expenditure controls: *budget* and *administrative*. Budget controls are geared to the appropriations and apportionments. Administrative controls are applied generically to specific operations of the agency, to ensure funds are spent correctly. Administrative controls are intended to prevent the waste or misuse of public funds at the operating level.

There are two types of budget controls: *allotments* and *reports*. Allotments were explained earlier in this chapter. They are a device to regulate timing of obligations and expenditures during the year. Reports are used to show what expenditures have been made and how this compares with what should have been made. A set of reports that could be used in many different governments is published by the Government Finance Officers Association.

There are a variety of reports commonly used: daily financial reports, monthly financial reports, quarterly financial reports, monthly performance reports, revenue reports, and annual reports. Daily financial reports are listings showing all transactions by department account. Monthly financial reports are cumulative daily reports that summarize (1) personnel costs by full-time, part-time, temporary, overtime, and other, and (2) costs by major object of expenditure. Quarterly financial reports point out variances between the current and prior year's expenditures. The monthly performance reports contain code numbers, descriptions, selected key work units, number of persons engaged in producing units, and explanations of significant variances. Common data elements include budgeted work units for the year, traits programmed for the current month, amount during the first prior year and current year, percent already completed, and percent of variance from that programmed to date.

There are two common types of administrative controls: *encumbrances* and *competitive bids*. An encumbrance is a claim on money; thus, encumbered money is not available for new commitments. The administrative reservation defined earlier is an encumbrance. The advantages of encumbrances are (1) they keep officials in government from overspending, and (2) the use of the concept enables officials to be certain of how much money is available for new commitments. Competitive bidding requires that the government solicit price quotations for goods or services from potential vendors or contractors. The normal advantages of competitive bidding are (1) the procedure tends to avoid careless and possibly costly awarding of contracts, and (2) the procedure reduces the danger that contracts will be awarded in return for kickbacks or political favors.

Expenditure controls and other administrative practices such as pre-audits should be carefully considered. The common reasons for detailed expenditure controls are to minimize fraud and to ensure that higher level policy is carried out. Detailed expenditure controls can also be called "red tape." The use of these controls means time and money must be used to write and review the reports. Also the controls tend to inhibit operating departments and their officials from taking initiatives and being creative because so much paperwork must be done.

A fraud/red-tape dilemma exists. Does the government wish to risk fraud (or cries of nonresponsiveness to political leaders) or add more red tape? Neither is pleasant, but the lesser evil is red tape. In the case of fraud, analysis can be used to determine the optimal point of cost control. Expensive administrative controls should be added up to the point that the cost of fraud is equal to the cost of the controls. Such an analysis would be difficult to accomplish given the uncertainties; but even if it were possible, the political wisdom of minimizing the possibility of fraud would tend to force administrators to opt for more controls—red tape. Politically, no politician wishes to be placed in the situation where any fraud was said to be condoned.

Cash Internal Control

The budget officer must be sure that proper cash internal control exists. Fraud and misuse of funds cannot be prevented completely, but they can be discouraged to the point where only rare cases occur. Twelve simple practices can make a significant difference.

1. All disbursements, except for petty cash, should be made by check. Cash invites theft and fraud because it is much more difficult to trace and associate with specific persons. Also, canceled checks provide a receipt. Petty cash is an exception in that detailed controls for small items can cost more than the items.
2. The signing of checks in advance should be prohibited. Signed checks are similar to cash. Delaying the signing of checks shortens the time they are negotiable and makes it easy to ensure that the checks do correspond to the purchase.
3. Checks should not be drawn to "cash." The checks should be used to create a trail so that if there is a fraud, investigators can isolate the illegal transaction. Also, a check

made out to "cash" is more difficult to associate with a specific voucher and invoice; thus, confusion is not lessened but compounded.

4. Bank accounts should be reconciled independently. If that is done, errors can be detected more easily because a second independent person is not likely to make the error in the same manner. More important, the likelihood of fraud is lessened because two people instead of one would have to he involved in the crime.

5. Checks should be reconciled with the statement using sequenced (numbered) checks. This permits tighter control of the checks and uncovers omissions much more easily. Also, if the checks are not numbered, theft of checks is much more difficult to detect.

6. Checks should be issued only on written authority. Checks should be traceable to invoices, purchase orders, and encumbrances. This is best done with a written record. More significantly, confusion about issuing of money should be minimized and written authority is the best way to avoid misunderstandings. The protection of the disbursing agent is enhanced if the agent can prove all disbursements were proper, and that can best be done with a written record.

7. An inventory control should exist over blank and voided checks. Without such control, fraud and theft is made easier, and a good criminal investigator would question the person who did not maintain such control for possible criminal involvement.

8. Separate bank accounts should be maintained for every fund. As explained in this chapter, each fund must be maintained separately, and this is done through separate bank accounts. This prevents a mingling of money and facilitates separate accounting and auditing.

9. Surprise counts should be made of the petty cash. Elaborate controls are by definition not desirable, but some means are necessary to encourage honesty on the part of those responsible for the fund. No one should be placed above or beyond suspicion. Surprise counting of petty cash is a sufficient and inexpensive control. Care should be taken to stress that the surprise count is a standard operating procedure which should not be taken as a questioning of personal honesty.

10. Checks should be matched with vouchers. If one cannot trace a check to an invoice to a purchase order, then confusion exists which can lead to paying bills twice, not paying some bills, and other problems.

11. Vouchers and supporting documents should be marked once a check has been issued. This prevents mistaken or fraudulent multiple use of the same justifying documents.

12. Cash receipts and deposits should be recorded daily. The logging of cash receipts provides an essential proof that money has been received and a record of when it was received. Depositing the receipts in the bank discourages large losses through theft. Also, once in the bank, the idle cash can be invested, thus earning extra revenue for the government. Even a day's interest on large sums is an extremely significant revenue source for a government.

Charles K. Coe and Curtis Ellis studied 127 cases of losses due to improper internal controls in North Carolina in 1986–88. The eight internal control failures noted were:

* not prenumbering receipts;
* improperly separating such accounting duties as the receipting, depositing, and reconciling of deposits;
* incompletely reviewing applications; not adequately securing assets such as checks, cashbooks, and equipment;
* not properly controlling inventories;

- insufficiently monitoring payments;
- not conducting an independent audit of a program; and
- having poor purchasing controls.

Exhibit 7–3 summarizes the findings by jurisdiction. Of the 127 problems noted, 49, or 39 percent, were identified as separating accounting duties improperly; for example:

- The same person was allowed to prepare the daily cash report, the deposit slip, and write receipts.
- The same person wrote the checks, paid the bills, opened the mail, reconciled the bank statements, and prepared the financial reports.
- A check co-signer signed blank checks so that the other co-signer would not have to inconvenience the first co-signer.
- An account clerk wrote the check and entered the check on the accounting books without confirmation that the accounting entry was made.

EXHIBIT 7–3   Internal Control Failure

LEVEL OF GOVERN- MENT	NO #ING	IMP. SEP. DUTIES	INC. REV. APPL.	INAD. SEC. ASSETS	LACK CONTROL	INSUF. MONT.	NO INDEP. AUDIT	POOR PURCH. CONTR.	TOT
State	3	18	3	4	4	13	1	7	53
Cities	6	19	0	0	2	1	0	4	32
Counties	3	12	2	1	3	1	0	4	26
Nonprofit	0	0	0	1	0	0	14	1	16
Total	12	49	5	6	9	15	15	16	127

Source: Charles K. Coe and Curtis Ellis, "Internal Controls in State, Local, and Non-Profit Agencies," *Public Budgeting and Finance,* 11, 3 (Fall 1991), p. 43–55.

Management Information Systems

Budget information can be part of a *management information system* (MIS) or it can be a separate system. An MIS uses sophisticated computerized procedures and routines. The advantage of a computerized system is that it offers speed and reliability in dealing with massive volumes of information. However, an MIS is only a tool which must be programmed correctly and given valid information. Ideally, a budget information system fosters the following:

1. *Control*: ensuring that operations take place in conformance with the budget and that funds are not expended in excess of available revenues.
2. *Planning and analysis*: evaluating with accurate, reliable, relevant information alternative allocations of resources and the efficiency of government operations.
3. *Accountability*: ensuring public monies are collected and disbursed properly and that an auditable record is kept of all transactions.

The parts of a budget information system depend on the complexity of the government. A few possible subsystems are *budget preparation, budget status, legislative tracking,* and *treasury.* A budget preparation subsystem would permit quick access to critical data. A budget status subsystem would provide current data on appropriations, administrative reservations, outlays, and so on. A legislative tracking subsystem would permit a quick comprehensive monitoring of legislative actions. A treasury subsystem would prepare the data and reports required on disbursements and outlays. If the data involved are not overwhelming, the agency or government may be wise to process such information manually. If speed or processing of large amounts of information is needed, then a computerized system should be implemented.

Pitfalls do exist. A good budget information system is complex and quite difficult to design, as every detail must be decided to program the computer properly. The budget process demands timely information, so system failures and breakdowns cannot be tolerated. Also, computer errors can often be most embarrassing as they tend to affect groups (for example, giving each member of a group too much money because a decimal place is misprogrammed). Computerized information systems can provide greater productivity to routine operations, but they require valid information and programmers who understand the complexities of budgeting.

In a few governments, *integrated financial management systems* (IFMS) are being used. The exact design varies, but Exhibit 7–4 is a good illustration of an IFMS. It was designed for New York City partly in reaction to that government's mid-1970s fiscal problems. Like other information systems, it accumulates, organizes, stores, and makes information available when needed. It contains a number of subsystems which are linked in the sense that information is shared among the subsystems.

The structure of the New York City IFMS is based on integrating elements and a group of subsystems. The integrating elements are a chart of accounts, standardized formats for transactions, and master tables. The chart of accounts is the basic dictionary for characterizing transactions throughout the system. The standardized formats for transactions permit the system to track and monitor its own activities. The master tables permit the cross-referencing of data. The group of subsystems is composed of budget and monthly plans, accounting, payroll, and purchasing. The first two subsystems are most important, as they provide guidance to the other systems. The make-up of the subsystem is suggested in Exhibit 7–4.

CASH MANAGEMENT AND INVESTMENTS

Cash Management

The government does not collect and disburse money at the same time. There is a time lag, and it is sometimes referred to as *cash flow.* A *cash flow problem* is when the amount that should be paid exceeds available cash even though there are

EXHIBIT 7–4   IFMS Integrated Data Base

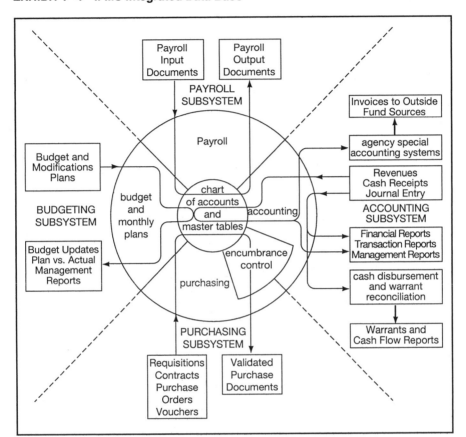

Source: Urban Academy, *An Introduction to IFMS.* New York: New York City Urban Academy, December 1976, p. 39.

enough government assets. Normally, those assets are in the form of obligations or taxes owed to the government that have not yet been paid or collected. The opposite of a cash flow problem is *idle cash.* Governments usually do not have cash flow problems unless they are highly dependent on transfer payments (for example, grants from other governments).

Cash management involves determining the best cash position so money is available for payrolls as well as for payment of debts, and through cash management, "extra" cash is invested until it is needed in the current year. For this to occur, forecasts must be made of the monthly cash balance needed to meet obligations. Government revenue does not come in evenly and is collected from several sources. For example, at the federal level, 25 percent of the revenue is not collected by the treasury. When and how much money is collected, as well as the expenditure rate, by month, for the government, must all be forecasted.

The *cash position* is determined by either of two factors. One is the minimum compensating balance requirement imposed by the commercial bank used by the government. The other is the self-imposed transaction balance developed considering risks and current interest rates on that idle cash. The desirable cash position is the larger amount determined by those two factors.

There are several approaches for determining the best balance. The most common practice is to hold a certain number of days' expenditure as a cash balance. The exact number of days will depend upon the judgment of the budget officer or treasurer. This practice is useful for most small governments. A second approach is called *Economic Ordering Quality* (EOQ). In this mathematical model (see Exhibits 7–5 and 7–6), carrying costs represented by the foregone earned interest are weighed against the total cost of the transactions. The government incurs an opportunity cost for holding rather than investing the cash. And, each bank transaction (for example, transferring from securities to cash) involves an administrative cost to the government. If the number of transactions drives up the cost, then more money can be saved by having a higher cash amount available. A formula helps determine the optimum-size cash balance.

EXHIBIT 7–5   Economic Ordering Quality Formula

$$P = b\left(\frac{T}{c}\right) + vT + i\left(\frac{c}{2}\right)$$

P = total cost of cash management

b = fixed cost per transaction of transferring funds from marketable securities to cash or vice versa

T = total amount of cash payments or expenditures over the period involved

c = size of transfer, which is the maximum amount of cash

v = variable cost per dollar of funds transferred

i = interest rate on marketable securities

The formula used to solve for the optimal transfer size and initial cash balance is

$$C = \sqrt{\frac{2bT}{i}}$$

The average cash balance is computed by dividing C by 2.

Source: J. Richard Aronson and Eli Schwartz, *Management Policies in Local Government Finance*. Washington, D.C.: International City Management Association, 1975, pp. 267–68, 271–272. Used by permission.

EXHIBIT 7–6   Illustration of the EOQ Formula

A city has total cash payments of $6 million for a six-month period. During this period, the payment (T) will be made at a steady rate, the cost per transaction (b) is $50, the interest rate (i) is 3 percent, and the cost per dollar of funds transferred (v) is 0.05 percent. Therefore:

$$c = \sqrt{\frac{2bT}{i}} = \sqrt{\frac{2(50)(6,000,000)}{.03}} = \$141,421$$

The optimal initial cash balance and transfer size is $141,421, and the average cash balance is $141,421 divided by 2 or $70,710. By dividing 6,000,000 by 141,421, the number of transfers (42) can be calculated. The total cost of cash management for the six month period is:

$$P = \$50 \; \frac{(\$6,000,000)}{\$141,421} + .0005 \; \frac{(\$6,000,000)}{} + .03 \; \frac{(\$142,421)}{2} = \$7,242$$

Source: J. Richard Aronson and Eli Schwartz, Management Policies in Local Government Finance. Washington, D.C.: International City Management Association, 1975, pp. 267–68, 271–72. Used by permission.

A third approach is called the *Miller-Orr Model.* The same basic concepts are involved except the focus is placed on the upper dollar limit needed for cash purposes. When the cash balance touches the upper boundary, then a predetermined amount of securities is automatically purchased. When the cash balance touches zero or an amount slightly above zero, then a predetermined amount of securities is sold, thus increasing the cash balance. The upper and lower boundaries are determined with transaction cost and lost earned interest in mind. The greater the likely cash fluctuations, the greater the control limits. The Miller-Orr Model is best applied when cash balances fluctuate randomly.

In order to maximize the investment earned on the cash balances, a cash budget with cash management policies should be developed. A system of prioritizing is needed to handle the more urgent and important spending by having it take precedent over less important needs. Administrative techniques and procedures should be designed to speed up cash management operations, minimize collection and holding costs, follow sound internal financial control, be attentive to good commercial relations, and make cash management more responsive to managerial decisions. Generally, cash usage priorities should be as follows:

- operation and maintenance of existing facilities and the fulfillment of legal obligations such as salaries, pensions, debt service;
- provision or restoration of working capital;
- replacement and renewal of plant and equipment necessary to sustain operations;
- construction or acquisition of equipment and facilities to upgrade current operations and maintenance; and
- expansion of public facilities to meet additional growth.

Cash forecasts should be made based on the likely pattern of receipts and disbursements over a period of time. Useful information for the forecast comes from both department heads and historical records on cash receipts and disbursements. This forecast is used to build a cash budget to determine the daily, weekly, monthly, and yearly cash position of the government. Such a budget should have a short- and long-term time frame. The long-term time frame is important for the higher interest paid for long-term investments. The short-term time frame is important for getting as much income out of idle cash as possible. Different strategies are used for each. Computerized software is available to build such cash budgets and help decide the best strategies to use.

Charles Coe reported on 1986 local government cash management in North Carolina which has a state agency assigned to helping local governments with cash management practices. Exhibit 7–7 shows the investment instruments used by the various types of local government. North Carolina developed the following five criteria to evaluate cash management practices:

EXHIBIT 7–7   Percentage of North Carolina Local Government Units Using Investment Instruments

GOVERN-MENT UNITS	PASS BOOK S.	CDs	NOW % MONEY M.	BAs	COM PAPER	REPOS	FED GOV	ST AG.	POOL
Cities									
50,000 +	30	60	50	50	80	60	70	60	90
10–49,000	31	80	57	14	46	40	17	31	80
2,500–9,999	38	79	78	2	3	14	0	4	46
1,000–2,499	39	67	74	0	2	4	1	0	21
500–999	47	61	68	0	0	2	0	0	10
499–	47	63	56	0	0	1	0	0	6
Counties									
100,000 +	54	85	38	46	77	38	62	62	92
50–99,999	31	92	73	8	35	42	8	12	81
25–49,999	39	83	70	0	26	13	0	9	78
24,999–	30	67	83	0	17	23	0	0	47
Public Author.									
Schools	25	62	88	1	10	23	0	0	32
Housing	28	69	85	0	0	0	1	1	0
Mental Hth C.	24	43	62	0	5	14	0	0	38
Sanitary Dt.	31	50	50	0	0	4	4	0	4
Reg. Airp.	21	36	57	0	7	14	7	7	0
Reg. Lib.	64	71	93	0	0	0	0	0	14
COG	6	24	59	0	0	6	0	0	50
Hospitals	51	69	72	3	26	23	18	5	21

Source: Based on 1986 Local Government Commission's Records reported in Charles K. Coe, "The Effects of Cash Management Assistance By States To Local Government," *Public Budgeting and Finance*. 8, 2 (Summer 1988), pp. 80–90.

- At least 90 percent of funds should be invested.
- Passbook savings should be no more than 10 percent of the cash management portfolio.
- Repurchase agreements (Repos) should be no more than 25 percent of the portfolio.
- Commercial paper should be no more than 50 percent of the portfolio.
- Money market or NOW accounts should be no more than 75 percent of the portfolio.

Exhibit 7–8 shows the percentage of government units that deviated from state norms. In general, Coe concluded that cities over 10,000 in population did a good job of cash management, but smaller cities and certain public authorities (that is, mental health centers, sanitary districts, regional libraries) had poorer cash management practices.

Accelerating the receipt of revenues is one component of cash management. At the state and local levels, receipts come from tax collections, agency collections, intergovernmental transfers, and bond proceeds. In some cases, tax collection policy are established in state laws or local ordinances, but sometimes administrative

EXHIBIT 7–8 Percentage of North Carolina Local Government Deviating from the State Norms

GOVERN MENT UNITS	TOTAL NO	UNIV. + 10%	PASS- BOOK + 10%	REPROS + 25%	COMM. PAPER + 50%	MONEY MARKET OR NOW + 75%
Cities						
50,000 +	10	10	0	20	10	0
10–49,000	36	11	3	3	14	0
2,500–9,999	99	21	7	3	2	9
1,000–2,499	119	34	13	3	0	19
500–999	109	44	22	1	0	12
499–	118	48	22	1	0	9
Counties						
100,000 +	15	7	7	7	20	0
50–99,999	26	8	4	15	12	0
25–49,999	26	15	8	4	12	0
24,999–	33	21	3	9	6	12
Public Author.						
Schools	130	9	2	15	4	14
Housing	99	17	9	0	0	6
Mental Hth C.	24	25	0	8	4	13
Sanitary Dt.	35	29	3	0	0	9
Reg. Airp.	18	22	6	6	0	17
Reg. Lib.	14	21	21	0	0	0
COG	18	28	0	6	0	11

Source: Based on 1986 Local Government Commission's Records reported in Charles K. Coe, "The Effects of Cash Management Assistance by States to Local Government," *Public Budgeting and Finance*, 8, 2 (Summer 1988), pp. 80–90.

action can speed collection. For example, taxpayers can be asked to mail their property tax checks directly to the local government's bank for deposit. Citizens can be allowed to pay their taxes with credit cards and can be given high late-penalty fees to encourage fast payments. The closing date of a bond is normally under the control of the government's finance director and that can be helpful in cash management. Intergovernmental transfer receipts varied widely with federal agencies, but the 1992 deadline of the federal Cash Management Improvement Act should impact significantly state and local governments. Agency collections are often enterprise activities (for example, water and sewer) like the private sector. Thus, such techniques as providing prompt payment discounts, hiring professional collection agencies, listing delinquents with credit reporting services, and sending monthly bills can be effective. In addition, local governments can use tax liens sent to employers and can ask state governments to subtract local tax bills from any state tax refund.

Commercial Bank Services

Which bank should a government use? There is a difference in earned interest and extra bank services which can lower government administrative cost. Also, there is the fact that local banks are likely investors in local or state government securities. Political factors must be weighed. Local banks do provide local jobs. Also, bank officials are often heavy political contributors. Often all those factors are weighed when decisions are made on which bank a local government should use. Because a government uses many accounts, one possibility is to spread the business among all the local banks.

An unusual service provided government is the *warrant*. (It is also explained in Chapter 8.) A warrant is a draft payable through a bank and it is used to slow disbursements. When a warrant is presented for payment, the bank will not pay until the warrant is accepted by the government. This device can be used in cash management to help regulate the amount of cash available. The disadvantage is the higher bank service charge and government cost to manage the use of warrants.

A practice that is becoming obsolete is "playing the float." A *float* is the difference between the total amount of checks drawn on a bank account and the amount shown on the bank's books. If the size of the float can be determined accurately, then the bank balance can be lower, and the idle cash can be invested. For small governments this is not significant; but for large governments, the amount of money can be large and the earned interest on only a few days' investment is significant and worth the effort.

The practice of playing the float is becoming obsolete with the greater use of electronic fund transfer systems, which tend to eliminate the float. The Federal Electronic Funds Transfer System illustrates the new practice. It was implemented by the Treasury Department and Federal Reserve System in 1976. A computer link is established between the Treasury Department and the New York Federal Reserve Bank. The system provides the capability for automatic receipt of fund transfers as well as computer-assisted generation of fund transfers among Treasury, Federal Reserve Banks, member banks, and others using the Federal Reserve Communication Systems. Thus, processing of checks can be done instantly instead of taking several days.

Lock box systems and *cash concentration accounts* can also be used to reduce negative float. Lock boxes are typically post office boxes used by banks in which taxpayers, user fee payers, and others deposit payments. Banks check the boxes several times per day and record the deposits. A concentration account is a regional account that is utilized by multiple funds for initial deposits, which are then processed into a concentration account and become available for immediate investment or wire transfer.

In "Cash Management in Texas Cities" by Robert L. Bland and Bobby Praytor (1985), the authors point out that the most common method of selecting a depository service bank was competitive bidding. Of the 101 cities surveyed, 86 used that approach, with an average of 2.3 bids and a range of 1 to 5 bids. The most common contract period was two years (used by 77 cities), but 6 cities used one year, 5 used three years, and 1 used four years. In the past, banks required a minimum bank balance and often did not charge for banking services, as their income came from investments. The advantage of so-called free service is that the bank arrangement need not be reviewed by the city council. The disadvantages are the lack of linkage between bank services provided and the lack of compensation from idle cash balances. The more desired practice today is for the bank to charge direct fees for the various services provided. The advantage of that practice is greater awareness of what services are provided, thus encouraging administrative care in being more cost-effective. In the survey, 46 cities used "free service," 11 used separate fees, 29 required a compensating balance, and 11 used a combination. ,

Wire transfers and *direct deposits* are important financial innovations for local governments. In the Bland and Praytor survey of Texas city finance directors, the authors reported that the state comptroller in Texas does not wire transfer the state's tax remittances from the state to the local governments. In order to overcome that ploy, many Texas cities maintain a *demand account* in an Austin bank that receives the monthly sales tax remittance checks. Those banks then wire transfer the funds to the respective city depository bank accounts. This innovation permits not only faster transfers but also better controlled transfers of monies. The result is that there is more income from invested idle cash.

The other innovation is direct deposits of the payroll. The city's payroll is deposited directly into the bank accounts of participating employees. The advantages to the city are the increased predictability of fund outflows, the lowered costs of payroll preparation, the enhanced security produced by reducing the chances of misplaced or stolen checks, and the increased amount of employee goodwill. The disadvantage is that there is less time to ride the float.

Two procedures that have proven particularly useful to local governments are using special handling procedures for large checks received in the collection process and using the *paying agent services* of a bank. Because large checks are sometimes a major portion of idle cash investment yield, developing special handling for them is often wise. In such a procedure, mail is opened as early in the day as possible. Large receipts are separated, bundled, and deposited before the bank's cutoff time for crediting deposits.

Often a local government can have its local bank act as the paying agent on the principal and interest of its bonds. This service includes authenticating and canceling bond certificates and coupons as well as disbursing payments to investors. For small- and medium-sized city governments, banks can perform those tasks in a more cost-effective manner due to their specialization. Thus, these procedures can be purchased by the cities from the bank at less cost than if the procedures were done internally by the finance office of the city.

Controlling Payables

Paying bills can mean saving money. Given the fact that idle cash is earning interest, bills should not be paid until they are due unless the discount for early payment is higher than the earned interest. In order to maximize earned interest, governments often make grants using a *letter of credit*. This enables the government to draw interest instead of the grantee.

Care should be taken to ensure that knowledgeable people are paying the bills. Normally, the management and control of payables is centralized to provide that expertise. In larger governments, another method is to use field units, with headquarters establishing spending and disbursement levels. The following general guidelines[1] are useful in tailoring agency or government disbursement and collectibles policies and procedures:

1. Each agency should have a carefully developed disbursement plan as a part of its forecast of outlays. The plan should be consistent with the agency's objectives, strategies, program plans, and budget.
2. A payment schedule and control system should be established.
3. Procedures should be established for evaluating economic factors, including the time value of money, in establishing payment schedules. Unless there are significant programmatic or policy factors, payments should generally be made at the time they are due.
4. Except for very large purchases for which special analyses might be warranted, cash discounts are usually desirable.
5. Procedures should be reviewed to ensure that payments to small vendors and for occasional purchases are not delayed beyond the due dates.
6. Fuller use should he made of letters of credit and other established procedures for managing the timing of payments for government programs.
7. Procedures should be established for regular comparison of actual and planned disbursements.
8. The causes and impact of significant variances from disbursement plans should be evaluated and plans adjusted when necessary.

[1]The guidelines were prepared by the U.S. Joint Financial Improvement Committee.

9. Agencies with significant amounts of receipts should have a collections plan that is a part of the overall forecasts and consistent with the agency's objectives, strategies, program plans, and budget.
10. Collection schedules and control systems for billing and cash processing should be established.
11. Economic factors, including the time value of money, should be considered in the development of billing cycles and collection procedures. The importance of prompt collection and deposit of cash should be recognized.
12. Procedures should be established for regular comparison of actual with planned collections.
13. The causes and impact of significant variances from planned collections should be evaluated and plans adjusted when necessary.

There are three procedures that have proven to be particularly valuable to local governments: pooling cash balances into one central concentration account, using zero-balance accounts for disbursements, and taking timely advantage of trade discounts. The pooling of cash balances into a central concentration account gives important information to the cash manager. This concentration account receives all cash deposits, and all investment purchases are made from it. The aggregation can be from a number of accounts in a single bank or from several banks. In addition, a zero balance is maintained in accounts such as payroll, vendor disbursement, debt service, capital project disbursements, and others. The advantage of concentration and zero-balance accounts is that it eases the task of monitoring cash balances; the monitoring and forecasting need to be done for only one account.

Normally, vendors should not be paid any earlier than (required for example, thirty days). The exception to this payable policy is when a vendor offers a discount for early payment. For example, an offer of "2/10 net 30" means the city may deduct 2 percent from the invoice if payment is received within 10 days. If not, full payment is expected in 30 days. This 2 percent discount is equivalent to a 36 percent interest rate and likely to be higher than interest income from normal idle-cash investments. Thus, the city treasurer should meet the fast payment terms and get the discount.

Investment in Marketable Securities

Once the cash and security position has been determined, the government is ready to invest the money for the desired short period of time. Often as much as 70 percent of the total liquid assets can be invested in securities. State law often limits the choice of securities to "safe" investments such as U.S. Treasury securities, U.S. agency securities, obligations of other municipalities within a state, and bank certificates of deposit. Permissible investments do not include common stock. The actual safety of some government securities is more questionable today—for example, New York City bonds would not have been a safe investment in 1975. Investing in such securities may be permitted under law, but such investments are unlikely until the risk of default on the securities is nearly eliminated.

Not all securities will earn the investor the same return on investment. That return is called "market yield," and it is determined by a combination of:

1. length of maturity;
2. default risk;
3. marketability;
4. call provision; and
5. tax status.

If a government is to invest, then the security market must be watched to determine what is a reasonable market yield, and that yield should be sought. *Long-term securities* tend to receive higher yields, but yields of fifteen to thirty years are not significantly higher. The key influence is the expectation of what will happen to the interest rate. Generally, when interest rates are expected to rise, the yield also rises. In poor market conditions, investors may be offered a risk premium to induce them to invest in long-term securities. Only when interest rates are expected to fall significantly in the future do long-term securities—currently yielding less than short-term securities—become attractive.

Default risk is the possibility that the borrower will fail to pay the principal or interest. All other factors constant, the greater the possibility the borrower will fail to meet the obligation, the greater the premium or market yield on the security. U.S. Treasury and U.S. government agency issues are considered default-free, so they establish the lower limit for securities. The creditworthiness of other issues is judged by the major security rating firms such as Moody's Investor's Service and Standard and Poor's. Sometimes investors demand a risk premium before investing in issues other than default-free securities.

Marketability involves the ability of the security owners to convert the security to cash. This is particularly important when idle cash is used to purchase the security, because the government may wish to convert the security quickly back into cash. Marketability concerns both the price realized and the amount of time required to sell the asset. The more marketable a security, the greater will be the ability of its owner to execute a large security transaction. Less-marketable securities require higher yields.

A *call provision* on a security allows the issuer to buy the security back at a stated price before maturity. The call provision is to the borrower's benefit because the borrower can refund the issue if interest rates move significantly lower. The investor is disadvantaged because the security is called in a period of low interest rates and the investor's funds must then be placed in securities returning a lower yield. Not surprisingly, investors demand a yield inducement and maybe a premium as well to invest in callable securities. Callable government securities are becoming more popular but are unusual in federal government securities.

Tax status has two effects on market yields. First, governments do not have to pay taxes on investment income, thus this is not an expense to them. Second, state and local government securities are tax havens for many private investors; this affects the government security market by driving the yield down. Generally speaking, the fact that local governments do not pay federal income tax means that they should invest in higher-yield federal securities rather than in state and local government securities. Another difference in investment strategy involves deep discount bonds and the tax rates on ordinary and capital gains. This distinction is significant to the individual who is a taxpayer but is not significant to the investing government. Thus, a government should not take advantage of the "bargain" yields on coupon bonds selling at par or above. In general, governments should simply invest in securities showing the highest pretax return.

Cities can contract their cash management investment activities to private companies, but those companies are sometimes massive fraud schemes. For example, Bear Lake, California hired Steve Wymer to invest its capital improvement fund. He promised to earn at least 2 percentage points more than neighboring towns because of his firm's sophisticated Treasury note trading. According to the *Wall Street Journal* dated January 22, 1992, (Gottschalk 1992), Mr. Wymer was arrested at his Newport Beach house and indicted by a federal grand jury for fraud. Mr. Wymer was charged with thirty counts of security fraud, mail fraud, money laundering, and making false statements. The federal government claims that fourteen cities and investment funds of over $113 million were involved. Contracting out cash management is a viable option, especially for small cities; but, obviously, care must be taken in order to avoid being a victim of fraud.

A 1990s intergovernmental approach to cash management for bond proceeds is the Virginia State Non-Arbitrage Program (SNAP), which was created as a reaction to the 1986 federal tax law. SNAP manages the cash from state and local bond proceeds, calculates the arbitrage for local bond issues, and rebates all necessary funds to the federal government to meet arbitrage requirements. This program manages over $1 billion, removes a major cash management burden from local government, has a greater chance of preventing possible arbitrage problems, and permits optimal professional cash management practices. SNAP is being copied in other states.

Types of Marketable Securities

State statutes commonly limit cash management assets to the highest credit quality securities, such as U.S. Treasury obligations, federal agency securities, repurchase agreements (REPOs), bankers' acceptances, and negotiable certificates of deposit (CDs). The two types of U.S. Treasury obligations are *treasury notes* and *treasury bills*. Treasury bills pay a low interest and are auctioned weekly for 91- to 182-day maturities. One-year bills are sold separately. Treasury bills carry no coupon but are sold at discount. These securities are extremely popular as short-term investments. The secondary market is excellent and transaction costs are low. Treasury notes hold one- to seven-year maturities, but they are used in the secondary market for short-term investments. In general, these two types of securities are the safest and most marketable, but they yield the lowest return on investment.

There are other types of securities issued by the federal government carrying the same assurances as U.S. Treasury obligations but having slightly better yields. Principal agencies issuing securities are the federal land banks, federal home-loan banks, federal intermediate credit banks, the Federal National Mortgage Association (called "Fannie Mae"), the Government National Mortgage Association ("Ginnie Mae"), and the banks for cooperatives. Maturities range from one month to fifteen years, but about two-thirds of the issues are for less than one year.

The *repurchase agreement* (REPO) is an innovation of government security dealers who recognize the selling potential of securities tailored to specific short time periods. With REPOs, dealers agree to repurchase the security at a specific future date, thus increasing the number of transactions and the resulting total fees from those transactions. Government investors benefit because they can get securities for the specific time periods they need, thus gaining the desired earned interest. There is little marketability, but that is unimportant because REPOs are normally only for a few days. There is no default risk because the securities are almost always U.S. Treasury securities.

Another commonly used short-term investment is the negotiable *certificate of deposit* (CD). A CD is the deposit of funds at a commercial bank for a specified period of time at a specified rate of interest. This investment device was originated in 1961, and normally it provides a yield better than treasury bills, with maturity in 30 to 360 days. A sizable secondary market exists, but marketability is usually nonexistent for small bank CDs. The default risk is related to the possibility of bank failure, which is normally a low risk for most banks. Commonly, local governments use CDs from local banks to support the region economically.

Portfolio

A *portfolio* is merely the collection of securities one holds. Government investors, as noted before, are limited to the legally sanctioned list of securities. The key consideration for a government's portfolio is to have the cash available when needed for the operations of the state, city, county, and so on. Default risk is minimal and a call risk is unusual. Taxability is not a direct factor; therefore, computations are simplified to the return on investment. Government investors should concentrate on maturity and marketability.

For the short term, needs are best satisfied by treasury bills, REPOs, and CDs. A significant portion of the emergency liquidity needs should be met with treasury bills and REPOs.

Intermediate and long-term needs are handled differently. Treasury notes and bonds, as well as U.S. securities, are used for intermediate purposes. Again, the key is to ensure that cash is available when needed, so maturities must be timed correctly or marketability must be excellent if the timing is not correct. U.S. agency securities provide better yields, but this advantage must be weighed against their marketability. In some cases, long-term investments are used, especially for larger potential emergencies or when funds are accumulated over years for a given purpose. In such cases, long-term treasury and agency securities are normally used. The most important consideration for long-term investments must be the future course of interest rates. The highest yield is not as important as the date of maturity or possible marketability. Often governments take the more conservative approach of confining their investments to short-term securities.

Exhibit 7–9 shows the short-term cash management investment instruments used by the finance directors of Texas cities in FY 1984. This exhibit not only shows the instruments used but also the number of cities out of the 101 surveyed that used the instruments. The exhibit also shows the average percent of cash held in each type of instrument and the range of cash held for each instrument. Note the popularity of the certificates of deposits. In this survey, conducted by Robert L. Bland and Bobby Praytor, 28 cities invested 100 percent of their idle cash in CDs. Administratively, CDs are easier to work with than T-bills; and, politically, investing locally is desirable. Also, in 1984, CD rates were competitive with Treasury bill (T-bill) yields.

EXHIBIT 7–9   Money Market Instruments Used by Texas Cities

TYPE OF INSTRUMENT	NUMBER OF CITIES USING INSTRUMENT	AVERAGE PERCENT OF CASH HELD IN INSTRUMENT	RANGE IN PERCENT OF CASH HELD IN INSTRUMENT
Certificates of Deposits	97	77.0%	10% to 100%
NOW Accounts	20	14.7	5 to 50
Super NOW Accounts	15	19.0	10 to 65
MMDAs	15	25.7	10 to 75
U.S. Treasury Bills	31	31.6	5 to 100
U.S. Treasury Notes	10	29.0	10 to 75
U.S. Agency Securities	3	15.7	2 to 35
Repurchase Agreements	6	39.2	10 to 75
Other	4	8.7	5 to 10

Source: Robert L. Bland and Bobby Praytor, "Cash Management in Texas Cities." Paper presented to the American Society for Public Administration, Indianapolis, Ind., March 24, 1985, p. 14. Used by permission.

In summary, investments of idle cash should be made, but expertise is needed to do it correctly. This section gives the reader some of the basics, but much more knowledge and experience are needed to deal properly in government securities. A better knowledge of both Chapters 7 and 8 will be obtained by reflection on the complementary character of the two.

ACCOUNTING FUNDAMENTALS

Accounting consists of *recording transactions* of an agency in financial terms, including classifying, summarizing, reporting, interpreting, and analyzing those transactions for the user of the data. The key words are "recording transactions." Transactions are financial decisions, such as obligating money, deciding to disburse, and setting aside funds for a purpose. Accounting is merely keeping track of and analyzing those transactions by using summaries and classifications. Accounting provides management with a means to evaluate management performance, to plan for future operations, and, lastly, to achieve financial control.

Principles of government accounting and reporting are deceptively simple. Since 1984, the primary rule-making body for state and local government accounting is the Governmental Accounting Standards Board (GASB), which stresses *accountability* and *interperiod equity*. Accountability is being obliged to explain one's actions and to justify what one does. Interperiod equity addresses the question if the current generation of citizens is shifting the burden of paying for current-year services to future-year taxpayers. GASB believes that accounting users should be able to assess whether current-year revenues are sufficient to pay for the services provided that year and whether future taxpayers will be required to assume burdens for services previously provided. GASB is moving toward requiring the collection of service efforts and accomplishment as a part of government accounting. Accounting principles stress that accounting should complement legal requirements and budgets. Fund accounting is used. Under the principles, government assets are not to be depreciated as in private sector accounting, and a modified accrual method of accounting is recommended. Standard classification, terminology, and reports are suggested. Financial reports are to show current conditions, and yearly reports should be prepared and published.

Government accounting is predicated on disclosure and integration with other management activities. Full disclosure of the financial results of government is essential, or abuse can go undetected. Accounting produces financial information for management purposes, which permits effective control over and ensures the accountability of all funds, property, and other assets. Reliable accounting serves as the basis for preparing and supporting budget requests, for controlling the execution of the budgets, and for providing needed financial information for reviewing groups. Government accounting, which is integrated and consistent with all accounting operations throughout the government, permits comparative analyses, thus strengthening the analytical ability of management. In addition, GASB is considering requiring the reporting of performance measures in order to strengthen accountability and improve management.

Accounting in the federal government was highly fragmented and decentralized prior to the 1990s. The GAO was responsible for prescribing government-wide accounting standards and certifying agency compliance. Their principles were to have (1) complete disclosure of agency financial activities; (2) adequate financial information needed for agency management; (3) effective control over, and accountability for, assets; (4) reliable accounting results and reports that are the basis for preparing and supporting agency budget requests and for executing the budget; and (5) suitable integration of agency accounting with the Department of Treasury's central accounting and reporting responsibilities.

Since 1990, accounting reforms have been aimed at standardizing federal accounting systems and principles, integrating accounting with other financial management activities, and linking accounting and budgeting systems. Other agencies concerned with federal financial management are the Department of the Treasury, the Office of Management and Budget (OMB), the Joint Management Improvement Program (JFMIP), and the Financial Accounting Standards Advisory Board (FASAB). The Department of the Treasury defines financial management requirements and practices because of its cash and debt-management operations. The JFMIP is a small professional staff which reports to a board composed of financial management leaders from GAO, OMB, and Treasury. In 1991, JFMIP created FASAB to help set standards for federal government accounting and reporting.

The Chief Financial Officers Act of 1990 was important legislation. It created in OMB the position of Deputy Director for Management to serve as the chief finance officer (CFO) for the federal government. In the major departments and agencies, the Act created an office of federal financial management which reports to the head of the agency on all financial management matters. Their duties include (1) developing and maintaining an integrated accounting and financial management system; (2) overseeing all financial management activities relating to programs and operations of the agency; and (3) monitoring the financial execution of the budget. The Act also directs the OMB to develop a five-year plan for improving financial management systems and report its progress in implementing the plan.

Accounting Norms and Budgeting

Certain norms are accepted in government accounting. The control accounts or fiscal accounts—which record receipts, obligations, and disbursements—must embrace the detail that supports the budget. If that is not the case, then the budget and accounting information cannot be related. Decisions on the forms of accounting records should be centralized, but the routine decentralized. Standard definitions and classification cannot be achieved without centrally controlled decisions on such matters, but the actual routine of accounting should be handled in the field where the action is taking place. Accounting must accompany a pattern of internal audit and control. Unless some inspections occur that verify that the required accounting practices are being used, the organization will not take the requirements seriously. Actual costs and measures should reflect management success and failure. Accounting is merely a reflection of performance and the reflection must show the good and bad news to help managers understand their true situation. Flexibility in accounting is desirable, but only in the context of overall uniformity. If useful summary information is to be compiled, then accounting uniformity is essential. On the other hand, accounting requirements can inhibit the organization from responding to its environment. This dilemma is always the challenge of top government accountants who must design the accounting systems.

A key step in accounting is *obligation*. If an item is being bought, then the agency normally issues a purchase order or a more formal contract. The purchase order is a valid offer. The vendor will send the goods requested and the bill to the agency based upon a valid purchase order or contract. In the case of personnel, a contract or a mere agreement to work for certain remunerations constitutes the obligation. The agency must pay for services rendered, and tenure protections commonly exist for government employees. Once an order is placed and has been accepted by the vendor, the government is obligated to pay—given that the contract is fulfilled by the vendor. At this stage, the agency records the order as an *accounts payable* item when the purchase order is sent. Normally, not all the money obligated must be paid because some orders are deficient in some manner and the government is not obligated to pay in such circumstances.

Once the goods have been received and placed in inventory, then an accrued expenditure exists until such time as the check is issued. This concept is useful if there is a large purchasing function because the demand on cash and government liability would be monitored more closely. In many other types of government functions, this concept is not needed. In this chapter the reports cited do not use "accrued expenditure" because the concept normally is not needed.

Expenditures is another step. This is when the invoice has been received from the vendor, and money—in the form of a check—is actually issued by the government. Today, expenditures are controlled closely. In the federal government, the rate of disbursement, especially on grants, is monitored and controlled for fiscal policy reasons. In all levels of government, but to a lesser extent in the federal government, the rate of disbursement is monitored and controlled to avoid shortages of cash and to take advantage of short-term idle cash investments.

Two additional budget and accounting concepts can also be applied. Once the goods are in hand but not being used, they are considered *inventory*. This concept is useful because inventory can be converted to cash if necessary; thus, separate treatment helps the decision maker have a better understanding of agency convertible assets. Another concept is *cost*. Once the goods are taken from inventory, they are considered used and are a cost. At this point, the item is no longer an asset.

Government accounting is keyed to the operating budget. Accounting is especially useful in tracking the obligations and expenditures against the budget. In government accounting, the term *encumbrance* is used. It is a claim on money. As soon as an obligation is made, the money needed to pay the obligation is set aside and no longer included in the balance of money available for new commitments. In budgeting for personnel costs, encumbrances are sometimes not essential because the cost is highly routine and regular in its flow. However, in budgeting for purchases of equipment, materials, supplies, other contracts, and grants, encumbrances are quite important, and the accounting system should provide data on those encumbrances as well as on later, related expenditures. This point shall be made again in the discussion concerning Exhibits 7–11 and 7–12.

In state and local government, a large share of the funds used comes from *grants* from the federal government. Federal requirements normally stipulate that each grant should be treated as a fund, with separate records maintained on all receipts and expenditures. The permitted cost and required supporting documents are spelled out in federal guidelines. Generally, the requirements are similar to those for normal government accounts. The appropriate local share of the grant is a unique feature of the federal guidelines. Normally, the local government can use cash gifts as well as value of goods and services for the local share. And, federal regulations include provisions for auditing of financial records plus acceptable internal control procedures such as those discussed later in this chapter.

FINANCIAL ADMINISTRATION

The key to good financial administration is to keep good account records. All financial transactions must be recorded. They must then be summarized and classified. Also, all such transactions must be related to the appropriate fiscal year.

Government accounting uses the fund concept. A *fund* is a sum of money set aside for a particular purpose and accounted for separately from the other monies of the government. The purpose behind fund accounting is to control the handling of money to ensure that it will be spent only for the purposes intended, such as highway construction. The concept is used extensively, but it does reduce management flexibility, thus making public management more difficult. The fund categories used by GASB are general, special revenue, fiduciary, and debt and capital projects. The federal government uses general and trust funds.

Government accounting uses a *modified accrual method* rather than the *cash method* of accounting. In the cash method, income is recorded when it is received, and expenditures are recorded when they are paid. In other words, transactions are recorded as of the date the cash changes hands. The advantages of the cash method are that it is easy to administer and the cash balance is easily determined. The critical disadvantage is that expenses and revenues cannot be related to the budget and its fiscal year. Thus, accountability is impossible.

In the accrual method of accounting, revenues are recorded when they are earned or billed and expenditures are recorded when they are obligated. The accrual method does permit accountability, but it also distorts the revenue and cash position of the government. The cash position must be calculated separately, as described earlier. Governments use a modified accrual method primarily because there are fundamental differences between a private enterprise operation and a government undertaking. This difference will become apparent when the various financial reports are discussed.

The modified accrual basis of accounting is required by the Governmental Accounting Standards Board (GASB) which established the General Accepted Accounting Principals (GAAP) for state and local government in the United States. GASB's standards are influential because (1) most states require local governments to follow GAAP, (2) the American Institute of Certified Public Accountants (AICPA) changed its guidance to auditors to recognize GASB as the primary standard setting body for state and local government, (3) the bond-rating agencies have indicated they expect annual financial reports to comply with GASB standards, and (4) the federal government required all governmental entities receiving federal funds to be audited in accordance with the Single Audit Act, which requires a statement as to whether the financial report complies with GASB standards. In general, accrual accounting is not required of the general fund but is required of funds that collect revenues for services rendered, such as water and sewer activities. As a means to further encourage GAAP accounting, the Government Finance Officers Association awards the Certificate of Achievement for Excellence in Financial Reporting. The certificate is earned after a government submits a Comprehensive Annual Financial Report (CAFR) and receives a positive recommendation from an impartial peer-review committee.

Accounting is built upon three operational tools: vouchers, journals, and ledgers. A *voucher* is a document that confirms the fact that a financial transaction has taken place. For example, payroll checks, purchase orders, receipts for rent payment, and even appropriation laws are vouchers. The *journal* is the first record book (now sometimes a computer printout) of the transactions. It is a chronological listing of the transactions and shows the date of the transaction's occurrence, the dollars, and a brief explanation of the transaction. A *ledger* is a group of accounts which pertain to the same subject, that is, a subject matter listing of information. These tools are important because together they provide the means to record usefully, summarize, and classify the transactions.

Basic Governmental Accounting

An important accounting convention is to use a double-entry system, with documents as the basic record. Original entries of transactions are recorded in journals and posted to general and subsidiary ledgers. Recording and posting are done with the objective of keeping both sides of the accounting equation always balanced. The fundamental accounting equation starts with *assets* equaling *equities*. Assets are owned items, such as cash, tax receivables, equipment, and buildings. Equities are claims against those assets; they include *liabilities* (for example, claims of creditors for goods and services purchased, amounts due to employees for unpaid wages, amounts due on loans) and *residual equity* (in the public sector, the latter is called *fund balance*). Some forms of equity are not available for potential obligation, and they are separated from fund balance and called *reserves*. The revised account equation, which can be seen in Exhibit 7–10, is as follows:

EXHIBIT 7–10   Revised Account Equation

$A = L + R + FB$
where
A = assets
L = liabilities
R = reserves
FB = fund balance

Source: Adapted from Khi V. Thai, "Governmental Accounting," *Handbook on Public Budgeting and Financial Management*, eds. Jack Rabin and Thomas D. Lynch, New York: Marcel Decker, 1983, p. 324.

The double-entry system is designed to isolate entry and arithmetic errors. In posting entries, each transaction must be both a debit and a credit. A debit of one account must be accompanied by a credit in the same amount on another account so that the accounting equation always remains balanced. As a rule, any increase in an account on the left side of the accounting equation must be debited, whereas an increase in the same amount on the right side is credited. For example, debits are increases in assets and decreases in liability accounts. Credits are decreases in assets and increases in liability. To check for errors, trial balances of the equation are used, but finding simple entry and arithmetic errors can be time-consuming. Fortunately, the use of the computer permits greater speed in calculation and reduces the likelihood of arithmetical error. Thus, the computer has become an essential tool for large accounting systems.

Accounting System Design

There are several factors to consider when designing an accounting system. Information should be timely, accurate, and objective. Obviously, this is an ideal and trade-offs must be made, especially between timeliness and accuracy. The system should be consistent with all legally established minimum requirements. Particular attention should be given to the collection and recording of information because this is the place where most errors occur. Care must be taken to design cross- and double-checks to isolate and correct such errors. Another concern is classification, summarization, and storage. Proper design here rests on an excellent grasp of how the information can best be used. Thought also goes into evaluating the use of electronic data processing. The advantage is speed and enhanced analytical capability. The risks to consider are computer-assisted fraud and the possibility of massive, extremely embarrassing mistakes.

The final factor to weigh in designing an accounting system is internal control. The system should fix responsibility on specific individuals. Policies and procedures should be written to avoid misunderstandings. Only designated personnel should be authorized to perform certain key functions such as disbursement. Forms should be considered carefully, so they reduce the likelihood of error and fraud. All reporting should be analyzed regularly and carefully, or the reports should be eliminated. Care must be taken to establish built-in cross- and double-checks of forms, people, and units in order to isolate errors and prevent fraud. For example, independent record keepers can be used to act as cross-checks on each other. A further safeguard is to use independent auditors. One final but key point to internal control is to get, train, and keep good people in the accounting unit.

Accounting systems should provide a standard, systematic method of communicating relevant, complete, and accurate financial information. The following activities become particularly important:

- classifying financial transactions and economic events,
- recording the economic nature of each event,
- summarizing the economic information in a meaningful way to policy makers and managers, and

- interpreting and communicating the results to appropriate decision makers and user groups.

REPORTS AND ANALYSES

Accounting is one of those subjects that can best be understood by example. The previous portions of this chapter explain accounting and financial administration fundamentals. This portion explains specific reports that illustrate some of the fundamentals and demonstrate the usefulness of accounting. The reports and analyses are drawn from Chapter 15 of Aronson and Schwartz, *Management Policies in Local Government Finance* (1975). The following five financial reports are discussed:

1. statement of revenue: estimated and actual;
2. appropriation and expenditure ledger account;
3. statement of encumbrances and authorization;
4. fund balance change; and
5. balance sheet.

Statement of Revenue

Exhibit 7–11 compares estimated with actual government revenue. This accounting report provides highly useful information to help analysts judge the accuracy of forecasting techniques. This report should be keyed to funds, tax source, and fiscal year. As the reader may recall, separate estimates must be made for each tax source, and separate accounting forces us to examine the estimates by funds and fiscal year. The recorded estimate should be the official one used by the government in computing its budget. Again, the reader may recall, the government should pass a resolution indicating the assumed (projected) revenue. The actual revenue should be that amount actually collected.

In examining Exhibit 7–11, the reader will notice where estimation errors were made. The important errors are those that result in significantly less revenue for the government. These errors are particularly harmful and result in using tax anticipation notes. If the revenue source is small, then large errors can be tolerated. If the revenue source is large, then even small, optimistic errors cannot be tolerated. In Exhibit 7–11, the intergovernmental revenue (for example, state payment, revenue sharing, or grant-in-aid) was significantly in error. Fortunately, the conservative estimates on the other revenue sources more than offset the mistake so that the entire estimate was off by about 9 percent. Exhibit 7–11 tells the analyst that more effort must go into forecasting revenue correctly.

The subsequent exhibits (7–12, 7–13, 7–14, 7–15) are complementary. Each tells the analyst a part of a story, but together they tell a reasonably comprehensive story about the whole government. For example, each is concerned with encumbrances and expenditures. If a question is raised on encumbrances in the balance sheet (Exhibit 7–15), the ultimate answer may be found in the appropriation and expenditure ledger account (Exhibit 7–12) or the statement of expenditures and encumbrances (Exhibit 7–13). The analyst must be able to read all the financial reports and understand their interrelationship.

EXHIBIT 7–11   Milesville General Fund Statement of Revenue—Estimated and Actuals, Fiscal Year Ending June 30, 2001

REVENUE SOURCE	ESTIMATED REVENUE	ACTUALS REVENUE	ACTUAL OVER- OR (UNDER) ESTIMATED
Taxes	$240,000	$ 290,000	$50,000
Licenses and permits	30,000	36,000	6,000
Intergovernmental revenue	120,000	90,000	(30,000)
Charges for services	40,000	45,000	5,000
Fines and forfeitures	6,000	9,000	3,000
Miscellaneous	4,000	10,000	6,000
Total	$440,000	$ 480,000	$40,000

Source: J. Richard Aronson and Eli Schwartz, *Management Policies in Local Government Finance*. Washington, D.C.: International City Management Association, 1975, pp. 267–68, 271–72. Used by permission.

Appropriation and Expense Ledger

Exhibit 7–12 is a subsidiary or partial appropriation and expenditure ledger account. As defined earlier, a *ledger* concerns a subject, and, in this case, the subject is a specific account (or fund), including information on encumbrances, expenditures, and essential voucher information. This report uses regularly and routinely collected voucher information.

Exhibit 7–12 tells us a story. On July 1, 2000, the fiscal year began with $125,000 being appropriated to the supplies account of the general fund. This meant that $125,000 was available to be obligated and spent. On July 10, 2000, some laboratory equipment was ordered which cost $25,000, thus reducing the amount to be obligated to a total of $100,000. Details of the order can be found on purchase order number 104, and this order constitutes a voucher. On October 15, 2000, an automobile or parts for automobiles were ordered, costing $10,000. This increased the encumbered balance to $35,000 and reduced the unencumbered balance to $90,000. On November 3, 2000, the ordered laboratory equipment finally arrived and was paid for. However, either some of the merchandise was damaged or a discount was given because the actual expenditure was $24,500. This meant that the total encumbrance was reduced by $25,000 to $10,000. The difference of $500 between the encumbrance and expenditure required a $500 upward adjustment in the unencumbered balance because that money was again available for obligation.

This type of financial report is quite useful. The analyst always knows how much money is available in each account for obligation, how much has already been spent, and how much is obligated but not yet actually spent. At any time in the

EXHIBIT 7-12 Milesville General Fund—Supplies Account Appropriation and Expenditure Ledger Account Starting July 1, 2000

| | | ENCUMBRANCES | | | EXPENDITURES | | APPROPRIATIONS | |
DATE	EXPLANATION	INCREASE	DECREASE	BALANCE	AMOUNT	TOTAL	AMOUNT	UNENCUMBERED BALANCE
Jul. 1	Budget						$125,000	$125,000
Jul. 10	Lab. equip.—P.O. #104	$25,000		$25,000				100,000
Oct. 15	Autos—P.O. #410	10,000		35,000				90,000
Nov. 3	Lab. equip.—P.O. #104		$25,000	10,000	$24,500	$24,500		90,500

Source: J. Richard Aronson and Eli Schwartz, Management Policies in Local Government Finance. Washington D.C.: International City Management Association 1975, pp. 267–68, 271–72. Used by permission.

current year, the operating budget may have to be revised. A summary appropriation and expenditure ledger account is essential for an intelligently done revision. Also the account tells managers how much they can plan on using and how much can be (or should be) spent before the end of the year.

Exhibit 7–13 is an elaborate summary statement of appropriations and expenditures. It is done for each separate fund and compares appropriations with expenditures and encumbrances involving a two-year period. This statement assumes that the fund balance is closed at the end of two years, thus providing sufficient time to pay obligations from the previous year. A two-year period is a reasonable time, but a shorter or longer time period can be selected. The reader may notice that the $800 "close to fund balance" and other information appear in Exhibit 7–14. The reader may also note that the information can be further subdivided into activities and objects.

Exhibit 7–13 helps identify expenditure forecasting errors, but a serious problem is not apparent in the example cited. Out of $425,000 appropriated, there was left unobligated only $11,200, or about 2 percent of the total. However, most of the money was in the welfare category, and the expenditure forecast error in that category was 16 percent. This error, coupled with a zero encumbrance, would raise a question for a budget analyst. The low 2001 encumbrances total is a pleasing sign that last-of-the-year spending was low and that proper pacing of obligations probably took place. The prior year's encumbrances total was even lower, so the manager might watch for a possible laxness developing in this area, but there certainly is no cause for alarm.

An analysis of the closing entries is particularly interesting. The sanitation function had negative closing entries; more money was spent than encumbered. This is a matter of note. Other interesting occurrences were the large $300 and $265 amounts in two categories. They represent 75 percent of one category and 48 percent of the other. Both percentages are high, but the amounts are low. Possibly, further investigation is warranted, but such an investigation is not recommended strongly. The total percentage of encumbrances to the closing entries is high at 16 percent, but the amount is low, so nothing extremely serious appears to be wrong beyond the antideficiency error.

Exhibit 7–13 also helps identify managers who may be obligating end-of-the-year funds in an attempt to argue that they needed all their requested appropriations. If the encumbered balances are large, this implies large last-of-the-year obligations that have not been paid yet. Also, large close to fund balances indicate sloppy purchasing practices which may be due to hasty obligations in the previous year. Analysts should check the ledger accounts to see when obligations were made and then confirm if they were necessary. An examination of increases in inventory would also be wise.

Fund Balance Change

Exhibit 7–14 focuses attention on available assets and the fundamental changes that occurred during a fiscal year. It is done for each separate fund and highlights the key additions and subtractions associated with the fund change during

EXHIBIT 7–13 Milesville General Fund Statement of Expenditures and Encumbrances Compared with Authorizations, Fiscal Year Ending June 30, 2001

	PRIOR YEAR RESERVE FOR ENCUMBRANCES	EXPENDITURES CHARGEABLE TO PRIOR YEAR RESERVE FOR ENCUMBRANCES	CLOSE TO FUND BALANCE	2001 APPROPRIATIONS	2001 EXPENDITURES	2001 ENCUMBRANCES	2001 UNENCUMBERED BALANCE
General government	$1,500	$1,500		$ 45,000	$41,000	$2,000	$2,000
Public safety	750	750		100,000	98,000	500	1,500
Highways and streets	450	400	$50	60,000	60,000		
Sanitation	250	275	(25)	40,000	39,000		1,000
Health	150	140	10	20,000	18,000	1,300	700
Welfare	1,000	800	200	30,000	25,000		5,000
Culture-recreation	400	100	300	16,000	13,200	2,000	800
Education	500	235	265	14,000	12,600	1,200	200
Transfer of funds				100,000	100,000		
Service fund	$5,000	$4,200	$800	$425,000	$406,800	$7,000	$11,200

NOTE: The NCGA would prefer breaking down expenditures by activity and object as well. This has been omitted for the sake of brevity. If there has been material revision of appropriations since the adoption of the original budget, this should be indicated here, with columns showing the original budget and revisions.

Source: J. Richard Aronson and Eli Schwartz, *Management Policies in Local Government Finance.* Washington D.C.: International City Management Association, 1975, pp. 267–68, 271–72. Used by permission.

the year. The excess of revenue over expenditure is added after it is adjusted upward for the prior-year reserve for encumbrances. Deductions are made from the reserve for encumbrances, and additions are made for increases in reserve inventory and supplies. The revenue in the computation is cited in Exhibit 7–11, and the expenditure is cited in Exhibit 7–13. And, the reserve for encumbrances can be found in Exhibit 7–13. The increase in reserve inventory and supplies is reflected in Exhibit 7–15, and will be discussed more later.

EXHIBIT 7–14 Milesville General Fund Analysis of Changes in Fund Balance, Fiscal Year Ended June 30, 2001

Fund balance, July 1, 2000		$ 84,500
Add:		
Excess of revenues over expenditures, 2001		
Revenues	$480,000	
Expenditures	406,800	
		73,200
Reserve for encumbrances, June 30, 2000	$ 5,000	
Less: Expenditures charged to prior-year reserve for encumbrances	4,200	
		800
		$158,500
Deduct:		
Reserve for encumbrances, June 30, 2001	7,000	
Increase in reserve inventory and supplies	2,000	
		9,000
Fund balance, June 30, 2001		$149,500

Source: J. Richard Aronson and Eli Schwartz, *Management Policies in Local Government Finance.* Washington, D.C: International City Management Association 1975, pp. 267–68, 271–72. Used by permission.

The fund balance tells us how much money can be spent without fear of overspending. It also explains the component parts of that figure. The revenue-less-expenditure figure tells us there is a 15 percent surplus, which is certainly unusual in most governments. The fund increases by $65,000, which constitutes a 177 percent yearly increase. Some questions about this increase should be raised by a budget examiner, as either taxes can be cut or expenditures can be increased. Certainly, the fund is in a healthy position in which to be starting the next year, unless some unusual expenditure increase is forecasted.

Notice the figure $73,200 in the analysis. That represents also the sum of (1) the revenue forecasting errors, (2) the expenditure forecasting errors, and (3) any deliberate unbalanced budget. In this case, the revenue forecasting error is $40,000, as can be seen in Exhibit 7–11. The expenditure forecasting error from Exhibit 7–14 is the sum of encumbrances and unencumbered balances ($7,000 plus $11,200) or $18,200. The deliberately unbalanced budget can be seen by comparing the total appropriations in Exhibit 7–13 and the estimated revenue in Exhibit 7–11. The first is $425,000 and the second is $440,000. In other words, the decision makers passed a surplus budget of $15,000. The math is as follows:

Revenue forecasting errors	$40,000
Expenditure forecasting errors	18,200
Unbalanced budget	15,000
Total	$73,200

Balance Sheet

The balance sheet is illustrated in Exhibit 7–15. The government balance sheet is similar to a private business balance sheet and is based on the simple formula: total assets equal total liabilities, reserves, and the fund balance. Assets include cash, short-term investments, property tax receivables, amounts due from other funds, and inventory. Liabilities include accounts payable and payroll taxes payable. Reserves include reserve for encumbrances and inventory of supplies. The balance sheet is designed to emphasize available assets, especially quickly available assets. A balance sheet must be prepared for each fund and each fiscal year.

The interesting feature of the government balance sheet is the items not found in it. The balance sheet does not include depreciation, profit, or stocks. Government accounting normally does not include depreciation. Capital items are reflected in the capital budget and debt administration. Government can have a surplus but not a profit. If money is returned to the taxpayer, it is called a *rebate*, but that is unusual. Government programs provide a service and also normally are not designed to make a profit. The initial capital or designated paper representing ownership in a private business is called *stock*. By definition, a government is owned and controlled by the people through the political process; therefore, the notion of private ownership is logically impossible. Instead, the fund balance is used to indicate available resources in the fund.

The balance sheet is informative, especially if it is presented in a comparative format. By examining Exhibit 7–15, one can see that the fund has grown significantly during the year, with little growth in total liabilities. One can also quickly see that not a great deal of money is held in cash and that idle cash is invested in short-term investments. The reader will note that the investment is cited at cost rather than at the higher market value. This is to provide the safest conservative estimate, but both cost and market value should always be shown. This information shows the loss of profit anticipated from the investment. It is also apparent that the amount of property tax receivables and allowances for uncollectible taxes has declined during this period. This is a good sign because it indicates a sound tax base and good collection practices. The inventory of supplies and its corresponding reserve have not grown radically, so unnecessary purchases probably did not take place. The significant increase was in the fund balance. An analyst would question this increase and wish to examine the fund balance in more detail.

EXHIBIT 7–15 Milesville General Fund, Balance Sheet, Fiscal Year Ending June 30, 2001

ASSETS		2001		2000
Cash		$ 15,000		$ 8,000
Short-term investment—at cost (market value $123,000)		120,000		50,000
Property taxes receivable	$35,000		$ 45,000	
Less:				
Allowance for uncollectible taxes	3,000	32,000	4,000	41,000
Due from other funds		1,500		2,200
Inventory of supplies		10,000		8,000
Total Assets		$178,500		$109,200

LIABILITIES	2001	2000
Accounts payable	$10,000	$ 9,200
Payroll taxes payable	2,000	2,500
Total Liabilities	12,000	11,700
RESERVES		
Reserve for encumbrances	7,000	5,000
Reserve for inventory of supplies	10,000	8,000
Total Reserves	17,000	13,000
FUND BALANCE	149,500	84,500
Total Liabilities, Reserve, and Fund Balance	$178,500	$109,200

In a balance sheet, the "due from other funds" amount is a significant item. In this particular balance sheet (Exhibit 7–15), there is no apparent problem, but problems can exist. The use of many funds means that some interfund transfers are necessary. It is possible to abuse these transfers for the purpose of confusing or hiding the real condition of the various funds. Fraud, poor management, or deliberate attempts to present a better picture of financial conditions are some of the reasons for an abuse of transfer. An analyst can be aware of this potential and can make an inquiry if the "due from other funds" amount distorts the total assets in the balance sheet. The inquiry would involve the legality and motivation behind any unusually high assets acquired as a result of the transfer.

The financial reports are an important use of the accounting system. They provide information useful in budget preparation, operating budgets, and auditing. Knowledge of the complexities of public budgeting and government are essential if the financial reports are to be interpreted correctly. Each financial report is read in the context of the other reports and with the knowledge of the budget process.

This section of the chapter explains the fundamental decisions to be made in computerizing an accounting system. Many small governments can save a significant amount of operating expenses and greatly improve their management capabilities by shifting from a hand-posted accounting system to computerized operation. Often, small governments may have only bank statements or small bookkeeping activities, which are difficult to maintain owing to high personnel turnover. A standard computer software package can be designed for small governments in each state. Such a system could be used by most cities in a state, require a minimum amount of effort to operate, and provide adequate financial data to local public managers. Such system was developed in Tennessee. Its computerized "General Ledger and Budgeting Accounting Program" costs $600 to $2,500 to operate, depending on the number of transactions. It serves as an example of what can be done.

A fundamental ingredient of the Tennessee system is a codification of the accounting fields based on the state uniform standardized chart of accounts. The use of the code does assume correct coding of the transactions. A qualified person is needed to analyze the reports, correct coding mistakes, and isolate problems in coding. The codification in Tennessee is as follows:

XX—XXX—XXXXX—XXX—XXX—XX

City code: to identify the city on the computer file;
Fund code: to identify groups and specific funds;
Basic account or purpose account: to identify accounts such as assets, liabilities, revenues, expenditures, reserves, etc.;
Object account: to identify primary and secondary objects of expenditures;
Optional code: for project cost accounting; and
Second optional code: to identify responsibility centers.

Input and Output

The input for the Tennessee system is in the form of vouchers. A copy of the checks plus entry information (for example, fund, function, object, debit, credit, description) go to the computer center. Cash reports on deposits, budget, and a general journal form (for corrections, adjustments, recordings of accounts payable, and encumbrances) are also sent to the computer center with the appropriate entry information. Data are batch-processed and the sending unit is responsible for the accuracy of the input. The computer center does run an input edit on the cards to ensure that (1) each transaction is entered dually according to accounting practice, (2) each expenditure and encumbrance has an object code, and (3) no code number has been used that is not in the chart of accounts. The edit is only for easily caught errors. More significant errors must be caught with an inspection procedure and an examination of the reports produced with this data.

The computer can generate an amazing number of useful reports based on the previously described input. These include:

1. the balance sheet;
2. trial balance;
3. general journal entry register;
4. budget entry register;
5. cash receipts journal;
6. cash disbursement journal;
7. deposit register;
8. analysis of change in cash on hand;
9. statement of estimated, realized, and unrealized revenue by specific source;
10. statement of expenditures compared by appropriation (function and object);
11. statement of object expenditures by account number; and
12. detailed general ledger analysis (helps trace transactions for each account).

Much more complex computerized accounting systems than the Tennessee example exist. By examining a simple system, however, the relationship of the computer to fundamental accounting concepts and financial reports can be understood more easily. And, the usefulness of computers becomes more apparent. The task of preparing reports on each fund is time-consuming. A computer can take much of the dull routine out of accounting work and do it much more accurately.

REVIEW QUESTIONS

1. Compare and contrast apportionment, allotment, and administrative reservations.
2. What are the common pitfalls one can anticipate in budget execution, and how can budget execution system design assist in minimizing these pitfalls? Compare and contrast budget and administrative controls.

3. Explain the fraud–red tape dilemma. Explain the importance of and how to achieve cash internal control.
4. Explain cash management and its importance. Why are guidelines for disbursement and collection significant, and what are their implications? What knowledge is particularly useful in investing idle cash?
5. Explain the fundamentals of accounting. How does accounting support budgeting?
6. Explain how one can go about making an analysis of a city's financial situation using each of the key financial reports discussed in this chapter.

REFERENCES

American Accounting Association. "Report of the Committee on Accounting for Not-For-Profit Organization," *Accounting Review*, Supplement to Vol. 46 (1971), 81–163.

APOSTOLOU, N. G., R. C. BROOKS, and W. B. HILDRETH. "Research and Trends in Governmental Accounting and Reporting," *International Journal of Public Administration*, 15, 5 (1992), 1121–1150.

APPLEBY, PAUL. "The Role of the Budget Division," *Public Administration Review*, 18, 3 (Summer 1957), 156–59.

ARONSON, J. RICHARD, and ELI SCHWARTZ (eds.). *Management Policies in Local Government Finance*. Washington, D.C.: International City Management Association, 1975.

BARTIZAL, JOHN R. *Budget Principle and Procedure*. Englewood Cliffs, NJ: Prentice Hall, 1942.

BATER, FRANCIS M. *The Question of Government Spending*. New York: Harper & Row, 1960.

BIERMAN, HAROLD, JR., and SEYMOUR SMIDT. *The Capital Budgeting Decision*. New York: Macmillan, 1966.

BLAND, ROBERT L., and BOBBY PRAYTOR. "Cash Management in Texas Cities." Paper presented to the American Society for Public Administration in Indianapolis, IN, March 24, 1985.

BLOCKER, JOHN GARY. *Budgeting in Relation to Distribution Cost Accounting*. Lawrence, KS: School of Business, 1937.

BUCK, ARTHUR EUGENE. *The Budget in Government of Today*. New York: Macmillan, 1934.

BURKHEAD, JESSE. *Government Budgeting*. New York: John Wiley, 1956.

COE, CHARLES K. "The Effects of Cash Management Assistance by States To Local Government," *Public Budgeting and Finance*. 8, 2 (Summer 1988), 80–90.

COE, CHARLES C., and CURTIS ELLIS. "Internal Controls in State, Local, and Non-Profit Agencies," *Public Budgeting and Finance*. 11, 3(Fall 1991), 43–55.

CRECINE, JOHN E. *Governmental Problem Solving: A Computer Simulation of Municipal Budgeting*. Chicago: Rand McNally, 1969.

ERNEST, E. "The Accounting Preconditions of PPB(S)," *Management Accounting*, 53 (January 1972), 33–37.

FISHER, G. W. *Financing Local Improvement by Special Assessment*. Chicago: Municipal Finance Officers Association, 1974.

FOUNTAIN, JAMES R., JR. "Future Changes in Financial Reporting: A Primer on GASB," *Intergovernmental Perspective*. (Fall 1990), 35–37.

FREEMAN, ROBERT J., and EDWARD S. LYNN. *Fund Accounting*, 2nd ed. Englewood Cliffs, NJ: Prentice Hall, 1983.

GOTTSCHALK, EARL C., JR. "Small Town Treasurers Rue the Day They Met Steve Wymer," *The Wall Street Journal*, January 22, 1992, p. 1.

HACKBART, MERL H., and JAMES R. RAMSEY. "Public Cash Management: Issues and Practices." In Thomas D. Lynch and Lawrence Martin (eds.), *Handbook of Comparative Public Budgeting and Financial Management.* New York: Marcel Dekker, 1993, 293–312.

HENRY, M. L., et al. "New York State's Performance Budget Experiment," *Public Administration Review*, (July/August 1970).

JOINES, W. W. "Computerized General Ledger and Budgeting Accounting Systems," *Government Finance*, 5, 2 (May 1976), 27–32.

KANE, THOMAS J. JR. "City Managers View Intergovernmental Relations," *Publins*, 14 (Summer 1984), 121–33.

LEMOV, PENELOPE. "How To Collect Every Last Dime," *Governing*, vol. 5, no. 4 (January 1992), 24–25.

MOAK, LENNOX L., and KATHRYN W. KILLIAN. *Operating Budget Manual.* Chicago: Municipal Finance Officers Association, 1963.

National Committee on Government Accounting. *Governmental Accounting, Auditing, and Financial Reporting.* Chicago: Municipal Finance Officers Association, 1968.

PITSVADA, BERNARD T. "Flexibility in Federal Budget Execution," *Public Budgeting and Finance*, 3, 2 (Summer 1983), 83–101.

RONDINELLI, DENNIS A. "Revenue Sharing and American Cities: Analysis of the Federal Experiment in Local Assistance," *Journal of the American Institute of Planners*, 41, 5 (September 1975), 319–33.

SCHICK, ALLEN. *Manual on the Federal Budget Process.* Washington, D.C.: U.S. Congressional Research Service, December 24, 1991.

STEIN, A. W. *Local Government Finance.* Lexington, MA: Lexington Books, 1975.

———. "Symposium: Performance Budgeting: Has the Theory Worked?" *Public Administration Review*, (Spring 1960).

THAI, KHI V. "Governmental Accounting." In Jack Rabin and Thomas D. Lynch (eds.), *Handbook on Public Budgeting and Financial Management.* New York: Marcel Dekker, 1983.

———. "Government Financial Reporting and Auditing." In Jack Rabin and Thomas D. Lynch (eds.), *Handbook on Public Budgeting and Financial Management.* New York: Marcel Dekker, 1983.

THIERANF, R. J., and RICHARD A. GROSSE. *Decision-Making Through Operations Research.* New York: Wiley, 1970.

TURNBUIL, AUGUSTUS. *Governmental Budgeting and PPBS: A Programmed Introduction.* Reading, MA: Addison-Wesley, 1970.

Urban Academy, *An Introduction to IFMS.* New York: New York City Urban Academy, December 1976.

U.S. Civil Service Commission, Bureau of Training, The Management Science Training Center, *Budget Formulation*, Washington, D.C.: 1976.

U.S. Joint Financial Management Improvement Program. *Money Management.* Washington, D.C.: U.S. Joint Financial Management Improvement Program, 1976.

U.S. Joint Financial Management Improvement Program. *Operating Budgets.* Washington, D.C.: U.S. Joint Financial Management Improvement Program, November 1975.

8

CAPITAL BUDGETING
AND DEBT ADMINISTRATION

This chapter discusses state and local debt, capital budgeting, and issuances. The concept of debt is defined and classifications commonly used are explained. Capital budgeting is contrasted to operating budgeting, with emphasis placed on capital facility planning and the capital budget cycle. The practical aspects of state and local bonding are explained, including designing an issue, the prospectus, notice of sale, debt records, reporting, and bond ratings. Capital budgeting and debt administration are introduced, with emphasis placed on the specific knowledge particularly useful to a person dealing with these challenging subjects. At the completion of this chapter, the reader should understand:

1. the commonly used definition of debt;
2. why debts are incurred;
3. alternatives to debt;
4. types and forms of debt;
5. revenue bonds;
6. creative capital financing and its origin;
7. nontraditional capital financing;
8. commonly used tests and limits on debt;
9. early warning guidelines for municipal financial operations;
10. significance of the New York City financial crisis on debt administration;
11. municipal bankruptcy, financial problems, and remedies;
12. the difference between capital and operating budgets;

13. capital facility planning and its significance;
14. the essential decisions and expertise critical in designing a municipal bond issue;
15. what is and should be in a bond prospectus and notice of sale;
16. investment syndicates and their significance;
17. the importance of good bond administration and data associated with debt reporting; and
18. bond ratings, what influences them, and why they are significant.

STATE AND LOCAL DEBT

Definitions

When persons charge items on Master Card or Visa, they are incurring a *debt*. They normally receive the items and pledge that they will pay for these items within a certain time period. When they get a bank loan for a car, they have incurred a debt. They have agreed to pay back the loan amount (called principal) plus an extra amount (called interest) for the privilege of borrowing the money over an extended period of time.

Governments also borrow money; thus, they incur short- and sometimes long-term obligations to pay back the principal and interest. However, some types of debt (for example, trade accounts payable and conditional repayment loans) sometimes do not involve interest payments. Debt constitutes an obligation that must be paid under the established legal conditions. The Bureau of Census uses the following definition, which stresses interest-bearing obligation:

> All long-term credit obligations of the government and its agencies, and all interest bearing short-term (i.e., repayable within one year) credit obligations. Includes judgments, mortgages, and "revenue" bonds, as well as general obligation bonds, notes, and interest bearing warrants. Excludes noninterest bearing obligations, amounts owed in a trust or agency capacity, advances and contingent loans from other governments, and rights of individuals to benefit from employee-retirement funds.

Governments incur debt for several reasons. In some cases, cash is needed before the actual revenue is collected. Debt is used to harmonize those divergent patterns of current expenditures and revenues. Often, the government wishes to finance a significant capital construction project or even large equipment purchases. Current revenues cannot pay for such large purchases, so a loan is negotiated. Sometimes a debt is incurred in order to refinance an existing (for example, short-term) debt. On occasion, debt is incurred to finance operating deficits. A form of debt that is not often recognized as such is a government's pension benefit obligation. Bonds are not normally sold for this purpose, but pensions are an increasingly significant government obligation that places severe financial pressure on governments.

Governments do not have to incur debts but the alternatives to debt are difficult to use effectively. One alternative is to accumulate funds over time, much like an individual's Christmas savings plan; this is called a *sinking fund*. The funds are invested until such time as the money is needed. Another alternative is to pay-as-you-go—to pay for the equipment or building costs out of operating expenses. The difficulty with both alternatives is that capital facility needs of governments often do not fit the pace of financing or the funding techniques. A city that needs to build a water-purification plant sometimes cannot wait the ten or twenty years required for a sinking fund or pay-as-you-go financing approach. Emergencies and irregular expenditure demands do occur, and debt is sometimes the only practical alternative under the circumstances.

New borrowings by consumers and private businesses far exceed government debt, but in 1991, the governmental share of the nation's debt load rose to nearly 36 percent. In the previous decade, it was 30 percent. In one decade, all debt outstanding rose to nearly $11 trillion from the previous $4 trillion level. In 1991, the debt equalled about $43,000 per person in the United States and exceeds 1.9 times the nation's gross national product. Spurring the trend was the large annual federal deficits of the 1980s and 1990s.

Classifications of Debt

Most of the liability items in the state and local government balance sheet are debts of the government. They include bonds, certificates of indebtedness, mortgages, notes, accounts payable, warrants payable, liens, judgments, unfunded pension obligations, and selected contingent liabilities. Excluded are contingent items and reserves for encumbrances.

The largest amount of debt is in the form of *bonds*. They are a written promise to pay a specified sum of money (called the face value or principal amount) at a specified date or dates (called the maturity dates) together with periodic interest at a specific rate. *Serial bonds*, which are the most common type of bond, are designed so that a specific number of bonds are retired each year. In contrast, *term bonds*, which are infrequently used, are normally designed to pay the interest over time but pay the principal when the loan period has applied. Sinking funds are normally used by the borrower to collect the necessary large principal payment at the end of the loan period. Before 1983, most bonds were payable to the bearer and they had detachable coupons representing the interest payments. Upon presentation of the matured coupon to the bond maker's paying agent, the proper interest represented on the coupon was paid. All bonds must now be registered on the books of the issuing government or paying agent to provide protection to the bond holder.

The other forms of debt are normally not as significant unless they happen to involve large obligations. *Certificates of indebtedness* vary from state to state, but they are frequently used in connection with agency resources or assets. *Mortgage bonds* use property to secure the obligation without transferring title, but most of them still do not give the government's creditor the right to foreclose. *Notes* are widely used to represent evidence of financial obligation, normally of a short-term nature. *Accounts payable* includes government firm liabilities such as wages earned but not yet paid as well as the common unpaid bills. The now uncommon *warrant* is a government-issued document to the bank upon which payment is made with the approval of the government. A *lien* is a claim on property arising from failure of the owner to make timely payment of a claim. A *judgment* is a court decision that the government has a liability or debt to a person who has sought redress through the courts. An *unfunded pension liability* is incurred when a government does not place sufficient funds in an appropriate pension fund but is still liable for those pensions. A *contingent liability* is incurred when an agreement stipulates that a liability will occur if a certain condition is met. For example, a city agrees with the area-wide transit board to help finance a transit system once the population density and traffic congestion reach a given level. Controversies often arise over the condition and the fulfillment of the agreement.

Debts can be classified by pledge of security. One type is the "full-faith-and-credit" debt in which a government's credit, including the implied power of taxation, is pledged unconditionally. For example, a city states it will pledge itself unconditionally to pay a bond obligation. Another type is debt in which the issuer or a guaranteeing government has a moral but not a legal obligation to pay. The financial community would rarely be interested in a moral debt unless a government was responsible for that debt. What commonly occurs is some government body (for example, a housing authority) pledges its user charges or some other revenue source to pay the debt and another unit of government (for example, the state) gives its moral backing to the debt. The financial community normally requires a default remedy to be spelled out by the government. The best pledge from the investor's point of view is a full-faith-and-credit obligation plus a specific user charge to pay the indebtedness.

Merl M. Hackbart and James Leigland (1990) classify long-term, tax-exempt state government debt obligations into the following four categories:

- *General obligation* (GO) debt is backed with an unconditional state government pledge of any and all revenue sources including the state's taxing power for the purposes of debt repayment.
- *Revenue* debt is nonguaranteed debt, but it is backed by one or more specific, pledged revenue sources (for example, user fees, special assessments, limited taxes).
- *Special authority* debt is issued by a special purpose governmental unit (for example, public authority, special district, board, bond bank, corporation) and is not a direct obligation of the state. Such debt is often backed by specific, pledged revenues of the state or governmental unit. Sometimes the obligation is secondarily backed by the state government.
- *Lease-backed* debt is structured like a revenue bond issue using *certificates of participation* or *lease revenue bonds* secured by lease-payment agreements. Although similar to revenue bonds, the distinction is made because some states do not recognize lease-backed obligations as state debt.

Exhibit 8–1 presents the types of debt used for each of the fifty states.

EXHIBIT 8–1 Types of Long-Term State Government Debt

STATE	GENERAL OBLIGATION	REVENUE	SPECIAL AUTHORITY	LEASE-BACKED
Alabama	X		X	
Alaska	X	X	X	
Arizona		X	X	X
Arkansas	X	X	X	
California	X	X	X	X
Colorado		X	X	X
Connecticut	X	X	X	
Delaware	X		X	
Florida	X	X	X	X
Georgia	X		X	
Hawaii	X	X	X	
Idaho			X	
Illinois	X	X	X	X
Indiana			X	X
Iowa			X	X
Kansas		X	X	X
Kentucky		X	X	X
Louisiana	X		X	
Maine	X		X	X
Maryland	X		X	X
Massachusetts	X	X	X	X
Michigan	X	X	X	X
Minnesota	X		X	X
Mississippi	X	X	X	
Missouri	X	X	X	X
Montana	X	X	X	
Nebraska			X	X
Nevada	X	X		
New Hampshire	X	X	X	
New Jersey	X	X	X	X
New Mexico	X	X	X	
New York	X		X	X
North Carolina	X	X	X	X
North Dakota		X	X	X
Ohio	X	X	X	X
Oklahoma	X		X	
Oregon	X	X	X	
Pennsylvania	X		X	
Rhode Island	X	X	X	X
South Carolina	X	X	X	
South Dakota			X	X
Tennessee	X		X	
Texas	X	X	X	
Utah	X	X	X	X
Vermont	X		X	
Virginia	X	X	X	X
Washington	X		X	
West Virginia	X	X	X	
Wisconsin	X	X	X	
Wyoming		X	X	
Totals	23	34	49	23

Source: Merl M. Hackbart and James Leigland, "State Debt Management Policy: A National Survey," *Public Budgeting and Finance*, 10, 1, (Spring 1990), p. 44.

M. G. Valente (1986) identified the following three broad categories of capital financing options:

- traditional, including current revenue, general obligation bonds, revenue bonds, special assessments, and tax increment financing;
- public-private, including tax-exempt lease purchases, sales lease-back, exactions, and privatization;
- creative bonds, including deep discount/zero coupon bonds, variable rate bonds, put option bonds, bonds with warrants, minibonds, and mininotes.

In 1986, C. Bradley Doss surveyed U.S. cities, asking them what methods they used to finance their capital projects. Exhibit 8–2 presents his findings. Current revenues, block grants, and general revenue sharing were the most used methods. Savings or reserve funds ranked seventh on the list. This survey was conducted before the 1986 federal tax reform act.

EXHIBIT 8–2 Methods of Financing Capital Projects in U.S. Cities (n = 851)— Percentage in 1986

METHOD	FRE- QUENTLY	FAIRLY OFTEN	OCCASION- ALLY	VERY SELDOM	NEVER USED	MISSING (N)
Current Revenue	48	21	17	9	3	24
Block Grants	27	26	23	11	10	29
Gen. Rev. Shar.	37	15	11	11	23	20
Fed. Catg. Gra.	15	25	30	18	8	32
G.O. Bonds	24	15	24	20	15	24
State Grants	13	25	38	16	5	28
Reserve Funds	15	16	22	20	23	47
Sp. Assmts.	15	14	22	23	22	29
Revenue Bonds	10	15	22	20	30	31
Lease Purchase	5	10	21	29	34	25
Other	3	1	2	1	5	742

Source: C. Bradley Doss, "Capital Budgeting Practices." In Thomas D. Lynch and Lawrence Martin (eds.), Handbook of Comparative Public Budgeting and Financial Management. New York: Marcel Dekker, 1993, p. 285.

Short-Term Debt

Short-term borrowing is normally done for the following reasons:

1. The community is short of the necessary revenue to pay for services. For example, the city forecasted the revenue incorrectly, and there is not enough money to pay for planned expenditures.
2. A brief loan is needed and will be paid back as soon as taxes are collected. The money owed to the city may have been collected, but obligations must be paid. A brief loan is needed to bridge this cash flow problem until the debts owed the city are paid.

3. The community has an emergency and necessary funds are not available.
4. The funds are needed to start a capital improvement project, but a long-term bond issue has not yet been approved.

At one time, short-term debt vocabulary included only *tax anticipation notes* (TANs), *revenue anticipation notes* (RANs), and *bond anticipation notes* (BANs). Under Internal Revenue Service arbitrage regulations and under specific circumstances, proceeds from government short-term securities can now be invested, yielding significant revenue. Thus, there is a fifth reason for short-term borrowing: to raise revenue, as the government can borrow at a lower rate than it can earn in the security market. In addition, there are new forms of short-term borrowing, including *tax and revenue anticipation notes* (TRANs), *grant anticipation notes* (GANs), and *tax-exempt commercial paper* (TECP), which will be explained later.

Given that they have very tight budgets and that they collect revenue primarily in the third and fourth months of a fiscal year, most large and many medium-size governments have discovered that short-term borrowing is essential. Because instruments such as TANs can actually be a money source—an added bonus—previous approaches by finance officers to short-term borrowing have been turned upside down. Certainly, BANs have become more popular, given their money-making potential plus their remarkably high long-term interest rates. Federal tax legislation in the mid-1980s has curtailed much of the money-earning potential of short-term debt. Regardless of the motivation for short-term borrowing, a formal payment calendar should be established so that the debt can be managed properly to maximize the benefits to the local government.

The average state and local long-term guaranteed debt in FY 1989 was $903 per capita, but the nonguaranteed debt was more than twice that at $2,241. In marked contrast, the short-term debt was only $72 per capita. The state with the largest per capita debt was Alaska.

Early Developments in the Debt Concept

Innovations and changes in the use of debt have been significant, starting with the innovative *revenue bond*. The most well-known innovative debt concept is the revenue bond. It was first used in 1897 to support the construction of the Spokane, Washington, Water Works. This debt mechanism, coupled with a means to raise revenue, was not popular until after World War II. Then court decisions held that authorities (for example, Port of New York and New Jersey and Triborough Bridge Authority) had separate legal status. People in government were seeking new ways to finance public facilities without increasing taxes, and revenue bonds provided an answer. Briefly, the reasons for increased use of revenue bonds are as follows:

1. Although revenue bonds had a higher interest cost than general obligations bonds, that cost decreased significantly.

2. There was more use of public authorities and an expansion of types of authorities (for example, airports, public parks, recreation areas and facilities, stadia and public sport facilities, power projects, housing, public markets, college dormitories, port facilities, and so on).
3. Restrictions on general obligations closed this mechanism, forcing the use of revenue bonds.
4. Obtaining revenue bond approval, especially because of the nonreferendum requirement, was relatively easy.
5. The ability to apply user charges to pay for debt services was appealing.

A lesser used version of the revenue bond is the *lease rental bond*. Let us say a school district cannot get voter approval for a bond issue. One ploy used is to create a nonprofit authority to build and then lease the new school to the school district. A long-term school board leases with the authority, thus providing the necessary security so that revenue bondholders know that debt services will be paid. The school is built and financed by a revenue bond. Because the authority is merely a financing mechanism, some financial groups treat these governments as general obligation bonds.

In order to attract industry to a city, region, or state, state and local governments started issuing *industrial aid revenue bonds* (IDBs). The concept was simple: governments pay less for bond interest, so a government would issue a bond and a new industry would pay the bond interest and use the proceeds to build a new factory which provided more jobs to the area. Although they were a useful state and local government tool to attract industry, the issuances of these bonds lowered federal income tax receipts because the interest on the bonds was tax exempt. The Tax Reform Act of 1986 essentially halted most of the use of that type of bond. Today, statewide caps exist on IDBs, and the tax-exempt privilege ended in December 1989.

An interesting cousin of the revenue bond is the *special obligation bond*. A revenue bond is tied to the revenue-generating capacity of a government's ability to produce a service, as well as to the demand for that service. A special obligation bond is tied to the revenue-generating capacity of a government revenue source, which can be entirely outside the control of the local government and may have no logical relationship to the reason for the bond. For example, general revenue-sharing receipts from the federal government can be the pledged revenue source for a special obligation bond, which can be used to build libraries, schools, roads, or piers.

Capital Financing in the 1980s

The early 1980s saw a remarkable change in the tax-exempt securities market. On the one hand, the need for state and local spending on public facilities became very significant (that is, $3 trillion). On the other hand, the supply of long-term investment capital decreased. No reasonably accurate estimates can be made of public facilities' needs, but Pat Choate, a senior economic policy analyst for TRTW, Inc., estimated in *America in Ruins: Beyond the Public Works Pork Barrel* (1981) that $3 trillion was needed for repair and replacement of existing public facilities and construction of new public facilities. This was in a period in which Reagan's Republican administration was successfully reducing federal domestic programs, many state and local areas were experiencing tax revolts which were limiting government revenue, and the economy was going through the worst recession since the Great Depression. This left state and local governments with debt as the only alternative in a very unstable credit market in which traditional debt instruments were inadequate.

The municipal bond market was affected both by the recession and by legal changes instituted by the Reagan administration. As a counter to high inflation rates prior to the recession, the Federal Reserve System had imposed extremely restrictive monetary policies. That, combined with the Reagan administration's massive yearly deficits, produced record high interest rates which came down slowly as economic recovery started to take place. Changes enacted in the Economic Recovery Tax Act of 1981 (ERTA) contributed to the higher interest rates by reducing the incentive for persons in higher tax brackets to use the municipal bond tax-shelter and by expanding other income-sheltering opportunities (for example, Individual Retirement Accounts and All Savers Certificates). In addition, ERTA permitted firms to sell tax benefits to the highest bidders, which created billions of dollars of alternative tax-shelter investment opportunities. Further, the Investment Tax Credit (ITC) and Accelerated Cost Recovery Schedules (ACRS) enhanced the after-tax rate of return on private investment, thus lessening the need for tax shelters because less income was taxable. The 1982 Federal Tax Act (TEFRA) further changed the municipal security market by the partial removal of the deductibility of bank interest costs used to finance tax-exempt securities and the requirement that all new municipal bonds must be registered. The latter change was extremely significant, as coupon bonds were very popular among investors.

The biggest influence on the market, however, was the poor economy, which resulted in lower business and individual profits that normally would have been attracted into the municipal bond market in tax shelters.

Given those environmental factors, the character of the municipal bond market changed radically. Demand for tax-exempt bonds by the two major institutional investors, namely commercial banks and property and casualty insurance companies, practically evaporated after 1979. The tax-exempt market reacted by stressing and more aggressively marketing to individual investors. The percentage of bonds held by individual and mutual funds in the tax-exempt market shot up in 1981 and 1982. This was particularly true for short-term tax-exempt paper, which appealed to the money market mutual funds. During 1981, tax-exempt money market holdings grew by $3 billion, which represented an increase of approximately three-fourths. By the end of 1982, there were $13.2 billion in aggregate holdings.

The factors cited above, plus the extensive use of private-purpose tax-exempt borrowing, narrowed the gap between the tax-exempt and taxable markets, with the notable exception of the short-term market. Historically, tax-exempt interest rates ran from 65 to 70 percent less than comparable taxable bond yields. In 1981 and 1982, the spread shifted to 80 to 85 percent. This meant that the arbitrage advantage did not automatically result in lower bond interest charges for local and state governments. The cost of borrowing for long-term issues was about the same for government as the private sector. This radical change was partially the result of industrial revenue bonds which induced its extensive and scattered defaults (for example, Washington Public Power Supply System), and shook investor confidence in revenue bonds. The result was higher tax-exempt borrowing rates.

The Tax Reform Act of 1986 brought significant changes to municipal debt, the most notable of which was the diminishing of total dollar volume of new issues from over $220 billion in 1985 to about $100 billion in 1987. Most of the decline was in nongovernmental or private activity bonds due to the legal constraints of the Tax Reform Act. But even in governmental purpose bonds, borrowing levels were lowered due to a pre-1985 rush to avoid the 1986 legal changes and the stronger arbitrage earning limitations of the 1986 law that sapped demand. For those governments that did borrow after 1986, they found lower interest rates with a spread a little over 80 percent from taxable securities. John E. Peterson (1988) summarized the impact of the 1986 act as follows:

- Fewer projects can be financed on a tax-exempt basis because of the restraints placed on borrowing, especially that involve nongovernmental entities.
- The municipal market is now a fragmented and complicated market because of the varying tax treatments for different classes of bonds.
- Fewer opportunities now exist to earn arbitrage income by investing bond proceeds.
- Currently, more burdensome procedures surround the issuance process.
- Stiffer competition among underwriters and thus lower profits and fewer firms exist because there are fewer deals and constraints on flotation costs.
- The low ebb of institutional investor demand meant that the individual investor became supreme in the tax-exempt market.
- Little likelihood exists that there will be a relaxation of federal restrictions and the return of rapid tax-exempt market growth.

The Tax Reform Act of 1986 created a new security called the *taxable municipal bond*. Its likely buyers are households influenced by the federal alternative minimum income tax. Unfortunately, 42 percent of the early issues were linked indirectly to the junk bond crisis associated with the fraud case of Mr. Ivan Boesky. Despite the early problems, a weak market exists for this new security. Interest rates are higher and are even higher than corporate bonds with comparable pledges.

The Tax Reform Act of 1986 also brought other significant changes to municipal debt. Congress severely limited the use of tax-exempt bonds to finance "essential" or "public purpose" projects as defined in the legislation. Thus, "private-purpose" projects and programs (such as loans to farms and small businesses) must turn to the new taxable municipal bonds for funding. John E. Peterson (1988), formerly of the Government Finance Officers Association, estimated that the new market could be 15 percent or higher than the dollar value of municipal securities. With the post-1986 federal caps (that is, limits) on industrial development bonds, the percentage could be higher.

After strong initial interest in these new securities, issuers and investors balked. Investors have felt the new and sometimes gimmicky nature of the early issues increased general investor concern about the subsequent demand for the taxable municipal bonds. Foreign investors, especially the Japanese, were evident as they sought investment diversification of their holdings. This new set of important investors from abroad adds the problem of currency exchange to the already complex municipal securities market.

There is a new world for the finance officer. At the beginning of the century, the municipal bond market was staid, straightforward, and conservative. Most financing was general obligation (GO) debt, with a gradually increasing use of revenue issues backed by either a user fee or a dedicated tax source. In 1960, total long-term financing was approximately $7.5 billion, of which 70 percent was general obligation. By 1975, non-GO debt accounted for 50 percent of the total new issues; and, by 1981, it accounted for 70 percent, a complete reversal of the 1960 situation. During recession periods, only the most popular subjects (for example, building of jails) tend to be financed by GO debt because they alone get voter referendum approval. In November 1991, more than half of the bond referendums on the ballots were defeated.

One type of creative capital financing still used since the 1980s is the *zero coupon bond* (ZCB). The federal tax law was changed significantly twice in the Reagan administration. The first change prompted many new creative and often complex local government bonding methods. The second change essentially stopped the use of most of those creative capital financing methods. ZCBs are bonds without current interest coupons, which are offered at a substantial discount from par value and provide return to investors through accretion in value at maturity. Thus, for example, they can be sold for $602 when issued and can be redeemed in five years for $1,000. This approach has potential appeal to households earning between $50,000 and $100,000 as they are looking for retirement or college education financing. A package of ZCBs could provide these investors with the equivalent of a tax-free annuity stream that would be attractive compared with taxable alternatives. Exhibit 8–3 provides an example.

NONTRADITIONAL

The nontraditional ways to package bond issues more attractively include *external credit supports, tax-exempt commercial paper, put option securities, original issue discount bonds*, including ZCBs; *variable-rate securities*, and *leasing*. These are means to attract new or retain old investors in the tax-exempt market. With these instruments, a negotiated sale may become superior to a competitive sale owing to the complexity of this type. Regardless, technical advice is important to obtain in meeting the following goals:

EXHIBIT 8–3   Tax-Exempt ZC "Annuity" Bonds

MATURITY (IN YEARS)	AMOUNT AT MATURITY	PRICE TODAY FOR ANNUITY PAYMENT	EFFECTIVE YIELD
1	$ 1,000	$915.73	9.00%
2	1,000	830.58	9.50
3	1,000	746.22	10.00
4	1,000	671.70	10.20
5	1,000	602.34	10.40
6	1,000	538.10	10.60
7	1,000	478.89	10.80
8	1,000	424.58	11.00
9	1,000	375.02	11.20
10	1,000	329.99	11.40
11	1,000	289.28	11.60
12	1,000	252.64	11.80
13	1,000	219.81	12.00
14	1,000	189.28	12.25
15	1,000	164.54	12.40
16	1,000	143.71	12.50
17	1,000	125.28	12.60
18	1,000	109.01	12.70
19	1,000	95.52	12.75
20	1,000	83.62	12.80
	$20,000	$7,585.84	11.76%

Equivalent Taxable Returns:

50% Tax Rate	$40,000	$7,585.84	26.11%
30% Tax Rate	28,710	7,585.84	18.16%

Source: Ronald Forbes and Edward Renshaw, "Tax-Exempt Zero Coupon Bonds." In John E. Peterson and Wesley P. Hough (eds.), *Creative Capital Financing.* Chicago: Government Finance Officers Association, 1983, p. 153. Used by permission.

1. targeting the investment vehicle toward a specific group of investors (those who have money and have a preference which can be satisfied);
2. designing the instrument features, such as where to place the put option, what index to employ in a variable rate, and how to construct a lease-purchase agreement (these will be explained later);
3. timing the transaction; and
4. considering objectively the alternative approaches.

The forms of *external credit support* include a bank line of credit, a letter of credit, municipal bond insurance, state credit assistance, and federal guarantees. A *line of credit* is a contingent loan arrangement with a bank in which the bank agrees to lend funds required by the government for a fixed time period. The similar *letter of credit* (LOC) is an unconditional pledge of the bank's credit to make principal and interest payments of specific amount and term on an issuer's debt. Both provide a guarantee that future liquidity needs will be met. Normally, they are used for smaller amounts than are found in bond insurance, and the size and type of issue are generally unrestricted; banks usually charge an annual fee for the LOC plus normal interest charges on the principal. An interesting development for American local governments starting in the mid-1980s is the increased use of Japanese and European banks instead of American banks. For example, Shelby County, Tennessee, negotiated successfully with Sanwa Bank (a Japanese bank), apparently resulting in an annual savings of $1 million on loan costs. In contrast, the *bond insurance premium* is a one-time, up-front fee. The LOC can lower interest cost because the creditworthiness of the bank is substituted. Also, it may be necessary to use the LOC in connection with other creative capital financing devices (for example, put options). A major private insurance group such as the Municipal Bond Insurance Association (MBIA) or the American Municipal Bond Assurance Corporation (AMBAC) can also assume the default risk of a government for a specific fee. Exhibit 8–4 presents selected features of the three private bond guarantee programs available to state and local governments.

EXHIBIT 8–4   Selected Features: Private Municipal Bond Guarantees

FEATURES WHICH ISSUES MUST POSSESS TO BE ELIGIBLE FOR GUARANTEE

PROGRAM	TYPE OF ISSUE*	SIZE OF ISSUE (IN MILLIONS)	QUALITY LIMITATIONS	COST OF GUARANTEE (PD. AT TIME OF ISSUE)
AMBAC	G.O.'s & Rev. Bds. of existing facilities	$0.6-$22.0 (tot. prin. & int.)	S&P BBB or better	1/2%–1-1/2% of original principal and interest
Indemnity Corp.	G.O.'s & Rev.'s	$0.6-$18.0 (tot. prin. & int.)	none	1/2%–3-1/2% of original principal and interest
MBIA Rev. Bds.	G.O.'s & Utility	$0.6-$20.0 (prin. only)	Generally, S&P BBB or better	1%–2% of original principal only

*With the exception of Indemnity Corp., all guarantees are for new bond issues. (Indemnity Corp. will also guarantee portfolios of outstanding bonds.)

Source: Michael O. Joehnk and David S. Kidwell, "Determining the Advantages and Disadvantages of Private Municipal Bond Guarantees." In John E. Petersen and Wesley C. Hough (eds.), *Creative Capital Financing.* Chicago: Municipal Finance Officers Association, 1983, p. 214. Used by permission.

The result of purchasing insurance should be a lower interest rate than could be obtained without insurance. That benefit, using a present-value method, must exceed the premium cost. Normally, the insurance premium accounts for 20 to 30 basis points (100 basis points equals 1 percent in interest). Cost savings can be as high as 40 to 95 basis points on new bond issues. States can provide *municipal credit assistance* by guaranteeing local debt issues, much as a private insurance company would do; by acting as a financial intermediate via a state municipal bond bank; and, finally, by providing grants to subsidize local debt service requirements. Each activity can lower subjurisdiction interest and, possibly, administrative costs. The last external source of support is the federal government, which has provided guarantees in the areas of housing and urban renewal.

Municipal bond insurance, which has grown rapidly, came into the municipal market in 1971. Insured municipal bonds were about 30 percent of the $41.1 billion of long-term tax exempt issues sold in the first four months of 1991. They tend to boost bond ratings and thus lower interest rates. The major municipal bond insurers are, in order, Municipal Bond Investors Assurance Indemnity Corporation (MBIA), American Municipal Bond Assurance Company (AMBAC), Financial Guaranty Insurance Company (FGIC), Bond Investors Guaranty (BIG), and Capital Guaranty Insurance Company. Each insured bond is rated triple-A either by Standard and Poor's Corporation Guide or Moody's Investors Guide, or it is rated triple-A by both. This reputation means that many issuers of bonds can really lower their costs and be more attractive to buyers by offering insured issues. Interestingly, they actually trade in price closer to double-A bonds than to uninsured triple-A bonds. In other words, insurance helps, but an earned triple-A is better than a triple-A obtained by insurance. Not all insurance companies will result in the same cost advantage. In the late 1980s, MBIA-insured bonds have been providing slightly lower yields, and FGIC- and AMBAC-backed bonds trade 5 to 10 basis points higher. If the insurer's rating slips, so does the rating of all issues that the company insures. As of January 1986, only AMBAC has admitted paying claims. Those claims included covering the default on Washington Public Power Supply System's four- and five-year bonds.

An interesting creative finance development is "loan-to-lender" financing, which marries federally insured certificates of deposit to tax-exempt industrial revenue bonds. An industrial tax-exempt revenue bond is issued, with the proceeds deposited in exchange for federally insured certificates of deposit with triple-A credit ratings. Those proceeds, which result from negotiation at the same rate and term as the industrial bonds, are used, by contractual obligation, to make mortgage loans to third-party developers to finance publicly desired projects (for example, low-income housing). These increasingly popular instruments carry low interest rates.

Tax-exempt commercial paper (TECP) can be used for purposes similar to those of TANs and BANs, but the paper must be supported by a bank line of credit which enhances cash liquidity. This new security has increased in popularity recently, especially because the interest earned is exempt from federal taxes. The variety of maturities available and the ready liquidity make TECP an especially convenient instrument for those wishing to tailor maturities to future needs. There is a drawback: TECP has higher start-up and operating costs than traditional short-term instruments have (for example, TANs and BANs). Thus, a government should have at least $25 million of short-term borrowing per year to justify the TECP costs. If the government has large short-term borrowing needs, TECP normally costs less than traditional short-term instruments. However, TECP must be retired when funds become available, and this may eliminate important reinvestment earning opportunities. The latter can be an important source of local revenue.

A *put*, or *tender*, *option* in the issue offering can attract long-term investors as well as take advantage of lower short-term interest rates. The tender option permits the investors to convert the investment to a shorter maturity, much as the call provision permits the government to do the same. The put option places liquidity demands on the issuer; hence, a letter of credit is needed. The "window put," or European option, can be exercised once during a certain period. In contrast, the "anniversary put," or American option, allows investors to put their bonds back to the issuer periodically, generally on a given date once every year. Other things being equal, investors should value a twenty-five-year bond with a five-year window put option higher than they would a traditional twenty-five-year bond. The former represents very strong protection against rising rates and falling bond prices. In high-interest periods, it saves the issuer at least 275 basis points. Besides external liquidity support, the put option requires a remarketing agreement with a bank or underwriter by which the option is exercised.

An *original issue discount bond* (OLD) is a long-term bond offered at a discount of the stated par value. The return occurs through gradual accretion to the bond's maturity when par is met. This is in contrast to traditional bonds, with which investors pay the par value to the municipality and receive back the principal plus the stated interest by the time of maturity. The IRS treats the difference between the par value and the purchase price as tax-exempt income. The "ultimate" original discount bond is the ZCB explained earlier. Another type of bond is the *compound interest bond* (also called the *municipal multiplier* and *capital appreciation bond*), which is initially sold at its par value. At maturity, investors receive payment of principal invested plus the amount of earned interest that has been accumulated over the life of the bond at a semiannually compounded rate.

Variable-rate securities attract investors who believe that market rates will continue to rise and who wish to maintain their investment capital value. This is accomplished by offering securities that have floating rates; the yield is tied by a formula to some other market factor, such as the prevailing interest rate on treasury notes. An added plus is the inclusion of a put option to increase liquidity as a trade-off for lower interest charges. The key to this type of issue is the choice of indexes by which the floating rates are determined and the frequency with which the rate is readjusted.

A nondebt instrument that can accomplish the same purpose as a debt is the *lease*. The category includes the *operating lease*, the *sale-leaseback*, the *safe-harbor lease*, and the *leverage lease*. In the past, a lease was merely an agreement between a government unit and a private owner for the use of property or services over a period of time in exchange for rent or a fee. With creative capital financing, there are much more complex agreements that take advantage of recently enacted federal tax incentives for private investment in capital goods. In a *true* or *operating lease*, a government unit acquires the use of an asset, with a private investor having title, a 20 percent equity investment (under IRS rules), and the use of a tax-exempt debt (for example, an industrial bond) to cover the other 80 percent. Often the government purchases the asset at fair market value when the lease expires. The result of this complex arrangement is that the private person is able to "share" the accelerated depreciation and investment tax credit advantages at a lower lease rate and an agreed-upon fair market value selling price.

A *sale-leaseback* involves the sale of government property to private investors, who receive tax advantages from the purchase while leasing back the asset to the government for its use. The value of the tax benefits can be shared, with the "sale" proceeds used to renovate the asset. In a *safe-harbor* lease, made possible by ERTA, the government sells property (for example, mass-transit vehicles) in a traditional sale-leaseback, with the advantage that the tax write-offs can be sold to and used by profit-making companies to reduce their taxes. At the end of the lease, the asset may be repurchased for a nominal amount. In a *leverage lease*, a third party finances a large purchase. The lessor uses borrowed capital to purchase the asset leased to the local government. The lender is repaid with a tax-exempt interest and a security interest in the property. Exhibits 8–5 and 8–6 present the investor's and the government's respective advantages from a possible sale-leaseback situation using the net present-value concept.

Two more ideas associated with creative capital financing—*warrants* and *small denomination bonds*—may also be useful in designing issues. Warrants have acquired an additional meaning with the use of that term by the Municipal Assistance Corporation's February 1981 issue for the City of New York. *Warrants* are special certificates attached to bonds that permit investors to purchase future bonds at the same price and interest as the original issue. This is normally referred to as an *option to buy.* Such certificates are treated as bearer-redeemable securities that may be detached from the original bonds and sold separately. Edward Anthony Lehan champions mini-municipal bonds, which are sold in $100, $500, and $1,000 par amounts rather than in the traditional $5,000 par amount. He points out that they have been successful when tried and that they give the added advantage of permitting local citizens to invest directly in their community more easily. The minibonds, in some instances, were modeled on U.S. savings bonds and were essentially mini-ZCBs.

Two new public finance instruments added by the 1990s were *certificates of participation* (COPs) and *swaps.* COPs raise money without issuing debt per se as they are based on lease-backed financing; thus, they avoid the need for referendum approval. With COPs, a government agrees with another entity such as a leasing company to have them acquire a capital item. The government then leases the capital item, and the leasing fee is considered an operating expense rather than debt service. As of 1990, there was a $5 billion-per-year market, primarily in California, to

EXHIBIT 8–5 Sale-Leaseback from the Investor's Perspective

TOTAL PRICE TO INVESTORS: $5,000,000
SOURCES OF FUNDS: $3,850,000 Industrial Revenue Bond
$1,150,000 Investor Equity

	YEAR 1	YEAR 2	YEARS 3–14	YEAR 15	TOTAL (000's)	NET PRESENT VALUE @ 15% (000's)
(A) Operating Expenses						
Rental Income	$ 585,000	$ 585,000	$ 7,020,000	$ 585,000	$8,775	$3,421
Sale Price at End of Lease	—	—	—	1,150,000	1,150	141
Administrative Expense	5,000	5,000	60,000	5,000	75	29
Debt Service on IDB	565,273	565,273	6,783,276	565,273	8,479	3,307
Income before Taxes	14,727	14,727	176,724	1,164,727	1,371	226
(B) Tax Advantages						
Tax Liability or Savings at 50% Bracket**	77,667	71,470	-11,535	-493,051*	-355	148
Investment Tax Credit	950,000	—	—	—	950	826
Total Return on Investment after Taxes (Income before taxes plus tax advantages)	$1,042,394	$ 86,197	$ 165,189	$ 671,676	$1,965	$1,200

*Includes capital gains tax.

**Tax on income after deductions for straight-line depreciation, administrative expenses, and interest paid on IRB.

Source: John E. Peterson and Wesley C. Hough, "Leasing." In *Creative Capital Financing.* Chicago: Municipal Finance Officers Association, 1983, p. 89. Used by permission.

EXHIBIT 8–6 Sale-Leaseback from the Government Unit's Perspective

	ANNUAL	15-YEAR TOTAL	NET PRESENT VALUE @15%
Cost of Sale-Leaseback Financing Alternative:			
(1) Lease Payments (net of ground lease)	$585,000	$8,775,000	$4,449,556
(2) Earnings from Escrow Account ($1 million invested at 11%)	110,000	1,650,000	836,669
(3) Repurchase of Building at End of Lease ($1.15 million less $1 million in escrow account		150,000	35,909
(4) Net Cost of Sale-Leaseback	$475,000	$7,275,000	$3,648,796
Cost of General Obligation Bond Financing Alternative:			
(5) Debt Service if $4 Million, 5-Year Bonds at 10% Were Issued	$525,895	$7,888,425	$3,999,999
Savings from Sale-Leaseback:			
(GO debt service tess total cost of sale-leaseback)	$ 50,895	$ 613,425	$ 351,203

Source: John E. Peterson and Wesley C. Hough, "Leasing." In *Creative Capital Financing.* Chicago: Municipal Finance Officers Association, 1983, p. 90. Used by permission.

circumvent their Proposition 13–type limits. The market does not tend to support COPs used for anything other than essential government purposes. *Swaps* are trading one kind of interest rate for another in order to hedge the issuers's risk against unexpected behavior. Swaps come into play after a bond is issued and are designed to deal with volatile interest rates. A swap is an agreement between an issuer and a third party to exchange interest payments—but not the principal—on an existing indebtedness. Generally, a swap is used for switching fixed and variable-rate payments.

Tests and Limits

At the local and state levels, questions are raised when an increase in the local or state public debt is contemplated. Some argue that no debt is best. Others say that if the services can be greatly increased by substituting capital for current expenditures such as labor costs, then such investments are wise. Others argue that capital expenditures benefit tomorrow's taxpayers and paying a debt appropriately shifts the cost of the project to them. Others use a more pragmatic test: If the government (1) can service the debt (that is, meet the payments as well as meet other normal expenses of government) and (2) can refinance its debt through the market, then the debt is acceptable.[1] Servicing a debt can be a tremendous burden on a community. A commonly used danger sign is when the debt service approaches 20 to 25 percent of the total budget. In some communities this limit is exceeded, but nationally the aggregate debt figures for state and local governments are less than 10 percent of the total budgets.

The government debt situation in the United States is mixed. For state and local governments, it is generally quite good. At the federal level, there is reason for some concern, but the situation is not a critical problem unless the trend for large annual deficits continues. Exhibits 2–7 and 2–8 show the federal situation from 1962 to 1991. Having a high *net interest paid* means less money is left for traditional government activities (for example, national defense and domestic programs), and federal tax resources are being transferred to wealthy Americans and foreigners who invested in U.S. bonds. The solution, which might take many years before it is passed, will be higher taxes and cuts in federal programs.

Governments that have the most difficulty in financing their activities are usually those experiencing weak economic growth. If an area is growing, then there is demand for borrowing, but there is an improving tax base with which to pay that debt. If the tax base is shrinking but the cost of government is increasing, then the government is more likely to be classified as weak and not able to attract investors when refinancing is sought. Another common problem is a loose state law that easily permits local governments to issue tax-exempt bonds. For example, in the wake of Proposition 13, legal changes in California made it difficult for communities to issue general-obligation bonds, but vague criteria made it easy for special districts to issue bonds. This situation, combined with an economic recession, reduces the values in the real estate market, and increases the likelihood that special districts will not be able to meet their debt payments.

An associated problem is refinancing the short-term debt, which must be either retired or refinanced each year. This places pressure from the market on weaker governments when refinancing needs are high and investor confidence is low. Weaker governments find themselves unable to pay off the short-term debts, so default becomes a very real possibility in spite of the fact that normally they can meet the interest payments.

Investors' views are significant. They wish to buy safe bonds or notes that will earn them some money. There are no ideal indicators; however, investors do use the following indicators in making decisions:

1. Does the ratio of debt to full value exceed 10 percent?
2. What is the ratio of debt to market value of the real property? How does that compare with other governments?
3. What is the debt per capita? How does this compare with other governments?

---

[1] Some argue that even this test is not appropriate, given the changing municipal market demands and conditions. There is no uniform acceptance of any single simple test.

4. What is the ratio of debt to personal income (per capita income)?
5. What is the ratio of debt service to total budget?

Standard and Poor's (a major bond-rating firm) has developed a series of early-warning guidelines which municipalities would be wise to consider carefully in monitoring their own financial operations. They are the following:

1. current-year operating deficit;
2. two consecutive years of operating fund deficits;
3. current-year operating deficit that is larger than the previous year's deficit;
4. a general fund deficit in the current position on the current-year balance sheet;
5. a current general fund deficit (two or more years in the last five);
6. short-term debt (other than BAN) greater than 5 percent of main operating fund revenues outstanding at the end of the fiscal year;
7. a two-year trend of increasing short-term debt outstanding at fiscal year-end;
8. short-term interest and current-year debt service greater than 20 percent of total revenues;
9. property taxes greater than 90 percent of the tax limit;
10. debt outstanding greater than 90 percent of the tax limit;
11. total property tax collections less than 92 percent of total levy;
12. a trend of increasing tax collections during two consecutive years in a three-year trend;
13. declining market valuations during two consecutive years in a three-year trend;
14. overall net debt ratio 20 percent higher than previous year; and
15. overall net debt ratio 50 percent higher than four years ago.

The International City Management Association has developed an analytical tool called the *Financial Trend Monitoring System* (FTMS). It does not provide concrete answers as to whether a particular financial trend indicates a fiscal problem, but it does help decision makers more objectively consider a local government's financial condition. As can be seen from Standard and Poor's list of indicators, evaluating a jurisdiction's financial condition can be difficult, and no single indicator tells the whole story. Some indicators are more important than others, but the analysts cannot be sure which one or ones are more important until all the key indicators are assembled. The FTMS has twelve factors, with indicators for each factor. The six financial factors are revenues, expenditures, operating position, debt structure, unfunded liabilities, and condition of the capital plant. The five environmental factors are community needs and resources, external economic conditions, intergovernmental constraints, natural disasters and emergencies, and political culture. The twelfth factor is legislative policies and management practices. Indicators are grouped by factors, and under FTMS historical profiles are displays for each indicator.

State constitutions and laws do establish artificial limits. They vary greatly from state to state as well as by type of local government. Normally, they express the limit as a percent of the property tax base. Often state laws add provisions so jurisdictions that tax the same citizens have lower limits. This avoids greater taxpayer liabilities for citizens from two or more overlapping jurisdictions. And, state laws sometimes establish artificial limits based on the tax imposed for servicing the debt. Another common state limitation is the procedural requirement calling for a referendum on long-term indebtedness bond issues.

Revenue bonds are treated by investors much like corporation bonds. State law often does not prescribe limits, and the limits are established by the market. Investors examine forecasts of income to ensure debt services will be met and their investments will be safe.

New York City Financial Crisis

In April 1975, New York City hovered on the brink of default on its obligations. With help from New York State, the federal government, and others, default was averted, but two significant consequences have emerged:

1. interest rates are higher for state and local government since the crisis; and
2. more elaborate financial disclosures are now required.

The effects of the New York crisis were felt throughout the nation, and North Carolina is one example. In *Southern City*, Kenneth Murray reported in January 1976 that

> A recent study by the Municipal Finance Officer's Association (MFOA) shows that the New York City financial crisis has already cost local governments in North Carolina $424,000 in first-year added interest costs on bonded indebtedness and $5.1 million total in interest over the life of municipal bonds issued in 1975.

Exhibit 8–7 shows the Moody's credit-rating change for New York City. Notice that from 1965 to 1975, the remarkable drop to a low of Caa. Also note that since 1977, the rating has improved.

EXHIBIT 8–7 Moody's Rating for New York City

DATES	RATINGS
7/16/65	A to Baa
5/03/68	Baa to Baa1
12/18/72	Baa1 to A
10/02/75	A to Ba
10/29/75	Ba to Caa
5/24/77	Caa to B
11/19/81	B to Ba1
11/09/83	Ba1 to Baa

Source: *Moody's Municipal Credit Report,* April 29, 1985. Used by permission.

In the precrisis era, state and local governments were able to sell their bonds without revealing much about their financial situation. Since the crisis, investors are demanding greater disclosure of facts about the community and bonds.

Government Financial Emergencies

There are rather clear warning signs for a municipality that is in financial trouble:

1. an operating fund revenue/expenditure imbalance, in which current expenditures significantly exceed current revenues in one fiscal period (a well-managed government, under some conditions such as an excessively large fund balance, could properly have this type of imbalance);
2. a consistent pattern of current expenditures exceeding current revenues by small amounts for several years;
3. an excess of current operating liabilities over current assets (a fund deficit);
4. short-term operating loans outstanding at the conclusion of a fiscal year, the borrowing of cash from restricted funds, or an increase in unpaid bills in lieu of short-term operating loans;
5. a high and rising rate of property tax delinquency;
6. a sudden substantial decrease in assessed values for unexpected reasons;
7. an unfunded or underfunded pension liability, unless done over a long period of time such as 40 years; and
8. poor budgeting, accounting, and reporting.

Once there is recognition of the financial problems, financial management improvements can be considered. The most common remedy is to eliminate the imbalance between revenues and expenditures. Often, an appropriate remedy is to develop safeguards against misuse of short-term operating funds. The remedy could be to fund the retirement system adequately. Commonly, improvements must be made in municipal accounting and reporting systems.

If self-remedies are ineffective, then more significant steps can be taken. Some states have administrative bodies created to assist troubled local governments. If that is inadequate, the courts can demand that consultants such as Morgan Guarantee Trust be hired and, if necessary, can arrange for direct agreements with creditors. This is usually adequate for temporary or technical financial emergencies. If the problem continues, states sometimes have the power to force special remedies on a local government. Agreements usually undergo state review, approval, and supervision. The federal role is to provide a means to devise financial adjustments that a majority of the creditors approve.

Under Chapter 9 of the federal bankruptcy law, a plan of composition or financial adjustments is developed. First, a voluntary petition for bankruptcy is filed by the eligible local government unit. A plan of composition must be filed with the petition. The plan must be accepted by those holding 51 percent of the securities affected by the plan. Upon filing, an order is entered by the judges either approving or dismissing the plan. If approved, the resources of the debtor come within the jurisdiction of the court, and a time and place is fixed for a hearing. Notice is given to the creditors, answers can be filed, and the hearing is held. After the hearing, the court may confirm a plan of composition that has been accepted by the creditors involved in two-thirds of the aggregate amount. The court may, but seldom does, continue jurisdiction after the confirmation of the plan.

CAPITAL BUDGETING

Operating versus Capital Budgeting

Most local and state governments have two types of budgets: operating and capital. The *operating budget* deals with everyday types of activities. The *capital budget* deals with large expenditures for capital items. They differ in the nature of items purchased, methods of financing, and even the accompanying decision-making process. In most instances, operating expenses are depleted in a single year. Normally, capital items have long-range returns and useful life spans, are relatively expensive, and have physical presences, such as a building, road, water-supply system, or sewage system. Exhibit 8–8 notes that as of 1985, 56 percent of American cities had a separate capital budget and 73 percent of cities over 100,000 had them. Exhibit 8–9 notes that in 1986, forty-two states had capital budgets. Interestingly, the U.S. federal government does not have a capital budget, but this reform is championed strongly.

EXHIBIT 8–8 Separate Capital Budgets (SCB) in U.S. Cities

POPULATION STRATA	NUMBER OF CITIES	PERCENTAGE WITH SCB	PERCENTAGE WITH CIP	PERCENTAGE MAYORAL	WITH SCB MANAGER
10–25,000	316	48	59	52	50
25–50,000	257	52	65	47	54
50–100,000	150	63	74	58	66
100,000 +	73	73	92	67	81
Total	851	56	68	55	60

Source: Based on 1985 data in C. Bradley Doss, Jr., "The Use of Capital Budgeting Procedures in U.S. Cities," *Public Budgeting and Finance,*7, 3 (Autumn 1987), pp. 57–69.

The most significant difference between an operating and capital budget is the method of financing. Capital budget items are often financed through borrowing, but they can also be funded by saving over a period of years for the capital item or by using grants, special assessments, and the general revenue fund. Because government debts are involved, state laws, not surprisingly, do establish debt limits (normally associated with the assessed value of property). Also, states often require equalization rates to ensure consistent treatment throughout each state. The debt limits vary from state to state, and there are exceptions to the limit and application of equalization rates.

EXHIBIT 8–9   State Capital Budgets

NUMBER OF STATES

States with Capital Budgets	42
Extent of Coverage:	
All Capital Included	9
Not Included	33
For the States with Capital Budgets, Nontransportation capital is included in the Capital Budgets if Financed by:	
Bonds (5 do not borrow to finance capital)	37
Own-Source Current Revenue	37
Federal Grants	28

Note: Tabulations do not include autonomous authorities.
Source: Based on a 1986 OMB study reported in Lawrence W. Hush and Kathleen Peroff, "The Variety of State Capital Budgets: A Survey" *Public Budgeting and Finance*, 8, 2 (Summer 1988), pp. 67–79. Used by permission.

Some local governments shift as many expenses as possible from operating to capital budgets. For example, in both West Point, Mississippi, and New York City, band uniforms have been called capital budget items by public officials. This tendency can lead to corruption of the concept of a capital item to such an extent that the government has two operating budgets, with one financed through borrowing. That situation, in turn, leads to overuse of bonding, greater government resources used for debt retirement, and proportionately less money used to meet operating budget demands. Eventually the debt can become large enough that payments cannot be met and the community must face the possibility of management bankruptcy. Traditionally, debt is used to finance items with a life expectancy that lasts as long as the debt payments. The effect of this practice is to limit the overuse of debt financing and to make the debt more defensible politically as the future taxpayers are able to identify how they benefited from the decision to finance the item by borrowing money.

In capital budgeting, planning and careful, deliberate action are essential. Planning is needed to integrate the capital items with the remainder of the physical structure in the community. Capital improvement plans are essential to coordinate the work by time, funding possibilities, and physical plans. If building is involved, then the process of executing decisions involves study of the possibilities, site selection and acquisition, and planning and design as well as construction financing. Delays translate to higher construction costs owing to inflation, especially rising labor costs; thus, delays are to be avoided. Also, the increased operating and maintenance expense incurred because of the new facility is an important factor that can be considered in the planning phase. Communities have built facilities they cannot afford to operate or maintain (for example, stadiums).

Capital Facilities Planning

Decisions to add a public facility or make extensive repairs can be made on the basis of understanding the needs of the community and the resources available. The best approach to identifying the resources is to inventory the existing public facilities. The next step is to catalog the proposed public facilities. The key facts in the catalog include: the location of the proposed facility, the year of construction, cost priority, project description, financing schedule, prior or sunk costs, projection of future related fund requests, operating costs, and savings in operating and maintenance costs. The inventory and file of proposed projects can be updated at least once a year to ensure that decisions are based on the correct facts.

Making decisions on proposed projects is not easy and can be aided greatly if there are clear, detailed answers to the following questions:

1. What is the relationship of the proposed project to the overall development of the city?
2. How many citizens will be helped by the project, and how many citizens will be harmed or inconvenienced if the project is not constructed? Which citizens?
3. Will the proposed project replace a present worn-out service or structure or is it an additional responsibility of government?
4. Will the project add to the property value of the area, thus increasing the value of city property and receipts from property tax? How much of an increase will be realized?
5. Will the construction of the improvement add to the city's operation and maintenance budget? How much?
6. Will the project increase the efficiency of performance? How much and where? What cost savings will result? Will the project reduce the cost of performance for a particular service? How much and where?
7. Will the project provide a service required for economic growth and development of the municipality?
8. Is the estimated cost of the improvement within the city's ability to pay?

Ultimately, priorities have to be decided and judgments have to be made. Sometimes analytical techniques such as cost-benefit analysis are useful, but judgment cannot be avoided. Some communities use a point system to establish priorities. One scale used is as follows:

1. urgent (highest priority);
2. essential;
3. necessary;
4. desirable;
5. acceptable; and
6. deferrable (lowest priority).

Capital Budget Cycle

The budget cycle for capital budgeting is similar to the operating budget cycle. The phases are identical. A capital budget call and calendar are needed just as in an operating budget. Detailed information must be collected. Illustrations of the forms can be found by consulting the publications of the Government Finance Officers Association noted in this chapter's references.

Many governments prepare a multiyear capital improvement program each year. This helps those relying on capital decisions to understand the likely physical facilities in the near future. The program is normally funded through borrowing, grants, and the operating budget. The government formally approves the capital improvement plan and passes an ordinance or law that clearly explains what is approved and the method of financing the program.

Capital budgets are reviewed carefully. Both budget analysts and planners review the plans for possible errors and potential problems. Public hearings are commonly held, especially if revenue-sharing money is used to fund the capital budget. Careful consideration goes into deciding the best financing plan. Ultimately, the capital budget is approved by the official government policy-making unit, such as the city council (and possibly even by the electorate, if a bond issue is involved).

BONDING

Designing an Issue

Once a government has decided to borrow money, bonding is usually undertaken. The bond disclosure rules of the Securities and Exchange Commission (SEC), which apply only to bond issues over $1 million, must be followed. Two approaches to bonding are possible: use competitive bidding or arrange a negotiated sale to a specific underwriter. Often, competitive bidding is used to seek the lowest bidder, especially in general obligation bonds; but negotiated sales have been more frequent in revenue bonds and very small general obligation bonds. Underwriters affect issuer's costs due to their differing profit spread and their ability and willingness to locate investors to repurchase the bonds.

Competitiveness tends to encourage underwriters to lower their profit spread and try harder to locate investors. With negotiated sales, tailor-made issues can be designed to meet the unique needs of specific interests or preferences of a particular underwriter. This may mean that the particular underwriter may be in a better position to offer a lower bid for the bonds. Six common reasons for choosing a negotiated sale are:

- a new credit instrument may need such a sale to get customer interest;
- sometimes issues are too large for only one syndicate to buy through competition;

- sometimes a government has a low credit rating, and it has no other choice;
- the issues are very small, and there is no interest in submitting a competitive bid;
- the securities market is very volatile, and few competitive bids will be received; and
- the issue is complex, and a negotiated bid can better deal with the complexity.

Prior to publishing the invitation to bid, decisions must be made on the maturity, the size of the issue, the call terms, the principal and interest return structure, the interest cost limit, and the option to reject the bids, plus a wide variety of financing considerations such as put options and ZCBs. Commonly, a financial advisor is used to help make these decisions. Maturities vary in length and size. Sometimes they are thirty years, but more commonly they are twenty years or less. Traditionally, the length of the maturity is no longer than the useful life of the capital facility that is being financed. Serial bonds can be divided on an approximately equal basis, but it is also possible to negotiate a deferral of payments during the first two to five years, resulting in a large final payment (called a *balloon*). If the issue is simple, it is called "plain vanilla" bonds; unusual or complicated bonds that require more effort to sell are called "story" bonds.

If the issue is to appeal to the larger banking and securities community, it should not be less than $1 million; $4.2 million is a normal size, but issues of more than $100 million do exist. With the changing federal tax laws, the make-up of the bond market has shifted. For example, the alternative minimum tax caused many banks to leave the bond market. If the insurance companies follow the banks, the market will consist only of private households, which tends to be the most volatile group.

Large issues require buyers to form *syndicates*, which are temporary financial partnerships to buy and sell securities. The primary buyer is called an *underwriter*; this can be a syndicate, which will eventually sell the securities to groups and even to other syndicates. The use of syndicates is commonplace. Interestingly, their complex million-dollar agreements are sometimes made by phone in a remarkably informal manner. If negotiated sales are planned, decisions must focus on the coupon interest rates so that an issue's yield curve will conform to the market yield curve for the appropriate grade of security, ensure the underwriter involved will properly promote and place the bonds so as to get the best possible price, and select an acceptable level of underwriting compensation. Underwriters should know several weeks in advance that it will have a specific product to sell. Thus, it can test the market and even change such things as a bond's size to improve the bonds marketability.

The provisions in the bond offering are important. Together with the credit standing, they largely determine the marketability of the issue. If many seek to invest in the security, then the government can get a lower interest rate. The variety of ways to structure the issue is remarkably complex. The key to the decision is to structure the issue to achieve the lowest price and other benefits for the government.

The real cost of interest payments depends on the time value of money. Further out in the future, the dollar is worth less to the investor than the near-term dollar. To accommodate the common preference for shorter-term maturity bonds, the issuer can issue "front-loaded" bonds that give high coupon rates on short-maturity bonds. Another consideration is that buyers seek specific maturities that are similar to what the market finds to be attractive. Thus, coupon rates should enable bonds to be sold at or near their par value. If this occurs, they are called "efficient." If they are not efficient, underwriters would have to resell bonds at prices that are substantially above or below their par value. Such a requirement normally makes such sales difficult and sometimes costly to the underwriter. Thus, an objective in designing an issue normally is having efficient coupon rates.

For most bidders, the fact that there is a tax advantage for municipal bonds is significant, but taxable government bonds do exist. Exhibit 8–10 illustrates the importance of municipal bonds to the two highest tax brackets. In nontaxable bonds, the interest income is exempt from federal income tax and is often exempt from the income tax in the state of issue. In *South Carolina* v. *Baker*, the Supreme Court ruled that the doctrine of reciprocal tax immunity does not apply, but the Congress has not repealed federal laws revoking tax immunity. However, if a state or local government improperly places the loaned proceeds in revenue-generating investments (for example, only for reinvestment purposes), then the Internal Revenue Service would call the bonds arbitrage and tax the interest income from the bond. Without such a rule, local governments would take advantage of their unique lower interest rates to invest in higher interest bearing bonds and make a profit from the difference in interest rates.

EXHIBIT 8–10   Advantage of Tax-Free Income
(for illustrative purposes only)

Tax-Free Yield	TAXABLE EQUIVALENT YIELD 1991 FEDERAL INCOME TAX RATES	
	28%	31%
6.25%	8.68%	9.06%
6.50	9.03	9.42
6.75	9.38	9.42
7.00	9.72	10.14
7.25	10.07	10.51

Source: Dean Witter Reynolds, Inc., 1991 "Tax Free Income."

The three basic methods used by bond-issuing governments for awarding bond issues to competing bidders are the *unrestricted net interest cost* (NIC) method, the *net interest cost with constraints* (NIC-C) method, and the *true interest cost* (TIC) method. Of the three, the newer TIC tends to minimize interest costs the best. The NIC method looks at the total coupon interest payments over the life of the issue. It takes special account of the time value of money. Thus, with this method, bidders are encouraged to front-load their bids and produce inefficient bids that result in penalty yields. NIC-C imposes constraints on the bidding process to overcome the shortcomings of the NIC method. For example, the constraint is established that the coupon rate on any particular bond must be at least as high as the rate on bonds having the shortest maturity. This constraint does help in terms of front-loading and penalty yields, but it can still result in bond issues awarded to bidders who do not bid the lowest true interest cost among the bids submitted. In the TIC method, bond bids are evaluated on the interest payments required in terms of their present value or present worth. Many states have laws that do not permit the use of the TIC method yet.

Other factors can also be considered before a bond is offered. The government may wish to establish an interest cost limit to protect itself from bids that are, as a group, unreasonable. In some circumstances, such ceilings can raise costs especially when tax-exempt yields are very high for a prolonged period of time. Such ceilings force postponement of projects and thus possibly raise project costs even higher. States are wiser to remove statutory interest rate ceilings or to have indexing of them. Governments sometimes add a stipulation that all bids may be rejected to protect themselves further. Other decisions include the bond date, the place and time of sale, payment dates for principal and interest, who will receive and read the bids, who will print the bonds to avoid counterfeiting and theft, and what to do if no bids are received.

Many local governments do not have the necessary expertise to handle bonding or special types of bonding. Thus, getting outside assistance is common especially for complex issues. Some states provide financial advisory assistance, but, normally, private advisory services are used. The amount and degree of assistance varies with the amount and kind of funding contemplated. In moderate-sized, full-faith-and-credit transactions, groups such as local commercial banks, investment bankers, bond counsels, and state agencies may provide the services at no direct or minimum charge on negotiated sales. However, the services would be minimal, and there might be the expectation that an advantageous relationship would be developed or protected. Often, the underwriter or potential underwriter can be helpful in suggesting approaches with a better market appeal.

Services of financial advisors include developing a sale schedule, sizing and structuring the issue, preparing the sale document, arranging for the rating, coordinating sale advertising, verifying bids/interest rates, and assisting with closing. Exhibit 8–11 presents the costs commonly associated with obtaining bond expertise. Frequently, financial advisors are paid on a flat fee-for-services basis, but they can be paid based on the amount of the debt issued. Payment is usually stated as a dollar amount per note or bond issue (for example, $.75 per $1,000 of the principal amount of the issue).

Some states permit pooling of debt issues of more than one local government to reduce costs and enhance marketability of the bonds. A state bond bank assists local governments to sell their debts. Since 1970, states like Vermont have created a state authority to pool the debt of small participating communities into a single larger authority issue. This permits the state's stronger credit to be used to provide small community access to national credit markets at reduced borrowing costs. Given the increasing need for government investments in infrastructure, state efforts to create infrastructure banks give local jurisdictions a sustained and predictable bond-proceeds revenue stream for capital improvements without burdening a state's own general-obligation borrowing capacity. Some states permit umbrella bond-insurance programs, thus reducing the riskiness of bonds and lowering borrowing costs.

EXHIBIT 8–11 Total Marketing Cost ($5 to $10 Million Issues, Cost per $1,000)

ITEM	GENERAL OBLIGATION	REVENUE	DIFFERENCE (REVENUE-GENERAL OBLIGATION)
Legal			
Local Attorney	$1.62	$3.75	$2.13
Bond Counsel	2.00	2.96	.96
Bond Election	.50	.45*	-.05
Total Legal	4.12	7.16	3.04
Financial Advisor	1.44	2.63	1.19
Accountant	.97	1.05	.08
Notice	.14	.12	-.02
Prospectus	.91	1.30	.39
Printing	.23	.25	.02
Rating	.53	.78	.25
Signature	.06	.03	-.03
Other	.21	2.19	1.98
Total	$8.61	$15.51	$6.90

*Mean for all revenue issues in the study.
Source: Philip J. Fischer, Ronald W. Forbes, and John E. Peterson, "Risk and Return in the Choice of Revenue Bond Financing." In John E. Peterson and Wesley C. Hough (eds.), *Creative Capital Financing*. Chicago: Municipal Finance Officers Association, 1983, p. 139–148. Used by permission.

Purchasers of bonds need to be assured the bond itself is legal, and they will not check the public record themselves. Therefore, a bond counsel is needed to certify (1) the legal existence of the government offering the bond, (2) the propriety of authorization of the bond, (3) the correctness of the procedures that have been followed in the conduct of the sale, (4) absence of litigation with respect to the validity of the bond issue, and (5) the correctness of the signatures on the bond. This assurance carries more weight if the bond counsel commands wide respect among investment bankers and investors.

Bond Prospectus, Notice of Sale, and Sale

Since the mid-1970s, a more elaborate bond prospectus has been required by investors. The prospectus is merely the information needed by investors to decide whether or not they wish to invest in the bonds. Key information in the prospectus often includes:

1. description of the bonds;
2. security for the bonds;
3. description of the government;
4. financial procedures pertinent to the issue;
5. fund revenues and disbursements;
6. explanation of the fund's budget;
7. local economic factors;
8. debt administration applicable to the issue;
9. description of the capital improvement program;
10. any contingent liabilities;
11. tax exemptions;
12. ratings;
13. certificates from necessary officials;
14. assessed valuation and tax rate;
15. tax levies and collections;
16. fund revenues and expenditures; and
17. comparative statement of financial conditions.

The GFOA "Disclosure Guidelines for Offerings of Securities by State and Local Governments" is the best guide to preparing a prospectus. It provides essential guidance and is recognized as the authoritative source. An excellent practical digest is presented in the Oregon Bond Disclosure Guidelines.

The prospectus is printed and distributed with the notice of sale. It is sent to investment bankers, a list of large investors, financial newspapers, and ratings and information agencies. The notice of sale includes:

1. the correct legal name of the issuing bond as well as the special law under which the government was organized and which gave it the authority to issue the bonds;
2. the type of bonds to be issued, the amount and purpose of the issue, the maturity schedule, and the call feature;
3. the date, time, and place of sale and the manner in which the bid is to be made;

4. limitations as to interest rate, payment dates of interest, and when and where the principal will be paid;
5. denomination and registration privileges;
6. basis for bidding;
7. amount of good-faith check required;
8. bid form and basis for award;
9. name of approving attorney and statement on legality;
10. provisions made for payment of principal and interest;
11. total tax rate in the government unit and legal limits;
12. methods and place for settlement and delivery of the bonds; and
13. the right to reject any or all bids.

Some practices are fairly well accepted in the bond market. Bonds are dated as near as possible to the delivery date to avoid improper interest charges. Bonds are normally issued in $5,000 denominations, except for odd amounts which should be retired the first year. Interest is paid semiannually, and bond owners often have the option of registering principal only or principal and interest. If the issue is sold on a wide market, then payments are made at large financial centers for the convenience of the bondholders. Payments must be prompt, or a default occurs.

Often large issues are bought by highly competitive investment syndicates organized just for the purpose of buying the issue. The practice of these partnerships is to resell the issues as soon as possible to other investors. The syndicate members make their profit on the slight difference of what they bought and sold for each issue. Thus, municipalities selling bonds should be aware of the factors (that is, maturity, coupon structure, points, rate limits) that permit easy syndicate reselling. If syndicates can resell bonds easily, then the municipality should be able to get a lower interest rate on its bonds.

Most of the information in this section assumes that open competitive bidding will be used rather than direct negotiations. Generally speaking, one is wiser to use open competitive bidding, but experienced governmental negotiators can often secure the lowest interest rates as well as better terms through negotiations. In a 1985 issue of *Public Administration Review*, Robert L. Bland noted that his research showed a positive correlation between experienced negotiators and lower interest costs, but there was a limit to the advantage of having more experience. He concluded by asserting that using experienced negotiators for sale of securities might be advisable, but they should not be used for first-time or very infrequent issuers.

For larger issues, a government might be wise to contract with a fiscal or paying agent. *Paying agents* are normally located in large financial centers, and they make the necessary principal and interest payments on the bonds. *Fiscal agents* have broader powers, including replacing lost or destroyed original bonds, exchanging coupons for registered bonds, canceling paid bonds and coupons, cremating canceled bonds and coupons, answering routine correspondence, and signing bonds. The advantage of having an agent at a financial center is the saving of time in the movement of credit, coupons, bonds, and checks, thus saving money.

Debt Records and Reporting

Reputation is important. The local government must develop a reputation among investors for accuracy and integrity so that full trust can be placed in its debt records, reports, and payment calendar. Surprises must be avoided. Scrupulous attention to each detail is essential. If such attention is not paid, the market automatically discounts the credit, and higher interest payments result on later issues. Reports are needed by the government bond dealers, bond-rating agencies, and, of course, the investors.

Essentially, the investor is interested only in the ability of the issuer to make timely payments of principal and interest. This judgment is often made on the basis of accounting data and reports. The National Committee on Government Accounting, in *Governmental Accounting, Auditing, and Financial Reporting* (1983), has established basic standards for reporting on debt. This information cannot be segregated from the other financial reports of a government because of the interrelationship of the data and the potential significance of other financial data in understanding the government's debt and financial condition. Briefly, the investor is concerned with the balance sheet, amount of debt outstanding, status of the debt reserves, ability of the government to meet the payments, willingness of officials to use their power to service debt, and the record of the community in debt and other financial management. Also the investor is concerned with assessments, the area's economic condition, the market value of its property, the tax habits of its citizens, and any overlapping of debt with other local governments.

Timely information is important to investors. Therefore, every reasonable effort should be made to provide reports promptly and frequently.

Bond Ratings

State and local government bonds are rated, and this does reflect the likely interest rate for new issues of that jurisdiction. The fact that a government spends less per capita does not necessarily mean higher bond ratings. There is some wisdom in the adage: "Reduce your debt and increase the value of taxable property." Investors do look at such ratios, and both factors may be within the control of the government. The use of budget controls or a certificate from the Government Finance Officers Association will not lower rates. However, as noted by Earl R. Wilson (1983), the use of budgets to plan and manage government does often result in lower interest rates.

The Standard and Poor's municipal bond-rating process involves four broad factors: *economic, debt, administrative,* and *fiscal. Economic factors* include the economic diversity of the tax base as well as the diversity and growth of area economic opportunities. *Debt factors* include debt burden, debt history, trend, and type of security. *Administrative factors* include tax rate, levy limitations, debt limits, and other information indicating likely ability to meet debt payments. *Fiscal factors* include the assets and liabilities in the balance sheet as well as trends in assets and liabilities, especially pension liabilities. In the fiscal factors, comparisons are made between assets and liabilities to see if assets exceed expenditures in the present and the foreseeable future. The bond-rating process does not proceed without the necessary information. Since the 1970s, more meetings on the issues, more extensive field trips, and more extensive analyses are commonly done to rate a state or municipal government. Rating decisions are based, in varying degrees, on the following:

1. likelihood of default: capacity and willingness of the obligator to observe the timely payment of interest and repayment of principal in accordance with the terms of the obligation;
2. nature of provisions in the obligation; and
3. protection afforded by, and relative position of, the obligation in the event of bankruptcy, reorganization, or other arrangement under the laws of bankruptcy and other laws affecting creditors' rights.

Moody's Investors Service considers factors similar to those considered by Standard and Poor's. It focuses on debt, economic, administration, and financial factors. The two most frequently used statistical ratios are *debt burden* and *net debt per capita.* The former is a ratio of the government's net debt (gross debt less bonds fully supported by enterprise revenues, and short-term debt plus overlapping debt) to the estimated full value of taxable property. Those ratios are helpful in understanding the total tax-supported debt. Both indicators are compared to national medians for governments of similar size. With inflation of property values, another supplemental indicator is debt service as a percent of local expenditures. A high or rapidly rising figure is often a significant warning. For revenue bonds, a commonly used measure is debt-service coverage (defined as net revenue) divided by principal plus interest requirements for the year. Another measure is the "safety margin" (that is, net revenue less debt-service requirements for the year divided by gross revenue and income). Moody's also looks at the government's fund balance. Generally, a fund balance of 5 percent of the budget is considered prudent and indicative of the capability to meet the debt obligation in a full and timely manner. See Exhibit 8–12 for the information required by Moody's to rate a debt issue.

The 1989 Moody's national distribution of general obligation bond ratings by category is: Aaa - 1%; Aa1 - 2%; Aa - 9%; A1 - 19%; A - 37%; Baa1 - 16%; Baa - 15%; and Ba1 and below - 1%. Exhibit 8–13 presents the 1990 Moody rating changes by region.

EXHIBIT 8–12 Moody's Information Requirements for Rating Debt

DOCUMENTS	TAX-SUPPORTED BONDS	REVENUE BONDS	BONDS ANTICIPATION NOTES	REVENUE BOND ANTICIPATION NOTES	TAX AND/OR REVENUE ANTICIPATION NOTES	LETTER OF CREDIT
PRIMARY:						
Official statement or prospectus	X	X	X	X	X	X
Notice of sale (if public)	X	X	X	X	X	
Annual reports or audits (last 3 years)[1]	X	X	X	X	X	
Most recent budget operations	X	X	X	X	X	
Capital budget or planning document	X	X				
Legal opinion	X	X	X	X	X	X
Law(s) under which notes are to be issued[2]			X	X	X	
Note resolution or ordinance			X	X	X	
Bond resolution or ordinance, trust indenture and any other legal documents relevant to the bonds and notes		X	X	X		X
Engineer's report (if available)		X	X	X		
Bond purchase commitment letter, if sale of the bonds has been prearranged (i.e., to an agency of the United States Government)			X			

Copy of local charter or document which describes governmental structure					X
For school districts; ten-year enrollment trend and projection; school plant description, including facilities and capacity					X
Cash flow statements[3]	X				
Financial feasibility study including projections if available				X	
Rate study (if available)				X	
SUPPORT: (for information not contained in any of the above documents)					
Maturity schedule for bond anticipation notes, including final statutory maturity date for this and outstanding notes		X	X		
Interest rate computation, 360 or 365 day basis		X	X		
Complete debt statement of issuer, including debt-incurring capacity		X	X	X	
Interest rate limitations on bonds and notes		X	X	X	
List of last five bond issues of type that will fund notes, including amount, sale date, number of bids received (if public sale), and net interest cost			X	X	
Enterprise system description[4]		X	X	X	
Descriptions of rate setting process; record of revisions for past five years		X	X	X	

EXHIBIT 8–12 Moody's Information Requirements for Rating Debt (continued)

DOCUMENTS	TAX-SUPPORTED BONDS	REVENUE BONDS	BONDS ANTICIPATION NOTES	REVENUE BOND ANTICIPATION NOTES	TAX AND/OR REVENUE ANTICIPATION NOTES	LETTER OF CREDIT
Investment policy; formal document or brief description of practices	X	X			X	
Public employees: number employed and trend, status of contracts, unions, pension funds, latest actuarial study, if available	X	X			X	
Tax assessment and collection procedures, including due dates and penalty rates	X				X	
Tax and levy limitations	X				X	
List of ten largest taxpayers, their assessed valuation and type of business	X				X	
Economic data for service area	X	X				
List of operating loan borrowings[5]					X	
Assumptions used in preparing cash flows					X	
Assessed valuation for last five years	X				X	
Equalization ratios last five years	X				X	
Current population and latest census estimates	X				X	

Statement of direct debt and debt overlapping debt issuers, including allocable share	X				
Future borrowing plans		X	X	X	X
Number of building permits—last five years, plus the dollar amount		X	X		
Local and area unemployment rates		X			
List of ten major empoyers, number of employees and type of business		X			
Area of the issuer (in square miles) and percentage of land that is developed		X			
Current number of government employees; whether unionized and contract status		X	X		
Debt (outstanding and new); segregate by security; actual principal maturities and interest requirements for each year, pro-forma debt service schedule for new debt including interest rate assumptions		X	X		
Letter of credit and reimbursement agreement					X
Loan or lease agreement					X
Bank counsel enforceability opinions (domestic and foreign)					X
Preference (bankruptcy) opinion					X

EXHIBIT 8–12 Moody's Information Requirements for Rating Debt (continued)

DOCUMENTS	TAX-SUPPORTED BONDS	REVENUE BONDS	BONDS ANTICIPA-TION NOTES	REVENUE BOND ANTICIPA-TION NOTES	TAX AND/OR REVENUE ANTICIPA-TION NOTES	LETTER OF CREDIT
Remarketing agent agreement						X
Tender agent agreement						X
Pledge and security agreement						X
Standby bond purchase agreement						X
Mortgage and/or other collateral documents						X
Other documents as applicable						X

[1]For revenue bonds, include interim financial results for recently concluded but unaudited period of year-to-date results and comparable period in prior year.

[2]This requirement is waived if the law(s) have been previously submitted and have not been subsequently amended.

[3]Include at least one full fiscal year actual; current fiscal year actual/estimate; and projections for the next fiscal year through note maturity.
Note: These are strictly cash basis and should not include or show negative receipts or disbursements or negative balances.

[4]For revenue bonds, include system capacity and trend of usage, particularly customers and consumption (output) by year for past five years, percent of service purchased by each major user.

[5]Over last five fiscal years, including type and amount issued in fiscal year, and amount outstanding at year end, and interest rates on the notes.

Source: Moody's Municipal Issues. Vol. 4, No. 1, February 1987. Used by permission.

EXHIBIT 8–13   1990 Moody Rating Changes

REGION	RATINGS ASSIGNED	RATINGS UP	RATINGS DOWN
New England	514	7	26
Mid-Atlantic	1,102	22	37
Great Lakes	1,211	47	42
Plains	719	14	22
Southeast	1,078	50	18
Southwest	725	10	24
Rocky Mountain	175	1	7
Far West	962	43	12

Source: Moody's Investor's Service, 8, 1 (June 1991), p. 14.

Ratings provide the investor and others with an informed opinion of the creditworthiness of a particular issue. Ratings do not establish interest rates, but higher ratings normally translate into lower interest cost to the issuer. Larger investors conduct their own analyses of issues, but the Moody's and Standard and Poor's rating services provide additional guidance on creditworthiness.

REVIEW QUESTIONS

1. What is a government debt? What are the various types and forms of debt? Why do they exist? What are the alternatives to debt and why are municipalities likely to incur debt?
2. Compare and contrast revenue bonds, general obligation bonds, short-term borrowing, and creative financing.
3. What criteria can be used to judge the correct level of state and local debt? Justify the criteria cited.
4. Explain the significance of the New York City financial crisis for (a) New York City, (b) other local governments, and (c) the bond market, including prospectus requirements (GFOA, federal, others).
5. Why is the term "bankruptcy" inaccurate and misleading for municipal governments? What can be done to anticipate and remedy a financial crisis?
6. How does the decision-making process differ in capital versus operating budgeting?
7. Why is judgment central to any capital budget decision? What analytical questions are especially useful and why?
8. What takes place in designing an issue? What is particularly important and why? Why are syndicates significant? Why is a prospectus important?
9. What can a government do if it gets low bond ratings?

REFERENCES

Advisory Commission on Intergovernmental Relations. *City Financial Emergencies: The Intergovernmental Dimension.* Washington, D.C.: Government Printing Office, July 1973.
———*Significant Features of Fiscal Federalism,* vols. I and II. Washington, D.C.: Government Printing Office, June 1976 and March 1977.
———*Understanding the Market for State and Local Debt.* Washington, D.C.: Government Printing Office, May 1976.
ARONSON, J. RICHARD, and ELI SCHWARTZ (eds.). *Management Policies in Local Government Finance.* Washington, D.C.: International City Management Association, Municipal Finance Officers Association, 1975.
BAKER, KEVIN. "Financing Government," *Governing,* (April 1990), 5A–22A.
BLAND, ROBERT L. "The Interest Cost Savings From Experience in the Municipal Bond Market." *Public Administration Review,* 45, 1 (January/February 1985), 233–237.
BLAND, ROBERT L., and LI-KHAN CHEN. "Taxable Municipal Bonds: State and Local Governments Confront the Tax-Exempt Limitation Movement," *Public Administration Review.* 50, 1 (January/February 1990), 42–48.
CHOATE, PAT. "Case for a National Capital Budget." *Public Budgeting and Finance,* 1, 4 (Winter 1981), 21–26.
CHOATE, PAT and SUSAN M. WALTERS. *America in Ruins: Beyond The Public Works Pork Barrel.* Washington D.C.:Council of the State Planning Agencies, 1981.
COE, CHARLES K. "Competitive v. Negotiated Sale of General Obligation Bonds: A State-Based Comparison." Paper presented at the SECOPA conference at Charlotte, N.C, 1991.
DOSS, BRADLEY C., "Capital Budgeting Practices." In Thomas D. Lynch and Lawrence Martin (eds.), *Handbook of Comparative Public Budgeting and Financial Management.* New York: Marcel Dekker, 1993, 269–292.
DOSS, BRADLEY, C. JR. "The Use of Capital Budgeting Procedures in U.S. Cities." *Public Budgeting and Finance.* 7, 2 (Autumn 1987), 57–69.
FISCHER, PHILIP J., RONALD FORBES, and JOHN E. PETERSON. "Risk and Return in Choice of Revenue Bond Financing." In John E. Peterson and Wesley C. Hough (eds.), *Creative Capital Financing.* Chicago: Municipal Finance Officers Association, 1983, pp 139–148.
FORBES, RONALD, and EDWARD RENSHAW. "Tax-Exempt Zero Coupon Bonds." In John E. Peterson and Wesley C. Hough (eds.) *Creative Capital Financing.* Chicago: Municipal Finance Officers Association, 1982.
GROVES, SANFORD M., W. MAUREEN GODSEY, and MARTHA A. SHULMAN. "Financial Indicators for Local Government," *Public Budgeting and Finance,* 1, 2 (Summer 1981), 5–19.
GROVES, SANFORD M. and VALENTE, MAUREEN GODSEY. *Evaluating Financial Condition: A Handbook for Local Government.* Washington D.C.: International City/County Management Association (ICMA), 1986.
HACKBART, MERL M., and JAMES LEIGLAND. "State Debt Management Policy: A National Survey," *Public Budgeting and Finance,* 10, 1 (Spring 1990), 37–54.
HUSH, LAWRENCE W., and KATHLEEN PEROFF. "The Variety of State Capital Budgets: A Survey," *Public Budgeting and Finance,* 8, 2 (Summer 1988), 67–79.
HUMPHREY, NANCY P., and DIANE RAUSA MAURICE. "Infrastructure Bond Bank Initiatives: Policy Implications and Credit Concerns," *Public Budgeting and Finance,* 6, 3 (Autumn 1986), 38–56.
LEHAN, EDWARD ANTHONY. "The Case for Directly Marketed Small-Denomination Bonds." In John E. Peterson and Wesley C. Hough. *Creative Capital Financing for State and Local Governments.* Chicago: Municipal Finance Officers Association, 1983.

LEMOV, PENELOPE. "The Brave New World of Public Finance." *Governing, February 1992,* *27–28.*

———"For Municipal Bonds, It's Not a Plain Vanilla World Anymore," *Governing,* June 1990, 52–58.

LEVITAN, DONALD, and MICHAEL J. BYRNE. "Capital Improvement Programming" In Jack Rabin and Thomas D. Lynch (eds.), *Handbook on Public Budgeting and Financial Management.* New York: Marcel Dekker, 1983.

MILLER, GIRARD (compiler). *Capital Budgeting: Blueprint for Change.* Chicago: Government Finance Officers Association, 1984.

MOAK, LENNOX L. *Administration of Local Government Debt.* Chicago: Municipal Finance Officers Association, 1970.

Moody's Investors Service. *Moody's Municipal Issues,* 2, 2, (May 1985).

Moody's Investors Service. *Moody's Municipal Issues,* 4, 1, (February 1987).

Municipal Finance Officers Association. "Disclosure Guidelines for Offerings of Securities by State and Local Governments." Chicago: MFOA, 1983.

MURRAY, KENNETH. "New York Crisis—Its Effect on North Carolina," *Southern City.* Raleigh, NC:North Carolina League of Municipalities (January 1976), p. 6.

National Committee on Government Accounting. *Governmental Accounting, Auditing, and Financial Reporting.* Chicago: Government Finance Officers Association, 1983.

PETERSON, JOHN E. "The Municipal Bond Market in a Changing Economy." *Public Budgeting and Finance, 8, 4 (Winter 1988), 22–34.*

PETERSON, JOHN E., and WESLEY C. HOUGH. *Creative Capital Financing for State and Local Governments.* Chicago: Municipal Finance Officers Association, 1983.

PETERSON, JOHN E., and PAT WATT. *The Price of Advice.* Washington, D.C.: The Government Finance Research Center of the Government Finance Officers Association, 1986.

STANFIELD, ROCHELLE L. "It's a Tougher World for City Bonds," *National Journal,* 9, 34 (August 20, 1977), 1300–1303.

Standard and Poor's *Credit Overview.* New York: Standard and Poor's Corp., 1983.

State of Oregon. *Bond Disclosure Guidelines, 1983.*

STEISS, ALAN WALTER. *Local Government Finance.* Lexington, Mass.: D.C. Heath, 1975.

U. S. Advisory Commission on Intergovernmental Relations. *Significant Features of Fiscal Federalism,* vol. 2, *Revenues and Expenditures, 1991.* Washington, D.C.: Government Printing Office, October, 1991.

VALENTE, MAUREEN G. "Local Government Capital Financing: Options and Decisions." *Municipal Year Book.* Washington D.C.: International City Management Association, 1986.

VASCHE, JOHN DAVID. "State and Local Government Options for Reducing Borrowing Costs." *Public Budgeting and Finance,* 3, 4 (Winter 1983), 42–56.

WILSON, EARL R. "Fiscal Performance and Municipal Bond Borrowing Costs." *Public Budgeting and Finance,* 3, 4 (Winter 1983), 28–41.

9

REVENUE SYSTEMS

There are two sides to every budget. One is expenditure and the other is revenue. This chapter discusses intergovernmental revenue systems, property taxes, and other revenue sources. The revenue side of budgeting is explained in an intergovernmental context involving the growth of government and the current patterns in government revenue. The most controversial yet most important local tax is the property tax. This chapter explains the tax, the controversy, and the administration of the tax. The same is done for income and sales taxes. At the completion of this chapter, the reader should know:

1. the latest trend in fiscal federalism;
2. the relative tax burden in the United States;
3. a definition of property tax and the major criticisms of it;
4. the major suggested property tax reforms, including the *Serrano* v. *Priest* decision and its implication;
5. how property is assessed as well as means to test assessments;
6. the assessment cycle, application of tax rates, and foreclosures; and
7. the definition, significance, issues, and administration of both income and sales taxes.

INTERGOVERNMENTAL REVENUE SYSTEMS

Historical Background

American government is a complexity of intergovernmentally financed programs, with the current pattern explainable by means of American political history. At the republic's beginning, state governments were the dominant form of government. But the federal government took on a more significant role by assuming the states' revolutionary war debt, financially assisting large transportation projects like canals, harbor improvement, and railroad expansion, plus supporting education through land grants. The federal government even used land grants for social purposes such as homestead programs. In the 1930s, the federal government involved itself extensively with social programs, but this time financed the programs with dollars. In the 1950s, new large grant programs, channeled through state governments, were designed primarily to help air and highway transportation. In the 1960s and 1970s, the number, variety, and type of grants expanded greatly. In the 1970s, grant consolidation was the theme, followed by the 1980s, with fiscal constraint as the theme.

John Shannon and James Edwin Kee (1989) argue that in 1978 a fundamental shift in American public finance took place which decidedly veered our intergovernmental system away from centralized federalism. This was due to five factors. The first was the disappearance of the federal government's fiscal advantage due to individual income tax reform, including using indexing for inflation. The second was the important legacy of President Reagan who accelerated the popular swing away from federal power towards increased state responsibility. The third was the resiliency of the state-local system which was able to rebound from the taxpayer revolts (for example, Proposition 13 in California), the early 1980s recession, and reductions in federal aid. The fourth was the emergence of relatively strong state-local revenue systems which are more balanced, broad-based, and have proportional tax structures. The last factor was state and local government institutional reforms, sometimes induced by federal actions such as *Baker* v. *Carr* ("one person, one vote") and civil rights laws.

The early 1990s created extreme budget pressures on many state governments due to the recession, demand for services—especially for Medicaid and prison construction—and fewer transfer payments from the federal government. For example, in fiscal year 1992, ten states were not able to start their fiscal years with a budget—highly unusual at the state level. In that year, states increased their revenues by $15 billion, which topped the $10 billion increase in fiscal year 1991. During that same period, spending growth was cut $10.2 billion, amid increasing demands for more services and lower taxes.

The tax burden is not constant from region to region or from state to state. According to the U.S. Advisory Commission on Intergovernmental Relations, more state and local taxes are collected per person in New England, the Midwest and the Far West and fewer taxes are collected in the Southeast and Southwest. In 1989, the highest state is Alaska because of its oil tax revenue at $3,922, but the District of Columbia is a close second at $3,714. The lowest was Mississippi at $1,184. The 1989 national average was $1,888. Exhibit 9–1 shows 1988 state capacity and effort indices and the revenue percent distribution by source. Some states have a relatively larger tax capacity, with Alaska, Connecticut, and

EXHIBIT 9–1   Total 1988 RTS and RRS Capacity and Effort Indexes by State

	REPRESENTATIVE TAX SYSTEM CAPACITY	EFFORT	REPRESENTATIVE REVENUE SYSTEM CAPACITY	EFFORT
Alabama	76	84	77	95
Alaska	159	127	255	122
Arizona	99	96	97	97
Arkansas	74	84	74	86
California	116	94	115	98
Colorado	107	89	106	94
Connecticut	143	90	142	83
Delaware	124	84	120	94
District of Columbia	123	154	126	137
Florida	104	82	103	87
Georgia	94	89	93	98
Hawaii	114	112	111	111
Idaho	76	93	76	98
Illinois	99	102	100	95
Indiana	87	93	88	96
Iowa	83	113	84	118
Kansas	91	104	91	104
Kentucky	81	88	80	89
Louisiana	83	90	84	97
Maine	98	105	97	99
Maryland	109	108	111	102
Massachusetts	129	94	131	89
Michigan	95	112	96	112
Minnesota	104	112	103	117
Mississippi	65	94	65	108
Missouri	90	86	89	86
Montana	85	102	84	102
Nebraska	90	98	89	106
Nevada	135	69	129	75
New Hampshire	126	66	123	66
New Jersey	124	101	126	95
New Mexico	83	99	88	103
New York	109	152	110	141
North Carolina	91	93	89	91
North Dakota	86	91	85	107
Ohio	91	97	92	98
Oklahoma	89	89	87	95
Oregon	91	99	91	104
Pennsylvania	94	97	95	93
Rhode Island	99	104	100	99
South Carolina	79	96	78	102
South Dakota	78	95	78	95
Tennessee	84	83	84	89
Texas	96	88	95	89
Utah	78	106	76	109
Vermont	105	100	102	100
Virginia	104	91	104	90
Washington	98	102	98	105
West Virginia	78	88	76	90
Wisconsin	90	119	90	117
Wyoming	123	94	118	105
U.S. Total	100	100	100	100

Source: U.S. Advisory Commission on Intergovernmental Relations, *1988 State Fiscal Capacity and Effort*, Information Report M-170. Washington D.C.: ACIR, 1990, p. 26.

Massachusetts having the highest. The lowest was Mississippi. The states with the highest capacity are not always equally high in tax effort. The states with the highest tax effort were the District of Columbia and New York. The lowest effort was New Hampshire. The state with the biggest positive spread between tax capacity and tax effort was Nevada, and the biggest negative spread was New York.

American federal, state, and local taxes have increased in dollars but are about the same as a percentage of the gross national product since 1976. After World War II to 1972, there was a slight increase, and the early 1980s saw a slight decrease. The federal, state, and local tax revenue in 1989 was 20.9 percent of the gross national product. What is more interesting is the distribution change. State and local tax revenue grew from 5.1 percent in 1948 to 9.0 percent in 1989. In contrast, the federal tax revenue shrank from 14.5 percent to 11.8 percent in that same period. If that trend continues, state and local tax revenues will equal and eventually surpass federal tax revenues. Property tax remains the important tax source for local government, whereas individual income tax and sales tax are about equally important to state government.

American federal, state, and local taxes have increased in dollars but declined slightly as a percentage of the gross national product since 1972. After World War II to 1972, there was a steady increase in the public sector to 21.7 percent of gross national product. Since 1982, it declined slightly to 20.9 percent by 1989. Exhibit 9–2 shows the tax revenue by major source, level, and type of government. Note the importance of income tax to both state and federal governments, with the latter very dependent on that tax source. Note also the importance of property tax to local governments and sales tax to state governments.

Significant New Trend

The Advisory Commission on Intergovernmental Relations uses the three Rs— the revolt of the taxpayers, reduced federal aid, and recessionary pressures with no federal bailout—to describe the reasons behind the latest trend in fiscal federalism. These three jolts came in rapid succession and created a new fiscally conservative perspective, especially for American state and local governments. Although California's Proposition 13, which rolled back property tax to 1 percent of market value, was not the first conservative tax reform, it was the most dramatic and served as the model for other states. Government growth shifted from a hefty 4.4 percent average annual increase in adjusted per capita expenditure to a revised 0.5 percent increase. The major state tax increases in the post–Proposition 13 era were due, not to "big spenders," but rather to severe fiscal crisis. The second R—reduced federal aid—began to occur in the second half of the Carter administration and was accelerated in the Reagan administration. The third R—recession with no federal bailout—was the big jolt because painfully large government shortfalls hurt state and local government programs severely. Traditional federal actions in a recession, such as a national economic stimulus program, would have bailed out state and local governments, but they were not forthcoming, especially during the Reagan administration. The effect was painful belt-tightening and politically unpleasant state and local tax increases.

EXHIBIT 9–2 Federal, State, and Local Tax Revenues as a Percentage of Gross National Product, Selected Years 1948–1989

	1989	1988	1987	1986	1985	1984	1983	1982	1980	1978	1976	1974	1972	1964	1956	1948
BY GOVERNMENT																
All Governments	20.9%	20.5%	20.9%	20.0%	20.0%	19.5%	19.5%	21.2%	21.0%	20.8%	20.1%	21.4%	21.7%	21.3%	21.4%	19.6%
Federal	11.8	11.5	11.9	11.2	11.3	11.0	11.2	12.8	12.8	12.2	11.3	12.5	12.7	13.9	15.2	14.5
State and Local	9.0	8.9	9.0	8.8	8.7	8.5	8.4	8.4	8.2	8.6	8.8	8.9	9.0	7.4	6.2	5.1
State	5.5	5.4	5.5	5.4	5.4	5.2	5.0	5.1	5.0	5.0	5.0	5.0	4.9	3.7	3.1	2.6
Local	3.5	3.5	3.5	3.4	3.3	3.3	3.3	3.3	3.2	3.6	3.8	3.8	4.1	3.6	3.0	2.5
BY TYPE OF TAX																
Federal[1]																
Individual Income	8.6	8.2	8.7	8.2	8.2	7.8	8.5	9.4	8.9	8.0	7.4	8.1	7.8	7.5	7.5	7.4
Corporation Income	2.0	1.9	1.9	1.5	1.5	1.5	1.1	1.6	2.4	2.7	2.3	2.6	2.7	3.6	4.9	3.7
Sales, Gross Receipts, Customs	1.0	1.1	1.1	1.1	1.2	1.3	1.3	1.4	1.2	1.1	1.2	1.4	1.7	2.3	2.4	2.9
Death and Gift	0.2	0.2	0.2	0.2	0.2	0.2	0.2	0.3	0.2	0.2	0.3	0.3	0.4	0.4	0.3	0.3
All Other	0.1	0.1	0.2	0.1	0.2	0.2	0.1	0.1	0.1	0.1	0.1	0.1	0.1	0.2	0.1	0.1
State																
Individual Income	1.7	1.6	1.7	1.6	1.6	1.6	1.5	1.4	1.4	1.3	1.2	1.2	1.1	0.5	0.3	0.2
Corporation Income	0.5	0.4	0.5	0.4	0.4	0.4	0.4	0.4	0.5	0.5	0.4	0.4	0.4	0.3	0.2	0.2

General Sales, Gross Receipts	1.8	1.8	1.8	1.8	1.7	1.7	1.6	1.6	1.6	1.6	1.5	1.5	1.5	0.9	0.7	0.6
Selective Sales, Gross Receipts	0.9	0.9	0.9	0.9	0.9	0.9	0.9	0.9	1.0	1.1	1.2	1.3	1.2	1.1	1.0
Motor Vehicle and Operators' Licenses	0.2	0.2	0.2	0.2	0.2	0.2	0.2	0.2	0.2	0.2	0.3	0.3	0.3	0.3	0.2
Death and Gift	0.1	0.1	0.1	0.1	0.1	0.1	0.1	0.1	0.1	0.1	0.1	0.1	0.1	0.1	0.1
All Other	0.4	0.4	0.4	0.5	0.5	0.5	0.5	0.4	0.4	0.4	0.4	0.4	0.4	0.4	0.3
Local																
Property	2.6	2.6	2.5	2.5	2.5	2.5	2.5	2.4	2.8	3.1	3.2	3.4	3.2	2.6	2.2
Sales and Gross Receipts	0.5	0.5	0.5	0.5	0.5	0.5	0.5	0.4	0.4	0.4	0.4	0.4	0.3	0.2	0.2
Local Income[2]	0.2	0.2	0.2	0.2	0.2	0.2	0.2	0.2	0.2	0.2	0.2	0.2	0.1	—	0.1
All Other	0.2	0.2	0.2	0.1	0.1	0.1	0.1	0.1	0.1	0.1	0.1	0.1	0.1	0.2	0.1

—represents zero

[1] Figures exclude user charges, utility and liquor store revenues, and social insurance contributions. In 1989, the federal government trust funds received $349.3 billion in social insurance taxes and contributions (OASDHI, railroad retirement, unemployment insurance, federal supplementary medical insurance, and employee retirement), and state and local government trust funds received $111.4 billion. User charges and miscellaneous general revenue equaled $316.0 billion for all governments in 1989.

[2] Local individual and corporation income taxes. For 1989, the local individual income tax revenues were $8,988 million and the corporation income tax revenues were $2,060 million. Nearly all of the local corporation income taxes are raised in New York City and the District of Columbia.

Sources: ACIR computations based on U.S. Department of Commerce, Bureau of the Census, *Government Finances in [Year]*. Exhibits from U.S. Department of Commerce, Bureau of Economic Analysis, *Survey of Current Business*, April 1991.

Since the tax revolt, state governments have followed a predictable series of actions. When unanticipated revenue shortfalls occur, the first step is belt-tightening; then user charges, including the semi-user-fee gas tax, are increased; the third step is increasing "sin taxes" (for example, cigarette taxes); and finally, the general sales or individual income tax is increased. The latter step is taken when political actors see a severe revenue shortfall. Interestingly, these major state tax increases are sometimes scheduled to self-destruct in a fixed time, such as six months to a year. The three Rs have had their impact on state legislative behavior.

PROPERTY TAX AND CONTROVERSY

A Simple Idea

Property tax is a simple revenue-generating idea. First, property is assessed locally so that property value is determined. Second, a tax rate is determined and applied on the basis of the property value. If the property owner fails to pay the taxes, then the owner can be fined and, as a last resort, the property can be taken by the government to pay the taxes.

This form of taxation is still one of the most significant revenue sources for most state and local governments. At one time, property reflected wealth; thus, a real estate property tax could have been a progressive tax. Today, wealth is not reflected in real property; therefore, this form of taxation cannot be used to tax wealth uniformly and progressively. There has been a decline in the relative significance of property tax as a revenue generator because it has not provided sufficient revenue by itself. Property tax is less significant today, but it is still highly important as a revenue generator.

Property tax is placed on personal and real property. Tangible personal property includes machinery, equipment, and motor vehicles. Intangible personal property includes stocks, bonds, mortgages, and money. Real property includes land as well as improvements to the land such as buildings. Normally, property taxes are administered locally. Not all property is taxed at a universal rate. In some cases, the tax is regressive, but special features can be added to minimize regressive burdens. Another interesting fact is that one person can be held responsible for taxes on both personal and real property. Also, a citizen may live in overlapping local governments and thus be taxed on the same property by two common jurisdictions. Double taxation has become an important fiscal issue in many local areas.

Criticisms

According to the U.S. Advisory Commission on Intergovernmental Relations, the property tax is the worst or least-fair tax and federal income tax is the second-worst. A 1991 poll showed that 30 percent of the nation's citizens regard property tax as the worst or least-fair tax. Twenty-six percent thought federal income tax was the worst. Taxes are never popular, but property tax beat the others in nonpopularity by a margin of two to one. Why?

1. This form of taxation bears down harshly on low-income households. Lower income families must pay a higher percentage of their incomes for real estate taxes.

2. Property tax is an antihousing levy. It discourages home ownership and does provide preferential treatment for shelter cost as commonly found in income and sales taxes. Also, as taxes increase, property tax is viewed by many as a threat to their continued home ownership. Property taxes increase as values go up, but the owner does not benefit from the "paper profit," as it is rarely converted to spendable income except for equity loans. This means that taxes are increased but the property remains the same.

3. The administration of property tax is difficult and often poorly done. At best, the assessment is an informed estimate, that is, a subjective judgment of market value. At worst, the assessment can be used for political or economic advantage.

4. The infrequent mass reappraisals in periods of inflation result in severe taxpayer shock and hardship. Taxes go up radically, and taxpayers may not be in economic positions to absorb sometimes doubling and tripling of tax bills. No other tax has such severe hikes.

5. Property taxes can be painful to pay. Often the property taxes are collected with the monthly mortgage payment charge. Such a "pay-as-you-go" technique is less painful for most taxpayers. Often, however, local government does not permit such practices, and payments must be made on a yearly basis, thus causing hardships.

6. Property tax does contribute to urban blight. If some houses must be foreclosed due to nonpayment of taxes, such houses are likely to be in marginal neighborhoods. The long foreclosure process will probably stimulate extreme negligence to the house, thus harming an already weak housing market. Values will drop, and the neighborhood will deteriorate.

One very complex problem is the perennial conflict between state valuation and local assessment practices. The property tax laws of most states require that all classes of property be assessed at the same percentage of current market value. This sounds reasonable, but most state tax administrators are unable to hold county assessment at any uniform percentage of current market value. The most frequent beneficiaries—not victims—of the extralegal assessment practices are farmers and homeowners. Farmland tends to be assessed at a lower percentage of market value than residential property. Income-producing property such as a factory site tends to be at a higher rate unless they have recently moved to the area. There are examples of the company in a "company town" benefiting, but that is not the common pattern.

There is a natural reluctance on the part of state officials to raise the assessments of all classes of property to the state valuation standard. Such reforms are grim politically to those officials. Local rate makers should cut back tax rates if the state hikes local assessment; thus, each taxpayer would pay about the same tax amount. However, local governments are pressed for added revenue, so by not lowering the tax rate, they can generate more income while placing the tax-hike blame on the state. Another problem for state leaders is the creation of a uniform tax policy, which means that they will be repealing the popular "little assessment break" given farmers and homeowners. Both headaches are political liabilities which state officials do not wish to bear. Tax reform designed to bring the law and practice into reasonable alignment does require heroic action. Thus, such reforms—when they do occur—take place normally because of court rather than legislative or administrative, action.

Property Tax Reforms

Given the number of criticisms of property taxes, no one should be surprised to find an active reform movement involving property tax. Few argue that the tax should be eliminated because it does generate large quantities of tax revenue. Many do argue for the less radical reforms designed to improve the process.

Some obvious improvements are to have better assessors and to use better assessment techniques. Better pay would attract more qualified people. Persons hired should be given added training. And, selection of assessors should be on the basis of professional merit, not ability to win local elections. Assessment can be improved by using cadastral maps and parcel information files. The work of assessment lends itself to data processing; thus, much routine work can be done by computers. Another technique is to use building permit data to alert assessors to important changes. Another useful device is to enact a real property transfer tax act which includes a provision requiring that the assessor be notified automatically of changes in market value. Statistical techniques like multiple regression analysis can be useful to identify market data which best indicate rapid changes in market value. Other reforms are to use professional consulting firms, especially for major reassessments.

Another reform involves government reorganization. Assessment districts often can be consolidated. This would lead to some economies of scale. It also would permit more specialization, better job development for assessors, and the use of sophisticated equipment that could not be justified in small operations.

A reform addressed to correcting the regressive character of property tax is called a *circuit breaker*. Circuit breakers are normally designed to aid the families with the lowest incomes or the elderly. The details of circuit breakers vary from state to state. Circuit breakers have covered only the aged, aided renters as well as homeowners, limited benefits to households with incomes below $5,000 with no assets test, and imposed a maximum total relief of $500 or less.

More radical reforms are advocated. One is the *site value approach,* which exempts reproducible capital from the property tax base. Proponents argue that there would be no tax loss, but taxing would be done in a different way. They say taxing the building as improved property tends to slow down renewal, whereas taxing only land does the opposite. Thus, urban areas would be improved. These debates will continue as long as there are legitimate criticisms of the property tax.

The most notable property tax reform was California Proposition 13 in 1978, which was copied in Idaho, Nevada, and Massachusetts. This reform radically cut California's property tax back to 1 percent of the market value and moved property assessment back to the 1975–76 rates. In addition, it provided for a 2 percent growth rate annually. California's property tax rate moved from a 2.21 percent average effective tax rate to a 0.98 percent rate with that single reform. Exhibit 9–3 shows the change in the average effective property tax rates. The U.S. average is 1.21 percent, with eight states near the 1 percent rate, five states at over 2 percent, and twelve at less than 0.9 percent. Reducing property-tax receipts does not mean a uniform decrease in state and local government services because some services rely more heavily on property tax than others. State government is not affected directly, but school districts and townships, which rely heavily on property tax, will be hurt the most as major cutbacks occur.

Serrano v. Priest

A particularly significant reform is shifting the property tax to the state level. Reformers point out that this would solve many of the problems commonly cited. In 1971, the State of California Supreme Court ruled in *Serrano* v. *Priest* that the relationship between a district's property tax wealth per pupil and its educational expenditure must be broken. In other words, the property tax may be administered locally, but the funds must go into a state-wide pool. The level of spending for a child's education may not be a function of wealth other than the wealth of the state as a whole.

This decision has remarkable property tax implications for the states that follow this policy. At least, in education, there is no longer such a thing as a rich or poor school district. The *Serrano* decision, strictly applied, would invalidate many existing patterns of real property school financing. The decision does not void real estate property tax, but does require a major design constraint on the tax.

In 1973, the U.S. Supreme Court in *San Antonio Independent School District* v. *Rodriguez* did not extend the *Serrano* decision to the national level. In a five-to-four opinion, the court ruled that education is not one of the fundamental rights; thus, it is not covered under the equal-protection clause of the Constitution. Interestingly, the lawyers for Rodriguez could have argued discrimination and equal opportunity and the court decision might have been otherwise. However, the court ruling meant that the *Serrano* decision did not apply on a national level. In a 1992 ruling, the U.S. Supreme Court, in an eight-to-one ruling, upheld California's Proposition 13 cap in spite of the equal-protection argument made in a class-action suit by shorter-term property owners in the state.

Nevertheless, more states are following the California reasoning, normally by court ruling. Some call this a "Robin Hood" approach, as the state serves to equalize the tax among the local districts. The *Serrano* decision continues to be influential and property tax is being revised around the country due to that decision.

EXHIBIT 9–3 Average Effective Property Tax Rates, Existing Single Family Homes with FHA Insured Mortgages, by State and Region, Selected Years 1958–85[1]

STATE AND REGION	EFFECTIVE PROPERTY TAX RATE, 1985	[HIGH = 1; LOW = 50][2] RANK	PERCENTAGE OF FULL MARKET VALUE							
			1984	1983	1982	1981	1977	1971	1966	1958
U.S. Totals	1.21%		1.23%	1.31%	1.26%	1.26%	1.67%	1.98%	1.70%	1.34%
New England										
Connecticut	1.64	11	1.68	1.60	n.a.	1.53	2.17	2.38	2.01	1.44
Maine	1.28	19	1.31	1.52	1.52	1.42	1.65	2.43	2.17	1.5
Massachusetts	1.33	15	1.57	1.85	n.a.	2.43	3.50	3.13	2.76	2.21
New Hampshire	1.87	10	2.02	2.23	2.39	n.a.	n.a.	3.14	2.38	1.81
Rhode Island	2.08	6	n.a.	2.01	n.a.	n.a.	n.a.	2.21	1.96	1.67
Vermont	n.a.	n.a	n.a.	n.a.	n.a.	n.a.	n.a.	2.53	2.27	1.63
Mideast										
Delaware	0.65	44	0.71	0.76	0.75	0.79	0.88	1.26	1.14	0.71
Washington, D.C.	1.19	22	1.14	1.17	1.15	1.22	n.a.	1.80	1.37	1.08
Maryland	1.30	16	1.26	1.38	1.37	1.25	1.69	2.24	2.05	1.47
New Jersey	2.47	1	2.62	2.54	2.55	2.53	3.31	3.01	2.57	1.77
New York	2.38	2	2.80	2.66	2.57	2.75	2.89	2.72	2.40	2.09
Pennsylvania	1.41	13	1.53	1.71	1.63	1.50	1.85	2.16	1.88	1.50
Great Lakes										
Illinois	1.57	12	1.63	1.72	1.59	1.47	1.90	2.15	1.96	1.35
Indiana	1.27	20	1.22	1.23	1.19	1.13	1.66	1.96	1.64	0.84
Michigan	2.27	4	2.78	2.68	2.68	2.74	2.63	2.02	1.81	1.45
Ohio	1.11	26	1.03	1.15	1.15	1.07	1.26	1.47	1.44	1.07
Wisconsin	1.99	7	2.00	1.90	2.01	1.75	2.22	3.01	2.31	1.82
Plains										
Iowa	1.96	9	1.63	1.67	1.64	1.75	1.76	2.63	2.12	1.34
Kansas	1.16	23	1.11	1.00	0.97	0.93	1.37	2.17	1.96	1.65
Minnesota	1.04	29	0.99	0.85	0.77	0.79	1.39	2.05	2.14	1.57
Missouri	0.98	32	1.02	1.09	1.17	0.95	1.59	1.79	1.64	1.12
Nebraska	2.29	3	2.11	2.12	2.23	2.31	2.48	3.15	2.67	1.90
North Dakota	1.26	21	1.25	1.26	1.10	1.01	1.26	2.08	1.81	1.54
South Dakota	1.96	8	1.63	1.75	1.77	1.69	1.79	2.71	2.64	2.01
Southeast										
Alabama	0.37	49	0.41	0.42	0.41	0.38	0.74	0.85	0.66	0.56
Arkansas	1.29	17	1.35	1.29	1.42	1.42	1.49	1.14	1.09	0.86

State	Rank									
Florida	39	0.81	0.79	0.92	1.03	0.92	1.13	1.41	1.09	0.76
Georgia	31	1.00	1.08	1.16	1.21	1.21	1.27	1.44	1.30	0.84
Kentucky	35	n.a.	0.95	1.02	1.11	1.14	1.25	1.27	1.03	0.93
Louisiana	50	0.22	0.16	0.14	0.15	0.28	0.61	0.56	0.43	0.52
Mississippi	37	0.81	0.77	0.82	0.76	0.86	1.10	0.96	0.93	0.66
North Carolina	30	n.a.	1.01	0.96	0.97	1.07	1.35	1.58	1.31	0.90
South Carolina	40	0.77	0.81	0.85	0.92	0.84	0.82	0.94	0.60	0.48
Tennessee	24	1.14	0.97	1.17	1.24	1.42	1.40	1.53	1.37	0.97
Virginia	28	1.07	1.00	1.28	1.44	1.39	1.21	1.32	1.13	0.90
West Virginia	43	n.a.	n.a.	0.68	n.a.	0.37	n.a.	0.69	0.71	0.56
Southwest										
Arizona	45	0.65	0.71	0.71	0.56	0.74	1.72	1.65	2.41	2.14
New Mexico	41	0.76	0.76	0.90	0.93	1.14	1.65	1.70	1.30	0.93
Oklahoma	36	0.95	0.95	0.89	0.74	0.82	0.95	1.35	1.11	0.86
Texas	14	1.36	1.32	1.36	1.40	1.68	1.84	1.91	1.62	1.36
Rocky Mountain										
Colorado	33	0.97	0.98	0.95	1.01	1.01	1.80	2.45	2.20	1.72
Idaho	38	0.81	1.01	1.02	1.04	0.94	1.46	1.72	1.23	1.14
Montana	18	1.28	1.14	1.17	1.14	1.08	1.31	2.19	1.70	1.32
Utah	34	0.96	0.87	0.97	0.92	1.03	1.03	1.49	1.52	1.05
Wyoming	48	n.a.	n.a.	0.45	0.48	0.47	0.87	1.38	1.34	1.17
Far West										
California	27	1.08	1.02	1.05	1.03	1.04	2.21	2.48	2.03	1.50
Nevada	46	0.60	0.63	0.68	0.77	1.13	1.71	1.48	1.47	1.06
Oregon	5	n.a.	2.22	2.27	2.06	1.56	2.25	2.33	1.98	1.55
Washington	25	1.14	1.01	1.03	1.01	0.95	1.75	1.62	1.14	0.92
Alaska	42	0.75	n.a.	n.a.	n.a.	n.a.	n.a.	1.61	1.42	1.12
Hawaii	47	0.51	0.51	0.60	0.48	0.36	n.a.	0.92	0.81	0.62

Note: These effective rates are for existing FHA insured mortgages only, which represent small and varying percentages (by state) of total single-family homes. The United States average tax rate for 1985 (1.21) indicates that, on average, the property tax on a home with a market value of $100,000 would be $1,210.

n.a.—Data not available.

[1] Effective tax rate is the percentage that tax liability is of the market value of the house.

[2] In cases where 1985 data were not available for a particular state, rankings were based on data for the most recent year for which data were available.

Source: Computed by ACIR staff from data contained in U.S. Department of Housing and Urban Development, Housing-HFA, Management Information Systems Division, Single Family Insured Branch, Data for States and Selected Areas on Characteristics of FHA Operations Under Section 203(b), various years.

ASSESSMENT AND TAXATION

Taxable Property and Assessment

Real estate property normally is defined to include the land, structures, and fixtures. The key test is "Is the item fixed?" (For example, the item nailed to the wall is "fixed.") If the answer to the test is yes, it is considered part of the real property for tax purposes. Repairs are not considered to add per se to the property value, but improvements do. Here, the test is: "Is the change an addition or alteration, as opposed to a restoration to a previous condition?" Both tests are difficult to apply, and much controversy arises out of using them. One common problem is how to handle mobile homes because, as the name implies, they are not fixed to the property. Most states supplement the test of being fixed by using the length of time the mobile home is on the property or other actions taken to indicate fixture such as removing wheels.

The first step in property taxation is to determine the tax base. An inventory must be taken. Normally this is done using owner declarations, surveys, and building permits. Care must be taken to record properly all relevant details, especially improvements to the property.

The assessment process is complex. It must be accurate and uniform, or charges of unfairness can be made, resulting in possible court action. Normally, assessment is based on a uniform fraction of market value or on full market value. Classes of property (for example, farms, vacant land, one-family residences, multiple residences) are taxed at different rates. Sometimes tax exemptions exist, such as homestead, elderly, sovereignty (for example, Indian tribe or foreign embassy), or meritorious service (for example, religious, charitable, educational, or veterans).

The assessment is normally made on market price. Whenever possible, the test used is the *market price* for the property. That is defined as the price at which a willing seller will sell and a willing buyer will buy where the seller is not forced to sell and buyer is not forced to buy. If the property was sold recently, then that price would probably constitute market price. Normally, the assessor does not find such a situation, and judgments are based on sales information. A *sales ratio*—that is, the ratio between price and assessed value—is developed based on sales reports. If the assessment is accurate, the ratio would be one for full market value assessment. Statistical measures, such as central tendency and dispersion, are applied to the sales ratios. This helps the assessor isolate current assessed value inaccuracies as well as determine the quality of assessment. These ratios can then be used to develop a percentage factor to adjust improper assessments. A more sophisticated approach is multiple regression analysis, which identifies variables that reflect market value. This approach could be used to find property value indicators and use them to update assessments. Another approach is to analyze market data to select independent variables that help to predict or estimate sales prices accurately, or identify comparable properties to determine property value.

In some situations, other market approaches must be used in making an assessment. One is the *cost* or *replacement cost approach*. This approach is a particularly useful means of evaluating large numbers of buildings. The stress is on how much it would cost to replace the building at the time of assessment. Data can be gathered from builders and others to determine reproduction cost of the building. Then, age and condition can be determined to recognize the depreciation factors. Next, land value is estimated. Finally, the replacement cost minus depreciation is compared with the recent sale price of similar property.

Yet another approach is the *income approach*, and it is seldom used as the sole basis for assessment. It is particularly useful in situations in which the market for the property is imperfect (for example, no willing buyer). Net income for the property is first calculated and then divided by the current discount rate to arrive at an estimated property value. This value should be validated by using the income approach on similar property that can be assessed by the market approach. The results should be comparable.

Assessments should be done frequently enough so that the assessment is comparable to the market price. In many assessing jurisdictions—which are sometimes not the same as taxing jurisdictions—the practice is to have extremely infrequent reassessments. This leads to the "welcome stranger distortion." People who move into an area are assessed automatically at the market price when their houses are bought. The residents who do not sell their homes are assessed at the lower past assessment. Thus, newcomers pay higher property taxes for comparable property.

A hardship sometimes caused by reassessment involves circuit breakers. As inflation occurs, an owner can move from nearly zero property taxes to significant taxes because the property exceeds the relief level. However, the circuit breaker can be carefully worded to provide a gradual increase in property taxes rather than a harsh drastic increase.

So-called tax havens do exist. Let us say a family owns an expensive, even highly assessed home. Normally, this would mean high property taxes. If that home is in a tax district that has a great deal of industry, then the tax rate may be low on residential property because enough revenue to run the government is generated from the industrial property tax owners. This would be a tax haven for the residential property owners. Taxes paid depend on both the assessment and the tax rate.

A state requires that a uniform property tax assessment exist throughout the state, but the practical problem is that there are many local assessing jurisdictions. One means to achieve the desired objective is for a state board of equalization to convert each local assessment into a uniform statewide assessment. This conversion process can be done by multiplying the local assessment by a ratio or rate much like the one used in the sales-ratio assessment approach. The *state equalization rate* is the ratio of assessed value of real property to market value. Exhibit 9–4 explains how a state determines the equalization rate.

EXHIBIT 9–4   State Equalization Rate Determination

Step 1: The assessed value of the property is established by using the local government assessment rolls.

Step 2: The market value of all property is established. This is done by examining sales information. An estimate for all the property is based on the sales information.

Step 3: The ratios are determined for all classes of property based on the assessed and market values.

Step 4: For each class of property, the total number of taxed properties and market-to-assessed-value ratio are determined for each county. The computation appears as follows for one class of property.

TAXING DISTRICT	MARKET VALUE	ASSESSED VALUATION	RATIO	NUMBER OF TAXED PROPERTIES	PRODUCTS
A	A_m	A_r	$A_m{:}A_r$	A_p	$(A_m{:}A_r)A_p$
B	B_m	B_r	$B_m{:}B_r$	B_p	$(B_m{:}B_r)B_p$
C	C_m	C_r	$C_m{:}C_r$	C_p	$(C_m{:}C_r)C_p$
N	etc.	etc.	etc.	$\dfrac{\text{etc}}{T_p}$	$\dfrac{}{P}$

$P \div T_p$ = state equalized ratio

Step 5: Inform each taxing district of the state equalization ratio for each class of property. They are required to apply (multiply) this ratio to the determined full market value in determining the state uniform percent of full market value applicable to the taxing district.

Source: Thomas A. Dorsey, *Understanding the Real Property Tax*. Syracuse, N.Y.: Syracuse Governmental Research Bureau, 1974.

The equalization rate serves as a measure of assessment quality. If the market value of a house is $40,000 and the equalization rate is 50 percent, then the assessment should be about $20,000. If it is not, then the house is either under- or over-assessed.

Testing Assessments

The assessment process is often highly controversial. People do not want to pay any more taxes than necessary, especially if the tax is increased as a result of a recent tax reassessment. Taxpayer "rebellions" occur when a large number of property owners protest increased reassessments. Considering the subjective nature of assessment, mistakes can easily be made, and differences of opinion can make a difference in the tax due. Individual taxpayer complaints and appeals are common. This section discusses several tests that can be applied to test the assessment process.[1] There are three key questions:

[1] This section draws heavily from Arnold H. Raphaelson, "Property Assessment and Tax Administration." In J. Richard Aronson and Eli Schwartz (eds.), *Management Policies in Local Government Finance*. Washington, D.C.: International City Management Association, 1975.

1. Has the assessor apportioned the property tax burden among owners on the basis of the value of their properties?
2. Does the assessor tend to favor or to discriminate against certain types of property?
3. Are the higher-priced properties underassessed?

The test for apportioning the tax burden on the basis of value is the *coefficient of dispersion* for the district. The coefficient reflects how closely the assessment values are to each other, relative to market value. The steps for calculation are as follows:

1. Determine the assessment ratio for each of a sample of properties sold. Let us say there are three parcels. Each is sold for $10,000 and assessed separately at $5,000, $6,000, and $7,000. The separate assessment ratios are:

50%   60%   70%

2. Determine the average of these assessment ratios for the sample of transactions. Average (or median) assessment ratio:

60%

3. Compute the average deviation of the separate assessment ratios from the average or median assessment ratio. Average deviation:

$(10\% + 0\% + 10\%) \div 3 = 6.6\%$

4. Relate the average deviation to the median or average assessment ratio. Coefficient of dispersion:

$6.6\% \div 60\% = 0.11$ or 11%

Note: Margin of 10% expected given imperfection in data.

In the above explanation, the test tells us the assessor has *not* apportioned the property tax burden among the owners on the basis of their properties' value. The coefficient of dispersion was 11 percent, which is 1 percent over the excusable margin. The problem is probably not significant, but a problem does exist.

The test for determining if the assessor is discriminating against some types of property is made by first identifying the median assessment ratio for each category of property. Second, the average of the median ratios is determined by adding the median ratios and dividing by the number of categories. Third, the average deviation is determined by averaging the deviation of each category from the average of median assessment ratio. Finally, the coefficient of dispersion is the average deviation divided by the average of the median assessment ratio. The calculations are similar to the ones cited previously. For example:

1. The assessment ratios for each category are:

   40%   60%   80%

2. Average of median assessment ratio:

   60 %

3. Average deviation:

   $(20\% + 0\% + 20\%) \div 3 = 13.3\%$

4. Coefficient of dispersion:

   $13.3\% \div 60\% = 0.22$ or 22%

   The coefficient for dispersion indicates definite discrimination.

The test to determine if higher-priced properties are underassessed is done by calculating the *price-related differential*. It is a measure of the relative accuracy of higher- and lower-priced property assessments. The steps for calculation are as follows:

1. Calculate the aggregate assessment-sales ratio, which is weighted by the values of the parcels in the sample. Let us say the following example exists:

SALE PRICE	ASSESSED VALUE	ASSESSMENT RATIO
$100,000	$20,000	20%
10,000	4,000	40%
10,000	4,000	40%
10,000	4,000	40%
$130,000	$32,000	140%

   The aggregate assessment-sales ratio is:

   $(\$32,000 \div \$130,000) = 0.246$ or 24.6%

2. Calculate the average of the assessment ratios of the separate parcels. The average assessment ratio of properties is:

   $140\% \div 4 = 0.350$ or 35%

3. Divide the mean of the assessment ratios by the aggregate assessment-sales ratio to determine the price-related differential. The price-related differential is:

   $35.0 \div 24.6 = 1.42$ or 142%

The deviation from 100 percent is the key concern in this analysis. If the calculations result in about 100 percent, then there is no under- or over-assessment. If the calculations result in more than 100 percent, then there is underassessment of higher-priced properties. If the calculations result in less than 100 percent, then there is underassessment of lower-priced properties. In the above example, 142 percent is significantly more than 100 percent; therefore, there is underassessment of the $100,000 property.

There are three types of improper assessment situations: *illegal assessment, inequitable assessment,* and *overvaluation. Illegal assessment* is when some specific legal rule or law is violated in the assessment process. *Inequity* is when assessed value exceeds the uniform percentage for the class of property. *Overvaluation* is when assessment exceeds the actual market value. The following illustrates the concepts:

	HOUSE A	HOUSE B	HOUSE C
Current market value	$20,000	$20,000	$20,000
Equalization rate	.50	.50	.50
Calculated assessed value	10,000	10,000	10,000
Actual assessed value	25,000	10,000	15,000
	overvaluation	equitable assessment	inequitable assessment

The assessor can expect complaints from the owners of both houses A and C.

Assessment Cycle, Taxation, and Foreclosure

The assessment cycle is built on an assessment calendar that is much like the budget calendar. By the taxable-status day, the assessor must determine the value of the property. By the tentative completion date, the assessment role is considered complete, and legal copies are filed. By the grievance day, formal petitions for change of assessment to the review board must be filed. The final completion day is the beginning of court reviews of review board decisions. Eventually, the state or local legislative body must certify the assessment. The final step is that the assessment roll becomes the tax roll. All this must be done each year.

The state or local government now must calculate how much revenue it needs and the tax rate needed to generate that amount of revenue. The government computes estimated expenditures and subtracts other revenue. The remainder must be generated by the so-called tax of last resort—the property tax. The needed revenue is divided by the assessed valuation, which is converted into a rate per thousand of assessed value. The tax rate is determined by the tax base and the amount of money needed to run the government.

The process does have its constraints. Often a law establishes a maximum tax rate. Certainly, there are economic constraints because high rates discourage commerce and discourage people from living in an area. There are also political constraints because high tax rates can lead to taxpayer rebellions which can force some officials out of office.

The yield from property tax is due both to the tax rate and to the assessed value. The tax yield can increase if the assessed value goes up or the tax rate is increased. If the local government is at the maximum tax rate, then pressures increase for reassessment, which is an often-neglected task. If a community has a growing tax base, then it has the advantage of getting a greater yield without necessarily increasing the tax rate or reassessing the established property. However, if a community has a shrinking tax base, then it has the unfortunate prospect of reaching its tax-rate limit and reassessing its property as much as possible. This tends to discourage commerce and to encourage greater flight from the community.

Taxes are collected in a variety of ways. Some governments demand a yearly or possibly a quarterly payment directly to the government. Most people must borrow money from a bank to buy a home, and they have monthly mortgage payments to make to the bank. Often the bank will also collect the property taxes as a part of the monthly payment. The tax amount goes into an escrow account until payment is due to the government. If the government does not receive payment, there is an extra interest charge or penalty amount added on to the already delinquent tax obligation.

If no payment is made, then a long, complex foreclosure begins. The process varies from state to state, but the following illustrates a typical situation. First, a *tax lien* is imposed, which includes the interest and the penalties. Tax liens are in the form of tax certificates. They are negotiable securities and can be sold, as they represent a debt that must be liquidated before clear title can be conveyed. The property serves as the security for the debt.

The whole process is designed to give the taxpayers a fair opportunity to save their property. Public notice on major foreclosure actions on the property in question must be given, but often individual notice is not required. At the sale, certificates on the title are given and the owner has one year to redeem or to lose the property. If it is not redeemed, then title is conveyed to the owner of the tax certificate unless there is actual occupancy of the property or the property is also subject to a mortgage. If those conditions exist, the tax certificate owner can foreclose. The process involves years. Often the property in question is neglected during this period. Its value goes down, and it becomes an eyesore to the neighborhood.

Property tax delinquency has not been a big problem in most places, and, normally, delinquent taxes are eventually paid. The Great Depression saw severe property tax delinquency with an average state and local delinquency rate of 20.5 percent. Exhibit 9–5 was compiled by Larry DeBoer (1990). It shows the comparative property tax delinquency rates for forty-seven major American cities. Notice that most cities had very low rates, but some cities, such as Houston, Newark, Portland (Oregon), and St. Louis, had and continue to have higher delinquency rates.

EXHIBIT 9–5 Property Tax Delinquency Rates in 48 Major U.S. Cities, 1933, 1950–74, and Recent Year

CITY	DELINQUENCY RATES 1933	AVERAGES, 1950–74	RECENT (YEAR)
Atlanta, GA	3.3	3.2	5.6 (84)
Baltimore, MD	14.9	2.9	0 (86)
Birmingham, AL	17.7	0.2	0.9 (87)
Boston, MA	8.4	9.2	0.7 (84)
Bridgeport, CT	14.1	2.1	7.2 (87)
Cedar Rapids, IA	n/a	0.4	4.3 (86)
Charleston, SC	n/a.	6.7	10.0 (82)
Chicago, IL	40.6*	10.9	5.3 (84)
Cincinnati, OH	n/a	2.1	4.1 (86)
Cleveland, OH	n/a	2.5	7.5 (86)
Dallas, TX	13.2	1.4	2.9 (86)
Denver, CO	10.6	0.7	0.8 (84)
Des Moines, IA	15.5	0.5	1.3 (86)
Detroit, MI	35.1	2.2	8.5 (86)
Fargo, ND	n/a	4.2	9.5 (86)
Ft. Wayne, IN	n/a	3.0	2.6 (85)
Hartford, CT	21.4	1.6	3.7 (86)
Houston, TX	22.3	11.0	29.7 (85)
Indianapolis, IN	n/a	2.1	2.6 (86)
Kansas City, MO	n/a	2.7	4.4 (87)
Little Rock, AR	n/a	3.0	4.6 (86)
Los Angeles, CA	10.1	2.0	7.8 (83)
Louisville, KY	6.6	5.5	6.6 (87)
Memphis, TN	23.6	3.0	3.7 (86)
Miami, FL	27.8	1.5	4.1 (86)
Milwaukee, WI	37.6	0.7	2.0 (86)
New Orleans, LA	15.4	1.9	7.1 (86)
New York, NY	10.4	5.1	5.2 (87)
Newark, NJ	19.4	9.2	17.1 (84)
Norfolk, VA	26.1	5.4	6.7 (87)
Oakland, CA	8.7	2.1	3.2 (82)
Oklahoma City, OK	22.3	2.5	7.8 (86)
Philadelphia, PA	15.5	3.1	9.9 (86)
Phoenix, AZ	n/a	2.1	7.0 (87)
Pittsburgh, PA	25.2	6.1	6.5 (86)
Portland, OR	24.6	7.5	10.3 (86)
Richmond, VA	5.1	3.7	2.0 (86)
St. Louis, MO	24.3	5.8	11.8 (87)
Salt Lake City, UT	n/a	3.8	6.2 (86)
San Francisco, CA	5.4	1.3	3.1 (87)
Seattle, WA	51.2	3.0	3.3 (87)
Spokane, WA	21.4	3.6	6.5 (86)
Toledo, OH	n/a	2.8	4.1 (86)
Topeka, KS	n/a	1.3	3.9 (86)
Tucson, AZ	n/a	3.0	8.4 (86)
Wheeling, WV	n/a	3.8	6.6 (85)
Youngstown, OH	n/a	4.6	1.2 (85)

*1932

n/a = not available

Source: Table prepared by Larry DeBoer and reported in "Property Tax Delinquency and Tax Sales: A Review of the Literature," *Public Budgeting and Financial Management*, 2, 2 (1990), p. 315.

OTHER REVENUE SOURCES

Income Tax

Income tax is thought of as a federal tax, but it is also a revenue source for state and local government. For example, in 1989, $672,710 million in income taxes was collected in the United States, of which $123,729 million was state and local income tax revenue. About $11,048 million was local income tax revenue. About 1.5 percent, or $7,000 million, was local income tax revenue. At the federal level, income tax is collected from both corporations and individuals, with the latter being much more significant. The federal tax is collected on all types of income, but there are many complex exceptions that are beyond the scope of this text. The state income taxes are normally related closely to the federal tax, with some specific changes mandated by each state's legislature. Local income taxes are normally flat-rate taxes on wages and salaries.

Like the property tax, the income tax is not without its issues. Prior to 1977, the complexity of the federal tax and the related "tax loopholes" were common issues. At the state and local level, taxation of nonresidents and taxation of nonlabor income are frequent subjects of controversy. Most agree that taxation should be a means to redistribute revenue among classes and among localities, but disagreement exists on how much should be redistributed and which localities should receive the benefit. One particular concern to state and local governments is that the tax can produce an out-migration of individuals and businesses to areas where taxes are lower.

Tax loopholes are now called "tax expenditures"—a legal reduction in effective tax rates for certain classes of taxpayers, resulting in lower taxes due from nominal tax burdens. This newer terminology emphasizes the granting of government largess to tax-expenditure beneficiaries who gain just as much as those people who receive regularly budgeted expenditures such as those on welfare or veterans. The public does not normally think of the IRS deduction for home mortgages and related taxes as similar to welfare or veterans' benefits, but each one is designed to benefit a certain targeted class or set of people. More affluent income classes and corporations tend to be the beneficiaries of tax expenditures because:

- Low-income groups often do not pay taxes and therefore do not benefit from tax expenditures.
- High-income groups often are in higher tax brackets and thus benefit more from tax expenditures.
- Politically sophisticated groups realize that tax expenditures are less visible governmental benefits to them.
- Tax-expenditure benefits continue indefinitely once enacted, whereas budgeted benefits do not.
- Tax expenditures tend to be held to a lower standard of performance than budgeted benefits.
- Tax expenditures reduce overall government revenue and thus correspond more easily to the conservative feelings of many high-income people.

The details of income-taxation administration vary, but the major features are *rates, base, withholding, administrative staff and equipment, revenue potential* and *implementation*. *Rates* can provide the progressive feature of the tax because higher-income persons are taxed at a higher rate. Federal and state income taxes have progressive rates, but most local income taxes are done on a flat rate. The *base* is that to which the rate is applied in order to arrive at the tax. At the local level, it is simply the wages and salaries combined. At the federal level, the base is difficult to calculate, but it is the net taxable income after various adjustments are made. The *withholding* is a key administrative feature of this tax because it makes tax payment less painful to the average taxpayer. Employers are required to deduct specific amounts from each employee's paycheck for taxes. Thus, an amount is set aside for the yearly taxes. The income tax is difficult to *administer* and qualified staff plus sophisticated equipment, such as electronic data processing equipment, are needed. The *revenue potential* is quite good for this tax, and sophisticated revenue-estimating procedures are often important, as explained in an earlier chapter. Tax administration involves maintaining a bookkeeping and audit staff and reporting forms, the continuing surveillance of tax collections, and prosecution of tax evasion and fraud cases.

Sales Tax

The sales tax is primarily a state tax, but some local governments use it. Out of $218,542 million in taxes collected in 1989 from sales, gross receipts, and customs, $138,248 went to the state level, $27,767 to the local level, and $52,527 to the federal level. A *sales tax* applies to goods and services normally levied at retail stores and expressed in percentage terms. Sales tax can be general (that is, broadly applicable) or selective (that is, limited to a few items). The use of this tax increased as a result of the need for greater revenue than the income or property tax alone could provide. It has proven to be a highly successful tax.

The policy issues related to sales tax include *jurisdictional liability, scope of coverage, loss of business*, and *compliance*. Should sales tax liability for a particular transaction be established at the *place of delivery* or at the *location of the vendor?* The *place of delivery* answer would result in added tax revenue but also added administrative headaches. One way to deal with the problem is the *use tax*. It is a tax levied in lieu of a sales tax on an item purchased outside the sales tax jurisdiction but still used and enjoyed in that jurisdiction. In practice, use taxes are poorly enforced and the *location of the vendor* is the most practical jurisdictional liability test to apply. A community does lose retail business if its sales tax is higher than that of adjacent areas. The best policy is to have sales-tax uniformity throughout a county or metropolitan area. Compliance problems always exist with contractors, itinerant sellers, installation workers, and multiple operations having locations in different cities.

Four other policy issues are *regressivity, overlapping governments, allocation*, and *expansion of tax to cover services*. Sales tax applies mostly to consumers, and the poor must consider all of their resources. Therefore, the sales tax will affect the poor to a greater degree. Sales taxes are *regressive*. One attempt to lessen regressivity is to exempt food and similar vital items from the tax. Often more than one government unit covers an area and each imposes a sales tax. Thus, there is an *overlapping of local sales taxes*. A potential sales tax policy conflict exists and certainly confusion for the retailers collecting the tax exists. Another issue is *allocation* because of the lack of correlation between the sales tax base and revenue needs. Areas with concentrations of retail stores, such as shopping centers, will benefit greatly from the tax, but the greater tax needs may be in the poorer neighborhoods, which have fewer stores. If the tax is statewide and placed in a general fund, this is not a significant problem. However, there are many local governments that collect sales taxes themselves. Expanding the *coverage of the sales tax to service industries* is becoming more common, but there is significant resistance, especially from the legal profession and the media, which relies on advertising revenues. The latter group is particularly powerful politically, and expansion of the sales tax to its activities is unlikely.

These issues are implicit in state and local sales taxes. There are approaches that one can take to mitigate the problems, but the problems do remain and must be weighed when decisions are made about how to administer this tax.

There are four steps in the administration of the sales tax. First, a list of vendors must be prepared and updated. Second, return forms explaining the tax collected by vendors must be prepared. Third, the returns or collections are mailed, with stress placed on speed. Return lists must be compared with the vendor list so delinquents can be isolated. Sometimes court action is necessary to get the returns. The fourth step is to have trained auditors examine a sample of vendor accounts and records. This is essential to maintain successful retail sales administration. Each step requires expertise and careful attention to detail.

User Charges

Another important revenue source for government is the *user fee, toll, license fee*, and *impact fee*. In many cases, due to the general public value of the service, a *user fee* is a charge that does not cover the cost of the service provided by government; however, many services are completely covered by a user fee. Accurate user-fee pricing assists the public in understanding the economic worth of a government service. Accurate pricing avoids subsidies of a particular group by the entire community or the reverse subsidy of a particular group to the general public.

Cost-volume-profit (CVP), or break-even analysis, often provides a means to determine user-fee charges more accurately. The focus of the analysis is on the interaction of the price, volume, and variable and fixed costs which produces a break-even point in volume or dollar value at which total revenue and total costs are equal. A detailed explanation of this type of analysis is beyond the scope of the text, but the following example illustrates its usefulness.

Stephen V. Senge (1986) discusses the proper charge for cars at a local government recreation area that caters to family groups who arrive by car. There are 7,500 carloads of people projected to use the park next year, the traceable fixed costs (for example, permanent salaries, insurance, equipment maintenance, and utilities) are projected at $40,000, and the allocated fixed costs (for example, park overhead and general government overhead) are $8,000. The variable costs (for example, clean-up, supplies, part-time workers) are projected at $2 per car. A subsidy of $18,000 is budgeted from the general fund.

The equation used is as follows:

$$P = \frac{VC + [\,(TFC + AFC) - S\,]}{Q}$$

Where P is correct user fee charge per car.

VC is the variable cost per car.
TFC is the traceable fixed costs.
AFC is the allocated fixed costs.
S is the subsidy.
Q is the total number of carloads of people.

Substituting values into the formula gives:

$$P = \frac{2 + [\,(40{,}000 + 8{,}000) - 18{,}000\,]}{7{,}500}$$

$$P = 2 + \frac{30{,}000}{7{,}500}$$

$$P = 2 + 4$$

$$P = 6 \text{ or } \$6 \text{ per car}$$

Another important tax source, especially in high-growth areas, is the *impact fee*. New development can have a significant impact on both infrastructure and community resources. Impact fees are intended to make the developers pay a part of those costs rather than letting the entire burden fall on existing residents. New development normally means added wastewater treatment, sewers, schools, local traffic, park usage, libraries, and so on. Commonly, impact fees are passed on to the new home buyer, thus forcing up the price of new homes. However, communities see impact fees as a means to raise needed revenue without raising taxes. Courts require a rational relationship between the fee and the improvements acquired from the fee. The five major communities with a history of broad impact-fee use are San Francisco, California; Palm Beach County, Florida; Montgomery County, Maryland; Boston, Massachusetts; and Minneapolis, Minnesota.

Other Taxes

Various other taxes and charges exist. For example, there are transfer taxes
and charges for legal transactions. Some states have utility and inventory taxes.
Special assessments also exist. The value-added tax (VAT) is commonly used as a
national level tax, but it has not been adopted by the federal government and has
only been adopted by a few state governments in the United States. If the federal
government decides to significantly add tax revenues to balance the yearly budget,
the VAT will be considered, especially if it is directed toward most businesses except
retail businesses or politically powerful business such as the media.

REVIEW QUESTIONS

1. What are the major trends in intergovernmental revenue systems? Explain the
   implications of those trends.
2. Why is the property tax considered to be an onerous tax? Explain why
   achieving a uniform, full-market-value property tax is extremely difficult.
3. What are the most easily adopted property tax reforms, and why is it difficult
   to achieve those reforms? Why is *Serrano* v. *Priest* an important case?
4. Explain why judgment is important in applying the key tests associated with
   property tax. Explain the various approaches to assessment and why it is a
   difficult judgment to make.
5. What are equalization rates in real property tax? How are they applied? What
   aspects of the assessment process should be tested, and how is this done? How
   is the tax rate determined?
6. How are property taxes collected, and what happens if taxes are not paid?
7. Compare and contrast the issues involving income and sales taxes. Compare
   and contrast income and sales tax administration.

REFERENCES

Advisory Commission on Intergovernmental Relations. *Significant Features of Fiscal Federalism, 1981–82*. Washington, D.C.: Government Printing Office, April 1983.
———.*Changing Public Attitudes on Governments and Taxes*. Washington, D.C.: Government Printing Office, 1982.
ANGELL, CYNTHIA, and CHARLES A. SHORTER. "Impact Fees: Private-Sector Participation in Infrastructure Financing," *Government Finance Review*. 4, 5 (October 1988), 19–21.
ARONSON, J. RICHARD, and ELI SCHWARTZ (eds.). *Management Policies in Local Government Finance*. Washington, D.C.: International City Management Association, Municipal Finance Officers Association, 1975.
ARRON, HENRY J. *Who Pays the Property Tax*. Washington, D.C.: Brookings Institution, 1975.
BLECHMON, BARRY E., EDWARD M. GRAMLICK, and ROBERT W. HARTMAN. *Setting National Priorities: The 1976 Budget*. Washington, D.C.: Brookings Institution, 1976.
BLINDER, ALAN S., et al. *The Economics of Public Finance*. Washington, D.C.: Brookings Institution, 1974.

BREAK, GEORGE F. *Agenda for Local Tax Reform*. Berkeley: University of California, Institute of Governmental Studies, 1970.

DEBOER, LARRY. "Property Tax Delinquency and Tax Sales: A Review of the Literature," *Public Budgeting and Financial Management*, 2, 2 (1990), 311–49.

DORSEY, THOMAS A. *Understanding the Real Property Tax*. Syracuse, N.Y.: Syracuse Governmental Research Bureau, 1974.

DUNCOMBE, SYDNEY, and THOMAS D. LYNCH. "Taxpayer Revolt." In Thomas D. Lynch (ed.), *Contemporary Public Budgeting*. New Brunswick, N.J.: Transaction Books, 1981.

ECKER-RACZ, L. L. *The Politics and Economics of State-Local Finance*. Englewood Cliffs, N.J.: Prentice Hall, 1970.

GALAMBOS, EVA C., and ARTHUR F. SCHREIBER. "The Analysis of Double Taxation," *Public Budgeting and Finance*. 1, 2 (Summer 1981), 31–40.

GROVES, SANFORD M. *Financial Trend Monitoring System*. Washington D.C.: International City Management Association, 1980.

MAXWELL, JAMES, and J. RICHARD ARONSON. *Financing State and Local Governments*. Washington, D.C.: Brookings Institution, 1977.

MIKESELL, JOHN L., and KENNETH OLDFIELD (eds.). "Special Issue on Property Taxes: A Symposium of Its History and Prospects For Improved Administration, Relief and Reform," *Public Budgeting and Financial Management*, 2, 2, 1990, 145–406.

PETERSON, GEORGE E. (ed.). *Property Tax Reform*. Washington, D.C.: Urban Institute, 1973.

RAPHAELSON, ARNOLD H. "Property Assessment and Tax Administration." In J. Richard Aronson and Eli Schwartz (eds.), *Management Policies in Local Government Finance*. Washington D.C.: International City Management Association, 1975.

SENGE, STEPHEN V. "Local Government User Charges and Cost-Volume-Profit Analysis," *Public Budgeting and Finance*, 6, 3 (Autumn 1986), 92–105.

SHANNON, JOHN, and JAMES EDWIN KEE. "The Rise of Competitive Federalism," *Public Budgeting and Finance*, 9, 4 (Winter 1989), 5–20.

U.S. Advisory Commission on Intergovernmental Relations. *Changing Public Attitudes on Government and Taxes*. Washington, D.C.: Government Printing Office, 1982.

———. *1988 State Fiscal Capacity and Effort*, Information Report M-170. Washington, D.C.: ACIR, 1990, p. 26.

WHICKER, MARCIA LYNN. "Evaluating State and Local Tax Expenditures." Paper presented to the Southeastern Conference on Public Administration, New Orleans, La., October 1987.

10

INTERNAL
SERVICE FUNCTIONS

This chapter covers three important financial management topics: (1) property management, (2) risk management, and (3) pension funds. The subjects are important and useful for a person working in budgeting. At the conclusion of this chapter, the reader should know:

1. the steps in a systematic preliminary review of property management;
2. what purchasing is and why a specialist in purchasing is useful to a government;
3. what competitive bidding is and its disadvantages;
4. the importance of standardization and specifications;
5. the usefulness of preventative group replacement, computing maintenance and equipment cost in purchasing decisions, and cooperative intergovernmental arrangements;
6. the usefulness of central stores and the challenge of inventory management;
7. the significance of property control;
8. the potential applications of bar-code technology;
9. what risk management is and why it is an important concern;
10. what exposure identification is and how one goes about risk evaluation;
11. what risk control is and its significance;
12. what self-insurance is and when it is appropriate;
13. what insurance is, how it is selected, and some general standards applicable to it;
14. the elements of administration related to proper risk management;
15. the significance of retirement plans to public budgeting;
16. the significance of pensions to budgets; and
17. policy issues relevant to public pension funds.

PROPERTY MANAGEMENT

Preliminary Review

A government may own extensive and valuable property which needs to be managed. In a systematic preliminary review of property management, the first step is to inventory the property, describing location, identifying its use, recording its value, and identifying persons responsible for the property. The second step is to determine if up-to-date and comprehensive regulations exist that ensure proper management, including a property accounting system and adequate frequency and scope of internal audits. Auditing should complement property management and a preliminary review should discern whether audits cover property management practices and whether audit findings are seriously considered. In addition, employees using the system are often the best source of ideas for improvement, and a preliminary review should check to see whether their opinions are sought and used effectively. One last review concern should be risk associated with the property. This subject will be covered later in the chapter.

A sound system ensures that no one individual or small group controls all aspects of property management transactions. Certain specific duties, such as purchasing, receiving, accounting for, paying for, and disposing of property, should be divided among different people to minimize the possibility of pilferage or misuse of property. Duties and responsibilities should be identified and documented so that each employee clearly knows his or her role. If separation of key functions is impossible, then management reviews and internal controls should be more frequent. In addition, personnel need to be adequately trained in their responsibilities, including care and protection of property, proper and safe practices, and the ethical implications of their jobs.

The following is a more detailed list of the duties that should be separated whenever possible:

1. requesting purchases;
2. authorizing purchases;
3. purchasing;
4. receiving and inspecting property;
5. maintaining physical custody of property or inventories;
6. maintaining property ledgers or detailed inventory records;
7. maintaining financial accounting records for property or inventories;
8. conducting physical inventories;
9. reconciling physical inventory counts with property book balances;
10. performing surveys for shortages, losses, thefts, or damage;
11. authorizing transfers or disposition of property;
12. reconciling property records with accounting records;
13. making payments for purchases; and
14. performing reviews and audits.

Purchasing

In an organization, goods and services must be acquired. This activity is called *purchasing*. Materials, supplies, and equipment must be procured that best suit the job to be done by the operating unit. Ideally, the correct quantity should be ordered and in the hands of the operator when the units are needed. This proper timing of orders should also anticipate potential emergency shortage situations. The goods, services (including technical services), or equipment should be purchased at the lowest possible price. Unneeded inventory must be disposed of appropriately.

A central purchasing agent should be in charge of the procurement. Purchasing requires a knowledge of supply sources, pricing, business practices, market conditions, and appropriate laws, ordinances, and regulations. The procurement system should be devised to ensure that discounts are taken, quality is tested, items are properly received and stored, and deliveries are prompt. Expertise is needed in dealing with salespersons, contractors, and people in the government seeking goods and services to get their jobs done. In other words, procurement is a separate administrative specialty and often can best be done by a central purchasing agent.

In spite of the obvious advantages, there are often serious problems in properly conducting purchasing operations. As a result of political pressure, contracts are sometimes awarded to favored persons or groups. Because of the enormous amount of money involved, corruption is always a threat. Another problem is that procurement approaches (discussed later) do not lend themselves to undisputedly proper purchases of services, especially if high levels of talent are being acquired. Also, the process can be so involved that quick purchases are simply not possible. In other words, procurement is not an easy administrative undertaking.

Procurement

Centralized and sometimes cooperative approaches to procurement are often taken. Centralization and cooperation lead to sufficient activity to justify hiring a specialist purchasing agent. A specialist can take the time to monitor delivery services better, develop a list of qualified vendors, and improve purchased items through standardization, use of standard specifications, better inspections, and testing. Responsibility for procurement can be established more easily in problem cases. And, greater fiscal control over expenditures for materials, supplies, and equipment can be achieved. These benefits are not automatic. Often, centralized purchasing can mean friction between the ordering department and the purchasing department as well as other problems if the purchasing department is inefficient, corrupt, or lacks sufficient budget authority.

In most governments, the law requires most purchases to be made by competitive bidding in order to minimize cost and to avoid corruption. Advertising for many bids and maintaining up-to-date lists of suppliers are essential if the spirit of the law is to be kept. The opportunity to bid should be unrestricted in most circumstances. The invitation or request for bids should involve related items and specify the conditions of delivery. The sealed bids should be opened publicly and awards to other than the lowest bidder must be clearly explained in terms of the previously stated criteria. Awards must be in accordance with the stated specifications. Care should be taken to discourage and, if necessary, prosecute seller collusion.

Sometimes competition is constrained. One common and wise device is to use the qualifier of "lowest responsible bidder" in order to disqualify vendors with a negative performance history. Another common and sometimes unwise legal constraint to competition is limiting vendors only from specific geographic areas such as U.S. firms, a firm doing business in the government's jurisdiction, or a firm from a minority area in the government's jurisdiction. These constraints are occasionally framed in terms of specific percentages of contracts awarded— for example, "no less than 20 percent of the contracts must be awarded to minority contractors." Competition is also limited by purchasing procedures such as not requiring professional service contracts to be selected competitively. Although competition for professional service contracts is often best, the nature of the requested work, which may mean disqualifying nonresponsible or unacceptable professionals, may be overly difficult in a competitive context. Care must be taken to avoid "back-door selling," which means gaining vendor favor by means of gifts, kickbacks, paid trips, friendships, or other favors. One last category of competition constraint is bidder anticompetition practices such as rotating the lowest bid among bidders and allocation of business based on a geographic location. Although often illegal, such bidder practices are hard to detect.

Competitive bidding has its disadvantages. It is inflexible and takes a great deal of time to process. It does not lend itself to small purchases, emergency buying, or contracts for professional services. If only one or even a few bids are received, the government must be able to refuse the bid, or the process may result in higher prices rather than lower ones. In such circumstances, negotiated bidding may be a better purchasing process.

Standardization and *specification* are important procurement activities. *Standardization* of purchased items can lead to reducing the number and kinds of items purchased, thus reducing costs through quantity buying. Exceptions to standardization exist, especially with highly specialized and technical goods. However, standardization is often desirable, as it leads to price savings, quality improvements, and lower administrative costs. A *procurement specification* is a product or material description upon which bids are solicited. An adequate specification must be accurate and complete, but not overspecific. It must describe the methods of inspection and testing; state special requirements such as packing; conform, if possible, to national standards; and be internally consistent and simply stated. Good specification should place all bidders on an equal basis, minimize disputes, and avoid expensive brand-name buying. Both standardization and specification require enormous work and a highly qualified staff. If these activities serve no practical purpose in a given context, however, they should be avoided as they should serve to increase, not lower, efficiency.

Goods should be inspected and tested. Were the goods delivered on time and in good condition? Were the goods received those that were ordered? Are the goods of the quality ordered? Inspection and testing answer these vital questions. Not all items need to be inspected, but a random sample should be taken.

Another purchasing department responsibility is disposal of property. If possible, reassignment of items should be made. However, the time comes when an item such as an automobile should be traded, sold at auction, or sold as surplus. The objective should be to save the government money by using items as much as possible and recovering any value for the goods after they have ceased being useful to the government.

The 1970s and 1980s saw advances in the field of purchasing. The American Bar Association published the Model Procurement Code which has stimulated public awareness and interest in improving government purchasing. The code recommends that the purchasing policy and operations be separated, with day-to-day purchasing headed by a chief procurement officer with at least eight years purchasing experience. Another advancement is an increased ethical awareness and additional laws, evidenced in the federal 1986 Anti-Kickback Act and the 1988 book *Ethics and Quality Purchasing,* by Stanley D. Zemansky. According to Charles Coe (1993), the 1970s and 1980s saw increased use of purchasing techniques such as:

- *value engineering* (analyzing a product or service so that its function can be performed at the lowest possible overall cost without sacrificing quality);
- *computerization;*
- *total cost purchasing* (looking at other factors such as cost of supplies, energy, parts, warranties, maintenance);
- *faxing;*
- *commodity coding* (a standard classification system developed by the National Institute of Government Purchasing); and
- *life-cycle costing* (considers the total cost of ownership of a commodity or building).

Selected Purchasing Challenges

One purchasing challenge is deciding if particular items should be replaced as a group or individually. A preventative maintenance program sometimes can result in overall savings by replacing all items in a given category (for example, light bulbs) at one time rather than individually. Group replacement can be cheaper because of efficiency in scheduling labor and quantity price discounts. If this is to be done, then a replacement cycle must be established so that buying and labor scheduling can be properly coordinated. And, some research is needed to decide the expected life of the item and the best replacement time.

Another challenge is including maintenance cost with the equipment cost so that total cost can be computed. The maintenance cost can be estimated by the supplier or the government. In fact, the contract with the supplier can include a proviso declaring the maximum maintenance cost and guaranteeing that any excessive maintenance cost would be reimbursed by the seller. Exhibit 10–1 is an illustration cited in Chapter 14 of Aronson and Schwartz (eds.), *Management Policies in Local Government Finance* (1975).

EXHIBIT 10–1   Total-Cost Purchasing or Least-Cost Purchasing

Three suppliers bid as follows on heavy equipment:

SUPPLIER	PURCHASE PRICE	TOTAL FIVE-YEAR GUARANTEED MAINTENANCE COST	REPURCHASE PRICE
A	$23,000	$11,000	$ 2,000
B	30,000	5,000	15,000
C	26,000	12,000	10,000

Supplier C has specified a five-year guarantee of $800 times the age of the machine each year. Suppliers A and B have agreed to apportion their guarantees evenly over the five years (i.e., $2,200 per annum for A and $1,000 per annum for B).

The formula to calculate total cost is as follows:

$$K = P + \left[\sum_{i=1}^{5} R_i \left(\frac{1}{1.2} \right) \right] - T \left(\frac{1}{1.2} \right)$$

where

K = net present value R_i = maintenance cost in year i
P = purchase price   T = repurchase price

Using a 20 percent discount, the formula results in the following:

SUPPLIER	PUR-CHASE PRICE	+	PRESENT VALUE OF MAINTE-NANCE COST	-	PRESENT VALUE OF REPUR-CHASED PRICE	=	NET PRESENT VALUE
A	$23,000		$6,579		$ 804		$28,775
B	30,000		2,991		6,029		26,962
C	26,000		6,318		4,019		28,299

The least expensive total-cost bid is B.

A third purchasing challenge is maintaining cooperative intergovernmental arrangements. Such arrangements can mean cost savings, but they should be undertaken with a clear understanding of all the factors involved. A basis for cost sharing must be negotiated. The level of service should be the same; or, if reduced, this must be accepted. Labor disputes can sometimes arise when jobs are eliminated. And, the parties must understand who controls the planning, specifications, and service availability. Cooperative arrangements are normally difficult to apply because of disagreements over uniform items, the need for detailed records, and the allocation of shared costs. Besides cost-savings advantages, cooperative programs lead to a better sharing of ideas and greater personnel growth opportunities. Some important services that can be contracted or shared include street lighting, garbage disposal, sanitation services, health services, tax assessment and collection, water supply, law enforcement, and street and highway maintenance.

Central Stores and Inventory

Central warehousing, including tanks and storage yards, can foster significant savings since it makes possible quantity buying at the right time and price. Central stores permit better use of lead time to stock for emergencies and to allow the management of uneven requirements for goods. The disadvantage of central stores is the administrative cost of operation. Thus, warehousing should be minimized. Problems to avoid include:

1. overstocking, especially if the goods can become obsolete;
2. a nonrestrictive inventory, not limited to substantial demand items;
3. failure to balance stocking cost against value of having the item in stock when needed; and
4. failure to consider the full range of cost elements.

The critical challenge of inventory is to calculate and to achieve the optimum amount of commodities so that necessary goods are available but storage costs are minimized. If supplies were available instantly and if purchase unit price did not vary by such factors as size of purchase, there would be no need for inventory. However, inventory is needed to reduce the likelihood of being out of needed goods and to obtain lower prices through bulk purchase and by taking advantage of fluctuations in market price. Those "savings" must be balanced against storage costs. This calculation is much like the decision to invest idle cash, discussed in an earlier chapter.

Safety stock must be determined. There are various ways to determine that level of stock, but they all should recognize the various inventory costs:

1. *ordering cost*—preparing specifications, obtaining competitive bids, negotiating, receiving items;
2. *incremental cost*—unique extra costs due to specific order;
3. *carrying cost*—deterioration, obsolescence, storing, issuing, theft, handling, interest, and insurance; and
4. *shortage cost*—associated with disappointing a client, legal settlements, lost labor costs, other costs due to delay or failure to provide service.

The solution for optimal safety stock is to keep the total of holding costs and expected shortage costs minimal. These calculations assume sound estimates, but once those costs are determined, the actual calculation for optimal safety stock is relatively simple, especially with a computer. Rules of thumb can be developed in terms of days of normal use. Ideally, these rules of thumb should be checked against the more sophisticated calculations.

Another calculation involves *ordering cost*. For this, the economic ordering quantity (EOQ) model is used. The ordering costs must be weighed against the holding costs that arise on account of the size of the order. The calculation is similar to the optimal safety stock determination. The optimum ordering quantity is reached when the total of the two types of costs are at a minimum. The following EOQ model is used:

$$Q = \sqrt{2\,C_0 D \div C_H}$$

where

Q = the optimum (that is, most economic) quantity to order
C_0 = the cost of ordering per order
C_H = the cost of holding per unit per time period
D = the quantity of units used or demanded in each time period

An example is as follows:

D = 110 cubic yards of gravel used per day
C_0 = $20.00 per order (ordering costs)
C_H = $0.02 per yard per day (holding costs)
$Q = \sqrt{2(20)110 \div .02} = 469$ yards [1]

Again, most analysts develop simpler rules of thumb. However, the results of those casual estimates should be tested against the more sophisticated approach discussed here.

Total desirable inventory is calculated by adding the EOQ and safety stock solution. A more accurate solution would use a simultaneous solution, but that higher degree of accuracy is not normally warranted.

The calculations described above use quantifiable costs, but often important government or social costs cannot be reduced to numbers. This should be understood when applying the techniques.

Property Control

A *property control* officer is needed to ensure that personal property and the equipment of government is being efficiently managed. No operational control is necessary, but procedures must be devised and practices must be monitored to ensure efficient management. This type of control should be applied only to cases in which poor use of items can easily mean inefficiency or corruption.

[1] This explanation and example are from Corcoran, "Financial Management."

Records control fixes actual responsibility for the care of an item. Periodic reports are needed on the condition of the item. Records help with insurance loss claims, preventative maintenance decisions, and reordering. Records should use identifying numbers, acquisition purchase orders, transfers, and repair and disposal orders.

An option to owning goods is leasing. This is an alternative that may be the best economic investment. The calculations to determine this are similar to the ones involving present value discussed in an earlier chapter.

Bar-Code Technology

In the early 1960s, supermarkets and their suppliers began using bar codes to identify items for automatic check-out and inventory control. Since then, bar codes and other machine-readable symbols (see Exhibit 10–2) have been used on material components, finished goods, shipping containers, warehouse bins, bills of lading, and other distribution documentation. Optical scanners are increasingly common in factories, private warehouses, and government agencies. Scanners convert the symbols into an acceptable computer input.

The hardware consists of the optical code reader and bar-coded labels. The reader is a small computer that records, stores, and transmits coded data to the main computer. The reader often uses a light pen to focus a light beam on the bar-coded surfaces to sense reflections. The reader may also have a cathode-ray tube (CRT) to display the data being scanned in its proper place on the record being updated. It may be on-line—interfaced directly with a large computer—or off-line, with interface devices used on occasion to transmit stored data. For inventory and property control, the portable, hand-held models are most widely used. Bar-code labels must be readable and durable and must adhere properly to the labeled items.

Great productivity gains in property management can result from bar-code technology. If faster and more accurate data entry is important, then this technology can lead to increased operational effectiveness. The following are some of the more common bar-code applications:

1. forms management;
2. document sorting;
3. tracking and locating work in progress;
4. production control;
5. order processing and automatic billing;
6. quality control inspection;
7. distribution or warehouse control;
8. mail operations, including sorting and tracking;
9. motor vehicle accountability and maintenance;
10. productivity measurement;
11. "job shops" for billing purposes;
12. libraries/central files;
13. security in controlling access to restricted areas; and
14. shipping and receiving control.

EXHIBIT 10–2 Examples of Bar-Codes and Machine-Readable Symbols

PROPERTY MAINTENANCE

Property maintenance, whether preventive or corrective, is an important activity of government. Upkeep and repair of equipment and facilities can result in significant savings, and both are necessary if the government is to work effectively and efficiently. The following factors have made maintenance even more important today:

- changing from slow- to high-speed process and production equipment;
- changing from manual to automatically controlled equipment that requires a higher-grade engineering talent for maintenance;
- increasing cost-per-hour of productive labor and thus a higher cost of equipment downtime;
- increasing cost of production, with greater management pressure to better utilize equipment; and
- increasing ratio of maintenance employees to production employees, with fewer people actually using the equipment and more assigned to keeping the equipment and facilities ready to operate.

A well-run maintenance department should have a systematic work-order system, employ material and manpower controls, maintain histories of equipment repair and repair cost, use cost-accounting procedures, employ work-sampling and work-performance measures, review costs through materials studies, and employ training to update old and create new employee skills. Because of the computer, much more effective use of information is possible. In particular, the following data are useful:

- trend studies in the cost of maintenance per unit of product or service;
- recorded histories of equipment use;
- status reports of backlogged work orders; and
- surveys of plant operating and housekeeping conditions.

The most significant advance in maintenance management has been the development of *preventive maintenance, corrective maintenance,* and *maintenance prevention. Preventive maintenance* involves (1) periodic inspections to discover conditions that lead to breakdowns or harmful wear, and (2) upkeep designed to rectify those negative conditions while they are still insignificant. *Corrective maintenance* is focused on high-repair-cost items. Once these items are identified, then effort is focused on either reducing or eliminating the conditions that cause high-cost repair problems or eliminating the aspect of the problem that makes it expensive. *Maintenance prevention* is minimizing maintenance itself by means of good equipment and facility design.

RISK MANAGEMENT

A Practical Necessity

Both public and private concerns are subject to significant risk, which could be costly. *Risk management* is merely deciding how to best to deal with those risks and to manage the problem accordingly. Insurance is one tool in dealing with risk, but the cost of it is often high, and sometimes it is not even possible to acquire. The risks or liabilities for government include civil damages, breach of contract, dishonesty protection, worker's compensation, activity interruption, and even health protection. What losses can take place? Property can be stolen. People can get sick. Each represents a loss that can cost a government a significant sum of money.

The most serious loss exposure concerns third-party liabilities. Liability damage awards can occur if a public employee is involved in an accident, the environment is polluted, or for other reasons. For example, the city of Tamarac was sued successfully when a tired drinking driver hit a 560-pound decorative limestone boulder placed in the road's median. Damages included $4.7 million paid by the city and $1.15 million paid by the county that placed the boulder on the median. An environmental example is the town of Hopewell, Virginia. It was sued for either actively or passively condoning the contamination of the James River by a small firm connected with Allied Chemical Company. New loss exposures are being defined in the courts today: Jail inmates have sued Dutchess County, New York, for providing inadequate medical treatment. The city of Los Angeles was sued by property owners near the airport because aircraft noise reduced their property values. The potential cost to state and local governments is high.

Exposure Identification and Risk Evaluation

The first step in risk management is the identification of government resources and the losses that are possible. What kind of damages to people and property could take place? What type of damage can result if the government's responsibility is not met? What happens if someone is in an accident, is sick, or is dishonest? This step requires an inventory of the government's resources and a careful evaluation of responsibilities and potential damages. This evaluation can be facilitated by a knowledge of the types of risk liabilities governments commonly experience and the types of claims currently found in the courts. This step must be done on a continuing basis by using checklists, questionnaires, interviews with employees, physical inspections, and a careful monitoring of the contemporary risk-management literature.

Part of exposure identification must be a full understanding of the *tort doctrine of government immunity*. This doctrine gave government immunity from many civil tort actions, such as negligence. However, this doctrine has been reconsidered since the 1940s, and governments are increasingly vulnerable. This means, for example, that governments can be sued for not maintaining property to prevent injuries. Care must be taken in these areas by governments, or costly judgments can occur. An awareness of state law is necessary to understand the status of the doctrine of government immunity in each particular state.

Information is the key to exposure identification. Accurate and timely data on costs must be available so that costs can be identified with specific departments and activities. Financial statements, especially involving capital projects, help identify property exposures and areas of new activity not analyzed for risks. Another useful source of data is analyses of operations. By following through the process, the risk manager can identify services that could be disrupted, potential hazards in procedures, health dangers, and equipment safety concerns. In looking over such data, the manager is concerned particularly with the likely frequency and severity of the exposure potential. Other concerns include neat storage of goods and equipment, proximity of storage to fire sources, freedom of movement so that people can escape from dangerous situations and proper officials can have easy access to them, and special handling of flammable liquids.

Exhibit 10–3 is a useful risk and insurance checklist. This checklist can aid in a systematic review of the exposures facing a government unit.

The measurement of potential losses is not accomplished easily. A complete inventory of property is needed, including distance from building location to hazards; proximity to highway, air, or rail traffic; available fire protection, including quality indicators such as water pressure; and a description of the surrounding property. The inventory should also include the construction details, specifics of safety protections used, and building and equipment replacement costs. In measuring liability exposure, an evaluation of the laws covering government immunity, a review of the current history of local claim awards, and a review of all contract terms are essential. In measuring fidelity exposure, careful examination must be made of cash receipts, opportunities to convert assets to cash, and potential for dealings between high officials and vendors or grantees. Periodic outside audits are essential. Risk managers must review (1) the audits, (2) accounting reports which show balances, (3) purchasing procedures, (4) electronic data processing concerning money, (5) the location and volume of cash, and (6) cash internal control procedures. Losses must be weighed in terms of exposure and severity.

Given the difficulty of gathering information and other aspects of risk management, previous government practice, not surprisingly, was to buy insurance and transfer the risk. This permitted the government officials to forget about the risk and pay attention to other, more pressing problems. Today, government cannot afford to handle risk in that manner because:

1. premiums are expensive and increasing in price;
2. some forms of coverage do not exist;
3. government immunity is shrinking;
4. damage awards are radically increasing beyond maximum insurance award limits;
5. preventative and safety programs can dramatically reduce exposure risks;
6. self-insurance is often a cheaper alternative than insurance; and
7. knowledge of insurance and exposure risks can translate into better insurance coverage at less cost.

EXHIBIT 10–3   Risk and Insurance Checklist

1. Real Property
   a. Buildings owned
      (1) Nature, use, and location
      (2) Value replacement and actual cash value
      (3) Rental value of space used
      (4) Income from space rented to others
      (5) Laws and ordinances for demolition and for replacement standards
   b. Buildings rented from others
      (1) Nature, use, and location
      (2) Value of improvements and betterments made by tenant
      (3) Total rent paid by tenant
      (4) Rental income derived from subletting space to others
      (5) Value of the lease (is the lease favorable?)
      (6) Type of insurance clauses and hold harmless agreements in the lease
   c. All buildings and other real property (includes a. and b. above)
      (1) Alterations and additions in progress or contemplated
      (2) Boilers and pressure vessels in operation
      (3) Power machinery in operation (switchboards, motors, engines, generators, etc.)
      (4) Cold storage vaults and other special provisions for maintaining controlled temperature or humidity
      (5) Electric or neon signs
      (6) Plate or ornamental glass
      (7) Elevators and escalators
      (8) Possible fire department service charges
      (9) Fire and other protection (sprinklers, alarms, watchmen)
2. Personal Property
   a. Stock, including packaging materials (each location)
      (1) Peak value and low values (month by month)
      (2) Susceptibility to crime loss
      (3) Values dependent on parts difficult to replace
      (4) Values susceptible to damage by lack of heat or cold
   b. Furniture and fixtures attached to the building
      (1) Those permanently attached to the building
      (2) Unattached furniture, fixtures, machinery, office equipment
      (3) Supplies and prepaid expense items
   c. Personal property belonging to others
   d. Personal property in the custody of others
   e. Coins and currency (maximum amounts)
      (1) Payroll cash (when)
      (2) Other cash
      (3) Cash in custody of each bank messenger
      (4) Cash in custody of each truck driver or collector   (continued)

        (5)   Cash kept in safes overnight
        (6)   Liability limit or armored car carrier

  f. Incoming checks (maximum amounts)
        (1)   On premises
        (2)   In safes overnight
        (3)   In custody of each bank messenger
        (4)   In custody of each truck driver or collector

  g. Bank accounts (locations, amounts, uses)

  h. Securities (maximum amounts)
        (1)   In safes
        (2)   In custody of each bank messenger
        (3)   In safe deposit vaults
        (4)   At other locations (specify)

  i. Especially valuable property (maximum amounts) (e.g., precious stones, fine arts, antiques, rare metals, isotopes, radium)
        (1)   In safes
        (2)   Elsewhere on premises
        (3)   In custody of each truck driver
        (4)   In safe deposit vault
        (5)   At other locations or in transit (specify)

  j. Valuable papers, documents, records
        (1)   Kind
        (2)   Where kept
        (3)   Value
        (4)   Protection afforded

  k. Accounts receivable
        (1)   Maximum and minimum values
        (2)   Where account records are kept
        (3)   How protected

  l. Automobiles, airplanes, boats, trains, buses (owned or used)
        (1)   Ownership
           (a)   Owned
           (b)   Nonowned
        (2)   Value and extent of concentration in one place at one time

3. Operations
  a. Central operations: principal services
        (1)   Nature of all services regularly provided
        (2)   Sources of materials and supplies used
        (3)   Flow of goods, steps or processes in provision of services: any bottlenecks
        (4)   Extent, nature, and location of goods on installment or similar credit arrangements
        (5)   Installation, demonstration, or servicing away from premises
        (6)   Quality control

  b. Service for employees

    (1)   Operation of a hospital, infirmary, or first-aid station
    (2)   Operation of a restaurant for employees
    (3)   Sponsorship of employee athletic teams
  c. Operation of a medical facility or other service in which a malpractice hazard exists
  d. Operation of a restaurant for the general public
  e. Work let out under contract
  f. Advertising signs, vending machines, booths, etc., owned or operated away from the premises
  g. Sponsorship of outside athletic team
  h. Liability assumed under contract
    (1)   Sidetrack agreements
    (2)   Leases
    (3)   Hold-harmless agreements
    (4)   Purchase orders
    (5)   Elevator or escalator maintenance agreements
    (6)   Easements
    (7)   Service agreements (for or by the entity)
    (8)   Other contracts
    (9)   Warranties
  i. Shipments (values shipped annually and the maximum value of any one shipment, both incoming and outgoing)
    (1)   Own trucks
    (2)   Truckmen
    (3)   Rail
    (4)   Railway express
    (5)   Air
    (6)   Parcel post prepaid and C.O.D.
    (7)   Registered mail
    (8)   Inland or coastal water
    (9)   Foreign
    (10) Marine cargo
  j. "Time element" exposures
    (1)   Payroll: key persons; "ordinary" payroll
    (2)   Cost of merchandise
    (3)   Cost of heat, light, and power
    (4)   Trend of revenue for current year; estimate for next year
    (5)   Maximum time required to replace facilities subject to damage
    (6)   Percentage of revenue that would be affected by a business-interruption loss
    (7)   The availability and probable cost of substitute facilities to reduce loss of revenue in case of damage to present facilities
    (8)   Extra expense to maintain operations following loss
    (9)   If plans are interdependent, the percentage of revenue affected by a stoppage at each such plant or location, assuming damage at only one location

(continued)

        (10) Extent to which operations are dependent on outside sources of heat, light, or power
4. Personnel
  a. Home-state employees
    (1) Duties
    (2) Use of automobiles
    (3) Estimated annual payroll
  b. Employees in other states
    (1) Residence state and states traveled
    (2) Duties
    (3) Use of automobiles
    (4) Estimated annual payroll
  c. Employees annual payroll
  d. Employees required to use or travel in aircraft
  e. Classification of employees according to duties
  f. Key individuals (individuals whose loss might seriously affect operations)
5. Principal Property Hazards (Probable Maximum Loss)
  a. Fire
  b. Earthquake
  c. Flood
  d. Other
6. Data Processing Machines
  a. Owned or leased
  b. Protection
  c. Lease to others?
  d. Disaster plan
  e. Analysis of extra expense costs

Source: Gerald M. Surfus, "Identifying and Evaluating Potential Risk," *Government Finances*, 6, 28 (May 1977), 28–29.

Risk Control

Risk control is the reduction of risk or loss through careful procedures and practices in security, personnel safety, fire prevention, auto safety, product safety, environmental protection, and emergency planning. For the most part, state and local governments do not perform adequate risk control. The National Safety Council uses lost workday cases, cases involving days away from work and deaths, nonfatal cases with lost workdays, lost workdays, and days away from work as indicators of industrial safety problems. Exhibit 10–4 presents the industrial averages for the major industrial groups, including government. Each indicator shows that the safety record for government is the worst and often significantly worse than industries considered traditionally dangerous such as agriculture, mining, and construction. This represents a record of inaction and inadequate attention to safety.

**EXHIBIT 10–4   Occupational Safety Risk
Incidence Rates per 100 Full-Times Employees in 1988**

INDUSTRY	LOST WORKDAY CASES	CASES INVOLVING DAYS AWAY FROM WORK & DEATHS	NONFATAL CASES WITHOUT LOST WORK	LOST- WORK- DAYS	DAYS AWAY FROM WORK
All Industries	3.58	2.17	5.20	72	49
Agriculture, etc.	4.22	3.50	6.35	82	56
Mining	1.43	1.06	3.93	46	36
Construction	4.28	3.32	6.68	93	77
Manufacturing	3.56	1.84	6.13	68	42
Transportation, etc.	3.76	2.75	2.85	83	63
Sales	3.46	2.16	3.16	64	46
Services	2.34	2.22	2.64	35	28
Government	5.10	4.67	6.75	106	96

Source: National Safety Council, *Accident Facts 1990 Edition.*

If the following sound risk-control programs were adopted more often, the safety record for government would improve significantly. Sound risk-control programs include:

1. *security*—preventative techniques and procedures to combat theft, burglary, and vandalism;
2. *personnel safety*—meeting occupational safety and health standards, setting work safety standards, monitoring work environment and record keeping on accidents, and maintaining safety training and safety committees;
3. *fleet safety*—systematic review of driving records and implementation of stringent defensive-driving courses;
4. *property conservation*—regular inspection by fire, electrical, police, and other officials to identify and to correct hazards to physical property;
5. *environmental protection*—procedures to dispose of solid, liquid, and gaseous wastes in accordance with state and federal standards;
6. *emergency preparedness*—plans for and practice in dealing with a wide variety of emergencies, such as bomb threats, national disasters including fires and floods, and nuclear war; and
7. *contract liability*—procedures to review likely contracts so that the government will not assume liability for others, as well as care to get contractors for public authorities who show evidence of adequate insurance to sign stiff hold-harmless agreements.

Over the years, the following safety beliefs have proven to be helpful: (1) unsafe acts and conditions lead to accidents and injuries; (2) reducing the frequency of injury will also lessen the severity of injury; and (3) safety means education, engineering, and enforcement. The key person for safety is the first-line supervisor. Postinjury investigations are essential to identify and remove unsafe acts and conditions. Safety programs translate to caring actively about safety and implementing the proper remedies. Safety plans should reflect those beliefs in most instances.

Risk control costs money, as does insurance. A public authority can approach decisions on risk control and insurance on the basis of lowest cost to the government. Exhibit 10–5 illustrates how the cost can be charted. The cost of risk control is calculated and related to the likely cost of insurance and self-insurance. The solution is the lowest joint risk control and insurance cost. Obviously, human compassion must be considered, and those values dictate that higher sums of money be spent for risk control than our economic analysis suggests. However, the chart does help to see the relationship between safety and insurance costs.

Risk Funding and Self-Insurance

Risk funding is providing for sufficient funds to meet loss situations, if they occur, by the most effective use of internal and external financial resources. A public body can retain the risk and pay losses through extraordinary means or the regular budget.

Another option is to transfer the risk through a pooling of insurance. The *self-insurance* or *partial self-insurance* option is often desirable because it is the most economical approach for a public body. Even the insurance industry is encouraging the use of high deductibles—that is, partial self-insurance—today.

EXHIBIT 10–5   Risk Control Plus Insurance

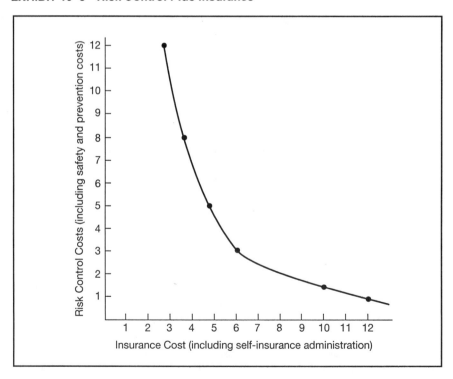

Insurance is merely the pooling of risks plus charge for administering that pooling. Insurance companies will generally collect from $1.50 to $2.00 in premiums for every dollar spent in claims. Some governments are larger than insurance companies and are in a better position to fund the potential losses than are the companies. A guideline to help decide the proper risk retention amount is that a government body should be willing to accept up to 1/10th of 1 percent of its operating budget in uninsured losses arising out of a single occurrence, or up to 1 percent of the operating budget as the aggregate of all such self-insured losses in a single fiscal year.

The following corollary objectives exist in risk funding:

1. Sufficient funds must be provided to meet the worst possible loss event. Some use a "maximum-foreseeable loss" criterion, and others also use a "maximum probable loss" estimate for the loss.
2. The management of risk funding should include proper use of idle cash reserves.
3. The maximum stability of risk funding should be maintained over time.
4. Administration should be both as efficient and as effective as possible.

Governments are in a much better position to absorb losses than most private concerns. They can use the following special factors:

1. federal disaster assistance (Public Law 93–288);
2. landed reserves or an insurance company created especially for that purpose;
3. spreading judgments over, say, a ten-year period;
4. bond issues;
5. special tax levies; and
6. citizen or group donations.

Another type of self-insurance option is pooling on a local, regional, or state basis. For example, the cities in Contra Costa County, California, have pooled together their liability and property risks. Pools for workers' compensation claims have been set up in Alabama, Texas, and Maine. This alternative does work well; and, as the liability insurance marketplace deteriorates, this joint action may become the only practical alternative. The biggest problem with pooling is the challenge of reaching administrative consensus on such matters as the cost allocation system. The accompanying chart is a useful guideline on risk retention:

TYPE OF RISK	RETENTION POLICY
Low frequency and low severity	This risk should be retained due to the low exposure.
High frequency and low severity	Normally, this risk should be retained as self-insurance.
High frequency and high severity	Handling this risk depends on the size of the government and insurance marketplace. Worker's compensation is a typical exposure of this type.
Low frequency and high severity	This risk normally cannot be absorbed; risk transfer by insurance is wise. An alternative is partial self-insurance. This can reduce insurance and total risk costs. Property and liability exposures are prime examples of this type.

Partial self-insurance can be practiced by selecting high deductibles and special insurance plans, which permit a sharing of risk with the insurance company. The decisions on this subject should weigh premium credits and administrative savings. Do not risk a lot for a little. A deductible should result in savings commensurate with the risk which is retained. However, the government should set the deductible at the level it can afford based on its own financial ability and not on the savings generated in any one year. An annual aggregate deductible should be used rather than a single occurrence deductible because this provides greater budgeting certitude. The following list addresses common practices by type of insurance:

1. *fire insurance*—high deductibles are often used. Normally, the deductible should be on a "per occurrence" basis and not on a "per loss" basis because single windstorm represents one occurrence but many losses. Also, an aggregate deductible should be used.
2. *workers' compensation*—most private bodies—and, increasingly, public bodies—use self-insurance for catastrophic loss (for example, over $100,000 on a per-occurrence basis).
3. *public liability*—the use of insurance above set limits is critical, but often insurance is difficult to obtain.

The planning process for self-insurance takes about six months. The first month is spent gathering data, especially on premiums and losses, as discussed earlier. In the second month, the maximum amount which can be retained should be determined. In the third month, the insurance bidding process should begin. In the fourth month, the bids should be reviewed or costs negotiated. In the fifth month, the contracts should be awarded.

A true self-insurance program means that the government performs all the various functions which would have been handled by an insurance carrier. These functions include accounting for premiums, a safety and loss control service, adjusting services, legal services, and funding for losses. A fund from which losses will be paid up to the retained limit must be established. Such funds are accumulated on a gradual basis, and the idle funds are invested. Also, the department incurring the loss should be charged back a predetermined amount of each loss. This serves to encourage department heads to be sensitive to their risks and the importance of risk control.

Insurance

Many public authorities require bidding for insurance. There is some controversy associated with bidding. Advocates point out that open competitive bidding gives every company a fair opportunity to receive the contract, and the process leads to the best price for the government. Those against the process point to several problems. Yearly bidding discourages long-term company-to-client relationships, thus negating a potential advantage and adding to the cost of overhead in the insurance industry. Increasingly, fewer companies are willing to bid; thus, artificially high bids do exist. If individual negotiations occur instead, that might result in lower bids. An alternative approach is limited competitive bidding, in which stress is placed upon selecting qualified agents or brokers. Two or three are selected and asked to submit firm quotations. The contract is awarded on the basis of those bids.

The forms of insurance include *property insurance, crime coverage, liability coverage*, and *employee benefits*. *Property insurance* includes both fire, "all risk" contracts on buildings, contents, and property, and other coverages. *Crime coverage* includes employee dishonesty, faithful performance bonds, and protection against burglary, robbery, and theft. *Liability coverage* includes all forms of public liability insurance, automobile insurance, and workers' compensation. Umbrella protection is essential and should include the governing body, all boards, commissions, elected officials, and employees, and even volunteers. *Employee benefits* are often subject to labor-management negotiations, but they can include health insurance, major medical insurance, long-term disability income insurance, accident insurance, group life insurance, and pension plans.

A few general standards apply to all insurance contracts. The named insured group should be consistent on all policies. Property limits should be updated to actual cash or replacement value. All insurance contracts should have a sixty-day written notice of cancellation, nonrenewal, or material reduction. Retention and participation in risk should be carefully spelled out in the contract. Proper notification of loss should begin after the risk manager is aware of the loss and payments on losses should be to the governmental body. Normally, all the contracts, or as many as possible, should expire at the end of the fiscal year. Cash flow arrangements should be made to the advantage of the government's idle cash plans.

Some general suggestions on content can be made. Coverage should be very broad because of the variety of risk exposures found in government. Large maximum limits should be used. Umbrella coverage is getting more difficult to obtain so some risks must be insured separately, such as airport, aircraft, and bus line liability.

Administration

A risk-management program requires continuous direction and careful attention. For larger governments, a full-time risk manager is essential and an additional safety staff would be wise. For smaller governments, this activity can be part of the budget office responsibilities. For both large and small governments, outside assistance can be quite valuable at times because of the complex nature of this subject.

A formal risk-management policy should be developed which sets out important understandings. The policy must have active top legislative and executive support. The policy should establish the goals of the program as well as define authority and responsibility in this area. The necessary types of interdepartmental coordination should be spelled out. Guidelines on risk retention should be stated in the context of the risk management philosophy of loss reduction and prevention. Insurance purchasing should be centralized. A model policy statement is presented in Exhibit 10–6.

Two keys to risk management are communication and cooperation. Risk identification depends on getting the necessary information for the governing body, the legal staff, the program units, the personnel department, purchasing, and others. A government has outstanding in-house expertise, which must be tapped. The expertise includes the fire department, police, inspection units, attorney's office, finance, personnel, and others. Each can be quite helpful. For example, the fire department can help devise a fire loss-prevention effort, and the finance office can help devise the best means to deal with idle cash resulting from the risk-management program.

EXHIBIT 10–6   Risk Management Policy

1. The function of risk management has as its purpose:
   a. Protecting the municipality from catastrophic losses
   b. Minimizing the total cost of accidental loss to the municipality
2. Risk management is to place the greatest emphasis on reduction rather than reimbursement of loss, through professional attention to loss-control techniques, motivational incentives, prompt claims payments, and other loss-prevention measures.
3. All insurance shall be purchased through the city risk-management department.
4. Subject to the risk manager's discretion, the amount of insurance purchased shall provide protection whenever a single accidental loss would result in property loss in excess of $50,000 per incident or liability judgment that would potentially exceed $50,000 per incident. Lesser amounts may be retained if financially feasible.

Source: "Risk Management in Local Government," *Government Finances*, 6, 2 (May 1977), 40.

The risk managers should report annually on their program to top management. The report should point out major changes in the program, the outline of new program departures in the future, and comparisons to programs with similar government units. The loss-prevention program should be presented, and total cost savings stated. The report should also contain an analysis of claims paid, reserves, and administrative and legal costs.

In conclusion, the risk manager should have responsibility for:

1. aiding units in analyzing risks, including accidental losses;
2. advising and adjusting major losses for all units on loss prevention, safety, and self-insurance levels;
3. allocating insurance and risk costs to the units;
4. maintaining records of losses, loss costs, premiums, and related costs;
5. reviewing all new contracts for hold-harmless requirements;
6. purchasing insurance; and
7. coordinating all activities involving risk.

PENSION FUNDS

Budget Concerns

Pensions are budget concerns. Salaries and wages constitute a significant portion of government expenses—especially for local governments—and half of the related fringe benefits are pensions and social security payments. Such costs vary, but some governments pay as much as 42 percent of salaries and wages for fringe benefits. In the court-determined contractual relationship between governments and their employees, such expenses represent a mandatory liability and an appropriation due former employees. Pensions thus have first or near-first demand on government revenue. Normally, governments establish special pension funds to which both the employer and the employee make payments in each pay period. Pension fund liability is usually covered wholly or partially from the pension fund, which receives its revenue from employer and employee payments plus investment income. There are approximately 6,000 public pension plans in the United States, with 90 percent of all employees belonging to the 100 largest plans. Pension assets exceed $135 billion and can have a growth rate of over 12 percent per year.

Like risk management, the key to pension funds is to spread liability among many people. With pension funds, the liability is the future pension benefits that will be received by each former employee from retirement until death. Thus, the future costs of the pension-benefit payments and associated administrative expenses must equal the combined employee and employer fringe-benefit payments, investment income from the fund, and any general fund subsidy. Many systems do have a partial or full subsidy. If the pension-benefit outlays are financed by existing member pension payments, a "pay-as-you-go" system exists. If the pension fund income is calculated to cover future likely pension outlays without present or future general fund subsidy, then the system is actuarially sound. The latter type of system is not always present, even though the municipal finance investment community, in judging creditworthiness, prefers and sometimes demands that pension plans be completely funded. However, fully funded pension funds are more costly in the budget year, whereas a pay-as-you-go strategy will meet immediate pension expenses and be less expensive in the BY. There is a strong temptation to use the less expensive approach and let future legislatures or city councils find the money to meet the future expenses. In summary, the case for a fully funded pension plan is as follows:

1. good fiscal management means knowing what programs cost;
2. it adds security to the pension obligation;
3. it protects employers from overgenerous benefit arguments in labor-management negotiations because the future pension burden on the budget is more easily understood; and
4. the financial community, in determining government creditworthiness, is increasingly demanding fully funded pension plans.

Both private and public pensions are so common today that their recent origin is surprising. The first public pension program was started in 1857 to cover the New York City police force. However, it was not until the turn of the century that pension systems became widely adopted in either the public or private sector. Today, pension plans are fragmented, with one city sometimes maintaining many separate plans for police, fire, sanitation, general administration, and other employee groups. Because the Tenth Amendment to the Constitution preserves the rights of states, there has been little federal regulatory oversight; but, at the state level, one finds increasing state oversight concern, even to the extent of having a state-administered pension fund in which both state and local employees participate.

Pension policy is often a concern of labor-management negotiations. Union negotiators often use a tactic called "leapfrogging," which means establishing higher benefits for one union and then demanding comparable features for another union. For example, the firefighters' union would argue for added benefits, and any success would be used by the police union in their negotiations. In the public sector, unlike the private sector, legislative policy makers are usually involved in setting pension policy. Thus, unions can and do lobby legislators for pension policy changes, in addition to negotiating for them. Rarely are pension policies major political issues because they require specialized skills and knowledge, have long-term implications, and have low visibility. In addition, pension systems have no general authoritative standards, and system growth has been haphazard. These conditions are ideal for negotiated settlements, which can have expensive, hidden long-term budget implications.

The Investment Process

According to Girard Miller (1987), the conceptual framework of the general investment process should consist of the following five parts:

- Identify and establish specific, explicit written policies on investor's opportunities, constraints, preferences and capabilities.
- Identify investment opportunities.
- Formulate and implement investment strategies on the purchase of financial securities and related instruments in the marketplace.
- Monitor, document, and report on the investor's circumstances, market conditions, and related security values.
- Respond to new objectives and changing circumstances by making portfolio adjustments.

Miller suggests the following cookbook approach to implement as the conceptual framework:

- Identify the entity's objectives, constraints, preferences and capabilities.
- Develop investment policies.
- Develop administrative systems and internal controls.

- Prepare a cash forecast.
- Determine the investment horizon.
- Establish an investment outlook and strategy.
- Analyze the yield curve.
- Select optimizing instruments.
- Monitor the markets and investment results.
- Report results.
- Adjust and rebalance the portfolio accordingly.

Policy Issues

Pension fund policy can be viewed in terms of benefits, investments, and administration. *Benefit policy* involves questions of how much money employees can collect and when they can collect it. *Investment policy* is concerned with questions of who controls the investments, limitations on investment, and investment performance.

Since the first public employee pension plan in 1857, the number of plans has grown to over 6,600 in the United States, with 90 percent of state and municipal workers enrolled in the 350 systems with over 1,000 or more members. The largest plan in 1992 was CALPERS, which invests $67.0 billion. In contrast, the AT&T pension fund had $38.9 billion. There are significant economic gains normally to be made by the consolidation of smaller systems into larger systems. Sometimes pension funds are directed to promote local economic development or social goals. For example, the $1.4 billion Wyoming Retirement System invested $10 million in Dow's Wyoming operation. Sometimes such investments lose money, such as the 1980s Alaska public employees and teachers' retirement funds loan for $165 million for multifamily houses, in which 40 percent went delinquent or resulted in foreclosures. The Alaska $4 billion pension fund was able to manage the loss.

With large funds comes economic power. Using such power, a public pension fund manager can rebuke a major firm such as Salomon Brothers for cornering the market on U.S. Treasuries. For example, CALPERS owns 1 percent of practically all the major publicly traded companies and thus can demand action with some success from the largest corporations. In New York State, the governor's business-labor task force recommended curbing the power of New York State's public pension fund. The task force felt that the fund managers should not oppose company management in takeover fights and proxy votes. They also opposed financing hostile leverage buy-outs or backing buy-out firms that do not promise to avoid them. By the year 2000, large pension funds are likely to own two-thirds of the corporate world, and, therefore, the mushrooming economic power of pension funds is an important public policy issue. One possible positive pension-management policy might be to require the funds to focus on the long-term health of corporations and the economy as a whole. Such a policy would significantly encourage American private companies to avoid focusing on short-term profits and instead focus on gaining market shares, conducting more research and development, training employees, and other long-term oriented policies.

Until the 1990s, public pension funds were fairly successful at fending off attempts to transfer their money to other funds. However, in tighter economic times, raiding pension funds has become an issue. Two common methods to raid pension funds are to (1) simply commandeer them and (2) cut back on the annual contribution to the funds. The first method is politically difficult and can lead to law suits. The second method is normally used, and it has two types: (1) change the actuarial and investment-income assumptions, thus lowering the government contribution to the pension fund, and (2) simply deferring the payments. The latter method is especially expensive as the state must not only pay the contribution but also the equivalent interest earned. A dramatic raid occurred in 1991, when Governor Pete Wilson of California transferred $1.6 billion from the state's pension fund to the general fund in order to balance the state's 1991 budget.

The major concern of those who deal with pension funds is the *benefit package*. The four major benefit policy issues are *wage replacement*, who pays *contributions* to the fund, *indexing*, and *double coverage*. Not surprisingly, employees would like retirement benefits to replace their wages, but that is costly. Exhibit 10–7 is an illustration of one common method of calculating retirement benefits. Normally, an average of the last three or five years is used to calculate retirement benefits. One government used the last day of regular employment and found that this produced an artificially high amount because overtime was added to the already high-salary last day.

The second concern of those who deal with pension funds is who contributes; employees prefer that all costs be paid by the employer. The third concern is inflation, which can particularly hurt retired employees living on a fixed pension. The solution is to link the benefits to a cost-of-living index such as the consumer price index. Not surprisingly, indexing is popular with employees, but it becomes very expensive in subsequent years. The fourth concern is double coverage, which normally results from an overlap with Social Security benefits—an employer option for state and local governments.

Three other pension issues not illustrated by Exhibit 10–7 are *vesting, portable systems*, and *disability/survivor protection*. What if you are fired just before retirement? Will you collect any retirement benefits? The answer depends on whether or not you are *vested* (that is, whether you have worked the number of years required before an employee can collect any money at retirement). Vesting varies from system to system. Normally, three to five years is used, but some systems use ten years. What if you are vested in one government pension plan but take a new job with another government? Can your new government contribute to your old pension plan? Normally, the answer is no, but some states have combined state and local systems that do permit some portability. What if you become disabled? Do you receive retirement benefits (or does your spouse, in the event of your death)?

Again, provisions vary. For example, if your disability was incurred while you were at work, benefits are computed in the manner described in Exhibit 10–7. If the disability was incurred outside the workplace, you may still be eligible, but other requirements must be met, such as a minimum of ten years of service. Survivor benefits are also common. For example, under one plan, if an employee dies in the line of duty, his or her spouse receives a monthly benefit of half the regular monthly salary until the spouse's remarriage or death. If an employee dies elsewhere, the spouse receives benefits calculated under the policy in force at the time of death.

EXHIBIT 10–7 Sample Calculations of Retirement Benefits

Step 1. Creditable Service and Percentage Value

	% VALUE PER YEAR OF SERVICE	TOTAL YEARS OF SERVICE	TOTAL % VALUE PER PLAN
Retirement up to Age 62 or 30 Years	1.60%	x_____ =	_____
Retirement at Age 63 or 31 Years	1.63%	x_____25_ =	__40.75__
Retirement at Age 64 or 32 Years	1.65%	x_____ =	_____
Retirement at Age 65 or 33 Years or More	1.68%	x_____ =	_____
Total Years		_____25	

Step 2. Average Final Compensation (AFC)

Mr. Smith worked 25 years under the system and retired at age 63. In this step we list his five highest fiscal year salaries and divide their total by five.	$11,257.00
	12,851.00
	13,201.00
	13,706.00
	13,904.00
	Total $64,919.00

$64,919.00 ÷ 5 = $12,983.80 = Average Final Compensation (A F C)

Step 3. Monthly Benefit Calculation

Average final compensation (step 2)	$12,983.80
Total % value per plan (step 1)	x .4075
	$ 5,290.90 Annual benefit
	$ 5,290.90 + 12 = $440.91 Monthly benefit

Investment policy debates center on who controls the investments, on what investment limitations should exist, and finally on the adequacy of the investment performance. Government pension funds are rarely controlled by unions, as sometimes occurs in the private sector. Recently, the dispute over control has centered on the issue of decentralized versus centralized state systems. The advantages of a centralized state system include uniform benefits, greater decision-making expertise, greater cost effectiveness, and potentially higher yields, given the advantage of size. Nevertheless, many local governments prefer to retain control over investments. This is especially true if the portfolio managers are concerned about making investments that will benefit the local community. Advocates of this policy stress that such investments achieve both important public policy goals and employees' economic security. One example is the use of pension funds for local mortgage projects. In the case of New York City, pension funds controlled by unions were used to buy city bonds when no other investors could be found.

State governments place some restrictions and limitations on pension-fund investments. The eleven major types of investment restrictions are as follows:

1. maximum percentage of fund assets that can be invested in *common stock*;
2. maximum percentage of fund assets that can be invested in the securities of any *one company*;
3. maximum percentage of fund assets that can be invested in securities of any *one industry*;
4. maximum percentage of fund assets that can be invested in *real estate mortgages*;
5. maximum percentage of fund assets that can be invested in *real estate equities*;
6. maximum percentage of assets that can be held in *cash reserves*;
7. minimum *size* of company in which investments can be made;
8. minimum total *rate of return* for income to be earned on investments;
9. minimum *quality of bonds* in which the fund can invest;
10. maximum *price/earning ratio* on common stocks in which the fund can invest; and
11. minimum number of consecutive years of *dividends paid* on common stock (divided-payment record).

The adequacy of investment performance is an important matter to budget officials because a stronger performance means a decrease in employer and employee contributions. In general, managers of public pension plans are cautious investors who prefer fixed income obligations rather than equity securities (for example, common stock). In a survey conducted by the Municipal Finance Officers Association in 1980, public pensions did better than private pensions, but that fact was attributed to the relatively greater use of equity securities by the private pension funds during a period of declining stock prices. One interesting finding was that public pensions outperformed private pensions in the rate of return of equities. Private pensions, however, outperformed public pensions on bond portfolios. Probably, public and private pension plans perform at about the same level.

Administrative policy disputes center on the largely unregulated and unknown status of pension funds. Controversy about disclosure practices has arisen because there is disagreement over what information should be made known, in what form it should be given, who should make it known, and who should receive it. Pension information can be expensive to prepare, but the expense must be balanced against the importance of acquiring especially for actuarial analysis. The frequency and quality of the latter are critical to the accuracy and value of pension plan financial disclosures. They inform employees and government policy makers of the relative soundness of the pension funds.

With the recessionary pressures on state and local governments in the early 1980s, concern grew that governments might not be able to meet future pension liabilities, that governments might be diverting pension funds to other areas such as the general operating fund, and that pension funds might not be properly invested. Unfortunately, the shortage of adequate data only increased fears. Not surprisingly, some have argued for federal regulations, but the Advisory Commission on Intergovernmental Relations (ACIR) has taken a position against federal regulation of public pension systems. Exhibit 10–8 presents the ACIR argument.

EXHIBIT 10–8 Advisory Commission on Intergovernmental Relations: Reasons for the Commission's Recommendation against Federal Regulation

In recommending against federal regulation of state and local pension systems, the Commission rested its case upon five major arguments.

- Our federal system with its emphasis on state sovereignty requires that states have full responsibility for determining all basic components of their public employees' compensation, and that of the local employees within the states.
- The unique and diverse nature of state and local retirement systems requires the kind of adaptation and fine tuning that only state and local government control and regulation can provide.
- State and local governments have made significant progress during the past few years in putting their own retirement systems in order.
- There is no convincing evidence that the federal government has any compelling "national interest" in regulating state and local public pension systems.
- Even mild or limited forms of federal regulations are undesirable, given the tendency for federal regulatory agencies and the courts to take a friendly piece of legislation and turn it into an unfriendly set of regulations.

Source: ACIR, *State and Local Pension Systems*, December 1980, p. 54.

The Government Accounting Standards Board (GASB) has taken a strong stand that more pension data should be disclosed. Such a ruling is politically significant to local governments because following the rule can make a local government appear to be over- or under-funded in their pension liability. The GASB position would require state and local governments to disclose their own unfunded pension liability using a GASB prescribed actuarial technique. Retirement systems can continue to use a different method to determine how much money to actually contribute to the pension plan. The GASB approach is designed to permit financial analysts, who are considering government securities, to compare pension systems more easily.

Public pensions are significant activities and they significantly affect government budgets.

REVIEW QUESTIONS

1. Explain what should take place in a preliminary review of property management. Explain also the challenge of procurement, including the difficulty of using a competitive bidding process.
2. Explain the administrative implications of bar-code technology on government property management.
3. Explain the relationship between risk control and insurance. Explain what factors should be weighed in deciding how much risk should be retained.
4. What type of knowledge and skill is needed for exposure identification and risk evaluation? What types of continuous direction and careful attention connote excellent risk management?
5. The proper funding of public pensions has budgetary implications. What are the concepts behind pension funds, the policy issues related to pensions, and the budgetary implications of pension funds?

REFERENCES

COE, CHARLES K. "Government Purchasing: The State of the Practice." In Thomas D. Lynch and Lawrence Martin (eds.), *Handbook of Comparative Public Budgeting and Financial Management.* New York: Marcel Dekker, 1993, 207–224.

CORCORAN, A. WAYNE. "Financial Management." In J. Richard Aronson and Eli Schwartz (eds.), *Management Policies in Local Government Finance.* Washington, D.C.: International City Management Association, 1975.

Government Finance Officers Association. *Guidelines for the Preparation of a Public Employee Retirement System Comprehensive Annual Financial Report.* Chicago: Government Finance Officers Association, May 1980.

———. "Pension Training Seminar," *Resources in Review*, 2, 1 (September/October 1979), 6–7.

———. "Public Employee Retirement," Number 3 in *Elements of Financial Management.* Washington, D.C.: Government Finance Officers Association, Government Finance Research Center, 1981.

HILDRETH, W. BARTLEY, and GERALD J. MILLER. "Risk Management and Pension Systems." In Jack Rabin and Thomas D. Lynch (eds.), *Handbook on Public Budgeting and Financial Management.* New York: Marcel Dekker, 1983.

International City Management Association. *Municipal Finance Administration*, 6th ed. Chicago: International City Management Association, 1962.

MILLER, GIRARD. "The Investment of Public Funds: A Research Agenda." *Public Budgeting and Finance, 7, 3 (Autumn 1987), 47–56.*

MOAK, LENNOX L., and ALBERT M. HILLHOUSE. *Local Government Finance.* Chicago: Municipal Finance Officers Association, 1975.

————. "Risk Management in Local Government," *Government Finances*, 6, 2 (May 1977).

PETERSON, JOHN E. *A Summary of State and Local Government Public Employee Retirement System Investment Practices and Policies.* Washington, D.C.: Government Finance Officers Association, Government Finance Research Center, December 1980.

————. *State and Local Pension Fund Investment Performance.* Washington, D.C.: Government Finance Officers Association, Government Finance Research Center, December 1980.

POPE, RALPH A. "Economies of Scale in Large State and Municipal Retirement Systems." *Public Budgeting and Finance,. 6, 3 (Autumn 1986), 70–80.*

ROSS, NESTOR R., and JOSEPH S. GERBER. *Governmental Risk Management Manual.* Tucson, Ariz.: Risk Management Publishing Company, 1977.

ROTHMAN, MATT. "CALPERS Director Is Financial Force to be Reckoned With," *San Francisco Examiner*, Sunday, February 23, 1992, E–1.

SURFUS, GERALD M. "Identifying and Evaluating Potential Risk," *Government Finances*, 6, 28 (May 1977), 28–29.

TWEEDALE, DENNIS G. "Risk Management in Local Government," *Government Finance*, 6, 2 (May 1977), 40.

U.S. Advisory Commission on Intergovernmental Relations. *State and Local Pension Systems.* Washington, D.C.: Advisory Commission on Intergovernmental Relations, December 1980.

U.S. Joint Financial Management Improvement Program. *Bar Code Technology: A Means to Improve Operational Efficiency and Internal Control.* Washington, D.C.: U.S. Joint Financial Management Improvement Program, May 1982.

————. *Property Management Evaluation Guide for Federal Agencies.* Washington, D.C.: U.S. Joint Financial Management Improvement Program, March 1982.

WHITE, JAMES A. "Panel Urges Curb On Pension Funds' Power," *The Wall Street Journal*, Thursday, June 22, 1989, C–1.

————. "Pension Fund Investments Get Strange," *The Wall Street Journal*, Friday, November 17, 1989, C–1.

ZEMANSKY, STANLEY D. *Ethics and Quality Purchasing.* New York: American Management Association, 1988.

GLOSSARY

Ability to Pay   The principle that the tax burden should be distributed proportionally among taxpayers, according to the size of their income. It is based on the assumption that as a person's income increases the person can and should contribute a larger percentage of his or her income to support government activities.

Accounting System   The total structure of records and procedures that record, classify, and report information on the financial position and operations of a government unit or any of its funds, balanced account groups, and organizational components.

Accounts Payable   Amounts owed to others for goods and services received and assets acquired.

Accounts Receivable   Amounts due from others for goods furnished and services rendered. Such amounts include reimbursements earned and refunds receivable. (*See also* Accounts Payable.)

Accrual Basis of Accounting   The basis of accounting under which revenues are recorded when earned and expenditures are recorded when goods are received and services performed, even though receipt of the revenue or payment of the expenditure may take place, in whole or part, in another accounting period.

Accrued Expenditures   Liabilities incurred during a given period that reflect the need to pay for (a) services performed by employees, contractors, other government accounts, vendors, carriers, grantees, lessors, and other payees; (b) goods and other tangible property received; and (c) amounts owed under programs for which no current service or performance is required (such as annuities, insurance claims, other benefit payments, and some cash grants, but excluding the repayment of debt, which is considered neither an obligation nor an expenditure). Expenditures accrue regardless of when cash payments are made, whether invoices have been rendered, or, in some cases, whether goods or other tangible property have been physically delivered.

Agency Generally, any department, independent commission, board, bureau, office, or other establishment of the government, including independent regulatory commissions and boards.

Allocations The amount of obligational authority from one agency, bureau, or account that is set aside in a transfer appropriation account to carry out the purposes of the parent appropriation or fund.

Allotment An authorization by the head (or other authorized employee) of an agency to his or her subordinates to incur obligations within a specified amount.

Annual Budget Revenues and expenditures for one fiscal year period.

Anti-Deficiency Act of 1906 Legislation enacted by Congress (a) to prevent the incurring of obligations or the making of expenditures (outlays) in excess of amounts available in appropriations or funds; (b) to fix responsibility within an agency for the creation of any obligation or the making of any expenditure in excess of an apportionment or reapportionment or in excess of other subdivisions established pursuant to 31 U.S.C. 665(g); and (c) to assist in bringing about the most effective and economical use of appropriations and funds.

Apportionment The distribution by the Central Budget Office of amounts available for obligation, including budgetary reserves established pursuant to law, in appropriations or fund accounts. In an apportionment, amounts available for obligation are divided among specific time periods (usually quarters), activities, projects, objects, or a combination thereof. The amounts so apportioned limit the amount of obligations that may be incurred.

Appropriation A legislative authorization that permits government agencies to incur obligations and to make payments out of the treasury for specified purposes. An appropriation usually follows enactment of authorizing legislation. An appropriation act is the most common means of providing budget authority, but in some cases the authorizing legislation itself provides the budget authority. (*See also* Backdoor Authority.) Appropriations do not represent cash actually set aside in the treasury for purposes specified in the appropriation act; they represent limitations of amounts that agencies may obligate during the period of time specified in the relevant appropriation act. Several types of appropriations are not counted as budget authority, since they do not provide authority to incur additional obligations. Examples of these include: (a) appropriations to liquidate contract authority—Congressional action to provide funds to pay obligations incurred against contract authority; (b) appropriations to reduce outstanding debt—Congressional action to provide funds for debt retirement; and (c) appropriations for refunds of receipts.

Appropriation Act A statute that generally provides authorization for agencies to incur obligations and to make payments out of the treasury for specified purposes. An appropriation act, the most common means of providing budget authority, generally follows enactment of authorizing legislation unless the authorizing legislation itself provides the budget authority.

Appropriation Limitation A statutory restriction in appropriation acts that establishes the maximum or minimum amount that may be obligated or expended for specified purposes.

Arbitrage Bonds The exemption from income tax of government bonds as long as state and local governments do not use the funds from the bonds for investment rather than for the prescribed public purpose.

Asset Any item of economic value owned by a government unit. The item may be tangible (that is, physical and actual) or intangible (that is, a right to ownership, expressed in terms of cost or some other value).

Audit An investigation of the accuracy and correct operation of an agency's accounting system, including validation of inventories and existing equipment, documentation of proper legal authority to carry out agency activities, adequacy of controls on fraud, waste, and mismanagement, and the effectiveness of the agency's programs.

Authorizing Committee   A standing legislative committee with jurisdiction over the subject matter of those laws, or parts of laws, that set up or continue the legal operation of programs or agencies. An authorizing committee also has jurisdiction in those instances in which backdoor authority is provided through substantive legislation.

Authorizing Legislation   Substantive legislation that sets up or continues the legal operation of a program or agency, either indefinitely or for a specific period of time, or that sanctions a particular type of obligation or expenditure within a program. Authorizing legislation is normally a prerequisite for an appropriation. It may place a limit on the amount of budget authority to be included in appropriation acts or it may authorize the appropriation of "such sums as may be necessary." In some instances, authorizing legislation may provide authority to incur debts or to mandate payment to particular persons or political subdivisions of the country.

Automatic Stabilizer   A mechanism having a countercyclical effect that automatically moderates changes in incomes and outputs in the economy without specific decisions to change government policy. Unemployment insurance and the income tax are among the most important of the automatic stabilizers used in the United States. Also known as a built-in stabilizer.

Backdoor Authority   Budget authority provided in legislation outside the normal appropriations process (that is, through appropriations committees). The most common forms of backdoor authority are authority to borrow (also called borrowing authority or authority to spend debt receipts) and contract authority. In other cases (for example, interest on the public debt), a permanent appropriation is provided that becomes available without any current action by Congress. Section 401 of the Congressional Budget and Impoundment Control Act of 1974 (31 U.S.C. 1351) specifies certain limits on the use of backdoor authority.

Balance of Payments   A statistical record of economic transactions between one country— for example, the United States—and the rest of the world. Balance of payments accounts normally distinguish among transactions involving goods, services, short-term capital, and long-term capital.

Balance Sheet   An accounting statement designed to balance total assets, total liabilities, and fund balance.

Balanced Budget   A budget in which receipts are equal to outlays.

Benefit-Cost Analysis   *See* Cost-Benefit Analysis.

Block Grant   *See* Grant.

Bond   A written promise to pay a specified sum of money (called the face value or principal amount) at a specified date or dates (called the maturity dates) together with periodic interest at a specified rate.

Bond Maturity   A set period of time at the end of which the principal on a bond is completely paid. The length of the maturity normally is not longer than the useful life of the facility that is being financed.

Bond Prospectus   The formal statement of information used by bond sellers to help investors decide whether or not they wish to invest in the bonds.

Borrowing Authority   Authority to spend debt receipts; statutory authority that permits an agency to incur obligations and to make payments for specified purposes out of borrowed monies. (*See also* Debt.)

Box-Jenkins   One of a class of models called ARIMA, for Auto Regressive Integrated Moving Average. Identifies possible useful models and checks each in turn against the time series until it finds the point that fits.

Budget   A plan for the accomplishment, within a definite time period, of programs related to established objectives and goals, setting forth estimates of the resources required and the resources available (usually in comparison with one or more past periods) and showing future requirements. Also, a request for funds to run the government.

Budget and Accounting Act of 1921 Federal legislation that provided for an executive budget for the national government and for an independent audit of government accounts.

Budget and Accounting and Procedures Act of 1950 Federal legislation that gave the president authority to prescribe the contents and arrangement of the budget, to simplify its presentation, to broaden appropriations, and to mandate progress toward performance budgeting.

Budget Authority Authority provided by law to enter into obligations that will result in immediate or future outlays of government funds; it does not include authority to ensure or guarantee the repayment of indebtedness incurred by another person or government. The basic forms of budget authority are appropriations, borrowing authority, and contract authority. Budget authority may be classified by the period of availability (one-year, multiple-year, no-year), by the timing of legislative action (current or permanent), or by the manner of determining the amount available (definite or indefinite).

Budget Call An announcement distributed by the budget office to all government departments and agencies, instructing them to prepare the budget and providing guidance on proper procedures to use. Much of the guidance is standardized and published in official bulletins and circulars.

Budget Execution System A set of procedures that gives direction to ongoing agency activities and allows for continuous and current reviews to determine if planned objectives are being met. One approach is to link an operating budget with management-by-objectives.

Budget-Wise Model An approach to budgeting in which all government decisions are perceived to be politically motivated, to the exclusion of all other factors. A person following this model stresses the futility of trying to make decisions on the basis of anything but political expediency and insists that a budget staff can do nothing but react to political events as they unfold.

Budget Year (BY) The fiscal year for which the budget is being considered; the fiscal year following the current year.

Built-in Stabilizer *See* Automatic Stabilizer.

Business Cycles The recurrent phases of expansion and contraction in overall business activity, evidenced by fluctuations in measures of aggregate economic activity, notably real gross national product. Both the duration and the magnitude of individual cycles vary greatly.

Call Provision The right of the borrower to buy back bonds at set prices regardless of the current market rate.

Capital In economic theory, one of the three major factors of production (the others being land and labor). Capital can refer either to physical capital, such as plant and equipment, or to the financial resources required to purchase physical capital.

Capital Budget A budget that deals with large expenditures for capital items normally financed by borrowing. Usually, capital items have long-range returns and useful life spans, are relatively expensive, and have physical presence (for example, buildings, roads, and sewage systems).

Case *See* Observation.

Cash Basis of Accounting The basis of accounting whereby revenues are recorded when received and expenditures (outlays) are recorded when paid, without regard to the accounting period in which the transactions occurred.

Categorical Grant *See* Grant.

Circuit Breaker A reform recommendation for property taxation that would reduce the regressive nature of the tax. Circuit breakers often provide for tax exemptions to families at the lowest income level or to elderly people on fixed incomes to relieve them of paying some of their property taxes.

Clientele Group The people who are perceived to be affected by an agency's programs and who take an active interest in its policies and actions.

Comprehensive Budget All revenues and expenditures included in the budget.

Confidence Interval A group of values used to estimate a statistical parameter. The confidence interval tends to include the true value of the parameter at a predetermined proportion of the time (for instance, 90 percent). The process of finding the group of values is repeated a number of times.

Congressional Budget and Impoundment Control Act of 1974 Federal legislation that was one of several reforms directed toward strengthening the legislative branch. It created the new Senate and House Budget Committees and the new Congressional Budget Office, required a current services budget, and required various reforms in the presidential budget and in presidential impoundment powers. It created a unified Congressional budget approach. (*See also* First Concurrent Resolution of the Budget *and* Second Concurrent Resolution of the Budget.)

Congressional Budget Office (CBO) Federal office responsible for presenting the Congress with reasonable and viable forecasts of aggregate levels of spending and revenue. The office also makes cost estimates for proposed legislation reported to the floor and provides cost projections for all existing legislation.

Consolidated Decision Package Package prepared at high organizational and program levels that summarizes and supplements information contained in decision packages received from subordinate units in an agency using zero-base budgeting.

Constant Dollar A dollar value adjusted for changes in prices. Constant dollars are derived by dividing current dollar amounts by an appropriate price index, a process generally known as deflating. The result is a constant dollar series as it would presumably exist if prices and transactions were the same in all subsequent years as in the base year. Any changes in such a series would reflect only changes in the real volume of goods and services. Constant dollar figures are commonly used for computing the gross national product and its components and for estimating total budget outlays.

Consumer Price Index (CPI) Either of two measures of change in the price of a fixed "market basket" of goods and services customarily purchased by urban consumers. CPI-U is based on a market basket determined by expenditure patterns of *all urban households,* while the market basket for CPI-W is determined by expensive patterns of *urban-wage-earner and clerical-worker families.* The level of CPI shows the relative cost of purchasing the specified market basket compared to the cost in a designated base year, while the current rate of change in the CPI measures how fast prices are currently rising or falling. Current rates of change can be expressed as either monthly or annual rates. Although the consumer price index is often called the "cost-of-living index," it measures only price changes, which constitute just one of several important factors affecting living costs. Both CPI-U and CPI-W are published monthly by the U.S. Bureau of Labor Statistics.

Contingent Liability An existing condition, situation, or set of circumstances involving uncertainty about a possible loss to an agency that will ultimately be resolved when one or more events either occur or fail to occur. Contingent liabilities include such items as loan guarantees and bank deposit insurance.

Continuing Resolution If a decision has not been reached on appropriations prior to the beginning of the new current year, then Congress can pass a resolution that says that the government can continue to obligate and spend at last year's budget levels or the lowest level passed by a chamber of Congress. The wording is usually framed to permit spending at the lowest amount the legislature is likely to pass.

Contract Authority Statutory authority that permits obligations to be incurred in advance of appropriations or in anticipation of receipts to be credited to a revolving fund or other account. Contract authority is unfunded and must subsequently be funded by an appropriation to liquidate obligations incurred under the contract authority, or by the collection and use of receipts.

Cost Accounting Standard A statement promulgated by the Cost Accounting Standards Board that becomes effective unless disapproved by Congress. These statements are intended to achieve uniform and consistent standards in the cost accounting practices followed by defense contractors.

Cost-Based Budgeting An approach to budgeting that is based on the costs to be incurred— that is, on the resources that will be consumed in carrying out a program, regardless of when the funds to acquire the resources were obligated or paid, and regardless of the source of funds (that is, the appropriation). For example, inventory items become costs when they are withdrawn from inventory, and the cost of buildings is distributed over time, through periodic depreciation charges, rather than in a lump sum when the buildings are acquired.

Cost-Benefit Analysis An analytical technique that compares the economic and social costs and benefits of proposed programs or policy actions. All losses and gains experienced by society are included and measured in dollar terms. The net benefits created by an action are calculated by subtracting the losses incurred by some sectors of society from the gains that accrue to others. Alternative actions are compared to determine which ones yield the greatest net benefits, or ratio of benefits to costs.

Cost-Effectiveness Analysis An analytical technique used to choose the most efficient method for achieving a program or policy goal. The costs of alternatives are measured by their requisite estimated dollar expenditures. Effectiveness is defined by the degree of goal attainment, and may also (but not necessarily) be measured in dollars. A comparison is made between either the net effectiveness (effectiveness minus costs) or the cost-effectiveness ratios of the various alternatives. The most cost-effective method may involve one or more alternatives.

Countercyclical Action Action aimed at smoothing out swings in economic activity. Countercyclical actions may take the form of monetary and fiscal policy (such as countercyclical revenue sharing or jobs programs). Automatic (built-in) stabilizers have a countercyclical effect without necessitating changes in government policy.

Crosswalk Any procedure for expressing the relationship between different classifications of budgetary data, such as between appropriation accounts and government programs.

Current Dollar The dollar value of a good or service in terms of prices current at the time the good or service was sold. This is in contrast to the value of the good or service in constant dollars.

Current Services Budget An executive budget projection that alerts the Congress—especially the Congressional Budget Office, the budget committees, and the appropriation committees—to anticipate specific revenue, expenditure, and debt levels, assuming that current policy is unchanged. It also provides a baseline of comparison to the presidential budget.

Current Year The fiscal year in progress.

Data Points The number of values a statistical software package can process in a procedure at one time. Often the allowable number of data points is equal to the number of variables allowed multiplied by the number of observations allowed.

Debt A government credit obligation.

Decision Package In zero-base budgeting, a brief justification document containing the information managers need in order to judge program or activity levels and resource requirements. Each decision package presents a level of request for a decision unit, stating the costs and performance associated with that level. Separate decision packages are prepared for incremental spending levels.

1. *Minimum Level.* Associated with performance below which it is not feasible for the decision unit to continue because no constructive contribution could be made toward fulfilling the unit's objectives.
2. *Intermediate Level.* Performance between the minimum and current levels. There may be more than one intermediate level.
3. *Current Level.* Performance that would be reflected if activities for the budget year were carried on at current year service or output levels without major policy changes. This level permits internal realignments of activities within existing statutory authorizations.
4. *Enhancement Level.* Level at which increased output or service is consistent with major objectives and at which sufficient benefits are expected to warrant the serious review of higher authorities. A series of decision packages is prepared for each decision unit. Cumulatively, the packages represent the total budget request for that unit.

Decision Package Set   A set of documents used in zero-base budgeting, consisting of the decision unit overview and the decision packages for the decision unit.

Decision Unit   In zero-base budgeting, that part or component of the basic program or organizational entity for which budget requests are prepared and for which managers make significant decisions on the amount of spending and the scope or quality of work to be performed.

Decision Unit Overview   In zero-base budgeting, that part of the decision package set that provides information necessary to evaluate and make budget decisions on each of the decision packages; eliminates repetition of the same information in each package.

Default Risk   The possibility that a borrower will fail to pay the principal or interest on a loan. All other factors being constant, the greater the possibility that the borrower will fail to meet the obligation, the greater the premium or market yield on the security.

Deferral of Budget Authority   Any action or inaction by an officer or employee of the government that temporarily withholds, delays, or effectively precludes the obligation or expenditure of budget authority, including authority to obligate by contract in advance of appropriations as specifically authorized by law.

Deficiency Apportionment   A distribution by the U.S. Office of Management and Budget of available budgetary resources for the fiscal year that anticipates the need for supplemental budget authority. Such apportionments may only be made under certain specified conditions provided for under the Anti-Deficiency Act, 31 U.S.C. 665(e).

Deficiency Appropriation   An appropriation made to an expired account to cover obligations that have been incurred in excess of available funds.

Deficit Financing   A situation in which the federal government's excess of outlays over receipts for a given period is financed primarily by borrowing from the public.

Definite Authority   Authority that is stated as covering a specific sum at the time the authority is granted. This includes authority stated as "not to exceed" a specified amount.

Deflation   A decrease in the general price level, usually accompanied by declining levels of output, increasing unemployment, and a contraction of the supply of money and credit.

Deobligation   A downward adjustment of previously recorded obligations. This may be attributable to the cancellation of a project or contract, to price revisions, or to corrections of estimates previously recorded as obligations.

Depreciation   The systematic and rational allocation of the costs of equipment and buildings (having a life of more than one year) over their useful lives. To match costs with related revenues in measuring income or determining the costs of carrying out program activities, depreciation reflects the use of the asset(s) during specific operating periods.

Deseasonalization   A method of removing any seasonal fluctuations that may distort the meaning of the data.

Devaluation   In a system of fixed exchange rates, the lowering of the value of a nation's currency in relation to gold, or to the currency of other countries, when this value is set by government intervention in the exchange market. (In a system of flexible exchange rates, if the value of the currency falls, it is referred to as depreciation; if the value of the currency rises, it is referred to as appreciation.)

Differencing   A method of taking out seasonality by subtracting the second data point from the first, the third from the second, and so on.

Direct Loan   A disbursement of funds (not in exchange for goods or services) that is contracted to be repaid with or without interest.

Discounting to Present Value   A method of adjusting dollar values in order to compare dollars expected to be received or spent in the future with dollars received or spent today.

Discount Rate   The interest rate that a commercial bank pays when it borrows from a Federal Reserve bank. The discount rate is one of the three tools of monetary policy used by the Federal Reserve System. The Federal Reserve customarily raises or lowers the discount rate to restrain or ease its money and credit policies.

Disposable Personal Income   Personal income less personal taxes and nontax payments to the federal government. It is the income available to persons for consumption or saving.

Durbin-Watson Figure   A model that determines if the variable in the equation is serially correlated, a condition that casts doubt on the reliability of the forecast.

Earmarked Revenue   Funds from a specific course to be spent only for a designated activity (for example, gasoline taxes that can be spent only for highway construction and maintenance).

Econometrics   The application of statistical methods to the study of economic data.

Economic Growth   An increase in a nation's productive capacity leading to an increase in the production of goods and services. Economic growth is usually measured by the annual rate of increase in real gross national product (as measured in constant dollars).

Economic Indicator   Statistics that have a systematic relationship to the business cycle. Each indicator is classified as leading, coincident, or lagging, depending on whether the indicator generally changes direction in advance of, at the same time as, or subsequent to changes in the overall economy. Although no one indicator or set of indicators is a wholly satisfactory predictor of the business cycle, taken as a whole they are valuable tools for identifying and analyzing changes in business cycles.

Economic Ordering Quantity   A means to determine total desirable inventory. The cost of ordering must be weighed against the cost of holding a sizable quantity of goods.

Eigenvalue   A scalar associated with a given linear transformation of a vector space.

Electronic Funds Transfer System   A communication system that provides the capability for automatic receipt of funds, as well as for computer assisted generation of fund transfers among the treasury, the Federal Reserve banks, member banks, and other institutions. Processing of checks takes an instant rather than several days, thus virtually eliminating the float.

Employment Act of 1946   Federal legislation that called for economic planning and for a budget policy directed toward achieving maximum national employment and production.

Employment Rate   In economic statistics, the total number of people who, during a specific week, did any work for pay or profit, or who worked for 15 hours or more without pay on a farm or in a business operated by a member of the person's family. Also included are those who neither worked nor looked for work but who had a job or business from which they were temporarily absent during the week.

Entitlement   Benefits mandated by law to be paid to any person or unit of government that meets the eligibility requirements established by such law. Authorizations for entitlements constitute a binding obligation on the part of the government, and eligible recipients have legal recourse if the obligation is not fulfilled. Budget authority for such payments is not necessarily provided in advance; thus, entitlement legislation requires the subsequent enactment of appropriations unless the existing appropriation is permanent. Examples of entitlement programs are Social Security benefits and veterans' compensation or pensions.

Expenditure   Payment of an obligation.

Exponential Smoothing   A method of transforming time series data for a better fit by creating a weighted average.

External Audit   An investigation carried out by separate independent agencies that examine accounts, check on the accuracy of recorded transactions and inventories, make on-site reviews of stocks, verify physical existence of equipment, and review operating procedures and regulations.

Federal Reserve System (Fed)   The central banking system of the United States, which operates to control the economy's supply of money and credit.

First Concurrent Resolution on the Budget   The annual resolution, containing government-wide budget targets of receipts, budget authority, and outlays, that guides Congress in its subsequent consideration of appropriations and revenue measures. It is required to be adopted by both houses of Congress no later than May 15, pursuant to the Congressional Budget and Impoundment Control Act of 1974 (P.L. 93–344, 31 U.S.C. 1324).

Fiscal Policy   Collectively, all federal government policies on taxes, spending, and debt management; intended to promote the nation's macroeconomic goals, particularly with respect to employment, gross national product, price-level stability, and equilibrium in balance of payments. The budget process is a major vehicle for determining and implementing federal fiscal policy. The other major component of federal macroeconomic policy is monetary policy.

Fiscal Year (FY)   Any yearly accounting period, without regard to its relationship to the calendar year. The fiscal year of the federal government begins on October 1 and ends on September 30. (Prior to fiscal year 1977, the Federal fiscal year began on July 1 and ended on June 30.) The fiscal year is designated by the calendar year in which it ends; for example, fiscal year 1980 for the Federal government is the year beginning October 1, 1979, and ending September 30, 1980. (*See also* Budget Year; Current Year; Prior Year.)

Fixed Costs   Those costs in any project or program that remain constant, regardless of the increase or decrease in units produced.

Float   The difference between the total amount of checks drawn on a bank account by the government and the amount shown for that account on the bank's books.

Formula Grant   *See* Grant.

Fourier Analysis   *See* Spectral Analysis.

Full Employment Budget   The estimated receipts, outlays, and surplus or deficit that would occur if the U.S. economy were continually operating at full capacity.

Full-Faith-and-Credit Debt   A long-term debt in which the credit (including the implied power of taxation) is unconditionally pledged by the government.

Full Funding   Provision of budgetary resources to cover the total cost of a program or project at the time it is undertaken. (The alternative is incremental funding, in which budget authority is provided or recorded for only a portion of total estimated obligations expected to be incurred during a single fiscal year.) Full funding is generally discussed in terms of multiyear programs, whether or not obligations for the entire program are made in the first year.

Functional Classification   A system of classifying budget resources by function so that budget authority and outlays of budget and off-budget entities, loan guarantees, and tax expenditures can be related in terms of the needs being addressed. Budget accounts are generally placed in the single budget function that best reflects its major end purpose (for example, national defense or health), regardless of the agency administering the program. A function may be divided into two or more subfunctions, depending upon the complexity of the need addressed by that function.

Fund Accounting The legal requirement for agencies to establish separate accounts for separate programs—that is, to segregate revenues and other resources, together with all related liabilities, obligations, and reserves, for the purpose of carrying on specific activities or attaining certain objectives in accordance with special regulations, restrictions, or limitations. The aim is to control the handling of money to ensure that it will be spent only for the purpose intended. Fund accounting, in a broad sense, is required by the government to demonstrate agency compliance with requirements of existing legislation for which funds have been appropriated or otherwise authorized.

General Accounting Office (GAO) The Congressional audit agency for the federal government. This agency reports directly to Congress. GAO investigates fraud, waste, and mismanagement. Its audits focus upon delegation of responsibility, policy direction and program evaluation, budget and accounting practices, and the adequacy of internal controls, including internal auditing.

GNP Gap The difference between the economy's output of goods and services and its potential output at full employment—that is, the difference between actual GNP (gross national product) and potential GNP.

Government Corporation Act of 1945 Federal legislation that directed the General Accounting Office to audit public corporations in terms of their performance rather than merely in terms of the legality and propriety of their expenditures.

Grant A transfer of funds from the federal government to another unit of government. The two major forms of federal grants are block and categorical.
1. *Block grants.* These are given primarily to general-purpose government units in accordance with a statutory formula. Such grants can be used for a variety of activities within a broad functional area. Examples of federal block grant programs are the Omnibus Crime Control and Safe Streets Act of 1968, the Comprehensive Employment and Training Act of 1973, the Housing and Community Development Act of 1974, and the 1974 amendments to the Social Security Act of 1935 (Title XX).
2. *Categorical grants.* These can be used only for specific programs and are usually limited to narrowly defined activities. Categorical grants consist of formula, project, and formula-project grants. Formula grants allocate federal funds to states or their subdivisions in accordance with a distribution formula prescribed by law or administrative regulation. Project grants provide federal funding for fixed or known periods for specific projects or for the delivery of specific services or products.

Grant-in-Aid For budget purposes, a grant-in-aid consists of a budget outlay by the federal government to support state or local programs of government service to the public. Grants-in-aid do not include purchases from state or local governments or assistance awards to other classes of recipients (for example, outlays for research or support of federal prisoners).

Gross National Product (GNP) The gross national product is the total productive activity in a country during a certain period of time. It is the sum of personal consumption plus gross private domestic investment plus government purchases of goods and services plus net exports of goods and services.

Identification Code An eleven-digit code assigned to each appropriation or fund account in the Budget of the United States Government that identifies (a) the agency; (b) the account; (c) the timing of the transmittal to Congress; (d) the type of fund; and (e) the account's functional classification. Such codes are common in budget systems.

Impoundment Any action or inaction by an officer or employee of the U.S. government that precludes the obligation or expenditure of budget authority provided by Congress.

Impoundment Resolution   A resolution by either the House of Representatives or the Senate that expresses disapproval of the president's proposed deferral of budget authority as set forth in a special message transmitted by the president, as required under Sec. 1013(a) of the Impoundment Control Act of 1974, P.L. 93–344, 31 U.S.C. 1403.

Income Tax   Revenue source used at all levels of government, but principally at the federal level. The tax is levied on the income of both corporations and individuals. It can be graduated or a flat percentage.

Incremental Budgeting   An approach to budgeting that focuses on the budget request, with emphasis on increases from the current year. Analysts of such a budget normally want information on all activities being planned in the budget year, but most of their attention will be on the program changes from the current year.

Incremental Funding   The provision or recording of budgetary resources for a program or project based on obligations estimated to be incurred within a fiscal year when such budgetary resources will cover only a portion of the obligations to be incurred in completing the program or project as planned. (The alternative is full funding, in which budgetary resources are provided or recorded for the total estimated obligations of a program or project in the initial year of funding.)

Indefinite Authority   Budget authority for which a specific sum is not stated but which is determined by other factors, such as the receipts from a certain source or obligations incurred. Borrowing authority that is limited to a specified amount that may become outstanding at any time (that is, revolving debt authority) is considered to be indefinite budget authority.

Indirect Cost   Any cost incurred for common objectives that therefore cannot be charged directly to any single cost objective. Indirect costs are allocated to the various classes of work in proportion to the benefit to each class. Indirect cost is also referred to as overhead or burden cost.

Inflation   A persistent rise in the general price level that results in a decline in the purchasing power of money.

Input   In a systems model, the resources used by a system to accomplish its work.

Internal Audit   An investigation of legality, effectiveness, and efficiency within the agency.

Internal Control   The plan of organization and all of the coordinating methods and measures adopted within a federal agency to safeguard the agency's assets, check the accuracy and reliability of its accounting data, promote operational efficiency, and encourage adherence to prescribed managerial policies.

Issue Assessment   A written presentation that identifies and describes the major features of a significant issue facing the government. The assessment is only a few pages long, but it clearly sets forth the ingredients that would be considered in preparing a study of a major issue.

Iterative   Refers to mathematical procedures that find an optimum figure by performing repeated calculations dealing with the same data.

Journal   A chronological listing of transactions, setting forth the date and dollar amount of each transaction and a brief explanation.

Lag   In regression calculations, observations for one of the variables may be "lagged" or shifted by one or more time periods to achieve a more realistic comparison between the variables. For instance, an advertising expenditure this month may affect sales for next month.

Least Squares   A basic method of fitting a regression line mathematically so that the sum of the squared errors is smaller than any other straight-line model.

Legal Reserve Requirement   One of the three tools used by the Federal Reserve to promote for economic stabilization. The Fed can tighten the money supply by requiring a greater reserve to be maintained, thus shrinking the amount available for loans. The converse normally increases the money supply.

Liability Amount owed for items received, services rendered, expenses incurred, assets acquired, or construction performed (regardless of whether invoices have been received); also, amounts received but as yet unearned.

Lien A claim on property arising from failure of the owner to make timely payment of a previous claim.

Line-Item Budget A budget format that presents the exact amount planned to be spent for every separate good or service to be purchased.

Macroeconomics The branch of economics concerned with aggregate economic analysis. Macroeconomics includes the study of the general price level, national output and income, and national employment.

Management by Objectives (MBO) A technique for establishing specific objectives for agencies; it requires regular periodic reports on the agency's progress toward achieving those objectives.

Method of Averages A technique of forecasting revenue by averaging the revenue generated over the last three to five years. It assumes the existence of a growth trend in the tax receipts and the economy.

Microeconomics The branch of economics concerned with the analysis of individual economic units, markets, or industries. Microeconomics includes the study of the prices of individual commodities, individual incomes, and the employment practices of individual firms. (*See also* Macroeconomics.)

Miller-Orr Model A method of determining a government's proposed fund cash balance that focuses on the upper dollar limit needed for cash purposes. When the cash balance touches the upper boundary, a predetermined amount of securities are automatically purchased. When the cash balance touches zero or an amount slightly above zero, then a predetermined amount of securities are sold, thus increasing the cash balance.

Monetary Policy Collectively, those policies affecting the money supply, interest rates, and credit availability that are intended to promote national macroeconomic goals, particularly with respect to employment, gross national product, price level stability, and equilibrium in balance of payments. Monetary policy is directed primarily by the Board of Governors of the Federal Reserve System and by the Federal Open Market Committee. Monetary policy works by influencing the cost and availability of bank reserves. This is accomplished through (a) open-market operations (the purchase and sale of securities, primarily government securities); (b) changes in the ratio of reserves to deposits that commercial banks are required to maintain; and (c) changes in the discount rate.

Money Supply The amount of money in the economy. The supply is divided into categories. M1-A consists of currency (coin and paper notes) plus demand deposits at commercial banks, foreign banks, official institutions, and the U.S. government. M1-B consists of M1-A plus other verifiable deposits, including negotiable orders of withdrawal and automatic transfers from savings accounts at commercial banks and thrift institutions, credit unions' shared draft accounts, and demand deposits at mutual savings banks. M-2 consists of M1-B plus savings and small denomination time deposits at all depository institutions, overnight repurchase agreements at commercial banks, Eurodollars held overnight by U.S. residents other than Caribbean branches of member banks, and money market mutual fund shares. M-3 consists of M-2 plus large denomination time deposits at all depository institutions and term repurchase agreements at commercial banks and savings and loan associations.

Monthly Treasury Statement (MTS) A summary statement prepared from agency accounting reports and issued by the Treasury Department. The MTS presents the receipts, outlays, and resulting budget surplus or deficit for the month and the fiscal year to date.

Mortgage Bond A type of bond that uses property to secure the debt obligation without transferring the title.

Moving Average   A method for using the average of past forecasting errors to calculate new forecasts.

Muckrakers   Journalists and book writers who document abuses and advocate reform; in the United States, their heyday was in the early twentieth century. As a result of their efforts, many government budgeting reforms were enacted successfully, especially at the municipal level.

Multiyear Authority   Budget authority that is available for a specified period of time in excess of one fiscal year. This authority generally takes the form of two-year, three-year, or some other yearly period of availability, but may cover periods that do not coincide with the start or end of a fiscal year. For example, the authority may be available from July 1 of one year through September 30 of the following fiscal year (15 months). This type of multiyear authority is sometimes referred to as forward funding.

Multiyear Budget Planning   A budget-planning process designed to make sure that the long-range consequences of budget decisions are identified and reflected in the budget totals.

National Income Accounts   Accounts prepared and published quarterly and annually by the U.S. Department of Commerce, providing a detailed statistical description of aggregate economic activity within the American economy. These accounts depict in dollar terms the composition and use of the nation's output and the distribution of national income to different recipients. The accounts make it possible to trace trends and fluctuations in economic activity.

Net National Product (NNP)   The net market value of finished goods and services produced by labor and property supplied by the residents of the United States. Net national product equals gross national product less capital consumption allowances, which are estimates of the value of the capital goods "used up" in producing the gross national product.

Nonguaranteed Debt   A long-term debt payable from earnings of revenue-producing activities, from special assessments, or from specific nonproperty taxes. The government does not guarantee its assets and earnings in support of the debt. Also known as moral debt.

No-Year Authority   Budget authority that remains available for obligation for an indefinite period of time, usually until the objectives for which the authority was made available are attained.

Object Classification   A uniform classification identifying the transactions of the government by the nature of the goods or services purchased (such as personnel compensation, supplies and materials, and equipment), without regard to the agency involved or the purpose of the programs for which they are used. Data category titles arranged by object classification are provided in an object classification schedule.

Obligational Authority   The sum of (a) budget authority provided for a given fiscal year, (b) balances of amounts brought forward from prior years that remain available for obligation, and (c) amounts authorized to be credited to a specific fund or account during that year, including transfers between funds or accounts.

Obligations Incurred   Amounts of orders placed, contracts awarded, services received, and similar transactions during a given period that will require payments during the same or a future period. Such amounts will include outlays for which obligations had not been previously recorded and will reflect adjustments for differences between obligations previously recorded and actual outlays to liquidate those obligations.

Observation   An individual value recorded for a variable. For example, in a list showing monthly telephone expenses for a year, the amount of the bill for any one month would constitute an observation.

Off-Budget Federal Entities   Certain federally owned and controlled entities whose transactions (for example, budget authority or outlays) have been excluded from budget totals by law. The fiscal activities of these entities are therefore not reflected in either budget authority or budget outlay totals. However, the outlays of off-budget federal entities are added to the budget deficit to derive the total government deficit that has to be financed by borrowing from the public or by other means.

Off-Budget Outlays Outlays of off-budget federal entities whose transactions have been excluded from the budget totals by law, even though these outlays are part of total government spending.

One-Year Authority Budget authority that is available for obligation only during a specified fiscal year and that expires at the end of that time. Also known as annual authority.

Open-Ended Expenditure Forecasting An approach to estimating future expenditures, based either on detailed work plans that often take months to prepare or on quick judgments involving a few minutes' preparation.

Open-Market Operations The purchase and sale in the open market of various securities, chiefly marketable federal government securities, by the Federal Reserve System for the purpose of implementing Federal Reserve monetary policy. Open-market operations, one of the most flexible instruments of monetary policy, affects the reserves of member banks and thus the supply of money and the availability and cost of credit.

Operating Budget The current year budget that guides agencies' everyday activities.

Outcome In the systems model used in this book, a benefit to individuals and society resulting from an agency program.

Outlay The liquidation of an obligation, usually by the issuance of a check or the disbursement of cash, but also by the maturing of interest coupons (in the case of some bonds), by the issuance of bonds or notes, or by increases in the redemption value of bonds outstanding. Outlays during a fiscal year may be for payment of obligations incurred in a prior year (prior year outlays) or in the same year. Outlays therefore derive partly from unexpended balances of prior year budget authority and partly from budget authority provided for the year in which the money is spent.

Output In the systems model used in this book, the specific products and services produced by a government unit.

Overhead Cost *See* Indirect Cost.

Oversight Committee The legislative committee charged with general oversight of the operation of an agency or program. In most cases, but not all, the oversight committee for an agency is also the authorizing committee for that agency's programs.

Performance Budgeting A budget format that presents government program input and output, thus allowing easy verification of the program's economy and efficiency.

Personal Income In the national income accounts, income received by persons (that is, individuals, nonprofit institutions, private uninsured welfare funds, and private trust funds) from all sources. These sources include production transfer payments from government and business and government interest, which is treated as a transfer payment. Personal income is the sum of wage and salary disbursements, other income from labor, proprietary income, rental income, dividends, personal interest income, and transfer payments, less personal contributions for social insurance.

Planning-Programming-Budgeting (PPB) An attempt in the federal government and some state and local governments to bring more analysis into the budgeting process. It is not itself an analytical technique, but it stresses the use of analytical tools in deciding budget issues related to specific government programs.

Policy Letter Document used in government to convey executive guidance and budget ceilings to the lower levels of the executive branch.

Potential Gross National Product An estimate of how much the economy could produce with full utilization of its productive resources and existing technology.

Prime Rate The rate of interest charged by commercial banks for short-term loans to their most credit-worthy customers.

Prior Year The fiscal year immediately preceding the current year.

Process Analysis   An analytical approach that seeks to determine if an agency's existing process makes effective use of resources and to identify idle or partly used resources.

Producer Price Index   A set of indicators that measure average changes in the prices received in all stages of processing by producers of commodities in the manufacturing, agriculture, forestry, fishing, mining, gas and electricity, and public utilities industries. Producer price indexes can be organized either by commodity or by stage of processing (finished goods, intermediate materials, or crude materials). Stage-of-processing indexes are more useful for analyzing general price trends. Formerly known as wholesale price index.

Productivity   A measure of efficiency, usually expressed as the ratio of the quantity of output to the quantity of input used in the production of that output. Usually it focuses on output per man-hour of change or on changes in cost per unit of output.

Program and Financial Plan (PFP)   A set of summary budget tables, categorized by major programs and activities. In the federal government, the PFP includes both obligations and disbursements. For some state and local governments, obligations alone or expenditures alone are sufficient. The information in a PFP covers the prior year, current year, budget year, and budget year plus five additional years. The PFP should reflect any policy changes; it is particularly useful prior to a budget call to forecast possible agency requests.

Program Budget   A budget format in which the budget material is arranged in such a way as to aid the executive and legislature to understand the broader policy implications of their decisions.

Project Grant   *See* Grant.

Property Tax   A revenue source for local and some state governments. Property (such as real estate) is normally assessed by the local government; then a tax rate is determined and applied on the basis of property value.

Quality Indicator   A measurement of characteristics, duration, content, extent, or degree used in evaluating outputs and outcomes.

Ratio Indicator   A measurement of the quantity of government service or product in relation to some larger entity such as population or area size.

Rational Decision-Making Model   An approach to budgeting that emphasizes (a) setting goals and objectives; (b) defining the alternatives: (c) analyzing the alternatives in terms of the established goals and objectives; and (d) selecting the best option.

Reactive Budget Decision Model   An approach to budgeting that is based on a stimulus-response pattern. Those who take this approach consider budgeting merely as a task to be done as defined in the job description. They act in response to the requirements of the budget calendar and the request, but give little thought to shaping events or making a difference.

Recession   A decline in overall business activity that is pervasive, substantial, and of at least several months' duration. Historically, recessions have been identified by a decline in gross national product for at least two consecutive quarters.

Registered Bonds   Type of bond that provides more protection to the bond holder because its ownership is registered on the books of the issuing government or its paying agent.

Regression   An analysis that expresses a dependent variable as the result of a formula approximation involving one or more independent variables.

Reimbursement   A repayment for commodities sold or services furnished, either to the public or to another government account, that is authorized by law to be credited directly to specific appropriation and fund accounts. These amounts are deducted from the total obligations incurred (and outlays) in determining net obligations (and outlays) for such accounts.

Reprogramming   Utilization of funds in an appropriation account for purposes other than those contemplated at the time of appropriation.

Repurchase Agreement   An innovation of government security dealers who recognize the selling potential of securities tailored to specific short time periods. Dealers agree to repurchase a security at a specific future date, thus increasing the number of transactions and the resulting total fees from those transactions.

Research and Development Research is systematic, intensive study directed toward fuller scientific knowledge or understanding of the subject studied. Development is the systematic use of the knowledge and understanding gained from research, directed toward the production of useful products or services.

Rescission The consequence of executive and legislative action that cancels budget authority previously provided by Congress before the time when the authority would otherwise have lapsed (that is, when appropriated funds would have ceased to be available for obligation). The Congressional Budget and Impoundment Control Act of 1974 (P.L. 93–344; 31 U.S.C. 1402) specifies that whenever the president determines that all or part of any budget authority will not be needed to carry out the full objectives or scope of programs for which the authority was provided, the president will propose to Congress that the funds be rescinded. Likewise, if all or part of any budget authority limited to a fiscal year—that is, annual appropriations, or budget authority of a multiyear appropriation in the last year of availability—is to be reserved from obligation for the entire fiscal year, a rescission will be proposed. Budget authority may also be proposed for rescission for reasons of fiscal policy or other reasons. Generally, an amount proposed for rescission is withheld for up to 45 legislative days while the proposal is considered by Congress. All funds for rescission, including those withheld, must be reported to Congress in a special message. If both houses have not completed action on the rescission proposed by the president within 45 calendar days of continuous session, any funds withheld must be made available for obligation.

Rescission Bill A bill or joint resolution that cancels, in whole or in part, budget authority previously granted by Congress. Rescissions proposed by the president must be transmitted in a special message to Congress. Under Sec. 1012 of the Congressional Budget and Impoundment Control Act of 1974 (P.L. 93–344), unless both houses of Congress complete action on a rescission bill within 45 days of continuous session after receipt of the proposal, the budget authority must be made restored. (*See also* Rescission.)

Reserve Requirement The percentage of deposit liabilities that U.S. commercial banks are required to hold as a reserve either at their Federal Reserve bank, as cash in their vaults, or as directed by state banking authorities. The reserve requirement is one of the three tools of monetary policy. Federal Reserve authorities can control the lending capacity of the banks (thus influencing the money supply) by varying the ratio of reserves to deposits that commercial banks are required to maintain.

Residuals The difference obtained when you subtract the forecast or "fitted" values from the actual values.

Revenue Forecasting Any of several systematic approaches used by governments to estimate the levels of revenue they can anticipate in future years.

Revenue Shaping The distribution, by formula, of federal funds to state and local governments, with few or no limits on the purposes for which the funds may be used and few restrictions on the procedures that must be followed in spending the funds.

Risk Control The reduction of risk or loss through careful procedures and practices in security, personnel safety, fire prevention, auto safety, product safety, environmental protection, and emergency resources.

Risk Funding The provision of sufficient funds to meet loss situations, if they occur, through the most effective use of internal and external financial resources.

Rule of Penultimate Year A technique for forecasting that calls for the forecaster to use the last completed year as a basis for estimating future revenue. This technique assumes growth in the economy and in related revenue sources.

Safety Stock The level of inventory that should be maintained for effective operations.

Scorekeeping A procedure for tracking the status of Congressional budgetary actions. Examples of scorekeeping documents are up-to-date tabulations and reports on Congressional actions affecting budget authority, receipts, outlays, surplus or deficit, and the public debt limit, as well as outlay and receipt estimates and reestimates. Scorekeeping data published by the Congressional Budget Office include, but are not limited to, status reports on the effects of Congressional actions (and, in the case of scorekeeping reports prepared for the Senate Budget Committee, the budget effects of potential Congressional actions), and comparisons of these actions to targets and ceilings set by Congress in the budget resolutions.

Second Concurrent Resolution on the Budget The annual resolution adopted by Congress that contains budget ceilings classified by function for budget authority and outlay and a floor for budget receipts. This resolution may retain or revise the levels set earlier in the year in the first concurrent resolution, and may include directives to the appropriations committees and to other committees with jurisdiction over budget authority or entitlement authority. The second resolution may also direct the appropriations committees to recommend changes in budget receipts or in the statutory limit on public debt. Changes recommended by various committees pursuant to the second budget resolution are reported in a reconciliation bill (or resolution, in some cases) on which Congress must complete action by September 25, a few days before the next fiscal year commences on October 1.

Serial Bond The most common type of bond It matures periodically (normally, every year).

Spectral Analysis Decomposing the data into a sum of trigonometric components to create waveform that is most appropriate for analyzing data with a pattern of repeating cycles.

Spending Authority The collective designation for appropriations, borrowing authority, contract authority, and entitlement authority for which the budget authority is not provided in advance by appropriation acts. The latter three authorities are also commonly referred to as backdoor authority.

Stagflation The simultaneous existence of high unemployment and high inflation.

State Space A forecasting technique that exploits the relationship of time series techniques to an advanced procedure called canonical correlation analysis.

Substantive Law Statutory public law other than appropriation law; sometimes referred to as basic law. Substantive law usually authorizes, in broad general terms, the executive branch to carry out a program of work. Annual determination of the amount of work to be done is usually thereafter embodied in appropriation law.

Supplemental Appropriation An act appropriating funds in addition to those in an annual appropriation act. Supplemental appropriations provide additional budget authority beyond the original estimates for programs or activities (including new programs authorized after the date of the original appropriation act) in cases where the need for funds is too urgent to be postponed until enactment of the next regular appropriation bill. Supplemental appropriations sometimes include items not appropriated in the regular bills for lack of timely authorizations.

Sunset Legislation Laws requiring the automatic expiration of government programs unless positive action is taken to renew them every few years by the legislature. In many cases, the sunset provisions permit the program to remain on the law books after the legal authorization for funds expires.

Tax Anticipation Note Borrowing by a local government against future anticipated tax revenue.

Tax Certificate A form of tax lien on property owned by a delinquent taxpayer. Tax certificates are negotiable securities and can be sold, as they represent a debt which must be liquidated before a clear title to the property can be given. At the sale of the property, certificates on the title are presented and the owner normally has one year to redeem them. If they are not redeemed, the property goes to the holder of the certificates.

Tax Credit Any special provision of law that results in a dollar-for-dollar reduction in tax liabilities that would otherwise be due. In some cases, tax credits may be carried forward or backward from one tax year to another; other tax credits lapse if not used in the year earned. Tax credits may result in a reduction of tax collections or an increase in the value of tax refunds.

Term Bond A bond that matures at one time. A sinking fund is normally used to accumulate the necessary funds over time.

Time Series The type of regression analysis employed in forecasting. It assumes that the data used was gathered at evenly spaced intervals in time. Box-Jenkins is an advanced form of time series analysis.

Transaction A financial decision, such as obligating money, deciding on disbursement, or setting aside funds for a purpose.

Transfer Payments Money moved from one government to another or to private persons. They often serve as automatic stabilizers built into the economy. These payments normally rise substantially during periods of recession and fall during periods of prosperity. For example, the unemployed receive unemployment compensation; in recessionary times they may eventually receive welfare and food stamps as well.

Transformation A mathematical adjustment made to a set of figures to improve the fit of the regression line.

Treasury Bills The shortest-term federal security. The maturity dates of treasury bills normally vary from three to twelve months. They are sold at a discount face value, instead of carrying a specific rate of interest.

Trend-Line Approach A forecasting technique that develops and extends an agency's trend line of expenditures or revenue from the past into the desired forecast period.

Unemployment Rate In economic statistics, the total number of people who, during a specific week, had no employment but were available for work and who sought employment within the past four weeks, were laid off from their jobs, or were waiting to report to a new job within 30 days; expressed as a percentage of the civilian labor force. (*See also* Employment Rate.)

Unemployment Rate, Insured The number of insured unemployed (that is, those persons who are eligible to receive unemployment compensation benefits) expressed as a percentage of covered employment.

Value The quantity of money, goods, or services that an article is likely to command in the long run as distinct from its price in an individual instance.

Variable An observable characteristic of an object or event that can be described according to some well defined classification or measurement scheme.

Volume Indicators The quantity of a government unit's service or products, such as the number of graduates from a university.

Voucher A document that confirms the fact that a financial transaction has taken place.

Wages and Salaries Monetary remuneration of employees, including the compensation, commissions, tips, bonuses, and receipts in kind that represent income to the recipients.

Warrant A banking service in which a draft is paid through a bank with the express permission of the government. It is used to slow and control disbursements. When a warrant is presented for payment, the bank will not pay until the warrant is accepted by the government.

Wholesale Price Index *See* Producer Price Index.

Wise Budget Model An approach to budgeting whose proponents recognize that politics is extremely important and sometimes of overriding importance. They also believe that, while analysis has its limitations, it can often help greatly in decision-making situations.

Zero-Base Budgeting (ZBB) An approach to public budgeting in which each budget year's activities are judged anew, with no reference to the policy precedents or dollar amounts of past years.

INDEX

Accelerated Cost Recovery Schedules (ACRS), 268
Accountability, 3, 128–31, 242
auditing and, 205, 207
management information system for, 227
Accountant's perspective on public budgeting, 4–5
Accounting, 8
budget execution and, 216
for financial administration, 245–48
accounting system design, 247–48
basic governmental accounting, 246–47
fundamentals of, 242–45
GAO principles of, 242–43
norms, budgeting and, 243–45
property accounting system, 329
reports and analyses, 248–57
appropriation and expense ledger, 249–51, 252
balance sheet, 254–56
fund balance change, 251–54
statement of revenue, 248–49
Accounts payable, 244, 263
Accrual method of accounting, 245
Accrued expenditure, 244
Accuracy, 80
in revenue forecasting, 144, 146–48
ACTION, 77, 78–79, 81
Acton, Lord, 83
Adaptive filtering, 150
Administrative controls, 224, 225
Administrative factors in municipal bond-rating process, 293
Administrative reservation, 224
Adoption of budget, legislative, 124–25
Advisory committee, 76
Advocates, reviews and, 93–94
Agency:
budget behavior, 82–85
defined, 71
interrelationships with other institutional roles, 71–73
as primary advocate, 93
role objectives and enemies of, 73–74
Agency budget format, 116
Agency budget office, duties of, 77, 78–79
Agency call, 115–16
Agents, fiscal or paying, 235, 236, 291–92
Aggregates in budget resolution, 56
Allied Chemical Company, 339
Allocation of sales tax, 324
Allotments, 12, 13, 219–24
Alpha factor weight, 150
Alternative choice models, 160–61
America in Ruins: Beyond the Public Works Pork Barrel (Choate), 267–68

American Bar Association, 332
American Continental Congress, 207
American Institute of Certified Public Accountants (AICPA), 207, 245
American Municipal Bond Assurance Corporation (AMBAC), 272, 273
American option, 274
American Revolution of 1776, 36, 37
American Society for Public Administration (ASPA), 175
Analysis applied to budgeting, 127–65
benefit-cost analysis, 159–63
crosswalks, 140–42
data measure constraints, 136–38
difficulties in, 134–36
mix-ups, 134
nonperformance option, 136
staff and service units, 135–36
with types of output measures, 135
elementary analysis, 138–40
defining relationships, 138
marginal cost and discounting, 139–40
expenditure forecasting, 148–52
bargaining and unit cost approaches, 148–49
expenditure econometric model, 151–52
time series methods, 149–51
planning and analysis phase of budget cycle, 10, 11
PPB as attempt to institutionalize analysis, 47
productivity analysis, 131, 152–59
budget justification and, 155–59
defining productivity, 152–53, 154
reasons for loss of productivity, 153
simple regression analysis, 153–55, 156
revenue forecasting, 142–48
approaches to, 142–44
econometric forecasts, 144–45
forecasting practices, 146–48
theoretical foundation for, 128–34
Budget System Approach and accountability, 128–31
program impact theory, 131–34
Analytical constraints, 159
Analytical processes, 166–212
budget examination, 166, 173–93
automation and, 190–93
code of ethics in, 174–78
detailed, 189–90
of emphasis and change, 182–84
exploring private options, 186–87
of forecasting, 187–88
information sources for, 174
of politically sensitive subjects, 188–89

of program effectiveness and efficiency, 185–86
of program inputs and outputs, 179–82
of responsiveness to policy, 184–85
of services performed, 178–79
process analysis, 166, 193–202
advantages of, 199–200
context in, 200–201
cooptation problems, 202
focus of, 193–99
honesty in, 202
needed interpersonal skills for, 201
program analysis, 166, 167–73
chief executive's role in, 173
commentary on, 170–72
issue assessment, 168–70
presentation of results of, 172–73
selecting issues, 167–68, 169–70
program evaluation, 166, 202–5
use of, 209–10
"Anniversary put," 274
Annual report on budget options, CBO, 57
Anti-Deficiency Act, 83, 84, 214
Anti-Kickback Act (1986), 332
Appropriation and expense ledger, 249–51, 252
Appropriation laws, 56, 124
Appropriations, 12–13
contingency, 218
permanent, 58
unobligated or disobligated, 95
Appropriation-to-unit crosswalk, 141
Aristotle, 207
Aronson, J. Richard, 230, 231, 248, 249, 250, 252, 253, 332
Arrogance of budget officer, 83
Articles of Confederation, 36
Assessment and taxation of property, 314–21
Assets, 246, 254
AT&T pension fund, 353
Audit agencies, 13
Audit and evaluation phase, 10, 13–14
Auditing, 166, 205–9
internal versus external audits, 206–7
principles, 207–9
property management and, 329
purpose of, 205–6
Authorizations, 12–13
bond authority, 12
borrowing authority, 58
contract authority, 12, 13, 58
operating budget, 215
reprogramming authority, 218
transfer authority, 218
Automation of budget preparation process, 190–93

Autoregressive models, 150
Autoregressive moving averages (ARMA), 150–51
Averages, method of, 143
Awards for Distinguished Budget Presentations, 105–7

"Back-door selling," 331
Backdoor spending, 58–59
Backlog of requests or tasks, pointing out, 96
Baker v. *Carr*, 303
Balanced Budget Act of 1985 (revised 1987), 66
Balanced budgets, 3, 17, 108–9
Balance of power between legislative and executive branches, 37
Balance sheet, 254–56
Balloon, 286
Bankruptcy law, Chapter 9 of federal, 281–82
Bank services, commercial, 234–36
Bar-code technology, 336–37
Bargaining approach to expenditure forecasting, 148
Barter economy, 23
Base, income tax, 323
Baseline budget projections, CBO, 55, 56
Beame, Abraham, 4
Beard, Charles, 39
Behavior, budget. *See* Budget behavior
Behavioral sciences, concepts from, 8
Belt-tightening, 308
Benefit-cost analysis, 159–63
Benefit package, 354
Benefit policy, 353
Bidder anticompetition practices, 331
Bidding. *See* Competitive bidding
Blair, Louis, 170
Bland, Robert L., 235, 241, 291
Boesky, Ivan, 269
Boiling, Richard, 61
Boll Weevils, 62
Bonafede, Dom, 31
Bond(s), 262
   capital appreciation, 274
   compound interest, 274
   "efficient," 287
   "front-loaded," 287
   lease rental, 267
   mini-municipal, 275
   mortgage, 262
   municipal, 268–70, 287
   nontraditional ways to package, 265, 270–82
   original issue discount (OLD), 274
   "plain vanilla," 286
   revenue, 263, 266–67, 269, 273, 280, 293
      industrial, 267, 269
      industrial tax-exempt, 273
      lease, 263

serial, 262, 286
small denomination, 275
special obligation, 267
"story," 286
term, 262
zero coupon, 270, 271
Bond anticipation notes (BANs), 266
Bond authority, 12
Bond counsel, need for, 289–90
Bonding, 285–99
   bond prospectus, notice of sale and sale, 290–92
   bond ratings, 292–99
   debt records and reporting, 292
   designing issue, 285–90
Bond insurance premium, 272–73
Bond Investors Guaranty (BIG), 273
Borrowing authority, 58
Botner, Stanley B., 192, 193, 209–10
Box-Jenkins method, 150–51
Break-even analysis, 324
Bricklin, Daniel, 191
Briefing books for hearings, 92
Brookings Institution, 39
Brownlow Committee, 41
Buck, A.E., 39
Budget, 5–6
   building, 112–16
      agency call, 115–16
      budget coordination, 112–14
      budget guidance, 114–15
      program financial schedule, 112
   operational definition of, 6–7
   origins of word, 35–36
   purposes behind, 44–46
Budget and Accounting and Procedures Act of 1950, 42
Budget behavior, 70–102
   politics and perspectives, 71–93
      agency budget behavior, 82–85
      agency budget office, 77, 78–79
      cultivation of active clientele, 75–76
      to develop confidence, 87–89
      institutional roles in, 71–75
      perspective of budget officer, 77–81
      preparing for hearings, 91–93
      reactions to normative theories, 85–87
      results and, 89–91
   strategies, 93–101
      cautions in, 100–101
      cutters' strategies, 97–100
      new programs, 96, 100
      reviewers vs. reviewed, 93–95
      spenders' strategies, 95–97
Budget call, 114–16
Budget controls, types of, 224
Budget cycle, 7–8, 10–14
   for capital budgeting, 285
   local government, 14
   nature of, 10
   phases of, 10, 11–14
Budget Enforcement Act of 1990, 66

Budget examination. *See under* Analytical processes
Budget execution system, 214–17, 218
Budget formats, 103–11
   of agency budget, 116
   distinguished budgets, 105–7
   as important means, 103–5
   influence of ends on choosing, 108–11
Budgeting and Accounting Act of 1921, 40–41
Budget justification:
   productivity measures melded into, 155–59
   program impact theory and, 132
Budget officer:
   behavior of, 82–84
   major concerns of, 105
   perspective of, 77–81
Budget preparation subsystem, 228
Budget realities, 7–9
Budget reforms, 8–9, 54–58
Budget resolution, 56, 121
Budget status subsystem, 228
Budget System Approach, 128–31
Budget-wise person, 87
Budget year (BY), 6
Budget year plus one (BY + 1), 6
Bureau of Census, 261
Bureau of the Budget (BOB), 40, 41, 42
Burke, Edmund, 38
Bush, George, federal budget process under, 63–66

Caiden, Naomi, 63
Calendar, budget, 112–14
California's Proposition 13, 278, 305, 311
Call:
   agency, 115–16
   budget, 114–16
Call provision, 238
CALPERS, 353
Capital appreciation bond, 274
Capital budgeting, 282–85
   capital budget cycle, 285
   capital facilities planning, 284
   operating budget versus, 282–83
Capital financing. *See also* Debt:
   in 1980s, 267–70
   nontraditional, 270–82
      government financial emergencies, 281–82
      methods, 270–77
      New York City financial crisis, 280–81
      tests and limits on debt, 277–80
   options, 265
Capital Guaranty Insurance Company, 273
Capitalism, 16–17, 21–22
Carrying cost, 334
Carter, Jimmy, 9, 30, 50, 61
Carter administration, 207, 305

Cash concentration accounts, 235
Cash flow, 228
Cash flow problem, 228–29
Cash internal control, 225–27
Cash management, 228–34
Cash Management Improvement Act,
    234
Cash method of accounting, 245
Cash position, 230
Cash receipts, logging of, 226
Categories, recasting budget into
    different, 95
Categorizations, 183
Causal methods of revenue forecasting,
    143–45
Cause and effect chain, 128, 129, 132
Causes, political, 10
Center for the Study of the States, 147
Central bank, 25–26
Centralized state pension system, 356
Central purchasing agent, 330
Central stores, 334–35
Certificate of Achievement for Excel-
    lence in Financial Reporting,
    246
Certificate of Conformance in Financial
    Reporting program, 105–6
Certificate of deposit (CD), 240
Certificates of indebtedness, 262
Certificates of participation (COPs),
    263, 275–77
Chang, Semoon, 144
Changes, examination of budget,
    182–84
Charles I and II, Kings, 36
Chase Econometrics, 144
Checks, control of, 225–27
Chelimsky, Eleanor, 205
Chief executive, 71
    briefing on budget, 117
    role in program analysis, 173
    role objectives and enemies of, 74
Choate, Pat, 267–68
Choice models, 160–61
Choice set, 159
Circuit breakers, 310, 315
City of Tamarac, liability damage
    awards in, 339
Classification Act of 1949, 42
Clientele:
    cultivation of active, 75–76
    defined, 71
    interrelationships with other
        institutional roles, 71–73
    role objectives and enemies of, 75
Clinton, Bill, 64
Code of ethics, 174–78
Coe, Charles K., 226, 227, 232–33,
    332
Coefficient of dispersion, 317, 318
Collectively consumed goods, adequate
    supply of, 27
Colonial America, public budgeting
    in, 37
Colorado, sunset legislation in, 63
Commercial bank services, 234–36

Commercial paper, tax-exempt
    (TECP), 266, 273–74
Commission on Economy and Efficiency
    Goals report, 40
Committee on Administration
    Management, 41
Commodity coding, 332
Communication, risk management
    and, 350
Communism, 16
Competitive bidding, 225, 291
    for bonding, 285
    constraints on, 331
    for depository service bank, 235
    for insurance, 348–49
    purchases made by, 330–31
Compound interest bond, 274
Comprehensive Annual Financial
    Report (CAFR), 246
Computers:
    bar-code technology and, 336–37
    budget preparation on, 191–93
    computerizing accounting system,
        256–57
Concentration account, pooling of
    cash balances into central,
    237
Conceptual model, 18
Conference committees, 94
Confidence in program and officials,
    building:
    of budget reviewers, developing,
        87–89
    hearings preparation and, 91–93
    professionalism and, 82–83
    results and, 89–91
Conflict, intralegislative, 94–95
Congress:
    audit and evaluation activities
        conducted by, 13
    unified and comprehensive approach
        to public budgeting, 38
Congressional Budget and Impound-
    ment Control Act of 1974,
    54–62, 119
    backdoor spending, control of, 58–
        59
    on impoundment powers, 59–61
    reconciliation provision of, 61–62
    reform motivations of, 54
    unified congressional budget
        reforms of, 54–58
Congressional Budget Office (CBO),
    24, 54, 55–58
    annual report sent to budget
        committees, 120
    baseline budget projections, 55, 56
    responsibilities of, 57–58
Congressional budget timetable,
    119–21
Consensus forecasting, 188
Consistency, crosswalks to determine,
    142
Constitution, U.S., 36
    Article I, Section 9 of, 37
    Tenth Amendment to, 352

Contingency appropriations, 218
Contingent liability, 263
Continuing resolution, 56, 120
Contract authority, 12, 13, 58
Contracting out a service to private
    sector, 187
Contract liability, 345
Contributions to pension fund, 354
Control(s), 3
    administrative, 224, 225
    allotments, 12, 13, 219–24
    cash internal, 225–27
    costs of, 46
    designing, 214–19
        budget execution, 214–17, 218
        current year adjustments, 218–
            19, 220–21
        fixing responsibility, 214
        pitfalls to avoid, 217–18
    expenditure, 224–25
    in local government budgets, 14
    management information system
        for, 227
    property, 335–36
    as purpose of budget, 44–46
    records, 336
    risk, 344–46
Cooperation, risk management and,
    350
Cooperative intergovernmental
    purchasing arrangements,
    333–34
Cooptation, 202
Coordination, budget, 112–14
Cope, Glen Hahn, 158
Corrective maintenance, 338
Cost(s):
    in accounting, 244
    direct, 182
    fixed, 139
    inventory, 334–35
    opportunity, 4, 160, 163
    recurring, 139
Cost approach to assessment, 315
Cost-benefit analysis, 159–63
Cost-effectiveness analysis, 159,
    185
Cost estimates required of CBO, 57
Cost-volume-profit (CVP), 324
Council of Economic Advisors, 24
Creative bonds, 265
Creative capital financing, 270–82
Credit:
    letter of (LOC), 236, 271–72
    line of, 271–72
    monetary policy and available, 26
Credit controls, selected, 26
Credits, debits and, 247
Crime coverage, 349
Cromwell, Oliver, 36
Crosswalks, 140–42
Current Services Budget, 120
Current services estimates, OMB, 55
Current year adjustments, 218–19,
    220–21
Current year (CY), 6

Cutback management, 98–100
Cutters' strategies, 97–100
Cutting budgets, rationales given for, 94

Daily financial reports, 224
Darwin, Charles, 24
Data measure, 133
  constraints, 136–38
Data Resources, Inc., 144, 151
Deadlines, 80
  congressional, 119–20
Debits and credits, 247
DeBoer, Larry, 320–21
Debt, 260–301
  beneficial aspects of large national
    public, 29
  bonding, 285–99
    bond prospectus, notice of sale
      and sale, 290–92
    bond ratings, 292–99
    debt records and reporting, 292
    designing issue, 285–90
  capital budgeting, 282–85
  nontraditional capital financing,
    270–82
    government financial emergen-
      cies, 281–82
    methods, 270–77
    New York City financial crisis,
      280–81
    tests and limits on debt, 277–80
  state and local, 261–70
    capital financing in 1980s, 267–
      70
    classification of debt, 262–65
    defining debt, 261–62
    early developments in debt con-
      cept, 266–67
    short-term debt, 265–66
Debt burden, 293
Debt factors in municipal bond-
  rating process, 293
Decision-making models, 18–21
  typical reactions to, 85–87
Decision packages in ZBB, 51
Default risk, 238
Deferral type of impoundment, 59,
  60
Deficit:
  growth in federal, 63–64
  as percent of GNP, 65
Deficit spending, 28–29
Delay as cutters' strategy, 97
Demand account, 235
Demand-responsive programs, 188
  budget examination of services
    performed in, 178
Democracy in U.S., 15
Depression, 22
Descartes, Rene, 132
Detailed budget examination, 189–
  90
Detailed revenue and expenditure
  estimates, 118–19
Diffusion of power, 15

Direct costs, 182
Direct deposits, 235
Directed programs, budget examina-
  tion of services performed in,
  178
Disability/survivor protection of
  pension, 354–55
Disagreements, minimizing or
  surfacing, 80
Discounting to present value, 139–40
Discount rate, 25
  in benefit-cost analysis, 162
Discounts, trade, 237
Disobligated appropriations, 95
Dispersion, coefficient of, 317, 318
Dorsey, Thomas A., 316
Doss, C. Bradley, Jr., 265, 282
Double coverage of pension, 354
Double-entry system, 246–47
Druker, Marvin, 99
Duncombe, Sydney, 2, 3, 84, 85
Dutchess County, New York, liability
  damage awards in, 339

Earmarked revenue, 58–59
Econometric model:
  expenditure, 151–52
  revenue, 144–45
Economic concepts, spender strategy
  using, 96
Economic factors in S & Ps municipal
  bond-rating process, 293
Economic growth, steady constant,
  27
Economic influences on public
  budgeting, 21–25
Economic Ordering Quality (EOQ),
  230–31, 335
Economic Recovery Tax Act of 1981
  (ERTA), 268
Economics, using concepts from, 8
Economist's perspective on public
  budgeting, 4
Education, property tax and, 311–13
*Effective Budgetary Presentations:
  The Cutting Edge* (Miller),
  105
Effectiveness analysis, 131
  budget examination of program
    effectiveness, 185–86
Efficiency, budget examination of
  program, 185–86
"Efficient" bonds, 287
Electronic spreadsheet, use of, 191–
  93
Ellis, Curtis, 226, 227
Emergencies, government financial,
  281–82
Emergency preparedness, 345
Emergency provisions, 218
Emergency public works programs,
  29
Emotional strategy, 96
Emphases, examination of budget,
  182–84
Employee benefits, 349

Encumbrances, 225, 244
England, Parliament versus king in,
  35–37
English Bill of Rights of 1688,
  36
Entitlement programs, 29, 58
Envelope budgeting, 52–53
Environmental protection, 345
Equalization rate, state, 315–16
Equities, 246
Ethics, code of, 174–78
Ethics and Quality Purchasing
  (Zemansky), 332
European option, 274
Evaluation:
  audits and, 10, 13–14
  program, 166, 202–5
  risk, 339–44
Executive. *See* Chief executive
Executive branch:
  Budget and Accounting Act of
    1921 and strength of, 40–41
  power of, under Reagan, 53
  tension between legislative branch
    and, 35–37, 54
Executive budget document, 118–19
Executive budget hearings, 116–17
Executive focus in public budgeting,
  46–53
  management-by-objectives (MBO),
    49
  planning-programming-budgeting
    (PPB), 46–49
  under Reagan and Bush, 53
  target-base budgeting (envelope
    budgeting), 52–53
  zero-base budgeting (ZBB),
    50–52
Executive legislative clearance
  process, 53
Executive Office of the President, 41
Executive Order 12291, 53
Expenditure controls, 224–25
Expenditure estimates, detailed,
  118–19
Expenditure forecasting, 148–52
  bargaining and unit cost
    approaches, 148–49
  expenditure econometric model,
    151–52
  time series methods, 149–51
Expenditures, 17, 244
Expert judgment, 143
Exponential smoothing, 150
Exposure identification, 339–44
External audits, 206–7
External credit support, 271–73
Externalities, 160, 162

Favors, minimizing granting, 89
Federal agency securities, 240
Federal budget (1992), 9
Federal budget cycle, 10–14
Federal Electronic Funds Transfer
  System, 234–35
Federal income tax, start of, 39

Federalism, 17–18
fiscal, latest trend in, 305–8
Federalist faction, 38
Federalist Paper No. 10, 15
Federal Reserve Communication Systems, 235
Federal Reserve System, 24, 25–26
Open Market Committee, 25
Federal Tax Act (TEFRA, 1982), 268
Feedback mechanisms, 128
Fidelity exposure, measuring, 340
Finance, using concepts from, 8
Financial administration, accounting for, 245–48
Financial advisory assistance in bonding, 288–89
Financial emergencies, government, 281–82
Financial Guaranty Insurance Company (FGIC), 273
Financial management. See Internal service functions
Financial Trend Monitoring System (FTMS), 279
Fire insurance, 348
Fiscal agents, 291–92
Fiscal analysis, CBO, 57
Fiscal factors in municipal bond-rating process, 293
Fiscal federalism, latest trend in, 305–8
Fiscal impact analysis, 148
Fiscal policy, 27–32
policy goals, 27
public budgeting and, 31–32
role of government in, 27–29
using, 29–31
Fiscal year (FY), 6
Fischer, Philip J., 289
Fisk, Donald, 170
Fixed costs, 139
Fleet safety, 345
Flexibility:
in budget execution, 218
gimmicks and, 82
Float, 234–35
Florida:
code of ethics for budget analysts in, 176–78
consensus forecasting in, 188
sunset legislation in, 63
Flow charting in process analysis, 194–98
Forbes, Ronald W., 271, 289
Ford, Gerald, 60
Ford administration, test of impound-ment process in, 60–61
Forecasting:
examination of, 187–88
expenditure, 148–52
bargaining and unit cost ap-proaches, 148–49
expenditure econometric model, 151–52
time series methods, 149–51
revenue, 142–48

approaches to, 142–44
econometric forecasts, 144–45
forecasting practices, 146–48
Foreclosure, 320
Format, budget. See Budget formats
Forrester, John, 146
Franchise to private firm, awarding, 187
Frank, Howard, 146
Frankston, Robert, 191
Fraud:
cash internal control to prevent, 225–27
contracting out cash management and, 239
Fraud/red-tape dilemma, 225
Friendships, professional, 88
"Front-loaded" bonds, 287
Full employment, 27
Full Employment Act of 1946, 42
"Full-faith-and-credit" debt, 263
Fully funded pension funds, 351
Functional allocations of spending in budget resolution, 56
Fund, 245
crosswalk between line-item and, 141
Fund balance, 246
Fund balance change, 251–54
Fund transfer, 95–96
Future needs, influence on budget, 5

Gallatin, Albert, 38
Gardner, Ella P., 192
General Accepted Accounting Principles (GAAP), 245
General Accounting Office (GAO), 41, 42, 206–7
audit and evaluation activities conducted by, 13
audit standards, 206, 207, 208
principles of accounting, 242–43
General obligation (GO), 263, 264, 270
Germany, hyperinflation of 1923 in, 23
Gimmicks, 82
Glossary, 361–79
Gold, Steven, 147
Gore, Al, 66
Gottschalk, Earl C., Jr., 239
Government, public's view of role of, 24
Governmental Accounting, Auditing, and Financial Reporting, 292
Governmental Accounting Standards Board (GASB), 129, 133–34, 242, 245, 357–58
Government Corporations Act of 1945, 42
Government Finance Officers Asso-ciation (GFOA), 67, 105–7, 133, 246, 285, 292
Code of Professional Ethics, 175–76

Government financial emergencies, 281–82
Grafton, Carl, 66
Gramm-Latta I and II, 62
Gramm-Rudman-Hollings Act (Bal-anced Budget Act of 1985), 66
Grant anticipation notes (GANs), 266
Grants, 187, 190, 244–45
Great Depression, 22, 24
Grizzle, Gloria A., 142, 146
Gross domestic product (GDP), 27, 28
Gross national product (GNP):
deficit as percent of, 65
defined, 27
1991, 28
tax revenues as percentage of (1948–1989), 305, 306–7
Group replacement, 332
Guarantee program, private bond, 272
Gubernatorial policy, executive budget document as instrument of, 3
Guidance, budget, 114–15
Gulick, Luther, 39

Hackbart, Merl M., 263, 264
Hamilton, Alexander, 37–38, 41
Hard data, 183
Harvard Business Review, 50
Hatry, Harry P., 168, 170, 173
Havens, Harry, 204
Hearings:
executive budget, 116–17
legislative, 122
preparing for, 91–93
Hegel, Georg Wilhelm Friedrick, 38
"Hidden" revenue, 97
Hills, Carla A., 60
History of public budgeting, 35–69
in colonial America, 37
in 1800s, 37–38
in England, 35–37
evolution of public budgeting, 39–46
approaches to budgeting by 1950s, 42–46
Budgeting and Accounting Act of 1921, 40–41
post–1940 reforms, 42
prior to 1921, 39–40
executive focus, 46–53
management-by-objectives (MBO), 49
planning-programming-budge-ing (PPB), 46–49
under Reagan and Bush, 53
target-base budgeting (envelope budgeting), 52–53
zero-base budgeting (ZBB), 50–52
legislative focus, 54–67
backdoor spending, 58–59
federal budgetary madness in: Reagan-Bush years, 63–66

impoundment, 58–61
1974 budget reform motivations,
54
reconciliation, 61–62
state and local challenges, 67
sunset legislation, 63
unified congressional budget
reforms, 54–58
Progressive reform movement, 16,
38–39
Hitch, Charles, 47
Honesty of budget analysts, 202
Hoover Commissions (1947, 1955),
42, 45, 46, 133
Hopewell, Virginia, liability damage
awards in, 339
Hough, Wesley C., 276, 277
House of Representatives
Appropriations Committee, 24, 38
appropriations subcommittees, 56
Budget Committee, 24, 54
origination of revenue and
appropriations matters in, 37
Ways and Means Committee, 24
*How Effective Are Your Community
Services* (Urban Institute),
204
Human rights, minority and
fundamental, 15
Hush, Lawrence W., 283
Hyperinflation, 22, 23

**Ideal-rational model of decision
making, 19–20, 21**
Ideology, influence of, 14–17
Idle cash, 229
investments of, 237–41
Illegal assessment, 319
*Immigration and Naturalization
Service* v. *Chadha*, 60
Immunity, tort doctrine of government,
339
Impact fee, 325
Impoundment, 12, 58–61
Improved programs, conditions for
funding, 184–85
Improvisational budgeting, 66
Income approach to assessment, 315
Income tax, 39, 308, 322–23
Incremental approach in expenditure
forecasting, 149
Incremental budgeting, 7, 44
Incremental change model of decision
making, 19, 20
Incremental cost, 334
Indexing of pension fund, 354
Industrial revenue bonds, 267, 269
Industrial tax-exempt revenue bond,
273
Inequitable assessment, 319
Inflation, 22–23
optimal, 27
pension funds and, 354
unemployment and, 23, 30
Inflation analysis, CBO, 57
Information sources, 174

Information to Applicants (Dept. of
Transportation), 72
Input(s), 128
budget examination of program,
179–82
Inspection:
of goods procured, 331–32
internal, 206
Inspector General Act of 1978, 207
Institutional roles in public budgeting,
71–75
interrelationships of, 71–73
role objectives and enemies, 73–75
Instrumentation, 204
Insurance:
competitive bidding for, 348–49
defined, 347
municipal bond, 273
risk management and, 340, 348–49
self-insurance, 346–48
Insurance premium, bond, 272–73
Intangibles, 161
Integrated financial management
systems (IFMS), 228, 229
Interagency and intraagency
cooperation, efficiencies
from, 186
Interest paid:
net, 278
to service federal budget, 65
Interest rates, monetary policy and,
26
Intergovernmental purchasing
arrangements, cooperative,
333–34
Intergovernmental revenue systems,
302–8
Internal audits, 206
Internal control:
accounting system design for, 247
cash, 225–27
failures of, 226–27
Internal inspections, 206
Internal Revenue Service, 266
Internal service functions, 328–59
pension funds, 351–58
budget concerns in, 351–52
investment process for, 352–53
policy issues in, 353–58
property maintenance, 338
property management, 329–37
bar-code technology, 336–37
central stores and inventory,
334–35
preliminary review of, 329
procurement, 330–32
property control, 335–36
purchasing, 330–34
purchasing challenges, selected,
332–34
risk management, 338–50
administration of, 349–50
exposure identification and risk
evaluation, 339–44
insurance, 340, 348–49
risk control, 344–46

risk funding and self-insurance,
346–48
International City Management
Association, 279
International Communications
Agency, 91
Interperiod equity, 242
Interpersonal skills of budget analyst,
201
Intralegislative conflict, 94–95
Inventory, 244, 334–35
Inventory costs, 334–35
Inventory of property, 329
for risk evaluation, 340
Investment:
in marketable securities, 237–41
portfolio, 240–41
types of securities, 239–40
for pension funds, 352–53
Investment policy, 353
Investment Tax Credit (ITC), 29,
268
Investors, indicators used by, 278–79
Issues for analysis:
assessment of, 168–70
selecting, 167–70

James II, King, 36
Jargon, avoiding, 172
Jasper, Herbert, 54
"Jawboning," 26
Jefferson, Thomas, 38
Joehnk, Michael O., 272
John, King, 36
Johnson, Lyndon B., 9, 29, 30, 47
Joint Economic Committee, 24
Journal, 246
Judgement, 263
Judgmental revenue forecasting,
143
Junk bond crisis, 269
Jurisdictions, overlapping of, 18

Kane, Thomas J., Jr., 216
Kee, James Edwin, 303
Kenney, Richard, 84, 85
Kidwell, David S., 272
Kimmel, Wayne, 170
King of England and Parliament,
struggle between, 35–37
Klay, William Earle, 142, 143, 146
Kramer, Fred A., 139

**Labor-management negotiations,
pension policy and, 352**
Laffer, Arthur B., 30
Laffer curve, 30–31
Laissez faire government, 24
Lauth, Thomas, 130
"Leapfrogging," 352
Lease, leasing, 274–75, 336
Lease-backed debt, 263, 264
Lease rental bond, 267
Lease revenue bonds, 263
Least-cost purchasing, 332–33
Least squares, method of, 153

Ledger, 246
    appropriation and expense, 249–51, 252
Lee, Robert D., Jr., 129–30, 131
Legal transactions, charges for, 326
Legislative adoption of budget, 124–25
Legislative analyst's review sheet, 122, 123
Legislative branch, tension between executive branch and, 35–37, 54
Legislative clearance process, OMB, 53
Legislative focus in public budgeting, 54–67
    backdoor spending, 58–59
    federal budgetary madness in Reagan-Bush years, 63–66
    impoundment, 58–61
    1974 budget reform motivations, 54
    reconciliation, 61–62
    state and local challenges, 67
    sunset legislation, 63
    unified congressional budget reforms, 54–58
Legislative program, budget as chief executive's, 5
Legislative tracking subsystem, 228
Legislature:
    budget consideration in, 121–24
    defined, 71
    interrelationships with other institutional roles, 71–73
    role objectives and enemies of, 74–75
Lehan, Edward Anthony, 104, 109, 275
Leigland, James, 263, 264
Letter of credit (LOC), 236, 271–72
Leverage lease, 274, 275
Liabilities, 246, 254. See also Pension funds
    contingent, 263
    contract, 345
    third-party, 339
    unfunded pension, 263
Liability coverage, 349
Liberal movement, 16
Lien, 263
    tax, 320
Life-cycle costing, 332
Line-item, 140–41
Line-item budgeting, 42–44, 105, 108
Line-item format, 104, 109
Line manager:
    establishing professional relationship between analyst and, 202
    proactive posture of, 201
    process analysis and improvement of, 199–200
Line of credit, 271–72
"Loan-to-lender" financing, 273

Lobbying, 15, 71, 73, 75
Local government budget cycle, 14. See also State and local governments
Lock box systems, 235
Logical positivism, 203
Long-term securities, 238
Loyalty to agency, 73–74, 82
Lynn, James T., 60

McCollough, Jane, 146
McKernan, John R., Jr., 147
McNamara, Robert, 47
Macroeconomics, 32
    goals in, 27
    role of government in, 27–29
Madison, James, 36–37, 64
Magna Carta, 36
Maier, Henry, 4
Maintenance cost, estimating, 332–33
Maintenance prevention, 338
Management:
    formats to improve government, 109
    impact of microcomputer on concerns of, 191–92
    process analysis and improvement of, 199–200
    as purpose of budget, 44, 46
Management-by-objectives (MBO), 49
    crosswalk between MBO objectives and program or appropriation structure, 141
    operating budget and, 13, 215
Management information systems (MIS), 227–28, 229
Management Policies in Local Government Finance (Aronson and Schwartz), 332
Marginal cost analysis, 139
Marketability, 238
Marketable securities, investment in, 237–41
    portfolio, 240–41
    types of securities, 239–40
Market price, defined, 314
Market yield, 238
Massachusetts Welfare Model, 151–52
Mattson, Gary, 100
Maxwell School of Syracuse University, 39
Mayo, OMB Director, 72
Median assessment ratio, 317, 318
Menson, Thomas P., 174
Message, budget, 118
Microcomputer, budget preparation and, 191–93
Milestones, budget, 119–20
Miller, Girard, 105, 124n, 352
Miller-Orr Model, 231–32
Minimizing disagreement, 80
Mini-municipal bonds, 275
Minority and fundamental human rights, 15

Model Procurement Code, 332
Modern budgeting, start of, 38–39. See also History of public budgeting
Modified accrual method of accounting, 245–46
Monetary policy, 25–26, 29, 30
Monthly financial reports, 224
Monthly performance reports, 224
Moody's Investors Service:
    credit-rating change for New York City, 280
    municipal bond-rating process, 293–99
Moral debt, 263
"Moral suasion," 26
Morgan Guarantee Trust, 281
Mortgage bonds, 262
Mosher, 207
Motawi, Magda H., 192
Moving averages, 150
    autoregressive (ARMA), 150–51
Muckrakers, 38
Multiple regression analysis, 155, 314
Municipal Assistance Corporation, 275
Municipal bond insurance, 273
Municipal Bond Insurance Association (MBIA), 272, 273
Municipal bonds. See also Bonding
    market in 1980s for, 268–70
    taxable, 269
    tax advantage for, 287
Municipal budget system, 39
Municipal credit assistance, 273
Municipal Finance Officers Association, 356
Municipal multiplier, 274
Murray, Kenneth, 280

National Association of State Budget Officers (NASBO), 174
National Center for Productivity and Quality of Work Life, 153, 154
National Committee on Government Accounting, 292
National Council of Governmental Accounting (NCGA), 207
National government, focus in budgeting of, 17
National Institute of Health, 76
National Municipal League, 39
National Safety Council, 344
"Necessity," political, 88–89
"Need for a National Budget" (report), 40
Negotiated sale to specific underwriter, 285–86
Net debt per capita, 293
Net interest cost (NIC) method, unrestricted, 287–88
Net interest cost with constraints (NIC-C) method, 288

Net interest paid, 278
New Deal, 24
New programs, 100
  conditions for funding, 184–85
  cutting, 98
  strategies for, 96, 100
New York Bureau of Municipal
    Research, 11, 39
  Program Memorandum, 46
New York City financial crisis, 280–
    81
New York Federal Reserve Bank, 234
Nixon, Richard M., 9, 30, 54
  impoundment by, use of, 59
Nixon administration, 49, 72
Nonreactive measures, 137–38
Notes, 262–63
Notice of sale of bond, 290–91

Object classification, 122, 218
  crosswalk between program and
    uniform, 140–41
Object classification budget, 39
Obligation, 224, 244
  general (GO), 263, 264, 270
Occupational safety risk, 344–45
Office of Management and Budget
    (OMB), 24, 47, 72, 214
  current services estimates, 55
  federal policy formulation and, 11,
    12
  influence of, increased, 53
  legislative clearance process, 53
O'Neill, Thomas P., 62
Open-market operations, 25
Operating budgets, 7, 13, 213–41
  budget concepts and reports, 219–
    28
    allotment and budget concepts,
      12, 13, 219–24
    cash internal control, 225–27
    expenditure controls, 224–25
    management information
      systems (MIS), 227–28, 229
  capital budget versus, 282–83
  cash management, 228–34
  commercial bank services and,
    234–36
  controlling payables, 236–37
  designing control, 214–19
    budget execution, 214–17, 218
    current year adjustments, 218–
      19, 220–21
    fixing responsibility, 214
    pitfalls to avoid, 217–18
  investment in marketable securities,
    237–41
    portfolio, 240–41
    types of securities, 239–40
Operating lease, 274, 275
Opportunity cost, 4, 160, 163
Option to buy, 275
Ordering cost, 334, 335
Ordinances, budget, 125
Organization size, process analysis
    and, 196–99

Original issue discount bond (OLD),
    274
Ostrowski, John W., 192
O'Toole, Daniel E., 105
Outcomes and outputs, 128
  budget examination of programs
    outputs, 179–82
  confusion of, 134
  staff and service units and, 135–36
  unsuccessfully defined, 136
Output measures, types of, 135
Overhead, 182
Overlapping of local sales taxes, 324
Overvaluation, 319

"Padding" a budget, 95
Partial self-insurance, 346, 348
Partisan bargaining, 15
Past experience, influence on budget,
    5
Payables, controlling, 236–37
Pay-as-you-go financing approach,
    262
"Pay-as-you-go" pension system,
    351
Paying agents, 291
Paying agent services of bank, 235,
    236
Pecuniary externalities, 162
Pension funds, 351–58
  budget concerns in, 351–52
  investment process for, 352–53
  methods to raid, 354
  policy issues in, 353–58
Performance budget, 42, 44, 45, 46,
    105, 109
  example of, 110–11
Performance budget format, 104
Performance measures, use of, 129–
    30, 133–34
Performance standards for operating
    budget, 216
Performance time analysis, 197–98
Permaloff, Anne, 66
Permanent appropriations, 58
Peroff, Kathleen, 283
Personal property, property tax on,
    308
Personnel safety, 345
Perspectives on public budgeting, 1,
    2–6
Peterson, John E., 145, 269–70, 276,
    277, 289
Petty cash, 225, 226
Phillips curve, 23, 30
Pitfalls, 172
Pitsvada, Bernard T., 218
"Plain vanilla" bonds, 286
Planning:
  budget as instrument for, 3
  as purpose of budget, 44, 46
Planning and analysis:
  executive focus on, 46–49
  management information system
    for, 227
  phase in budget cycle, 10, 11

Planning-programming-budgeting
    (PPB), 11, 46–49
"Playing the float," 234–35
Policy
  responsiveness of budget to, 184–
    85
  risk-management, 349–50
Policy analysis. See Program analy-
    sis
Policy Analysis in Public Policy-
    making (Lynch), 72, 86
Policy execution and reinterpretation
    phase, 10, 12–13
Policy formulation phase, 10, 11–12
Political event, budgetary process as,
    4
Political leader's perspective on
    public budgeting, 4
Politically sensitive subjects, 188–89
Political "necessity," 88–89
Political realities, 9–10
Political risk, spenders' strategies
    constituting, 96–97
Political science, using concepts
    from, 8
Politics, public-interest, 64. See also
    Budget behavior
Pooling:
  of local debt issues, 289
  self-insurance by, 347
Portable pension systems, 354
Portfolio, 240–41
Positivism, logical, 203
Post-audit, 206
Power(s):
  balance of, 37
  diffusion of, 15
PPB (planning-programming-bud-
    geting), 11, 46–49
Praytor, Bobby, 235, 241
Pre-audits, 206
Presentation(s):
  budget, 9
  at hearings, 92–93
  of results of program analysis,
    172–73
Present value, discounting to, 139–
    40
President, Bureau of the Budget as
    arm of, 40, 41. See also Chief
    executive
President's budget, submission of,
    55–56
President's Commission on Budget
    Concepts, 42
Preventive maintenance, 332, 338
Price-related differential, 318–19
Price stability, maintenance of, 27
Primary benefits, 161
Prior or past years (PY), 6
Private bond guarantee program,
    272
Private sector:
  exploring involvement of, 186–87
  use of ZBB in, 50
Privatization strategies, 100

Proactive posture of analyst and line manager, 201
Problem-solving model of decision making, 19, 20–21
Process, 128
Process analysis, 166, 193–202
advantages of, 199–200
context in, 200–201
cooptation problems, 202
focus of, 193–99
honesty in, 202
needed interpersonal skills for, 201
Procurement, 330–32
Procurement specification, 331
Productivity:
bar-code technology and, 336
microcomputer and, 192
Productivity analysis, 131, 152–59
budget justification and, 155–59
defining productivity, 152–53, 154
reasons for loss of productivity, 153
simple regression analysis, 153–55, 156
Professional development, budgeting for, 186
Professional friendships, 88
Professionalism, 116
codes of ethics and, 174–78
confidence through, 82–83
criteria for, 88
Professional service contracts, competition for, 331
Program analysis, 166, 167–73
chief executive's role in, 173
commentary on, 170–72
common mistakes in, 171
issue assessment, 168–70
presentation of results of, 172–73
selecting issues, 167–70
Program-and-authorization crosswalk, 141
Program and financial plans (PFP), 183–84
Program and policy analysis, CBO, 57
Program and uniform object classification, crosswalk between, 140–41
Program budgeting, 44, 105, 109
Program classification, 122
Program evaluation, 166, 202–5
Program Evaluation and Review Technique (PERT), 188
Program-evaluation objective— program-structure crosswalk, 141
Program financial schedule, 112
Program format, 104
Program impact theory, 131–34
Program structure, 47
Progressive reform movement, 16, 38–39
Property conservation, 345
Property control, 335–36
Property insurance, 349

Property maintenance, 338
Property management, 329–37
bar-code technology, 336–37
central stores and inventory, 334–35
preliminary review of, 329
procurement, 330–32
property control, 335–36
purchasing, 330–34
purchasing challenges, selected, 332–34
Property tax, 308–21
assessment, 314–21
assessment cycle, taxation, and foreclosure, 319–21
conflict between state valuation and local assessment practices, 309–10
taxable property and, 314–16
testing, 316–19
average effective rates (1958–1985), 312–13
criticisms of, 308–10
delinquency on, 320–21
reforms, 310–13
as simple idea, 308
Proposition 13, California's, 278, 305, 311
Prospectus, bond, 290
Public administration, 8, 39
Public budgeting:
budget cycle, 7–8, 10–14
local government, 14
nature of, 10
phases of, 10, 11–14
budget realities and, 7–9
context of American, 14–21
decision-making models, 18–21
federalism, 17–18
ideology, 14–17
economic influences on, 21–25
fiscal policy and, 31–32
history of. See History of public budgeting
main purposes of, 3
monetary policy and, 26
operational definition of, 6–7
perspectives on, 1, 2–6
political realities and, 9–10
Public goods, 16
adequate supply of, 27
Public-interest politics, 64
Public liability insurance, 348
Public manager's perspective on public budgeting, 5–6
Public Policy Institute of New York, 146
Public-private capital financing, 265
Public relations, budgeting as, 3
Public trust, sense of, 215
Purchasing, 330–34
procurement and, 330–32
selected challenges in, 332–34
Pure reactive person, 86–87
Put option, 274
Pyhrr, Peter A., 50

Qualitative (judgmental) revenue forecasting, 143
Quarterly financial reports, 224

Rand Corporation, 47
Raphaelson, Arnold H., 316n
Rates, income tax, 323
Ratio data scales, 136–37
Rational model of decision making, 19–20, 21, 44, 47, 48. See also Planning-programming-budgeting (PPB)
true rational believer in, 86
Reagan, Ronald, 9, 30, 31, 53, 61, 62, 303
federal budget process under, 63–66
Reagan administration, 268, 270, 305
Real estate property, defined, 314
tax. See Property tax
Rebate, 254
Recession, 22, 23, 58, 305
Reconciliation instructions in budget resolution, 56
Reconciliation provision of 1974 Act, 61–62
Recording transactions, 242
Records, debt, 292
Records control, 336
Recurring costs, 139
"Red tape," 225
Reform, budget, 8–9
1974 reform motivations, 54
Progressive reform movement and, 16, 38–39
unified congressional, 54–58
Reform, property tax, 310–13
Reformation period (England), 36
Regression analysis, 196
multiple, 155, 314
simple, 138, 153–55, 156
Regressivity of sales tax, 324
Regulation of pension funds, 357
Rehearsals for budget hearings, 92
Relationships between variables, defining, 138
Renshaw, Edward, 271
Reorganization Act of 1939, 41
Replacement cost approach to assessment, 315
Reports:
accounting. See under Accounting
debt, 292
risk management, 350
types of, 224
Reprogramming authority, 218
Repurchase agreement (REPO), 240
Reserve requirements, changing, 25–26
Reserves, 246, 254
Residual equity, 246
Resources, process analysis and use of, 193, 199
Responsibility, fixing, 214

Results, budget support due to demonstrable, 89–91
Retirement benefits, 354–55. *See also* Pension funds
Revenue(s), 17
earmarked, 58–59
"hidden," 97
statement of, 248–49
tax rates and tax, 30–31
Revenue Act of 1964, 29
Revenue anticipation notes (RANs), 266
Revenue bond, 280, 293
industrial, 267, 269
industrial tax-exempt, 273
lease, 263
reasons for increased use of, 266–67
Revenue debt, 263, 264
Revenue enhancing strategies, 100
Revenue estimation, 14
detailed, 118–19
Revenue forecasting, 142–48
approaches to, 142–44
econometric forecasts, 144–45
forecasting practices, 146–48
Revenue potential of income tax, 323
Revenue systems, 302–27
intergovernmental, 302–8
other revenue sources, 322–26
income tax, 39, 308, 322–23
other taxes, 326
sales tax, 308, 323–24
user charges, 187, 308, 324–25
property tax, 308–21
assessment cycle, taxation, and foreclosure, 319–21
criticisms of, 308–10
reforms, 310–13
taxable property and assessment, 314–16
testing assessment, 316–19
Reviewers, budget:
developing confidence of, 87–89
strategies of the reviewed versus, 93–95
Reviews, budget, 116–24
congressional budget timetable, 119–21
executive budget document, 118–19
executive budget hearings, 116–17
legislative considerations, 121–24
Reynolds, Lloyd G., 23
Rickards, Robert C., 107
Rights, minority and fundamental human, 15
Risk:
in benefit-cost analysis, 162–63
default, 238
Risk and insurance checklist, 340, 341–44
Risk funding, 346, 347
Risk management, 338–50
administration of, 349–50

exposure identification and risk evaluation, 339–44
insurance, 340, 348–49
risk control, 344–46
risk funding and self-insurance, 346–48
Risk manager, 349–50
Risk retention, guideline on, 347
Robinson, Betty, 99
Roosevelt, Franklin D., 24, 41
Rounding, practice of, 95
Rubin, Irene S., 53, 146–47

"Sacred cows," political, 9
Safe harbor lease, 274, 275
Safety programs, 345–46
Safety risk, occupational, 344–45
Safety stock, 334
Sale-leaseback, 274, 275, 276, 277
Sale of bond, 291–92
Sales ratio, 314
Sales tax, 308, 323–24
Salomon Brothers, 353
Samuelson, Robert J., 30
San Antonio Independent School District v. *Rodriguez*, 311–13
Satisficing model of decision making, 19, 20, 80
Scatter diagram, 138, 196
Schick, Allen, 61, 66
Schwartz, Eli, 230, 231, 248, 249, 250, 252, 253, 332
Scientific method, 203
Secondary benefits, 161
Second Hoover Commission (1955), 42
Securities, marketable, 237–41
Securities and Exchange Commission (SEC), 285
Security, 345
Selected credit controls, 26
Self-insurance, 346–48
Semi-judicial process, budget process as, 3
Senate:
Appropriations Committee, 24
appropriations subcommittees, 56
Budget Committee, 24, 54
Finance Committee, 24
Senge, Stephen V., 325
Separation of key functions in property management, 329
Separation of powers, 37
Serial bonds, 262, 286
Serrano v. *Priest*, 311–13
Service Effort, and Accomplishment (SEA) categories of performance measures, 134
Service industries, coverage of sales tax to, 324
Service units, budget analysis handling of, 135–36
Severe unemployment, 22
Shannon, John, 303
Shkurti, William J., 145, 147
Shortage cost, 334

Short-term debt, 265–66
Sigelman, Lee, 74
Simon, Herbert, 128
Simple regression analysis, 138, 153–55, 156
Simplified Governmental Budgeting (Lehan), 104
Simulation, 151
Single Audit Act, 246
Sinking fund, 262
"Sin taxes," 308
Site value approach, 310
"Sleight-of-hand" tricks, 95–96
Small denomination bonds, 275
Smith, Adam, 24
Smith, Linda, 55
Social Darwinism, 16
Socialism, 16, 21–22
Social Security benefits, 354
South Carolina v. *Baker*, 287
Southern City (Murray), 280
Special authority debt, 263, 264
Specialist purchasing agent, 330
Special obligation bond, 267
Specification, 331
Spencer, Herbert, 24
Spenders' strategies, 95–97
Staff analysis, 197
Staff units, budget analysis handling of, 135–36
Stages of problem solving model of decision making, 19, 20–21
Stagflation, 30
Standard and Poor's:
early-warning guidelines for municipalities, 279
municipal bond-rating process, 293
Standardization, 331
State and local debt, 261–70
capital financing in 1980s, 267–70
classification of debt, 262–65
defining debt, 261–62
early developments in debt concept, 266–67
short-term debt, 265–66
State and local governments:
cutback management in, 98–100
focus in budgeting of, 17–18
interrelationship of institutional roles in, 73
meeting challenge of budgeting, 67
national government cooperation with, 17
use of analysis in state budgeting, 130–31
State equalization rate, 315–16
Statement of revenue, 248–49
State Non-Arbitrage Program (SNAP), 239
Statistical analysis, 138
Stewart, J.D., 128
Stipak, Brian, 105
Stock, 254
Stock, safety, 334
Stock margin requirements, 26

"Story" bonds, 286
Strategies. *See under* Budget behavior
Subsidy to private sector, 187
Subunits to attract clientele, agency, 76
Success, measure of budget, 84, 85
Sullivan, Mrs., 72
Summary of budget, 118
Sunset legislation, 63
Surfacing disagreement, 80
Surfus, Gerald M., 344
Survivor benefits of pension, 355
Swaps, 277
Syndicates, 286, 291
Systems theory, automation and, 190

Taboos in hearings, 93
Taft, President, 40
Target-base budgeting, 52–53, 108–9
Taxable municipal bond, 269
Tax advantage for municipal bonds, 287
Tax and revenue anticipation notes (TRANs), 266
Tax anticipation notes (TANs), 266
Tax collection, 18
Taxes. *See also* Revenue systems
income, 39, 308, 322–23
property. *See* Property tax
revenues as percentage of GNP (1948–1989), 305, 306–7
sales, 308, 323–24
"sin," 308
tax burden by region and state, 303–5
tax rates and tax revenues, 30–31
tax rebates, 28
value-added (VAT), 326
Tax-exempt commercial paper (TECP), 266, 273–74
Tax-exempt market in 1980s, 268–69
Tax havens, 315
Tax lien, 320
Tax loopholes (tax expenditures), 322
Tax Reform Act of 1986, 267, 269–70
Tax revolts of 1980s, 268, 305
Tax status of securities, 238–39
"Team player," analyst as, 201
Technological externalities, 162
Temporary loan of help from private firm, 187
Tender option, 274
Tenth Amendment to Constitution, 352
Term bonds, 262
Thai, Khi V., 246
Third-party liabilities, 339

Time as limitation of process analysis, 196–99
Time series approaches
to expenditure forecasting, 149–51
to revenue forecasting, 143
Tinbergen, Jan, 144
Tort doctrine of government immunity, 339
Total-cost purchasing, 332–33
Trade discounts, 237
Traditional capital financing, 265
Transactions, recording, 242
Transfer authority, 218
Transfer payments, 29
Transfer taxes, 326
Travel Expense Act of 1949, 42
Treasury bills, 240
Treasury notes, 240
Treasury subsystem, 228
Trend-line approach in expenditure forecasting, 149
True interest cost (TIC) method, 288
True lease, 275
True rational believer, 86
Truman, Harry, 42
Trust, public, sense of, 215
Trust programs, 190
Turn-downs, techniques for, 89

Umbrella coverage, 349
Uncertainty in benefit-cost analysis, 162–63
Underwriter, negotiated sale to specific, 285–86
Unemployment, 22–23, 24, 27, 30
Unexpended balance, 59
Unfunded pension liability, 263
Unified congressional budget reforms, 54–58
Unit cost approach to expenditure forecasting, 148–49
United States:
built-in fiscal stabilizers in economy, 29
ideologies in, 15–17
U.S. Advisory Commission on Intergovernmental Relations, 303, 305, 308, 357
U.S. Bureau of Prisons, 76
U.S. Department of Agriculture, 50
U.S. Department of Defense, 47
U.S. Department of Transportation, 72
United States Information Agency, 75–76
U.S. Maritime Administration, 72, 73
U.S. Supreme Court:
on impoundments, 60
on property tax, 311–13
U.S. Treasury Department, 24, 38, 40, 234

Bureau of the Budget in, 40, 41, 42
U.S. Treasury obligations, 240
Unobligated or disobligated appropriations, 95
Unrestricted net interest cost (NIC) method, 287–88
Urban Institute, 133, 167, 168, 173, 204
Urban Mass Transportation Administration, 72
User charges, 187, 308, 324–25

Valente, M.G., 265
Value-added tax (VAT), 326
Value engineering, 332
Values in benefit-cost analysis, 163
Variable-rate securities, 274
Vesting, 354
Veto, impoundment used as, 59
Vietnam, war in, 29–30, 47
Views and estimates report, 56
VisiCalc program, 191
Volunteers, tasks done by, 187
Vouchers, 187, 226, 246

Wage replacement, 354
Warehousing, central, 334–35
War on poverty, 29–30, 47
Warrant, 234, 263, 275
Watergate crisis, 54
Ways and Means Committee, Congress, 38
"Welcome stranger distortion," 315
Weld, William R., 148
Wharton Econometric Forecasting Associates, 144–45
Wildavsky, Aaron, 84, 108
William and Mary, 36
Willoughby, Katherine, 84
Wilson, Earl R., 292
Wilson, Pete, 354
Wilson, Woodrow, 39, 40
Windfalls, 172
"Window put," 274
Wire transfers, 235
Wise budget person, 87
Withholding, income tax, 323
Workers' compensation, 348
World War II, 42
depression and, 24
Wyoming Retirement System, 353

Zemansky, Stanley D., 332
Zero-balance accounts for disbursements, 237
Zero-Base Budgeting (Pyhrr), 50
Zero-base budgeting (ZBB), 7, 50–52
Zero coupon bonds (ZCBs), 270, 271
Zingale, James, 148